D0209499

DECISIVE BATTLES
of the
CIVIL WAR

Eng⁴ by John Halpin.   Photo. by Gurney

U. S. Grant

Dick & Fitzgerald, New York.

DECISIVE
BATTLES
of the
CIVIL WAR

William Swinton

PROMONTORY
PRESS

All rights reserved. No part of this work may be
reproduced or transmitted in any form or by any means,
electronical or mechanical, including photocopying,
recording, or any information storage and retrieval
system, without permission in writing from the publisher.

Published in 1986 by

Promontory Press
166 Fifth Avenue
New York, New York 10010

Library of Congress Catalog Card Number: 86-61038

ISBN: 0-88394-064-7

Printed in The United States of America

INTRODUCTION.

DURING the late War it was common to speak of the "indecisiveness" of its greatest battles. In one sense, the reflection was just; since the very occurrence of so many engagements showed that no one had been finally decisive. But in the more important sense, the comment was false; and its error lay in forgetting that a battle inconclusive as to the whole problem. of the war may yet be conclusive as to one stage of that problem This distinction could not easily be drawn during the heat and ferment of actual conflict; and especially when popular criticism was more in the way of impatient complaint against the conduct of operations than of thoughtful study of their weight and meaning.

The Sadowas of history are few, since few are the wars wherein the antagonists concur to expend all their gathered powers in one blow, and, having set their fortunes on a single cast, resolve to stand the hazard of the die. More commonly, whether by reason of near equality in the combatants, or of geographical, social, political obstacles to easy conquest, or by reason of the intense passions aroused, or from whatever cause, wars are long-continuing and dubious, stretch over many campaigns, and embrace many great battles. Of such sort was the American War of Insurrection.

Where a Tours or a Waterloo is in discussion, the question regarding its results is quickly settled, the most unreflective appreciating them at a glance. But where, in the other class of wars, the final issue can be traced back to no single field, but many great and sanguinary ones are on the record, the study of the comparative influence of each joinder in battle upon the grand result becomes far more attractive, profound, and useful. A hasty critic will aver that all the battles of such a contest were indecisive; a more judicious observer discriminates between them, and assigns to each its proper historic value.

But what rule of judgment shall be adopted, so as to select from the throng of battles those which may be pronounced decisive? The rule should be to choose such as settled the fate of campaigns, the possession of great strategic points, the capture or dispersion of armies, the success or defeat of grand invasions, and, in brief, such battles as, though not final upon the war itself, were final upon the successive stages through which the war was fated to pass.

My purpose in this volume has been to describe, according to this principle, the decisive battles of the late War in America. It is not probable that all, or even the majority of my readers, will agree with me in all the battles I have selected; nor would all, or perhaps any greater number, agree in any other selection or combination. Each student of the war, from his peculiar turn of mind, or habit of thought, or from pardonable local prejudice, or from special sources of information, may honestly form his own opinion on the decisiveness of its battles. Besides, the events themselves are so recent, that the deceptive haze surrounding them may not yet, in all cases, have furled away. Still, with regard to most of the battles here set forth, there must needs be substantial unanimity; and with regard to the rest, I am convinced, from much examination, that they will stand the test of criticism. Possibly, he who objects to the presence or absence of this or the other battle in the list may find his neighbor quite satisfied on that point, while the latter, in turn, regrets an omission or insertion which had greatly pleased the former.

During the war, many operations at first appeared trivial which brought forth the largest results; while others, like those on the coast of North Carolina or west of the Mississippi, whence great things were expected, sank in value, though prosecuted to success. So, too, actions in which victory was claimed, for the moment, by both parties, like Shiloh or the naval fight in Hampton Roads, proved to be not dubious, but decisive in their fruits: others, thought to be overwhelming, like Fredericksburg, did not essentially vary the time or the manner of the war's conclusion. But the mist which immediately enveloped both events and actors, could not but distort the former from their true bearings, some being greatly magnified, others as greatly diminished; nor could they take on their just size and relations until they lay in the perspective of history.

Of the twelve decisive battles, Bull Run made known that the contest was to be a war, not a "sixty days" riot: Donelson conquered the western Border States for the Union: Shiloh overthrew the first, and Murfreesboro' the second, of the Confederate aggressive campaigns at the West: Antietam overthrew

the first, and Gettysburg the second, of the Confederate aggressive campaigns at the East : the fight of the Monitor and Merrimac settled the naval supremacy of the Union: Vicksburg re-
opened the Mississippi, and, as it were, bisected the Confederacy :
Atlanta opened a path through Georgia, and, as it were, trisected
the Confederacy : the battle in the Wilderness inaugurated that
dernier resort of " hammering out " which made an end of the
Insurrection : Nashville annihilated the Confederacy at the West :
Five Forks was the initial stroke of that series under which it
toppled at the East, and so the continent over.

Many battles there are, only a little less lustrous than these, as
worthy of record in a complete history, and seeming for the time
as decisive, but which, in fine, assumed each a different aspect
when, in the progress of events, another battle was required to
solve that part of the problem which they had been designed to
solve.   Thus, Fredericksburg did not substantially alter the relations of the combatants, sanguinary as was the shock of arms,
but left them facing each other for a more decisive grapple.
Thus, Chancellorsville, conclusive though it then appeared, did
not settle that summer's campaign, as was seen when, a few
weeks later, it was decided on the heights of Gettysburg.   Thus,
the magnificent conquest of New Orleans did not open the great
river, but that result waited for the triumph at Vicksburg, while
on the other hand the trans-Mississippi campaigns to which it
gave rise, and whence so much was expected, affected but slightly
the development of the war.   Thus, the expulsion of Bragg from
the crest of Missionary Ridge left his army to make front again
beyond the Georgia line, and it was Sherman's campaign that
drove it into and out from Atlanta.   Thus, that first prolonged

and terrible measure of strength between the Army of the Potomac and the Army of Northern Virginia, which began with the Peninsular campaign, was not ended there betwixt the York and the James, but very far away, on the banks of the Antietam. Nor did the Peninsular struggle, nor the passage of arms with Pope that succeeded it, give the right clue to the final and decisive battle of the varied campaign. Thus, Spottsylvania, North Anna, and Cold Harbor, were features of a campaign which did not end the war, but was prudently abandoned for a better ; and though all were startling expressions of a decisive element in the war, namely, that of unceasing " attrition," yet this element had been introduced at the previous battle of the Wilderness, and had stamped it as a decisive action.

It only remains to subjoin a word upon the method and manner of the present volume. A somewhat close military study of the war from its beginning to its end, and indeed up to this writing, many facilities in the possession of documents and verbal information communicated to me by busy actors in the drama, joined with some personal observation of a part of the battle-scenes here depicted, induced its publication. In a former work I purported to set forth a " critical history " of one of the great Union armies. My aim now is to give a series of battle-sketches designed more for popular than professional instruction. It seemed to me that from many of the books on the war a wrong impressions of the event described would be left on the mind of the reader. I have endeavored to give a true and impartial account of the battles here recorded, that the perusal might neither mislead nor be devoid of profit. And in order to gain for the book a readier acceptance I have labored, while holding to strict accuracy, to avoid some details which might be appropriate to more elaborate technical histories, but which to this would add diffuseness without picturesqueness.

In dividing each sketch into three sections, the Prelude, the Battle, and the Results, I aimed not only to describe the day of the battle, but to thoroughly explain the train of events which led up to it, and the circumstances under which it was fought; and then to show what it accomplished or failed to accomplish. In this way, too, a continuous thread of description will be found to run from the beginning to the end of the war, wherein are strung conveniently its Twelve Decisive Battles.

I must express my obligation to many general and field officers for valuable manuscript material, and also to G. E. Pond, Esq., for aid in its redaction. It has not been thought advisable to incumber the pages with notes of reference, the book not being in the least of a controversial character. An analytical index will be found at the close of the volume.

W. S.

CONTENTS.

V.

MURFREESBORO.

VI.

THE MONITOR AND MERRIMAC.

VII.

VICKSBURG.

VIII.

GETTYSBURG.

IX.

WILDERNESS.

X.

ATLANTA.

PORTRAITS.

MAPS AND PLANS.

THE TWELVE DECISIVE BATTLES OF THE WAR.

I.

BULL RUN.

I.

PRELUDE TO BULL RUN.

THE night of the 20th of July, 1861, two officers sat in earnest conference in a farm-house within the hamlet of Manassas, Virginia. Their discussion, as well might be, was grave and anxious; for into their hands, as its two most famous soldiers, the insurgent South had committed the fortunes of its untried army and the fate of its new-born Confederacy. Of these men one was General Beauregard, lately called from Fort Sumter to lead the army now lying encamped along the neighboring stream of Bull Run. The other was General J. E. Johnston, who, responding to his associate's appeal, had hastened to unite his Army of the Shenandoah with the one at Manassas, in order to meet the massive array which, long menacing, had at length launched forward from the Potomac, and which that night announced, in a thousand bivouac fires, its presence along the heights of Centreville. The single subject of council was the procedure of the morrow, before whose close it was manifest must be decided the great initial struggle between the armies of South and North. A map of the country lay before the generals; and by its aid they planned how best they might or parry or strike. Impulse and conviction alike prompted the latter course : it was resolved to assume the offensive, and, with this intent, what remained of night was spent in determining the method of attack. But, while this project was taking shape, the army at Centreville was already in motion. Throughout the hazy midsummer's night, the Union columns wended their way through the moonlit forests towards the stream of Bull Run, inspired by a like purpose of offence. Thus in action and in council the night hours wore away. And when, with the first light of dawn, Johnston hastily signed the orders of attack, the boom of a single gun, startling the stillness of the Sabbath air, proclaimed that the Union force already confronted the Confederate army at Bull Run.

It was the signal-gun of Manassas.

If we may imagine to ourselves a dispassionate observer, who, regarding the two "points of mighty opposites" here arrayed against each other, should have attempted to forecast the issue of the contest about to be joined, it is easy to see how futile must have been his sagest speculations. The animosities engendered by political quarrels, checked but to gather fresh fury by repression, had at length burst into a war that rent in twain the American Republic. Instantly from sea to sea the continent had swarmed with armed men ; and, with that fierce intensity of hate which comes only of changed love, the strife between brothers began. As northward and southward thronged the combatants to the brink of the chasm which had cleft the Union, peaceful America seemed peopled in a day with a race of soldiers.

What was chiefly manifest at the outset was the energy with which the war promised to be waged. It took rise in those passions which stir the profounder depths of human nature, provoking men to the verge of possibility in action and in self-sacrifice. Searching for historic precedent to guide his judgment upon the giant quarrel between the North and South, the reflective observer would find no parallel thereto in the world's record. It came of no royal spleen, or restless ennui, or lust of money or power; not of the theft of a necklace, or of a monarch's spouse; its source was not in the *spretæ infuria formæ* of a despised court beauty, nor in a favorite's malice nor a minister's jealousy. It was even no affair of grand diplomatic intrigue or of overleaping national ambition, with its specious popular hallow of right. Of such wars an end can be awaited when the burden and the blood shall have wearied rulers and ruled, and made alike loathsome the end and the means of strife.

But this struggle between North and South stretched its roots too deep down into ultimate human motives, and laid hold too tenaciously of principle, for such termination. It lacked not, indeed, the stimulus of glory, of national conquest, and of that powerful emotion symbolized in the banner of the country. And verily the material considerations put at issue were on so grand a scale as to ennoble the cause only less than an ethical impulse. In lieu of going "to gain a little patch of ground that had in it no profit but the name," the moiety of a continent lay the territorial prize between the combatants. If the struggle was in part political as well as moral, at least it meant life or death for a Republic of thirty millions of people, the rehabilitation or the ruin of the broadest scheme in modern state-craft, and the governmental destinies of the America of the future, teeming with its hundreds of millions. While, underlying all these vast considerations, that honor was at stake which causes men "greatly to find quarrel in a straw;" — and underlying both national pride and national aggrandizement, were influences more universal and more potent. For, granted that base motives impelled many leaders and many followers, as, of blind hate, of cunning, blood-thirstiness, greed of money or of rank — from no such selfish ends did the embattled nation resort to the sword.

On the one hand was a mighty tempest of indignation against what was conceived and held to be heaven-defying injustice, violation of faith pledged three generations gone, despotic oppression : which hot passion, in its return fitful, subsided to the steady aspiration for independence and for a new Union untrammelled by the traditions of the old. Towering up against this cause stood the strong cause of the North — marvellously compact of the sterner and the milder motives, of duty with high emotion, a blending of flame and fire : the integrity and sovereignty of the majestic Union, the defence of the government received from the fathers, the supremacy of the Constitution of the Republic, the honor and dignity of the Nation, — to which motives were superadded the cry of humanity, and a glow caught from a vision yonder, along the yet untrodden path, of liberty guarded by law.

Whoever should cast a parallel between such a war and the methodical conflict waged betwixt the swollen body-guards of two European princes, set upon each other at the wave of a single hand, and heedless of the cause of their mutual slaughtering, would preposterously err. There were, indeed, no standing armies worth consideration, it being that deadliest of struggles, a national war, millions against millions, and every soldier comprehending its cause and its aim — a war, therefore, in which fresh levies spring joyfully forward as the earlier are exhausted, and which terminates only when one of the combatants, never yielding nor ever compromising, lies spent and helpless at the other's feet.

With such fell intensity of purpose it was that North and South rose up and grappled in the spring of 1861. And, as if incentive enough were not present, in touching all the better of the fundamental springs of their humanity, fraternal affection curdled to maddening hatred in their veins. For it is a law of human nature, that the more tightly the bonds of concord have united men in society, the deeper is the hate when once they are parted.

Accordingly, from the hour when the Union flag ran down from Sumter, one incessant drum-roll seemed to echo through the streets of every city, along every hillside and valley, sounding the alarum. No act or thought thereafter seemed worthy but thought and act of war. Trade stopped in its channels, and the myriad callings of peace were thinned of their followers; for to wage war or prepare for it was the only duty of the hour. Men too old or feeble to give life could at least give property to the cause, and children too young to march might at least wear the colors and chant the battle-songs; while, more memorable than aught else, wives, mothers, daughters, impelled by a sublime sentiment, weepingly gave all that they held dearest to the common cause. Amid such emotion the people rendezvoused unbidden to the rival banners in multitudes so great, that, no equipments being ready for them, by the thousand they were turned away. Despite all horrors lying in wait, grim and ghastly in the gloom ahead, — perhaps from the consciousness of such horrors, — the spectacle of America in the spring of 1861 contained something more inspiring than anything in her past history. With a proud step, as if rejoicing to be accounted worthy of such sacrifice, the nation, stimulated by the noblest motives and with faith in God, marched on to the baptism of blood.

But the very intensity of the emotions under which the nation rushed to arms prevented a cool estimate of the military probabilities of its issue, much more of the chances of the first fruit of battle. On each side was perfect faith in its troops, in its leaders, and, above all, in the heaven-born justice of its cause. That one side or the other must be fatally deceived was a truth, which, as usual, did not, from either, exact an instant's pause for reflection. This confidence in success was stimulated somewhat by the noisy vaporing and boasting common to humanity, but more especially by the popular ignorance existing North and South of how wars are waged and battles won. Half a century of comparative peace was just ending for America, and, in the interval, not only military training and military knowledge, but even military traditions, had greatly died out. The garrisons were slender, the standing armies almost nominal, the State militia but feeble *cadres*, if not empty names. In the undrilled, undisciplined, and flimsily-organized "mobs of town-meetings," which took the field at the first drum-call, a keen eye could discern magnificent soldiery; but it was soldiery in prospective. Such antecedents would, of themselves, cloud the issue of any contest between two armies of volunteers, with little but their sinewy frames and their matchless patriotism to recommend them. This uncertainty was enhanced by the very character of the war, which was not only a national or people's war, but the war of a Republican people; and not only that, but a war within the American Republic, where, more than anywhere else, the people is king. Grant that little was to be apprehended from such mobile and fickle democracies as were wont in Athens to arbitrarily lengthen and shorten and wage her wars, yet at least the independent life of the American people, their great freedom from the restraints of close-fitting laws, their daily custom of following largely individual will and sense of right, rather than the despotic commands of a strong, controlling government, might greatly disconcert all military predictions. The very conduct of the war, too, would be doubtless submitted, at first, to popular criticism and decision: so that even military orders must be countersigned, as it were, before execution, by the people as commander-in-chief. Howbeit these considerations, and such as these, puzzling the opinion of an impartial observer, had little popular lodgment North or South. Each section, looking at its aim, its means, and the zeal and constancy of its people, half suspected of disloyalty a man who could prognosticate a wearisome and bloody contest. Rejoicing not only in the integrity of its cause, and its rallying shout of the law of the land, the North also properly confided in its exhaustless resources of men, money, materials, and all the appliances of war, which made ultimate victory, with constancy, as sure as the rising of the sun. But it forgot the South's chances for prolonging the war until that constancy should give way, chances quite threefold, independent of the power of the Southern people. First, in a recognition of its right to self-government by trans-atlantic powers ; secondly, in the alliance or the possession of the border states ; thirdly, in fatal dissensions at the North. Each possibility led into the other, also ; and on the maturity of one, both the others would come to fruition. The four million slaves, fancied at the North to be a fatal weakness, the South would make a tower of strength, using them as producers of the means of waging war ; and thus that great contingent of able-bodied Northerners, retained in shop and field to toil and spin for the clothing and food and arms of the troops at the front, the South would match in its blacks. Nay, the slave system itself, audaciously heralded by its Vice-President as the cornerstone of the Confederacy, chill though it might all foreign sympathy, would at least consolidate the South into one grand military organization, cohesive, mobile, adamantine.

While North and South thus carefully summed up its own resources, each as persistently shut its eyes to the military possibilities of the other, and soon ventured to deride its powers. For, with strange forgetfulness of the common blood flowing in their veins, the common soil which had nurtured them, and the historic glories wherein Northern and Southern fames were indistinguishedly blent, each antagonist made pretence to despise the other's valor. The one was easily cajoled into the notion that on the mere show of the first fruits of its strength, and the measureless resources lying untouched behind, its disheartened adversary would throw up his hands in submission. The other nursed the monstrous conceit that one of his own men was a match for five opposing warriors. Accordingly, popular speculation, avoiding as far as possible all serious thoughts of what might be the beginning of the war, fondly dwelt on what ought to be its ending. In place of discussion upon the organizing, disciplining, and handling of vast armies, the choice of lines of operation, the possible plans of campaign, there were chiefly current windy generalities, based upon fanciful distinctions in the diverse ancestry — Cavalier or Roundhead — and the diverse occupations — Maine lumberman or Georgia planter — of the contestants. Something of this idle generalization, and much of tempestuous haste, were observable in leaders as in led, on both sides; and the former marshalled their arrays in a supreme confidence which agitated rather than steadied the flame of popular enthusiasm. The Southern people were encouraged to believe that one blow would bring Washington and Baltimore to their feet, a second Philadelphia, and, ere long, a treaty of peace should be signed on the banks of the Susquehanna. The government at Washington, on the other hand, did not seek to conceal its conviction, that, in sixty days or ninety days, the waters of oblivion would roll over the insurrection. In truth, however, the military knowledge or insight of statesmen was but little removed, in those early days, from the ignorance of the laity.

Thus, then, confident in success, North and South, when once the gauntlet was flung down, rivalled each other in eagerness to precipitate the contest, firmly believing that an overwhelming triumph might be seized from the very initial measurement of strength. But where should the decisive blow be struck? The military topography of America had hardly been broached as a science of serious study; and, so far as essayed, concerned almost exclusively the Coast Defences, — that is, the methods of foiling the attacks of the ocean expeditions of foreign powers. It never contemplated the lines of operations or strategic positions of armies within the continent — that would have anticipated the dread contingency of civil war. But while the geographical problem was, for a moment, in abeyance, the rapid drift of political events seized and drew the unformed military campaigns into its current.

On the 16th day of April, 1861, the honored flag was hauled down from Fort Sumter; and on the same day President Lincoln, compelled thereto by the decisive tidings from Charleston Harbor, called 75,000 militia into the field to maintain the sovereignty of the Union. At that great epoch, the strip of Southern "border states," comprising Virginia, North Carolina, Tennessee, and Arkansas, had not joined the fortunes of the Confederacy; but the convulsions of such a movement powerfully shook these States, already trembling on the brink of the gulf which had torn the Union asunder. Virginia first plunged over, and drew after her, necessarily, Tennessee, Arkansas, and North Carolina. Such was the secondary secession movement — the secession of the southerly border states. The northerly border states — Maryland,. Kentucky, and Missouri — long tottering, yet withstood this second convulsion like the first, and then settled by slow degrees, firmer and firmer, on the the rock of the Union. Accordingly it happened, that, from first to last, the river Potomac formed the• northeasterly boundary between the antagonists, and in a natural impulse both leaped forward at once to its shores. By the most unfortunate of chances, on this river was located the national capital, and this fact shaped the entire course and character of the war. The 75,000 three-months' militia, gathering from farm and forge, armed or unarmed, poured, on all railroads, straight to Washington at the cry of "the Capital is in danger." Two days after Sumter, the Virginia Convention passed its ordinance of secession; and three days later, the vanguard of the armed 75,000 militia, the Massachusetts quota, fought its way through the city of Baltimore, whose pavements, upon the 86th anniversary of Lexington, ran with the first blood of the civil war. The militia had not too much hastened, though they had left the plough clinging in the soil, and the half-smelt iron glowing in the furnace fire. But, then, it was theirs to save Maryland, and therewith, the paths which lay across it to Washington; and, above all, to avert the ineffable disgrace of the fall of the national capital.

So, then, it fell out that the very site of the governmental capital was such as forced the Northern troops to converge thereon, turning Washington and its environs, before midsummer, into a crowdedly garrisoned city, with a multitude of outlying camps. Meanwhile, on the further bank of the Potomac, the Confederate forces gathered an opposing head, drawing up from the whole South to a focus in Virginia. Neither was their choice of position fortuitous, and, indeed, it was based on several reasons, each alone sufficiently substantial. Two schemes were of possible suggestion — the one to seduce the offensive army far down from its northern bases, and deliver battle in the interior of the Confederacy — the other to plant the standard of revolt on the outer wall, and dispute stoutly from the first every foot of soil claimed to be Confederate. The latter was infinitely more inspiring and more dignifying to its cause, since at the outset territorial occupation by an enemy carried with it a moral weight altogether disproportionate to its military meaning. And this truth quadrupled in force when thereto was added the state-pride of Virginia, which never would have brooked the uncontested abandonment of her soil. And again, successful retention of the Southern border states would attract the northerly border states, whose presence as guests in the Confederate mansion, was not only yearned for but expected for many months or years. But, while a swoop from the border might some day, perchance, gather Kentucky and Maryland into the fold, these States would not long attend a deliverer who was fighting for life hundreds of miles away; and the slender reward which welcomed Virginia's espousal of the Confederacy, by instant abandonment to Northern conquest, would become warning sufficient for other States against casting in their lots with the refluent South. Finally, the more Virginia was regarded, the more admirable a field did it present for the purpose of the Confederates. Time was soon to show that its stubborn defence was repaid and repaid many times by a stimulus of state pride and home love, which in addition to the Confederate sentiment animated those vast quotas of admirable soldiers whom Virginia poured forth unstintingly, filling up the battle-gaps till all were gone.

The Virginia Convention, as has been seen, passed, on the 16th of April, its ordinance of secession, with the proviso that the people should ratify or reject it by a vote on the 23d of May. But this vote the Convention instantly forestalled, by decreeing on the 24th of April, that, pending the popular decision, "military operations, offensive and defensive, in Virginia, should be under the chief control and direction of the President of the Confederate troops." At once, therefore, while Virginia volunteers were rallying in great numbers under the plea of State defence, Confederate troops were suffered to cross the frontiers of the State and take position within her borders. Not able even to await the popular vote in Virginia, the Confederate Government, on the 20th of April, removed its seat of authority from Montgomery to Richmond. In truth, however, the presence and operations of Confederate armies within her limits had already so long compromised Virginia and so thoroughly committed her to the Southern cause, that the removal of the Confederate capital to the seat of her area could not more effectually do so. But the latter movement, at once bold and wise, swept off, when consummated, all doubt, if any were still remaining, that Virginia was to be the great battle-ground of the war. The shifting and quivering lines of operations heretofore proposed at the North were at once absorbed and steadied in one clear, straight path, and aimless plans and quests gave way to a fixed objective. The army at Washington, which had long since rendered meaningless by its presence there its first rallying-call, turning its eyes from its own capital to that of the insurgents, audaciously thrust into their northernmost State, now raised a fiercer and more clamorous battle-cry, and people and rulers swelled the shout of " Onward to Richmond."

II.

THE BATTLE OF BULL RUN.

MIDSUMMER came before North and South had joined in the long-expected battle. The feverish rate at which the nation had been living, the intensity of popular feeling, and the vastness of that still doubtful stake for which the game of war was playing, had united to make the preceding Spring longer than a decade of ordinary years. A taste of battle, wherein the advantages were divided, set the edge of thirst for deadlier combat. The skirmishes at Big Bethel and Vienna, won by the Confederates, had been more than balanced by McClellan's brilliant minor campaign in West Virginia. But these affairs, though popularly magnified into monstrous proportions, were even then felt to be trivial prologues to an unknown drama. Impatient of what seemed unprecedented delay, the people had, by their excited Congressmen, and, indeed, by most of the public men of the day, beset the leaders of the Union troops for a forward movement, until the latter, against their better judgment, and with plentiful protests of the necessities of further preparation, sent their army into the world, literally " before its time, scarce half-made up," to seek its fortunes on the battle-field.

In the early days of July, a plan of operations having been matured by General McDowell, and accepted by the President and his cabinet, was put in train of execution. At that time the main Confederate Army, about 20,000 strong, lay encamped, under General Beauregard, along the stream of Bull Run. His head-quarters were at Manassas Junction, the point where the great railroad running between Washington and Richmond is joined by the one leading down from the Valley of the Shenandoah. A force here obviously covered Richmond by planting itself across the direct line of march from Washington; menaced the latter city; suspended the Virginia railroad system; and kept open two lines of railroad supply, of which the westerly one communicated with the rich Shenandoah valley, and with the army guarding it. The latter, about 8,000 strong, lay, under the command of General J. E. Johnston, at Winchester, and was so posted as to hold the valley, observe Harper's Ferry and the Union forces in its front, menace McClellan, approaching from the west, and, if need be, join Beauregard. At Hampton, Magruder had a few thousand men holding the peninsula between the James and York rivers.

Now, facing and menacing these bodies were the Union forces, under direction of Scott. Foremost was the " Grand Army," under General McDowell; which, on the night of the same 23d of May, when Virginia declared for secession, crossed into that State, and began the long task of reconquering it to the Union. It was 30,000 strong, and made up of the three-months' militia, a few advance regiments of the three-years' men, for whom the President had already called, and a handful of regulars. At Fort Monroe General Butler had a small column of troops; while near Harper's Ferry, menacing Johnston, General Patterson commanded a force of 18,000 of the same unkneaded and heterogeneous sort as that of McDowell. The latter officer, surveying the field of war, and estimating the forces then upon it with a soldierly coolness and precision quite rare in those early days, declared his ability to march against and dislodge the chief Confederate army, under Beauregard, provided he had the promise that the outlaying forces under Patterson and Butler should engage the attention (as they might easily do from their numerical superiority) of Johnston and Magruder.   This assurance was emphatically given by General Scott, and the 9th July fixed for the march.   Patterson was instantly ordered to again cross the Potomac, and so demonstrate against Johnston as to prevent his joining Beauregard.

McDowell crossed the Potomac, to use his own words, "with everything green": he could "with difficulty get any officers," and was "obliged to organize, and discipline, and march and fight, all at the same time."   He found difficulty alike in getting the troops and transportation designed for the expedition; and a part of the latter crossed the Potomac to him, raw and undrilled, on the day of the start, while the trains did not move until still later.   However, by great exertions, employing himself even with details which usually fall to the duties of subordinate commanders and staff-officers, he got his army, such as it was, in hand, and, on the afternoon of July 16th, moved it out from the works on the southerly bank of the Potomac, leaving Runyan's (Fifth) Division as garrison.   The marching force was about 30,000 strong, nearly all three-months' men, whose terms of service were expiring — the object of their rally having been the defence of Washington.   These all spiritedly marched to open the offensive campaign; and even some regiments entitled to discharge nobly remained, only two leaving — a Pennsylvania regiment and a New York artillery battalion — who, going back at Centreville, left McDowell still a little over 28,000 strong.   In this force were about 800 regulars, of various regiments, clustered into a battalion under Major Sykes.   There were four divisions in the column — the First under General Tyler, the Second under Colonel Hunter, the Third under Colonel Heintzelman, the Fifth under Colonel Miles. The advance struck Fairfax Court House next day, and found that Beauregard's outposts there had taken the alarm and vanished; thence it moved onward to Centreville. The troops were unaccustomed to marching, and did not understand the value of dispatch, while their officers were mainly ignorant of how to march them: so that the army did not reach the latter point till the 18th, a day after McDowell's intention. Tyler's advance thence pushed immediately down to Bull Run, which, as we have seen, was Beauregard's line of defence. Now, the plan of battle had been to turn Beauregard's right, under cover of a demonstration made straightforward from Centreville, on the road to Manassas Junction, against Beauregard's centre. But Tyler was one of those numerous officers in whom, confident of success, zeal outran discretion; and, believing from the success of his advance thus far that he could push straight through to Manassas with his single division, he moved forward to Mitchell's Ford, and opened a sharp artillery fire, which provoked a response from the Confederate batteries. Not content with this reconnoissance, which, so far, was harmless, Tyler deployed his infantry brigade along the stream at Blackburn's Ford, and let them fire into the opposite woods. Of course the Confederates at once returned a hot reply, this being their strong position, and, in a few exchanges, put to flight the troops opposing. So far as material result was concerned, the affair was trifling, the Confederate loss being 68, and the Union about 100; but it had a great effect on the *morale* of the main attacking army, who recommenced their familiar speculations on "masked batteries." Something, however, was learned of the Confederate position. The next day, the 19th, the troops all got into position, and their rations, which were in the rear, also came up. The 19th and the morning of the 20th were spent in reconnois-

sances, which determined McDowell to abandon the project
of turning the enemy's right, and to make a new order of
attack designed to turn his left.

Meanwhile, however, the Confederates were losing no
time. Johnston having received directions from Richmond
to join his corps to that of Beauregard, withdrew from
Patterson's front, marched through Ashby's Gap to Piedmont,
and thence transferred his infantry by rail to Manassas.
This point Johnston, with ten regiments, reached on the 20th.
Superior in rank to Beauregard, he adopted unhesitatingly
the former's dispositions and plans in the emergency. There
were now eight brigades positioned on the line of Bull Run,
a distance of eight miles : General Ewell's on the right at
Union Mills Ford, General Jones's at McLean's Ford, General
Longstreet's at Blackburn's Ford, General Bonham's at
Mitchell's Ford, Colonel Cooke's at Bull's Ford, about three
miles above, and Colonel Evans's at the extreme left at Stone
Bridge. The brigades of General Holmes and General
Early were in reserve in rear of the right. So skilfully and
rapidly had been the tranfer of Johnston's force that a great
part of it was already in position, and it was accounted
certain that the few remaining thousands would reach the
ground by noon of the morrow, thus giving an available
strength of 27,000 men for the defence of the Confederate
position.

That this force could decisively repulse a column of equal
size, — for even if nothing had been left in reserve at his
trains, full twenty-five thousand men were at McDowell's
disposal, — was beyond all doubt. The choice of position
and the friendly aid of abatis and of artillery in position,
had put the matter beyond question, it was thought, especially
against raw troops ; and the whole ground, of which his opponent was ignorant, was familiar to the inquiring mind of
Beauregard, who been occupying his camp, and intrenching it so far as he thought necessary, since the latter part of

May. There was, however, a difficulty at this point: it supposed an immediate attack by McDowell. It was prudent to consider that, so soon as Johnston's withdrawal had been learned by Patterson, the news must instantly have been telegraphed to Washington, and thence sent to McDowell, who would, accordingly, delay his attack until he should also be reinforced, either by Patterson's army or other troops, and until the numerical superiority on which his plan of attack was based, should be restored. It was possible that McDowell already knew the position of affairs, and it was also possible that, if he did not know it, some other cause would delay his attack, like want of rations, or the attending of reinforcements, until it did become known. What was unpleasantly certain was that already after having once burst at the line of Bull Run with the head of his column, he had now delayed in inaction more than two days.

With such probabilities but one true course remained for the Confederate generals: it was to advance instantly to the attack before any reinforcements could come up to their adversary. This plan would, to be sure, sacrifice the supposed advantages of position and superior knowledge of the ground; but these latter might become useless by holding them until McDowell should be strong enough to overcome them; and equally fatal might it be to delay in the hope that McDowell would disclose his intentions. A bold offensive was the soldierly course — a method which suited the instincts of both officers as well as the crisis of affairs. So far as numbers were concerned they could safely rely before nightfall of the next day, on no important disparity; while by effecting a surprise, and getting the advantage of successful attack, victory could be even earlier counted on. It was therefore decided by Johnston and Beauregard, on the night of the 20th, to cross Bull Run on their right, at the lower fords, and attempt to turn the Union left at Centreville. They relied on the spirit of their troops, now greatly encouraged by

Longstreet's repulse of Tyler at Blackburn's ford.   What might have come of this plan, it is idle now to speculate, for when the orders to put the brigades in motion had been executed, on the morning of the 21st, a delay of several hours in their transmission by the staff officers occurred, and, in the interval, McDowell had passed Ball Run, handsomely turned his opponent's left flank, and thrown him on the defensive.

McDowell's plan of battle was one unusually sensible and soldierly for that early day, and perfectly worthy of commendation at the present.   The reconnoissances of Major Barnard and the other engineer officers, during the 19th and 20th, had disclosed the facts on which it was based.   The stream called Bull Run ran south-easterly about equidistant between the Confederate head-quarters at Manassas and the Union head-quarters at Centreville.   The main road between these points crossed the run at Blackburn's ford, three miles from Centreville, while, on either side, a lower and an upper road, diverging from Centreville, struck the run respectively at Union Mills Ford and the Stone Bridge.   Here, then, were naturally located the right, the centre, and the left of the Confederate position at Bull Run.   The Warrenton turnpike road, the one from Centreville to Stone Bridge, was four miles long, and of course the Confederates had placed artillery and obstructed the adjacent ground on their side of the stream by heavy abatis.   Two miles above, however, beyond the Confederate left, carelessly guarded, a good ford was discovered at Sudley Springs, and though no road led thither, the intervening woods were passable.   McDowell's plan of attack was to pass this Sudley Springs ford with his right, under pretence of attack in front, and, having gained the rear of the position at Stone Bridge, to dislodge the enemy, and throw himself on the railroad between Beauregard and Johnston ; for he had not learned of their junction.   Miles's division was to remain in reserve at Centreville, holding the position, and strengthening it with earthworks and abattis, and demonstrating with one brigade against Blackburn's ford in artillery fire. Tyler's division was to move on the pike to Stone Bridge, threatening it, and afterwards crossing it. The main body, the two divisions of Hunter and Heintzelman, was to march across the country to Sudley Ford, and turn the enemy's left flank.

The time of starting was fixed for half-past two o'clock of Sunday morning, July 21st, and soon after midnight the troops were all astir. But unused to the swift mechanical manœuvres of veterans, and with the officers as unskilled as the men, Tyler's advance division was not out upon the road till long after the time, and the other two, Hunter's and Heintzelman's, which had to march behind it on the turnpike for some distance, were thereby fatally delayed. Hunter could not digress from the Warrenton turnpike till six o'clock, and, the route through the woods to Sudley Ford being longer and harder than was thought, the head of the flanking column did not reach the stream until half-past nine, three hours later than the time fixed. Meanwhile, Tyler had reached Stone Bridge on the turnpike, and at the appointed moment, half-past six, fired his signal gun.

It was a signal gun for the Confederates, too, who, intent on other things, and anticipating either to attack or be attacked far down the stream, on their right, had only Evans's demi-brigade, or regiment and a half, at the turnpike bridge. Even the latter hardly responded to Tyler's fire, except in some slight musketry exchanges between the skirmishers on the banks of the run. Yet, from so slight a circumstance, McDowell appears to have divined the fact that the mind of the Confederate commander must be occupied with some dangerous scheme concerning the other flank; and he instantly withdrew from Tyler Keyes's brigade to where, two miles back from the run, on the turnpike, the road forks to

Manassas, holding also in reserve one of Heintzelman's brigades, "in case we should have to send any troops back to
reinforce Miles's division." For it had already "become a
question" with McDowell, whether the Confederate general
"did not intend himself to make an attack, and make it by
Blackburn's Ford."

But the clamor of Tyler's guns had roused the Confederate commanders to a true sense of their position, and
dropping yet unmeshed the toils which they were knotting
for their opponent, they hastened to cut through those which
menaced to entangle themselves. His morning's tardiness
enabled them to do so. Hunter, having thrown the head of
his column across Sudley Ford, at half-past nine, turned and
marched down to take the works at Stone Bridge in reverse.
For the first mile, the region around the road leading from
Sudley Ford to the Warrenton turnpike, which the run
crosses at Stone Bridge, is thickly wooded, with some cleared
fields on the right. Thence, however, to the turnpike the
ground is open, with rolling fields on both sides of the Sudley road. Colonel Hunter's column was strung along the
road in the ordinary march by the flank, and it was quite ten
o'clock when its advance brigade, Burnside's, emerging from
the wood, spread out into this open space. Its leading regiment was very quickly greeted by two pieces of artillery,
succeeded by the musketry rattle of Evans's brigade. The
Confederates had saved themselves. Evans had, as we have
seen, held the extreme Confederate left on the Warrenton
turnpike and at Stone Bridge. The light cannonade of
Tyler had been successful, as designed, in occupying his
attention for three hours; that is, till half-past nine o'clock.
At that time, however, he plainly saw that a large force
crossing the river, was moving through the woods to his rear;
and, sending for reinforcements, he moved back his brigade,
consisting of a regiment and a battalion, and two pieces of
artillery. The Sudley Spring road crosses the turnpike

little more than a mile back from the Stone Bridge. Of course, therefore, Evans had not far to move, and in half an hour the whole of his change of front was easily made. A petty tributary of Bull Run, called Young's Branch, shoots northerly over the turnpike near this crossing of the Sudley Springs road, and thence bending forward in a wide curve around the base of an elevation over which the turnpike runs, flows along back across the turnpike near Stone Bridge. Evans, throwing his demi-brigade out to meet Hunter, found, north of the turnpike and of the bend of Young's Branch, very good ground for his purpose. His right rested in a long and narrow grove in front of Young's Branch; his centre crossed the Sudley road, some distance north of the pike, and his left was concealed among some houses, sheds, hay-stacks, and fences, on the farm of one Dogan. What with artillery and musketry he had a good fire down the slope at his enemy, whenever he might debouch from the woods many hundred yards distant.

The moment the head of Burnside's brigade appeared, Evans opened fire; and the former, too eager and too untrained to form proper line of battle, sharply responded. A brisk, but irregular and unimportant skirmish went on for half an hour between Burnside and Evans, while the former was getting his troops in hand. Porter's brigade, coming out of the woods, formed on Burnside's right, and Sykes's eight hundred regulars were sent to his left, while Griffin's battery got into position and attacked the Confederate artillery, and then the general battle began. Evans, meanwhile, had got up similar welcome reinforcements. A part of Colonel Bee's brigade, which had come from Johnston's army, was despatched to him, and a part of Colonel Bartow's, with six more pieces of artillery, of Imboden and Richardson. And, meanwhile, other supporting forces were arranging a second position in the rear. Bee and Bartow having crossed to Evans, the fight was sharply carried on. Hunter's left, in

3

which was Sykes's battalion, pressed rapidly against the grove in front of the Confederate right, and drove it back upon the road.   More tenaciously Bee, who was now in command, clung to his left.   But the Union force managed to keep its early advantage ; and, pressing along with vigor, Hunter at length drove the Confederates back right and left, carrying with it the grove and the house ; and finally sweeping across Young's Branch, across the turnpike, where the Sudley road reaches it, he forced the Confederates up the slopes to the heights beyond.   At the turnpike, Colonel Hampton's legion had been thrown in to the assistance of Evans, Bee, and Bartow ; but it was too late to check the progress of Hunter, and could only, according to General Johnston, "render efficient service in maintaining the orderly character of the retreat from that point."   Up the slope to a plateau on its crest rushed Bee's discomfited troops, and there found, solid and strong, and dressed in line, a full brigade holding the heights, and awaiting the rolling shock of battle. It was the brigade of Colonel Jackson — already a great soldier, since already he was possessed of those moral qualities which made him chiefly what he is now in history. Here, rallying his men, Bee pointed them for encouragement to their fresher comrades : "There is Jackson, standing like a *stone wall;* " and one word of the pithy exclamation became immortal.

In this way Hunter's division auspiciously opened the battle of Bull Run.   A still greater success was awaiting the Union army.   The brigades of Colonel W. T. Sherman and General Schenck, of Tyler's division, had been lying quietly on the turnpike in front of Stone Bridge.   By ten o'clock, however, it was perceived from tree-tops that Evans's brigade, on the other side, which had been drawing back from the bridge for half an hour, was now nearly all gone up the turnpike, and thence out to meet Hunter, the head of whose column could also be discerned from the same rude observatory. Hunter's fire drew nearer and nearer as he forced Evans back; but at length, almost an hour later, clouds of dust showed that the five supporting regiments of Bee and Bartow, with their artillery, had reached Evans, having crossed the turnpike, and that Evans was holding his ground. Tyler accordingly now ordered Sherman to cross the run, and Keyes to follow him, to Colonel Hunter's left. The quick eye of the former had earlier seen a horseman fording at a point above, and, having noted the place, he now led thither his brigade, and crossed without difficulty. The firing guided his march; but Hunter's success was already assured, and Sherman, reporting to McDowell, was simply ordered " to join in the pursuit of the enemy, who was falling back to the left of the Sudley Springs road." Keyes came up and formed on his left, while Heintzelman moved over the conquered field, crossed Young's Branch, and marched up the turnpike road beyond.

At this time the fortunes of the Confederates were in a critical condition. Their left had been turned, the Warrenton turnpike taken from them, uncovering Stone Bridge, and their line driven back a mile and a half since morning. The loss of this ground had allowed Tyler to cross two thirds of his division to Hunter's aid, while Heintzelman had already got into position. While McDowell had thus worked nearly all of his three divisions into good position, and was advancing nearly 18,000 strong, the Confederate lines had been thrown into confusion, and it was doubtful for a time whether an equivalent force could be quickly enough hurried forward to check the very much strengthened columns with which the enemy was now about to renew the conflict. But Johnston and Beauregard, ordering up the brigades of Holmes, Early, Bonham, and Ewell, and the batteries of Pendleton and Albertis, hastily rode to the scene of conflict, four miles distant from their head-quarters, to rally their disheartened forces. "We came," says Johnston, "not a moment too soon," for "the long contest had greatly discouraged the troops of Bee and Evans." He found "that the aspect of affairs was critical;" but by great efforts, "and some example," the "battle was re-established," and, after a time, "many of the broken troops, fragments of companies, and individual stragglers, were re-formed and brought into action." The tide of fugitives, with their wild stories of disaster, which had begun to set from the Confederate ranks, in the custom of raw troops, was checked; and an inexplicable lull in the Union attack (inexplicable except from the newness of the experience of the Union commanders) afforded golden minutes to the anxious Confederate generals.

The position on which the Confederates had now made a stand was a broad table-land elevated from 100 to 150 feet above Bull Run, and rising at its most advantageous points still higher. Around its northerly and easterly bases runs Young's Branch, while another creek encloses the northerly side; along the westerly side is the Sudley Springs road, nearly parallel with Bull Run at this point, and from it about a mile and a half distant. The main plateau is generally bare, and broken into rugged ridges; but its southerly and easterly heights are thickly wooded with pines, and at its westerly crest the Sudley road runs through a forest of oaks. In this opening victory the Union troops had seized the slopes leading up to the plateau from the turnpike. They now fought, in general, to sweep the Confederates from the crest and the plateau beyond. The latter had rallied and re-inforced their line, and the brigades of Bee, Evans, Bartow, Bonham, Jackson, Hampton's legion, and Fisher's regiment, were put in line of battle, with the batteries of Imboden, Pendleton, Albertis, and others.

To carry the position, McDowell now had the brigades of Wilcox and Howard on the right, supported by part of Porter's brigade, and the cavalry under Palmer; the brigades of Franklin and Sherman in the centre and up the road, and

Keyes's brigade on the left. Ricketts's and Griffin's batteries were on the right, and the Rhode Island battery on the left. It will thus be seen that Heintzelman's division was on the right, a part of Hunter's (now under Porter, Hunter being wounded), in the centre, and two brigades of Tyler on the left. Schenck's brigade and Ayers's battery were still on the other side of the river, and Miles's division, 9,000 strong, back at Centreville. McDowell had, however, 18,000 men with him on the field of action; from which, nevertheless, he had to deduct the losses of the morning and some withdrawn troops, like Burnside's brigade. The force which Johnston could bring immediately to bear was even less than this, for McDowell's demonstrations with the reserves of Miles and Richardson detained several Confederate brigades at the lower fords of Bull Run, from fear of a crossing at that point. Indeed it was not until three o'clock that the withdrawal of a part of these forces, and the arrival of Johnston's first troops from the valley, gave to the Confederates numerical equality, and at length, in their turn, superiority.

Accordingly, until three o'clock, the tide of battle steadily continued to turn against the Confederates. On the Union left, Keyes's brigade charged up the slope from the turnpike; and, finding itself in sharp conflict with both cavalry and infantry, succeeded nevertheless in reaching the crest and seizing the buildings known as the Robinson House on the plateau above: a position, however, which had soon to be abandoned. The great contest meanwhile was on the Union right, where, not far from the Henry house, some annoying Confederate batteries had been planted, and upon which from a neighboring crest, carried earlier in the day by the Union troops, the batteries of Griffin and Ricketts played. Between and around these batteries, from one o'clock till three, a fierce conflict raged, and forward and backed surged the opposing lines, the westerly edge of the plateau and the Sudley wood and the neighboring woods — nay, the two Union batteries themselves, passing alternately from the grasp of either antagonist into that of the other. Three times the Confederates overran Griffin's battery, and three times they were repulsed; while thrice also the Union forces surged in vain against the Confederate position. The Union advance seemed, at three o'clock, effectually checked, and an alternate roll forth and back in the attempts to carry or to hold the high plateau which formed the Confederate position, appeared to be the fate of the rest of the day.

Had the assaulting army been what it late was when it streamed up Marye's heights or stormed the salient at Spottsylvania, had its brigade and battalion commanders been already the trained soldiers who later manipulated *corps d'armee* or stood at the head of great armies, the plateau would inevitably have been carried; for it was really an untenable position. But had the raw Confederates been the fire-tempered troops who threw themselves on Cemetery Ridge, and passed through the terrific musketry of Antietam, they would have repulsed their assailants; for the latter were already exhausted, and, besides, were fighting without definite plan. But in truth, their later skill, the offspring of experience, was wanting to both leaders and soldiers on both sides.

So, then, from noon of the sultriest day in the year, scorched by the merciless sun, the parched and panting combatants fiercely grappling, writhed hither and thither over an indecisive field. For hours, on the slopes leading up to the table-land, nought was discernible, amid the choking clouds of dust and the heavy, slow-wreathing volumes of cannon-smoke, but the unsupported and fruitless attacks of gallant subdivisions — brigades or battalions shooting out here or yonder in a brief spurt of triumph, to be forced back in as sure a retrograde. Three o'clock had passed. McDowell still felt that the day, begun with prosperous omens, could be made his own. The Confederates, unwillingly compelled to throw in everything in the desperate attempt to hold the plateau, had stripped even the lower fords of their proper defences, and, in a choice of threatened evils, had resolved to risk the menace of Miles and Richardson, in order to meet the actual and present peril offered by McDowell. Accordingly, Ewell's brigade had been hurriedly ordered up from Union Mills Ford; Holmes's brigade came in from the rear of Ewell's; Early's marched up from McLean's Ford, bursting in at the very crisis of the battle; two regiments and a battery of Bonham had been early taken from Mitchell's Ford, and a third regiment followed. The brigades of Evans, Cooke, Bee, Jackson and Bartow were all in. It was absolutely necessary to leave Jones and Longstreet at the lower fords, to watch the entire reserve division of Miles. While the Confederates were thus pressed for more troops, McDowell had two brigades almost fresh, besides Burnside's, in reserve since noon. Howard's brigade was accordingly marched up to the front, and prepared to take part in the contest, and, meanwhile, Tyler having marched down to Stone Bridge, and dislodged the batteries there, had just succeeded, with his engineers, in clearing of abatis the whole length of the turnpike, and seizing the country adjoining. Then McDowell, ordering Schenck's fresh brigade across Stone Bridge to turn the Confederate right, prepared to make what might yet prove a final and triumphant effort.

At that moment, the loud cheers of fresh troops and a heavy rattle of musketry were heard directly on the right flank and rear of the Union forces who were struggling over the ridge at the Henry house. It was the van of the long-awaited column from the Shenandoah Valley, whose advance brigade, Elzey's, led by Kirby Smith in person, had plunged into the battle at its very critical point. Alive to the momentous consequences hanging on a single hour's delay of these troops, Johnston himself had gone to hasten them forward, and had sagaciously ordered that, instead of continuing down the railroad to the Junction, the cars should be stopped opposite the battle-field, and the troops marched across the country to his hard-pressed left. The plan was even wiser than it seemed; for, in the mean time, the Union troops had so far fought onward in "striving," as Johnston says, "to outflank and drive back our left, and thus separate us from Manassas," that Smith's brigades, on arriving, instead of joining on the Confederate left, struck full upon the flank and rear of the Union right.

In a moment, the battle was ended. The raw militia, exhausted by ill-conducted marching since midnight, and by a five hours' battle, faint from lack of food and thirsting for water — results of their own improvidence — broken up in organization by their successful advances, as well as by the day's losses — did not for an instant resist the impact of the fresh foe hurled full upon their flank and rear. Under the sweeping cross fire of Elzey's and Early's brigades of infantry, Stuart's brigade of cavalry, and Beckham's battery, the right wing, which had thitherto clung to the slopes, or surged forward on them, at once melted away. Like wildfire ran from man to man the cry that "Johnston's troops had come!" Crushed alike by the knowledge and the physical experience of that new presence, the Union troops gave way in absolute and irretrievable disorder. At once their commander saw that all was lost, and, knowing well the composition of his forces, felt that the escape of anything must be a matter of fortune, the chance in his favor being the equally raw composition of the forces opposing. Howard's brigade had been swept back in the tide of retreat, but it was of no consequence, for McDowell had no longer the offensive purpose for which he was beginning to use it. Schenck had not crossed the bridge; but it was idle for him to do so. McDowell wisely contented himself with throwing his seven hundred and fifty or eight hundred regulars on the hill opposite the one surmounted by the Henry house, to cover as well as he might the confused retreat.

The news of Kirby Smith's arrival had spread as quickly through the Confederate as the Union ranks, there producing as much relief and joy as to their opponents it had carried despair and ruin. With exulting shouts, the whole army rose and pressed forward in pursuit. But the work was already entirely over, and, save an exchange of shots with Sykes's sullen and stubborn handful of regulars, as they closed in behind the beaten army, nothing remained but to pick up here and there the exhausted or wounded stragglers in the flight. No longer now a triumphant army, but a disorganized collection of men, the Union troops finally abandoning their oft-captured and oft-recovered artillery, streamed confusedly over the Warrenton turnpike, crowding that and the fields adjoining, and recrossed Bull Run. The fording of that rivulet wrecked what faint shadow of organization there had been on retreating from the battle-field. Like the waters bursting from a broken dyke, the troops spread over all roads and fields, and so swept back to Centreville. There an assemblage of camp-followers, Congressmen, correspondents and civilian teamsters, was collected. A stray shell or two from an advanced Confederate battery run forward to Cub Run, burst among the wagons of the hireling teamsters, and instantly began a groundless panic there, a hundred-fold greater than the defeat of the troops on the field; and, blocking the road with their abandoned wagons, and flinging away property in their flight, the throng of civilians and teamsters streamed back on Washington. Thither also the soldiers, soon coming up, continued their retreat; for McDowell, observing the condition of the army and its lack of supplies, saw that little could be gained by an effort to rally at Centreville. Leaving, therefore, the greater part of three divisions to wander unorganized back to their works on the Virginia side of the Potomac, McDowell bent himself to the task of covering the retreat with the very large reserves which had not been in the battle. This was easily accomplished: Miles had foolishly withdrawn from Blackburn's Ford to Centreville, endangering the retreat of the whole army. On the heights, however, he remained, and there Schenck's brigade, too, of Tyler's division, being tolerably uninjured, and the handful of cavalry were drawn up to check the expected pursuit. Howbeit no pursuit of importance was made. The Southern troops, excepting the fresh arrivals, were as badly used up as their adversaries, and in getting hastily over Bull Run, had also, like them, almost broken up what organization they possessed; nor did the commanders dare to go too far with their raw troops. They moved a few miles over the field to Cub Run, and then stopped on observing beyond, as Gen. Johnston says, " the apparent firmness of the United States troops at Centreville, who had not been engaged, which checked our pursuit." These latter waited and watched till the great broken army behind them had rolled off out of sight, talking over the battle as they marched, and till the victorious Confederates, heedless of pursuit, were seen to be content to pick up the trophies dropped by their discomfited enemy. Then, at midnight, the cavalry which had bivouacked in the same field it occupied the night preceding, was roused up, and the Union rear-guard formed column and marched away from sight and sound of the battle-field.

III.

RESULTS OF BULL RUN.

Such was Bull Run — a battle which, being fought soon after the rise of the war, so entirely effected its subsequent course, that it is hard to picture what might have been its sequel, but for this event. What Hallam declares so strongly of Charles Martel's victory at Tours, in its import upon the world's destiny, may be averred of the influence of the battle of Bull Run upon the entire struggle of North and South : — " a contrary event would have essentially varied the drama in all its subsequent scenes." Indeed, eliminate its record, and the key seems lost to all ensuing military history of the rebellion, many of whose phenomena are only explicable by an earlier, all-controlling experience.

Before considering, however, the larger results of Bull Run, it will be necessary to glance at its immediate fruits, prefacing this summary, also, with some explanations: for upon no other battle in America was ever launched so much false, irrelative, and trivial comment, as was at the time put forth both officially and unofficially, and equally on both sides, concerning Bull Run. Much of the mis-statement of the official reports was doubtless deliberate, and for future military purposes, it being deemed expedient, for personal or patriotic motives, to conceal or distort facts which history is already reporting aright. In addition, however, most general officers of that day were entirely raw in the exercise of commands as large as those which were necessarily thrust upon them, and made astounding blunders concerning the numbers and plans of their adversaries, and the nature and strength of geographical positions. Such being the truth with regard to professional soldiers, nothing need be said of the shallow, ignorant, and flippant lay-writers, who, of course, must be expected to go still wider astray in accuracy and pertinency. Nine tenths of all the profuse generalizations about Bull Run, flooding the English and American press after its occurrence, are already in oblivion, their absurdity having been exposed by subsequent campaigns and battles, compared with whose terrific grandeur, this affair at Manassas was but a reconnoissance and a skirmish.

The battle of Bull Run may be placed at once among those conflicts whose issues are, until decided, the most doubtful and accidental, and yet, when decided, most easily comprehensible and explicable. Being fought on both sides by raw troops (for the handful of regular troops are alone excepted), it was impossible at the outset to predict the result. The con-

centration of Confederate troops, producing at length a substantial equality in numbers, made the incertitude still stronger.
Even the choice of position would not solve the difficulty, —
for its real importance was greatly over-estimated. What can
be averred, however, is, that the chances of accident were
greatly increased by the character of the combatants, and,
when fortune seemed inclined to one or the other of the banners, the rout of the other would probably be universal.   It
was left for the shock of battle to determine which of the armies
should be dispersed. Passing thence to the actual occurrence, we find the Union plan of campaign very well formed.
It never could in any event have accomplished what civilian
enthusiasts expected, an unimpeded march into Richmond
— not even if its triumph on the battle-field had been as
complete as its repulse ; but an initial victory it was well calculated to secure. On the other hand the rapid and delicate
withdrawal of Johnston's forces and their junction with Beauregard is equally worthy of praise, inasmuch as it precisely
checkmated McDowell's plan of campaign, and again took
away the latter's assurance of victory. Here again, the
meed of censure must not be passed upon the Union commander at Manassas, but upon those who permitted his plans
to be thwarted while he was necessarily ignorant of the result.
Coming now to the tactical conduct and the phenomena of
the battle-field, we find the troops on both sides standing up
to the work with the blood of their race ; and, nevertheless,
on both sides there were the strongest proofs of how much
was to be learned of the sóldier's art, in camp, on the march,
and in battle itself, and in those thousand skilful devices, and
that familiar acquaintance with danger, which make the veteran soldier more valuable, though not always more intrin-
sically manly, than the recruit. Amongst the officers on
both sides, of all grades, this fact was still more palpable,
even amongst those who subsequently rose to great and well-
deserved distinction, after having at Bull Run put forth

evidences of genius. For it is a very shallow judgment, as well as a very doubtful eulogy, which, led astray in biographical zeal hesitates to admit that its subject can learn anything by experience in the military as in other arts, and prefers to loudly protest that the perfect hero has made no mistakes from beginning to end. Most of the commanders did not at first understand how to conveniently march troops in large bodies; and, on the Union side at least, where the motion was of necessity greater, the preliminary movement to Centreville, the exhausting flank march from 2 o'clock on the battle-morning, and the manœuvres under the terrible sun of the day, doubtless exhausted thrice the energy they would have required, from being ill-timed and ill-conducted; and this ignorance alone, other things being equal, can easily lose a battle. The troops had not learned at that early day, as they did later, to supply the defects of their division, and brigade, and regimental officers, in this respect, by their own self-taught veteran devices for ease in marching, for rest, and for refreshment. On the contrary, while excitement or ignorance of probabilities had kept the Union troops sleepless, their unthinking improvidence caused them to fling away haversacks and canteens in the hot morning march, and left them without rations during the long toils of the day.

On the actual field, to the Union troops and most of their officers, it honestly appeared that their opponents were intrenched in an inexpugnable Gibraltar, hopeless to attack; while, in reality, the position was untenable against skilful attack. So, in the reports of many officers, as well as in the talk of their men, there were innumerable "masked batteries," which seemed a terrible, and almost an unfair advantage accorded to their enemy. The troops, fighting bravely, yet became disorganized by their own advance almost as much as by repulse. Individual impulses had not yet been drilled out of them; straggling occurred here and there, without much sense of its enormity on the part of the offenders; and, finally, when even routed, the whole body marched off without attempt at organization, talking over the causes of their defeat, and many deliberately dropping the accoutrements, and even the guns for which they had decided there could be no further use.   The troops on the Confederate side, gallant and disposed to fight as they were, were equally thrown into the confused state common to undisciplined volunteers, by severe repulse.   It has been described how dangerously they were demoralized by their hard fight, when Johnston and Beauregard rode among them to rally the lines, while victory was inclining to the Union cause.   A sympathetic eye-witness on the Confederate side, wrote that, at two o'clock, "the fortunes of the day were dark.   The remnants of the regiments, so badly injured, or wounded and worn, as they staggered out, gave gloomy pictures of the scene."   These stragglers — not cowardly but undisciplined — poured in dangerous numbers from the field, as two hours later did the whole Union army.

But the want of experience of which we speak was quite as observable among the officers on both sides.   The opening tactical manœuvres, on the Union part, whether in consequence of erroneous reconnoissances, or of the bad handling of the troops, were delayed three hours, and the victory thus shut out, as it were, from the troops, before they could fire a gun.   Then again, perilous lulls occurred in the battle — one of them during the all-important half-hour when the Confederate generals were rallying their troops in great distress — because the brigade commanders hardly knew what to do next. And when their attacks were afterwards made on the Confederate key position, they were made by brigades at a time, and without concert or cohesion.   Indeed, Hunter's first attack, in the morning, was a fire from the head of column. Many minor instances of inexperience in Virginia wood-fighting occurred; of which, by way of a single example, may be mentioned the first seizure of Griffin's battery by Stonewall Jackson. The Union chief of artillery thought the regiments which Jackson moved forward to take the battery was only the two regiment of supports, which he expected from the same quarter; and, allowing them to approach without fire, in an instant the cannoneers and horses were shot down, and the pieces, till recaptured, left in Confederate hands. So, on the Confederate side, the great mistake was made by Beauregard at the outset, of supposing Bull Run to be a defensive line, to be passed only at the fords. Again, the morning of the battle revealed to him that his whole left flank was either actually turned, or being turned — and this, in spite of the facilities for observing the marching of troops in the neighborhood of Sudley Springs; and, in spite of the delays of the Union column, and a pause of a part of it for half an hour at the ford. Moreover, his line was so constituted, that its left was driven back more than a mile before it become firm again; and his forces being, though less than 30,000 in number, strung over a range of eight miles, before the right could get up to the left, the day had nearly gone against the Confederates. His own opening dispositions for attack, also, had so absorbed attention that McDowell meanwhile had easily got the offensive; and so defective was the staff-system, that Beauregard and Johnston were wondering for some hours, ignorant that the orders had not been delivered, why their right brigades did not move forward to the attack. Here, on the other hand, it is equally clear that the Confederate generals were justified in making no attempt to pursue. It would have required an attack on the Union reserves, comprising a full third of McDowell's troops, who lay in good position on the heights of Centreville, covering the retreat of the other two thirds. This attack might well have been regarded as dangerous, especially to those knowing, as Beauregard and Johnston did, the demoralization of their forces, even after the arrival of reinforcements. "Pursuit," said General Johnston to the writer of this sketch, after the war ended, "could not be thought of; for we were almost as much disorganized by our victory as the Federals by their defeat." Indeed, making all allowances for the magniloquent reports of those early days, it had been, to use the words of Mr. Davis, "a hard-fought field," and the victors were in no condition to pursue.

The material fruits of the Confederate victory at Bull Run were the possession of the field, and of many prisoners and spoils, the precise figures, however, being, for causes already rehearsed, difficult to fix. The official Confederate loss in the battle was 378 killed, 1489 wounded, and 30 missing — a total of 1897; the official Union loss was 481 killed, 1011 wounded, and an unknown number of missing and wounded and missing. The Confederate reports showed a total of 1460 Union prisoners, wounded and unwounded, captured during and after the action. Besides these, there were many stragglers who never came back; so that the total Union loss may be safely put down, in round numbers, at from 3500 to 4000 men. The Union troops abandoned on the field and in their retreat, 28 guns, about 5900 muskets, nearly half a million cartridges, 64 artillery horses, 26 wagons, ten colors, and much camp equipage and clothing.

But the victory at Bull Run gained more than a field: it won a campaign. Midsummer passed, autumn came and went, winter at last found the Union and Confederate troops in Virginia in their peaceful log-camps. The year 1861 slipped entirely away without another forward movement in Virginia; the new year opened silently there; spring came again before the spell which Bull Run had thrown was broken up. Nor was this true of Virginia alone, but of the whole West; incessant skirmishes and desultory engagements by detached forces occupied the time and strength which had been designed for grand operations; for these latter were repressed at their beginning, and the military year of 1861, from which so much had been hoped, came to its end at the battle of Bull Run.

Nevertheless, the immediate and material consequences of this initial battle were dust in the balance, contrasted with its grand moral influences. Then, for the first time, the North knew that long and bloody war lay before it, for which it had not made adequate preparation. Much reliance it had hitherto placed on what it regarded as the supreme justice of its cause and on the matchless enthusiasm of its million defenders. By virtue of the one bitter cup quaffed at Manassas, it saw with clear eyes a truth proclaimed by universal history, that, whatever the intrinsic dignity of a national cause, when once it falls under the dread arbitrament of the sword, its surest hope of success is in the resort to the laws of war and the application of military science. Numbers will not supply the place of discipline, nor will enthusiasm allow the rules of war to be contravened. It is military strategy, it is the tactics and logistics of campaigning, it is in short the profession of war to which a cause, deserving to find in its own nobleness defence sufficient, has to be entrusted; and, as a client rests his fortunes in his patron's hands, to be submitted to the dull, mechanical channels of an unsympathetic professional routine, with all the law's delay and with new chances of failure from the superior professional talent of the opposing advocate suffered to intervene, so was the North forced to intrust its honor and very existence to the watch-care of a professional soldiery. With the first unwelcome consciousness of that necessity, there came a momentary pang of disappointment and a flutter of incertitude; for it had been thought that an upright cause would, in some indefinite way, prove its own advocate. It had been imagined, also, that nothing but that sublime self-sacrifice, and that supreme devotion of all which makes life worth the living, which could be seen at countless hearthstones, from ocean to ocean, were required to trium-

phantly vindicate the integrity of the Union. The initial
shock of general battle had taught a different lesson, and had
declared not only that mere numerical strength could not
avail, in itself, against an adroit enemy, but also that neither
the highest inspiration of patriotism, nor the profoundest
devotion to duty, no, nor yet the wildest enthusiasm reinforced by the call of duty, could win battles and decide the
issue of campaigns. But this battle taught something more
and more important, by disclosing that if the heart of the
North was pledged to its cause, not less entirely was the
heart of the South given to that opposing cause which, after
long and anxious doubt, it had now made its own. Many
scenes had the Union troops to relate, on returning to Washington, in which dying Southern soldiers, tasting the grateful
drop of water which humanity did not refuse even in the
ferocity of battle, said : " You have fought for your country ;
I die for mine."

Learning, then, therefore, not only that ill-directed enthusiasm would not avail, even against the most unscrupulous
and unprincipled opponents, and convinced, moreover, that
whatever might be true of Southern leaders, Southern men
with muskets in their hands were not without principle or
without a cause — that indeed, they would overmatch enthusiasm by enthusiasm — the North began to gird itself to a long
and sanguinary contest. In the change which then came over
its spirit, a reaction almost as remarkable and as violent as
its first impetus with regard to the conduct of the war, succeeded. The restless leaders and demagogues who had encouraged the people to fancy that a mere *levée en masse* and
a popular crusade against the South, like that which Peter
the Hermit and Walter the Penniless directed upon Jerusa-
lem, would gain them Richmond and the South, were covered
with confusion. With patience and docility the people now
submitted to tedious military manipulations, while their volunteers, all aglow with fire, were hammered and tempered

into drilled and veteran soldiers.   Reflective observers, looking beyond the trivial and accidental occurrences of Manassas,
saw that patriotism had not so much lowered at the North as
deepened, and if the thin leaping flames of excitement had
subsided, it was but to the white heat of fixed and unquench-
able purpose.   Its baptism of blood was also for the North
its reconsecration.   It had learned from experience what a
philosophical historian proclaims to be a fundamental truth
of military history, and a canon to which, strange as it may
seem, there is no real exception : — "One of the most certain
of all lessons of military history," says Dr. Arnold, "although
some writers have neglected it, and some have even disputed
it, is the superiority of discipline to enthusiasm.   The
first thing, then, to be done in all warfare, whether foreign or domestic, is to discipline our men, and till they are
thoroughly disciplined to avoid above all things the exposing
them to any general action with the enemy.   History is full
indeed of instances of great victories gained by a very small
force over a very large one ; but not by undisciplined men,
however brave and enthusiastic, over those who were well
disciplined, except under peculiar circumstances of surprise
or local advantages, such as cannot affect the truth of the
general rule."   Impressed with this truth, the North devoted what was left of summer with the autumn and the
winter to the levying and disciplining of great armies,
the accumulation of material of war, and meanwhile busily
arranged formal campaigns.   In place of the comparative
handful of untrained three-months' militia, who had once
been thought more than adequate to overrun the South before
their term of service should expire, the new campaign was
begun with a round half million of soldiers, enlisted "for
three years or the war."   In Virginia the broken mass of
fugitives who marched from Bull Run to Washington, became, when swelled and moulded into symmetry under the
hand of a skilful organizer, the Grand Army of the Potomac.

Every arm was increased and made efficient. Three companies
of cavalry were all that crossed the Potomac with McDowell's
army in May of 1861; seven companies were absolutely
all that marched with it to Bull Run — two companies
being left behind in Washington. "People years hence,"
said the commander of one of these companies, "will hardly
believe this; but it is, nevertheless, strictly true." Such
was the petty nucleus of the splendid corps of twenty thousand horsemen who, under Sheridan, swept through the Shenandoah Valley and took so glorious a part at Five Forks
and Culpepper Court House. Instead of seven companies,
McClellan took with him to the Peninsula alone ten regiments
or thereabouts, of Stoneman's cavalry, and as great a force
was left in other parts of Virginia. In place of nine imperfect
batteries of thirty guns, which remained from Bull Run as the
entire artillery of the Army in the East, spring found ninety-
two batteries, of five hundred and twenty guns, with a corps
of twelve thousand and five hundred disciplined artillerists.
Two hundred thousand volunteer infantry, many of them
seasoned since the opening of autumn by drill and exercise
in camp and garrison, were ready for march. The engineer,
the quarter-master, the ordnance, the commissary and the
medical departments, had been raised to a proportionate size
and efficiency.

If upon the South the influence of Bull Run was less immediate, it was not the less powerful. The first emotion
inspired by the result was commingled of relief, of joy, and of
confidence in the future. A great burden had been lifted;
for despite the braggart professions of superiority indulged
by the more vainglorious of its mercurial population, thoughtful men in the South had felt that infinite consequences, possibly the fate of the war, pivoted on its first great battle; and
that the issues of this battle were absolutely beyond the scope
of prediction. Now was at least to be war, not a mere riot.
Best and most inspiring of all, Bull Run had secured for the

South a period of probation during which infinite results might be compassed. A whole year had been gained. A whole year? and in less time than that States had been founded which flourished through ages!

Thus the result first in importance of the victory of Bull Run was to furnish the South with that element of visible success which was needful to unify the South, for there were tens of thousands of rich, of brave, of patriotic and of greatly influential men whose minds had never been thoroughly made up to permanently accept the Confederacy. Deprecating at the outset the effort at secession, partly on the ground of right, partly on the ground of expediency, these men could not find it in their consciences, certainly not in their discretion, as men of the world, to espouse a government which, in their eyes, was neither a *de jure* nor a *de facto* authority. To enrol this influential class, and thereby to take from the loyal North its plausible hopes from " Southern Unionists," and, weld the South into a homogeneous nation, with but a single sentiment and aim, there was wanting a victory in the field. That victory was won, and thereafter thousands of those who before had refrained from the strife out of no selfish motives, but from loyalty to law, till law should be hopelessly disowned, and a greater law take the vacant seat and by visible proofs support a claim to sovereignty, these men threw, at length, their swords into the scale, and with them life, fortune, and honor.

The uncounted hundred millions who from across the ocean gazed on through four years with never-ceasing wonder, upon the mighty drama whose stage was a hemisphere, were not less affected than the actors themselves by its opening scene. Sympathy indeed was quickly distributed to one or other of the combatants, according to the character, or sensibilities, or understanding of the onlookers. But it was only or chiefly after the struggle at Bull Run that, for the South especially, Transatlantic sympathy took practical shape, and manifested its sincerity in supplies of money, ships, arms, munitions of war, and whatever other material assistance could be sent across the water. The tendencies of foreign governments also to recognize as a belligerent power the nascent Confederacy, which had before been chiefly inclinations matured to more positive acts; and, above all, the people of Europe exerted upon their governments a strong pressure for the absolute recognition of the Southern Confederacy. This favorable sentiment being reflected across the Atlantic, had its full effect in raising the hopes of the insurgent South.

Nor do we yet reach the limits of the general results of Bull Run. Something I shall perhaps be expected to say of the general and well-grounded confidence which Bull Run gave to the South in the valor of its troops. Had this sentiment risen no higher than was justified by a sensible review of the circumstances of the victory, it might have simply acted as a stimulus to the South. But in the temper in which it found the people, it afforded so colorable an excuse for still more extravagant and ridiculous assertions of Southern prowess as to damage most seriously the cause they had at heart.

In tracing the connecting links in the complicated chain of cause and effect that runs through war, it will frequently be discovered that results the most momentous go back to influences seemingly the most remote. Of this truth the aspect and prospect of the rebellion, in so far as regards the military resources of the South at the opening of the campaign of the following year, furnish a striking illustration. It was in no slight degree the victory of the Confederates at Bull Run that in the following spring prepared for them a crushing defeat on the Cumberland and the Tennessee. Inflated with pride at their triumph in the first clash of arms, the Southern leaders no less than the Southern people, anticipated no other result whenever it might please the men of the North to test their prowess: so that while the North during the succeeding autumn and winter was forming a colossal armament, the Confederates, reposing in vainglorious confidence, contented themselves with preparations little proportioned to their actual needs. This apathy especially prevailed at the West. It was in vain that General Sidney Johnston, who commanded the Department, labored to produce a realizing sense of the requirements of his situation. " I appealed," says he, in an epistle of lamentation, written after the fall of Fort Donelson, " I appealed in vain to the War Department and the Governors of States —the aid given was small." It thus came about that at the opening of the spring campaign of 1862 the entire force garrisoning his very extended line of three hundred miles, from the Cumberland Mountains to the Mississippi River, numbered some 37,000 men. The result was, as will hereafter appear, that when Grant moved against Johnston his line, everywhere weak, was easily broken, and with the fall of Donelson the whole western system of defence fell in ruins to the ground. The high-blown confidence of the people was then succeeded by demoralization and a distrust of ultimate success that prevented the Confederate Government from ever evoking the full military strength of the west.

Regarding the great lessons of the battle fought on the plains of Manassas and the marvellous scope it instantly lent to the American conflict, it may be truthfully asserted that the cannon of Bull Run echoed henceforth on every battle-field of the war, — aye, down to the very surrender at Appomattox Court House.

II.

DONELSON.

I.

PRELUDE TO DONELSON.

THROUGHOUT the vast extent of territory enclosed between the Alleghanies and the Mississippi, the year 1861 passed without military operations of moment, but not without preparations for war on a colossal scale. The beginning of 1862 saw in the West a mighty armament and a formidable fleet ready to move against the enemy. Events had clearly determined the theatre of the war, which indeed was already marked out by the controlling lines of physical geography.

The centre zone presents a striking natural peculiarity, which not only shaped the lines of military operation, but which was bound up with a series of natural influences that powerfully affected the course of the war. This region is divided by the Tennessee River into two distinct parts, which may be called the upper centre zone and the lower centre zone. In the latter the water-shed carries all the rivers into the Gulf of Mexico; in the former, enclosed between the Tennessee and the Ohio, and embracing the States of Tennessee and Kentucky, the rivers, rising in the Alleghanies, flow westward and northward and swell the volume of the Father of Waters.

Now it is worthy of note, that while the States of the lower centre zone were carried into secession by a kind of political gravitation as potent as the propulsive force that hurries their waters to the Gulf, Tennessee resisted the primary secession movement, and only fell into the secondary movement inaugurated by Virginia, and that Kentucky, after a brief dream of neutrality, resisted altogether, and adhered to the Union.

Kentucky's loyalty marked out that State as the theatre of war in the West, for it was soon seen by the insurgents that, as the great water highways of the Tennessee and Cumberland, which conduct to the very heart of the South, flow northward through that State, and empty into the Ohio, the loss of Kentucky must be the loss of all the territory north of the Tennessee. When, therefore, Kentucky committed herself definitively to the side of the Union, the insurgents crossed her borders, seized and fortified Columbus, on the Mississippi, obstructed the Tennessee and Cumberland, intrenched themselves at Bowling Green — in a word, sought to gain the dominion of the whole upper centre zone, by anticipating control of the Mississippi water-shed.

The defensive line taken up by the Confederates embraced a very extended front, stretching through Kentucky from the Mississippi to the Cumberland Mountains. The control of this theatre of operations had since September, 1861, been in the hands of General Albert Sydney Johnston, an old officer of the service of the United States, and popularly esteemed at the time the ablest of those who had linked their fortunes with the revolt.

The left flank of Johnston's line rested on the Mississippi, at Columbus, twenty miles south of the mouth of the Ohio, where, upon a range of bold and jutting bluffs, a fortified camp was formed, and powerful batteries were erected to close the navigation of the river. The force at this point was under General Leonidas Polk, a whilom bishop of the Episcopal Church, who had exchanged the crozier for the weapons of carnal warfare. Running eastward from Columbus, the line passed through Forts Henry and Donelson —

two works, placed the one on the right bank of the Tennessee and the other on the left bank of the Cumberland (forty miles from where these rivers empty into the Ohio), with the view of obstructing the Union advance by those highways of communication. It then took a forward leap to Bowling Green — a strongly intrenched camp, covering Nashville and the Louisville and Nashville Railroad. Finally, the right flank was posted at Cumberland Gap, where the Confederates held the gateway to the mountain region of East Tennessee.

To act against this defensive cordon, and to open the Mississippi, two Union armies were assembled on two widely separated lines of operation. At the point where the Ohio joins the Mississippi, the wedge-shaped figure of Southern Illinois, thrust forward in a sharp salient between the States of Missouri and Kentucky, ends in a tongue of land upon which stands the town of Cairo. It is an unlovely, amphibious region, scarcely satirized in Dickens's famous description; but its commanding strategic importance had caused it to be made a point of rendezvous for a land and naval force destined to operate in the valley of the Mississippi. The naval force, consisting of a fleet of gun-boats and river iron-clads constructed in the workshops of St. Louis and Cincinnati, was placed under the charge of Commodore A. H. Foote, an officer distinguished alike for the unaffected piety of his character and his daring inspirations as a commander. The command of the land force had in August been assigned to a certain Brigadier-General U. S. Grant — a quiet, unimposing, and unostentatious officer, whom, at the time, neither the public voice nor the whisperings of his own prophetic soul marked out for that astonishing career that was to link his name with the mightiest achievements of the war. When, in November, 1861, General Halleck took command of the "Department of Missouri," he enlarged the "District of Cairo" to include all the southern part of Illinois, all that part of Kentucky west of the Cumberland, and the southern counties of Missouri south of Cape Girardeau, and Grant proceeded energetically with. the task of organizing an army for the impending campaign in the Mississippi valley.

The other Union army had been gathered on the Ohio, at Louisville, and thrown forward into Central Kentucky along the line of the Louisville and Nashville Railroad, and into Eastern Kentucky towards Cumberland Gap. The region covered by the activities of this army constituted the Department of the Ohio. Its command was for a time entrusted to General Robert Anderson, but, in October, it was transferred to General W. T. Sherman. That officer's pregnant military views, however, so far outran the short-sighted enthusiasm and crude experimentalism of the time that he was prouounced "crazy," and he was displaced (November 12) by General Don Carlos Buell — a soldier whose convictions certainly could not have sensibly differed from those of Sherman, but who was by temper more reticent in their expression. Buell immediately began putting forth all his energies to prepare movable columns for an advance upon Nashville and East Tennessee. By the end of December he had collected troops enough to organize four divisions — about forty thousand men. Two of these divisions were on the Louisville and Nashville Railroad — the one at Mumfordsville and the other at Bacon Creek; a third division was posted near Green River; the fourth division, forming Buell's left, was at Lebanon, under command of General G. H. Thomas.

If with this view of the relative situation of the opposing forces, we consider the problem to be solved by the Union armies, it will appear that, in its general stragetic aspect, there were two forces operating upon two independent lines against two other bodies holding an interior position. Grant, at Cairo, threatened the Confederates at Columbus and the forts of the Cumberland and Tennessee; while Buell, on the Louisville and Nashville Railroad, menaced Bowling Green and East

Tennessee.   But Johnston, with a direct line of railroad from Bowling Green to Columbus, was in position to concentrate at either point more rapidly than Grant and Buell could unite the one with the other.   Besides, the duty devolving on each of the Union commanders seemed beset with difficulties.   The position at Bowling Green, strengthened as it was by fortifications on both sides of Barren River, and covered by a formidable stream, might be supposed to be inassailable by direct attack, while it could hardly be turned.   In addition, the Cumberland Mountains, running almost parallel with Buell's line of operations, gave the Confederates a great facility for incursions into North-Eastern Kentucky.   These were of frequent occurrence, and difficult to prevent; and they were, in fact, only checked at last by the brilliant stroke of Mill Spring (January 18, 1862), where General Thomas first chained a victory to the Union standard, and began that splendid series of solid and substantial achievements with which his name is associated.   Howbeit, this success, though very valuable morally in inspiring the Union troops, had no direct bearing on the problem before Buell, which was to dislodge Johnston from Bowling Green.   The obstructions to an advance against that "Manassas of the West," as it was called, presented so formidable a front that it was difficult to see how they were to be overcome.

Nor, seemingly, was the situation of the army at Cairo much more promising.   Columbus was known to be powerfully fortified, and in the high-flown language of the time, it had acquired the appellation of a "Gibraltar."   It was connected, too, by unpleasant asssociation with Belmont, to which place General Grant had made an expedition in November, 1861.   After he had burnt the insurgent camp, the Confederates, crossing from Columbus, which is directly opposite Belmont, drove the Union force with a considerable loss to the shelter of its transports, and compelled it to return to Cairo.   One or two subsequent advances, or shows of advance towards Columbus, by the Kentucky side, had each been followed by a retrograde movement, the effect of which was unfavorable to the *morale* of new and high-spirited troops. If it had been possible to lay Columbus under siege, the operation would have been embarassed by the menace to the Union force offered by the presence of the garrisons of the forts on the Tennessee and Cumberland. Finally, its capture, without the capture of the force it contained, could have been of slight value, and would have decided nothing.

But while the Union commanders thus confronted each his special task, and counted with prudent calculation the stops and limitations that beset an advance, and planned with wise devisement how they might be overcome, a new solution of the whole problem presented itself. The conception of what afterwards proved to be the true method of initiative in the West, presented itself to so many minds almost simultaneously, that it is not easy to say to whom primarily belongs the credit. It is certain that General Buell, in a communication to General Halleck, suggested the plan as early as the very beginning of January, 1862; and it is equally certain that soon afterwards General Grant, without knowledge of what Buell had advised Halleck, but acting on the result of reconnoissances made by General C. F. Smith and Commodore Foote, requested permission to execute the identical operation proposed by Buell. Taking note of the remarkable course of the Tennessee and Cumberland rivers, and knowing that at the season of high water these streams are naviagble to large vessels to the very heart of the South, the officers named saw that if the obstruction to the navigation of the Cumberland and Tennessee could be removed, nearly the whole upper centre zone must become untenable to the enemy. Their plan, accordingly, was to employ the land and naval force that had been assembled at Cairo in reducing Forts Henry and Donelson, which held the gateway of these water lines; for it was plain that if these could be opened, both

Columbus and Bowling Green would be taken in reverse, that Johnston's line of communication would be severed, that the whole of the Confederate front of defence, as then drawn, must fall to the ground. This plan met the approval of Halleck, who on the 30th of January, 1862, gave to Grant and Foote the eagerly-awaited *laissez aller.*

On the morning of the 2d of February the fleet of gun-boats and iron-clads, followed by a long line of transports, freighted with troops, left Cairo to test their metal against the river strongholds of the enemy. Steaming up the Ohio to Paducah, the vessels by night turned their prows into the Tennessee, and next morning they anchored a few miles below Fort Henry, against which it was resolved to make the *coup d'essai.*

The Tennessee and Cumberland rivers, after a great curve by the south and west, turn northward: as they near the Ohio they approach very close to each other. At the boundary line between Kentucky and Tennessee these streams are separated by only twelve miles, and it was at points immediately south of this line that the Confederate commander had raised his bulwark of defence — Fort Henry being located on the right bank of the Tennessee, and Fort Donelson on the left bank of the Cumberland. Both were bastion earthworks, armed with heavy guns to defend the water faces, and enclosed in an extended line of infantry breastworks. A direct road connected the two forts. After two days spent in debarking the troops and in reconnoissances, it was decided to make a combined land and naval attack against Fort Henry on the morning of the 6th. The fleet was to move up the stream and open fire at twelve o'clock; Grant, whose forces lay encamped three miles below the work, was to march at eleven; and he believed that he could readily get his troops up to the rear of the fort in time to intercept the retreat of the garrison, if the fire of the fleet should be such as to induce the Commandant to abandon it. Confident in his iron-clads, Foote declared he would reduce the fort in an hour, and urged Grant to make an earlier start or he would be too late : but Grant thought otherwise. At the appointed time the Commodore steamed up toward Henry, his four iron-clads leading and followed by three wooden gun-boats. Opening fire at a thousand yards, he gradually closed on the fort, with daring gallantry running his vessels to within six hundred yards of the enemy. The armament of Fort Henry consisted of seventeen guns, twelve of which bore well on the river. These were of the following description : one ten-inch Columbiad, one rifled gun of 24-pound calibre, two 42-pounders, and eight 32-pounders, all arranged to fire through embrasures, formed by raising the parapet between the guns with sand bags carefully laid. The line of rifle-trenches guarding the land approaches was held by a garrison of 3,200 men, and the whole was under command of Brigadier-General Tilghman.

The fire of the fleet was for a time returned with spirit by the fort; but the extraordinary vigor of Foote's attack soon made itself felt, and several accidents occurred to disconcert the enemy. In a short time the rifled cannon burst, killing three of the men at the piece, and disabling a number of others. Then all the gunners at another piece were wounded by a shell that passed through the embrasure. Soon afterwards a premature discharge occurred at one of the 42-pounders, killing three of the men; and finally the Columbiad was rendered unserviceable by the breaking of a priming wire in the vent. The artillerists then became discouragad, and some even ceased to work the smaller guns, under the belief that their shot were too light to produce any effect on the iron-clad sides of the Union vessels. Tilghman exerted himself to the utmost to encourage and urge his men; but they had become thoroughly demoralized, and when he made an effort to get men from the outer lines to take the place of his

exhausted gunners, he failed in the attempt. He then instructed the commander of the troops to withdraw them to
Fort Donelson, while with the artillerists, numbering less
than a hundred, he remained to surrender the work. Foote
had declared he would reduce the fort in an hour, and he
kept his promise, for in five minutes after that time the white
flag appeared on the parapet. When Tilghman asked what
terms would be accorded him, the Commodore formulated
the conditions in two words, "unconditional surrender"—
a phrase which, inaugurated by that brave sailor, served
afterwards as the blazon of many a splendid victory at the
West. The only serious damage sustained by the fleet
was experienced by the iron-clad Essex, which received a
shot in its boiler, resulting in the scalding and burning of
twenty-nine officers and men, including Commander Porter.
The land force which had been much delayed in the miry
roads did not arrive till some time after the surrender: the
fugitive garrison, therefore, made good its escape and hastened in dismay to ensconse itself behind the bulwarks of
Fort Donelson. Thither, also, the propitious fate now plainly
pointed the way for the Union force.

I have thus traced the process by which the dim outlines of
the first western campaign grew into definite shape in the
brilliant plan of breaking Johnston's defensive system by a
perpendicular force moving on the river lines of the Cumberland and Tennessee; and I have shown with what success
this plan was initiated at Fort Henry. Before passing to the
recital of the weightier triumph at Donelson, it will be per-
tinent to examine the precise condition of the Confederates
in respect of the material resources they had wherewith to
meet the massive force arrayed against them, and the method
of action adopted by the Confederate commander.

From the time when Albert Sydney Johnston assumed the
command of the Western Department, he had limited his
views to the maintenance of a simple attitude of defence. To

this course he was led from the inadequacy of his strength;
for although he succeeded in giving both Buell and Grant the
impression that he confronted each with an overwhelming
force, his army was in reality pitifully slight.   On the eastern
line, at Bowling Green and its dependencies, he had of troops
not quite 22,000; and on the western line, at Columbus and
the forts of the Tennessee and Cumberland, about 15,000.
The total aggregate was some 37,000 men, and with this
force he attempted to defend a line three hundred miles in
length, stretching from the Cumberland Mountains to the
Mississippi.   In this condition, outnumbered on both lines,
Johnston does not appear to have comprehended that a defensive attitude could only result fatally to him — that his sole
ground of hope rested in taking advantage of his interior
position to concentrate the gross of his force at a single point,
and assume the offensive against one or the other of the two
Union armies.   Connected with this is a piece of secret
history, revealed to me by General Beauregard since the close
of the war, which will not be out of place here.

Towards the close of the first month of the year 1862 General Beauregard was transferred from Virginia to the West, to
take charge, under Sydney Johnston of the defence of the
Mississippi valley.   *En route* he visited Johnston at his head-
quarters at Bowling Green, and between the two officers a
prolonged conference ensued touching the best method of
action.   It was with the liveliest concern that Beauregard,
who had understood at Richmond that Johnston's force num-
60,000 men, learned that it was in reality little over one half
that aggregate.   But that officer was always essentially aggressive in his military inspiration, and he now proposed that
the works at Columbus should be so reduced that their defence
might be sustained by two or three thousand men; that the
remaining twelve thousand should be brought to Bowling
Green and joined to the twenty-two thousand there, and that
with the united force, a vigorous, and if possible a crushing

blow should be dealt Buell's army, which was regarded at the time as the most menacing, for Grant and Foote had not yet moved.   Johnston fell in with this plan, and Beauregard proceeded to Columbus to put it in train of execution.   Scarcely, however, had he started for Columbus when the thunder of Union guns on the Tennessee apprised him that it was too late, and by the time he reached the Mississippi, Fort Henry had fallen.   The clamor of those guns, like the knocking at the gate that affrighted the soul of Macbeth, startled Johnston with the omen of doom; for it, too, was a knocking at the gate — the gate which once broken down, exposed the very citadel of all his strength.

"Then," says he, "I resolved to defend Nashville at Donelson."

II.

THE SIEGE AND FALL OF FORT DONELSON.

When, on the night of the 6th of February, Johnston received tidings of the fall of Fort Henry, it was plain to him that not only was his position at Bowling Green seriously jeopardized, but that Nashville itself must become untenable unless the key of the Cumberland could be securely held. That key was Donelson, which had the character of a fortress thrust out on the flank of Nashville and Bowling Green.   In order, therefore, to insure so solid a defence that hostile efforts should not prevail against that stronghold, Johnston ventured upon parting with the major part of his own force.   He accordingly detached the commands of Buckner, Pillow, and Floyd, to Donelson, which raised the effective of the defending force to 16,000, while at Bowling Green he retained but 14,000 to confront Buell and cover Nashville.   In a word, he resolved "to defend Nashville at Donelson."

Had General Grant been in condition immediately after

the fall of Fort Henry to move upon Donelson, he would have had the advantage of striking at a time when the position was in a very imperfect state of defence. But not only was it necessary to await the accumulation of supplies for the intended change of base from the Tennessee to the Cumberland: it was requisite to allow time for repairing the damage suffered by the gun-boats, the importance of which auxiliary was, from their brilliant achievement at Fort Henry, very naturally magnified. Accordingly, though Fort Henry was captured on the 6th of February, it was the 12th before General Grant put his columns in motion towards Donelson, before which he drew up his force on the afternoon of the same day — the distance between the two works being but twelve miles. But on the 9th, the garrison of Fort Donelson, composed chiefly of those who made their escape from Fort Henry, was reinforced by the command of General Pillow; and on the 12th it received a further accession of several thousand men, brought by General Buckner from Bowling Green. The following day General Floyd arrived, bringing with him his brigade; and as that officer was the senior Brigadier, he assumed command of the whole Confederate force.

Fort Donelson, the stronghold, that thus became the object of attack and defence by the forces we have seen converging upon it, was situated on the left bank of the Cumberland, forty miles from the embouchere of that river in the Ohio. It consisted of a large field-work of irregular *tracé*, drawn on a commanding hill near the town of Dover, and enclosing nearly a hundred acres; while on the hill-side, riverward, were two powerful water-batteries, with an armament of eight 32-pounders, three 32-pounder carronades, one 10-inch and one 8-inch Columbiad, and one rifled gun of 32-pounder calibre. These batteries were admirably placed to control the river approaches, and the position was flanked both above and below the fort by small tributaries of the Cumberland, which had been converted by the high water into deep sloughs.

But while Fort Donelson had excellent command of the river front, it was ill-placed and, in fact, untenable with reference to attack from the rear or land side, by which General Grant was approaching from Fort Henry. From that side the site was completely commanded by a range of hills around the work. When, however, it was seen that attack was imminent, the Confederates hastened to anticipate possession of this ground and drew thereon a line of infantry-cover consisting of earthworks, rifle-trenches, and abatis. As reinforcements arrived, heavy details were employed in the construction of these defences, and by the night of the 12th, when the Union forces arrived, these were in readiness. The line was about two miles and a half in extent, and enclosed within its left flank the little town of Dover, in which were the enemy's commissary and quarter-master's stores. The ground is much broken by hills and ravines, and in most part heavily wooded; but the works were laid out by a skilful Engineer, and formed a very formidable line of defence. The troops under Buckner garrisoned the right, and those under Pillow the left of this line.

The force with which General Grant approached Fort Donelson on the afternoon of the 12th consisted of two divisions of about 15,000 men — the First division of four brigades under Brigadier-General J. A. McClernand; the Second division of three brigades under Brigadier-General C. F. Smith. The brigades of the First division were commanded by Colonels Oglesby, W. H. L. Wallace, McArthur, and Morrison; those of the Second by Colonels Cook, Lauman, and M. L. Smith. Six regiments were to be transported by water from Fort Henry to Donelson, and united with other regiments brought from Cairo and South-land, formed the Third division under Brigadier General

Lew Wallace. Smith's division immediately took position on the left; McClernand's on the right.

The men who followed Grant in what was really both his and their maiden campaign, were green soldiers; but they were men of the West — large, free, hardy, open-handed, brave, and from their very first campaign they showed that they had already many of the qualities and aptitudes of veterans. It was seen, for example, that the adventurous habits of the men that composed the Western army gave it a great mobility, and as its functions were to be offensive rather than defensive — as it had no Washington to cover, but, on the contrary, had resolved to hew its way to the Gulf, — that army early took and retained through all its career a kind of conquering, crusading spirit, a freedom and confidence in large aggressive operations, never possessed by the great army of the East. Already, in their first campaign, these men, as they boldly pressed up against the enemy's stronghold of the Cumberland, gave promise of that mettle they showed in the colossal operations that were to fill the coming years.

By the night of the 12th the line of investment was drawn closely around the enemy's defenses; and at dawn of the 13th hostilities began with a furious cannonade and sharpshooting, and in the afternoon an assault was made by four regiments with the view to carry a height near the enemy's centre; but though executed with great vigor, it resulted in a complete repulse, with a considerable loss. Nevertheless, the assault was, under the circumstances, a judicious measure; for this bold front served to impose on the enemy in regard to the Union force, which, in reality, did not at this time exceed that of the Confederates. Next day, Friday the 14th, Foote's fleet of iron-clads and gun-boats, together with transports bearing supplies and ammunition and a powerful reinforcement of 10,000 men, arrived, amid the joyful cheers of the army. The fresh troops were formed into a division under General Lew Wallace, and assigned a position in the centre of the line, between the divisions of Smith and McClernand.

The new accession to his strength received by Grant established a preponderance of force on the Union side, and it was resolved to make an immediate combined attack by the fleet against the water batteries and by the army against the defensive line of the Confederates. But it required all day of the 14th for the newly-arrived troops to get into position: so that in the afternoon the fleet alone was in position to begin operations. As, however, the success at Fort Henry had inspired the greatest confidence, both in the offensive power and the capacity for resistance of the floating batteries, Foote, without further delay, moved forward to the attack with four iron-clads and two wooden gun-boats. The firing was opened at a mile and a half, and continued steadily until the vessels had approached within less than four hundred yards of the fort. During all this time the vessels met no response from the batteries, the Confederates reserving their fire till the fleet had come within point blank range. All the guns in the water batteries, twelve in number, then opened fire, and a strenuous contest began between fleet and fort. But it soon became manifest that, as the conditions of attack and defence differed materially from those at Fort Henry, so also was the result destined to be different. The water batteries, from their position, had a most effective plunging fire on the fleet, and while the shot and shell of the ships produced no impression on the powerful sand embankments that protected the guns, the Columbiad and 32-pound rifle told with fatal effect on the iron-clads. "Two unlucky shots," says General Grant, "disabled two of the armored gun-boats, so that they were carried back by the current, and the remaining two were very much disabled." Thirty-five shots had struck the Louisville, thirty-five the Carondelet, twenty-one the Pittsburg, and fifty-nine the St. Louis, which was the flag-ship. Fifty-four persons were killed and wounded, and the Commodore himself received a severe hurt in the foot. After an hour and a half's fighting, the brave sailor was obliged to hoist the signal for retiring. It remains to add, that in this remarkable contest the Confederate batteries were uninjured, and not a man in them was killed.

The result of the two days' operations against Fort Donelson was far from encouraging; and seemed to reduce the Union army to a position of complete dead-lock. The partial assaults upon the defensive line of the Confederates had met so decisive a repulse as to augur ill for any future attempts of that nature; and the damage to the fleet deprived the Union commander of an auxiliary upon which he had confidently counted to greatly simplify the problem before him. In a word, the entire combination of effort for the reduction of Fort Donelson was to all appearances undone; and it became necessary to form new plans. It was accordingly resolved in a conference between General Grant and Commodore Foote, on the evening of Friday, that the commodore should return to Cairo, repair and augment his fleet, and return with a naval force adequate for a new and stronger attack. In the mean time Grant was to perfect the investment, and await the arrival of reinforcements from Cairo and Louisville.

But while the Union commanders thus planned operations that looked to a successful issue only at a distant day, the enemy had formed a resolve that precipitated an immediate crisis and hastened his own ruin. While, on Friday night, Grant and Foote were consulting with reference to their ulterior purposes, Floyd also called a council of his officers, and it must be said that if to the Union commanders the prospect as it presented itself to them was far from encouraging, to the Confederates the outlook, as they consulted together, was altogether gloomy. They had seen that very afternoon a numerous fleet of transports arrive with heavy reinforcements to an army which they already magnified to double its actual strength; they knew that the whole available Union force in the Western States could speedily be concentrated against Fort Donelson; and they perceived that as they were completely enveloped by the line of investment, and every avenue of exit and entrance from the land side cut off, it would be easy for General Grant, by extending his right and erecting batteries on the Cumberland above Fort Donelson, to cut off their one remaining source of supply by water, when they must be reduced to capitulation.

In this state of facts the Confederate officers unanimously agreed that the only course which held out a rational hope of escape was to recover, by a vigorous offensive stroke, the roads leading to Nashville, and thus open the way for their retreat. It was determined to make this attempt the following morning, and the plan of operation was as follows: From the position enclosed within the Confederate lines of defence two roads lead towards Nashville — the one called the Wynn's Ferry road, runs from Dover through Charlotte; the other, an obscure and bad road, crosses the flats of the Cumberland. But as the latter was at this time submerged by the overflow of the river, and considered impracticable for infantry and artillery, it only remained to force open the Wynn's Ferry road, covering which was planted the division of McClernand, forming the right wing of the Union line of investment. In the method of action resolved upon, Pillow's division, forming the Confederate left, was to make a vigorous attack upon the Union right flank; and Buckner's division, leaving in the intrenchments on the Confederate right a minimum of force, was to be moved over to strike at the same time the Union right centre planted on the Wynn's Ferry road. It was hoped that if Pillow's attack was successful it would roll back the Union right (McClernand) on the centre (Wallace) when the shaken mass, taken in flank by Buckner, would be thrown back in confusion on the left (Smith). In the latter case Grant's force would be routed and driven to its transports; but in any case it was at least expected to uncover the Wynn's Ferry road, and thereby an avenue of escape. The plan was not ill conceived, and its execution up to a certain point was, as will now be seen, a complete success.

Pillow's column, eight thousand strong, was formed before dawn of Saturday the 15th, and moved forward at 5 A. M. It was hoped to make the movement a surprise, and it has been commonly, though incorrectly, written down as such. But in point of fact the head of the hostile column was greeted by a fire from the Union force before Pillow had time to assume a line of battle, and his force suffered severely for an hour while making its formation. This being accomplished, there ensued a strenuous contest, in which the Confederates strove to force the Union position, but were unable to make any impression upon it. In the disposition of McClernand's division its three brigades were placed from right to left in the order of McArthur, Oglesby, and W. H. L. Wallace. Pillow's line covered the front of the two right brigades, and extended a considerable distance beyond the flank. After much unavailing effort, it occurred to one of Pillow's brigade commanders, Colonel Baldwin (who appears to have what his chief had not, a correct eye for ground), to direct the left of the line to advance under cover of a ravine, swinging round parallel with the Confederate front. This manœuvre brought the force directly on and in rear of the naked Union right flank. The movement was supported by the whole Confederate line, all the regiments on the left throwing forward their left wings; so that Pillow succeeded in making a change of front to the right, and the Union brigade on the extreme right being taken *en revers* was at once swept from its position.

While Pillow's attack thus fell upon the two right brigades of McClernard's division, Buckner, who had meanwhile moved

over from the extreme right of the Confederate line to support the assault of Pillow, had formed his troops opposite
McClernand's left brigade, under Colonel W. H. L. Wallace:
so that the whole hostile mass was concentrated against one
third of the Union force. Buckner, however, met with less
success than his colleague; for when he advanced to attack
the brigade of Wallace, he struck so steady a front of infantry and received so severe a fire from the Union batteries,
that his troops fell back greatly demoralized to their trenches.
Meantime, Pillow proceeded to follow up his first successful
stroke, and by direct and steady pressure, succeeded in
driving back the next brigade on the right, — the brigade of
Oglesby. Pillow pays a deserved tribute to the stubborn
bravery of the Union troops, when he says that "they did
not retreat, but fell back fighting and contesting every inch
of the ground," for every step gained by the enemy, a heavy
price in blood was exacted. Nevertheless, in the relations
of the contending forces, it was open to the Confederates by
simply advancing to continually outflank the Union line; and
when after an extremely obstinate resistance to the left brigade of McClernand, under Colonel W. H. L. Wallace, found
its right completely uncovered, and saw itself assailed in
overpowering force by the troops of Buckner (who succeeded
in stimulating his men by the news of their comrade's success
to renew the attack), it also gave way, and by nine A. M.
the whole position occupied by Grant's right division was in
the hands of the enemy. And the Wynn's Ferry road — the
avenue of escape — was open!

With the whole hostile mass hurled against one third of
Union force, was it wonderful it went down? Not wonderful,
indeed; but yet it would hardly be possible to imagine a situation more critical than that in which the whole army was
now placed. Moreover, the imminence of the peril was increased by an accidental circumstance. General Grant had
gone on board a gun-boat to consult with Commodore Foote,

and during all these pregnant hours there was no officer who could combine and conduct the forces upon that fearful field. The division of General Lew Wallace, which held position next on the left of McClernand was indeed called up by the sound of battle on the right; but the inference drawn was that it was McClernand attacking. At length about 8 A. M. Wallace received a message from that officer, asking assistance; but not deeming he had authority to take the offensive he forwarded the despatch to head-quarters, from which, however, the commander was still absent. Soon, another message reached him from McClernand that disclosed the full extent of the disaster. He then promptly forwarded one of his two brigades, under Colonel Cruft, to the assistance of the right. It only reached the scene of action in time to make a brief resistance, and then share the fate of the whole right wing. What that fate was, soon became apparent to Wallace; for flocks of fugitives from the battle-field came crowding up the hill in rear of his own line, bringing unmistakable tokens of disaster. Seeing now how critical the situation was, Wallace promptly put in motion his remaining brigade under Colonel Thayer. The movement was made by the right flank at double quick. The column had marched but a short distance when the retiring brigades of McClernand were met withdrawing to the left, — retiring indeed, but coolly, and without confusion, complaining chiefly that their ammunition was exhausted, to which circumstance the men attributed their mishap. The enemy was following, though without much cohesion: so that Wallace had time to deploy his brigade on the crest of a hill which crossed the line on which the enemy was making towards the left and form a line of battle at right angles with his former front before the Confederates could make dispositions to renew the assault.

And here we may pause a moment to note how the enemy, led away by his very success from the primal object for which this effort had been made, was hurried forward to his own destruction. The purpose of the Confederates was already fully accomplished — all that part of the Union army that barred their exit from the *cul de sac* in which they found themselves placed was driven away, and the door was open for their departure. But in their then exultant mood such a measure seemed but a lame and impotent conclusion for so brilliant a prelude. They had rolled back their antagonist's right on his centre : let them now drive the confused mass violently against his left and the swift-flowing Cumberland — would not that be a consummation which would cause Floyd and Pillow to strike the stars with their sublime heads? And so those worthies resolved.

But little did they reck in their high-blown fancies of the mettle of the men with whom they must try conclusions in the issue of this great emprise. Enraged at the untoward fortunes of the morning, and determined to regain whatever of honor they had lost, the troops of the right wing had no sooner refilled their cartridge-boxes than they returned and reformed behind the firm front which Wallace now presented. And when immediately afterwards the Confederates again advanced, and began to ascend the crest, they were met by a fire before which their line staggered and broke : so that the officers could only rally them out of range. They then essayed another charge; but this met a still more disastrous repulse, and then their officers could not rally them at all. Many fled precipitately to their works ; the rest were brought to a stand upon the ground wrested from McClernard.

So stood affairs when General Grant reached the field of action. Bitter as must have been the pang experienced by that commander at the sight of his wrecked and stranded lines, his resolve was instantly taken; and this resolve, then taken upon his first field, presents a complete illustration of that trait of character to which General Grant owes most of his achievements. It has frequently been seen that gener-

als have accomplished great things who, devoid of high
mental parts, have nevertheless possessed an immovable will,
and an offensive temperament.   That steady will, that per-
tinacious temper, that quality of "hammering continuously,"
which have been noted as the dominant traits of Grant's mind,
he already possessed upon the field of Donelson.   And it is
here worthy of note that of the motives that then prompted
him, General Grant afterwards gave an interesting revelation.
In the crisis of the greater disaster at Shiloh, that officer
visited the division of Sherman, and, in speaking of the situation of affairs, recurred to his experience at Donelson.
"On riding upon the field," said he, "I saw that either side
was ready to give way if the other showed a bold front.   I
took the opportunity and ordered an advance along the whole
line."

Such indeed was the order that now went forth to the division commanders both to the right and left — to Wallace on
the right, to retake the ground lost in the morning ; to Smith
on the left, who had not been engaged at all, to storm the
enemy's works in his front.   The manner of execution is now
to be seen.

So weighty had been the accumulation of force on the enemy's left for the grand effort of the morning, that the whole
right of the line, originally held by the troops of Buckner,
was left comparatively unguarded.   General Smith's division
confronted this flank, and the prompt manner in which the
initiative was seized gave that officer the advantage of this
circumstance at the first onset.   The storming force was
formed of Lauman's brigade in column of battalions, with
Cook's brigade in line of battle on its left to cover that flank,
and make a feint against the fort.   It was led in person by
General Smith, an officer of distinguished gallantry, under
whose inspiring example the troops moved steadily forward
to the assault.   The preparations for the attack had, however,
been seen by the enemy, and Buckner's command was hastily

summoned back to the defence of the works vacated in the morning. These were approached just as Smith's column was moving up the crest; but the Union force, having the advantage in that it had completed its dispositions, met the head of the hostile column with so determined a fire that it was continually staggered; and the Union troops, tearing away the abatis, rushed forward and seized the breastworks. Buckner, after a vain effort to dislodge the intrusive force, was fain to fall back and take refuge within the outworks of the fort, surrendering to the assailants all the high ground on the Confederate right — ground which completely commanded the main work, and saw in reverse a great part of the Confederate lines. We return now to the operations against the other flank, where the success was no less complete.

When Pillow's troops retired from the assault of the position where Wallace had thrown his force to check their further advance, they reformed upon the ground originally held by the Union right. To dislodge the enemy from this position, and drive him back within his works, was the duty assigned to Wallace. The advance was made with a force of two brigades and two battalions, and was executed in so spirited a manner and with so bold a front, that the enemy, after a brief resistance, abandoned the ground, and hastily recoiled to his own lines. And thus affairs stood at sunset; the integrity of the line of investment was restored complete in all its parts, and on the left, a commanding position was held within the enemy's works. The day's conflict had cost, as near as may be counted, a sacrifice of about two thousand killed and wounded on each side.

When the operations of Saturday closed, General Grant made his dispositions for a general assault at daylight the following morning. But circumstances otherwise determined the event.

Late that same night another meeting of the Confederate leaders took place at the head-quarters in Dover, where Floyd, Pillow, Buckner, and their staff-officers assembled to counsel together as to their fortunes. These were certainly sorry enough. Until late at night, it had been hoped that they would still be able to extricate their commands from the trap in which they found themselves; for they were not aware that the Union force had reoccupied its lines of the morning.

When, however, the scouts, who had been sent out to re-connoitre, returned with tidings of the real state of the case, there ensued a scene which, even as portrayed in the Confederate official reports, would seem to have resembled less a council of war than a conclave of ruined gamesters. After a good deal of bickering touching a proposition made by Pillow to cut their way out, the bitter conclusion was reached that surrender was inevitable. But who should make the surrender? Pillow said, "As for myself I will never surrender—I will die first." Floyd, whose guilty conscience caused him to see everything through a noose, added, "Nor will I. I cannot and will not surrender; but I must confess, *personal reasons control me.*"—"Then I suppose, gentlemen," said Buckner, the only one of the trio that seems to have had any sense of honor; "I suppose the surrender will devolve upon me?" Floyd replied, addressing himself to Buckner, "General, if you are put in command, will you allow me to take out my brigade?"—"Yes, sir," responded Buckner, "if you leave before the enemy act on my proposition of capitulation."—"Then, sir," said Floyd, "I surrender the command;" and Pillow, who was next in command, added quickly, "*I pass it.*" Thereupon Buckner called for writing materials and a bugler; and Floyd and Pillow hastened off to save their precious persons.

During the night, two small steamers had come up the Cumberland: Floyd seizing them, succeeded in carrying off fifteen hundred men of his own brigade.   Pillow and his staff made good their escape to the opposite shore in a skiff, and Colonel Forest, with three or four hundred of his troopers managed to traverse the slough through which the infantry could not pass, and got away by the river road.

It was by this time dawn of Sunday, and Buckner having completed his writing, forwarded, under flag of truce, to Gen. Grant, a communication asking the appointment of commissioners to settle upon terms of capitulation, to which end he requested an armistice till noon.   To this Grant promptly penned his characteristic reply : " No terms other than an unconditional and immediate surrender can be accepted.   I propose to move immediately upon your works."   Buckner, demurring at what he called these " ungenerous and unchivalric terms," was, nevertheless, obliged to accept them.

In the early morning nine thousand men laid down their arms, and the Stars and Stripes floated over the stronghold of the Cumberland.

III.

RESULTS OF DONELSON.

The fall of Donelson was to the Confederate system of defence in the West like the removal of the key-stone from an arch : it bore the whole structure in ruin to the ground. It will be proper, therefore, in estimating the degree in which Donelson is to be considered a *decisive* field, to set forth first of all what were its direct military consequences.   These will, at the same time, afford a striking illustration of the train of evils that in war follow dispositions originally faulty.

As soon as General Johnston learnt that the fort at Donelson was invested by the Union army, he became so fearful of the consequences which must result from its fall that he evacuated his stronghold at Bowling Green as a position

much too far advanced for prudence. With his force of
14,000 men he fell back to the north bank of the Cumberland,
opposite Nashville, and there awaited the issue. Buell then advanced along the line of the Louisville and Nashville Railroad,
occupied Bowling Green, and prepared to press on towards
Nashville. At midnight of the 15th of February, Johnston
received news of a glorious victory at Donelson — at dawn of
the 16th he was met by tidings of a defeat and a capitulation.
The blow was decisive. He immediately crossed the Cumberland to Nashville. But neither could Nashville itself be
held. Situated in a wide basin, intersected by the Cumberland, the key to which had just been wrenched from the Confederates, approached from all directions by good turnpike
roads, and surrounded by commanding hills, involving works
of at least twenty miles in extent, the capital of Tennessee
was untenable by a less force than fifty thousand men.
There was no alternative : Johnston abandoned Nashville amid
the wildest panic and terror of the people, and retiring
southward took position at Murfreesboro', where he endeavored to collect an army fit to offer battle. Buell promptly
pushed on from Bowling Green; and, on the 23d of
February Nashville was occupied by the vanguard of the
Army of the Cumberland.

While such was the effect of the fall of Donelson upon
the right of the Confederate cordon, it was felt not less sensibly at its extreme left, where that flank rested on the Mississippi. By that event Columbus was turned and became
untenable. Instead of being any longer part of a system of
defence, giving strength to and receiving support from the
other parts of the line, it was left an isolated outwork, thrown
out of all just position and relations. It was accordingly not
long before Polk received instructions from General Beauregard to "evacuate Columbus and select a defensive position
below." With this view, choice was made of the position
embracing Island No. 10, the main land in Madrid Bend, on

6

the Tennessee shore, and New Madrid. The work of removing the large stores of supplies and numerous siege guns
was begun the 25th of February and completed on the 1st
of March, without molestation. The following day Columbus was occupied by the Union force. But even this new
position at Island No. 10 was simply designed as a temporary
resting-place, the tenure of which was to be entirely contingent on future actions in the field.

Such were the astonishing events that, in a territorial point
of view, followed this brilliant stroke. To say that it carried forward the whole Union front of war two hundred miles
further south is not even an adequate statement. It was the
downfall of a *system* of defences. It cleared Kentucky completely of all insurgent force. It threw the Confederates back
into the centre of Tennessee, the capital of which was brought
under Union dominion. It unbound the Cumberland and
the Tennessee. In a word, it brought practically under the
Union control the whole upper centre zone.

Nor was its moral effect less remarkable. This is to be
estimated both in reference to the North and the South.

Consider that it was the initial campaign in the West, and
judge of the measureless content diffused throughout the
whole North by results so brilliant. Consider, too, its relations to the course of the war as a whole. The last trial of
strength had been Bull Run, the sting and humiliation of
which were still bitterly felt at the opening of this campaign ;
for it had been followed by entire inaction at the East —
inaction which however much imposed by sound military
considerations, was at the time little understood by the people. Is it true, then, men had begun to say to themselves
that there is really something in the vaunted Southern
prowess and invincibility? But how quickly such doubts
and fears vanished when the story of Donelson was told ! It
was then seen by palpable proof that not only were the men
of the North equal to them of the South in courage, but that

they had superior steadfastness and endurance; that they could not only storm works, but stem the current of disaster with unflinching front; and it was seen, too, that Northern generals could plan and manœuvre, and that by judicious disposition great results might be achieved with comparatively slight sacrifice of life. Thus, while darkness covered the East, there suddenly flashed from the Western horizon an auroral light that overspread all the land with the day-spring of hope.

Throughout the South, on the contrary, the events of this campaign produced universal terror and alarm. These sentiments were due not only to the patent results of the campaign, — to the capture of an army and the breaking up of a whole system of defence, — but to a certain element of *mystery* in the agencies by which these results were produced, and the mistrust thereby engendered in the minds of the people of the South touching the value of their whole military procedure. From the success of Beauregard in holding his position in Virginia there had grown up what may be called the Manassas theory — the theory of the impregnability of great intrenched camps. Hence Bowling Green and Columbus were each named a "Manassas of the West"; and it was never doubted that these strongholds could be held indefinitely. But when the Southern people saw both these positions fall without either of them being directly attacked at all, this delusion was rudely dispelled, and in its place, in obedience to that Roman maxim, so true to human nature, *Omne ignotum pro magnifico*, — there arose a vague terror that magnified the peril. This sentiment of alarm spread through all the borders; and when, two days after the fall of Donelson, the so-styled "permanent Congress" met in its first session at Richmond, Mr. Davis was forced to confess, in a message of lamentation, that the South "had attempted too much." In point of fact, however, the South had rather attempted ill what it had undertaken than attempted too much. With the revelations already made of the actual condition of Confederate military strength at the West, it needs no recondite process to reach the root of their disasters. But these were undoubtedly hastened and augmented by the ill-judged method in which that strength was used. A brief exposition of this will perhaps show that the Confederate commander, General Albert Sidney Johnston, scarcely merits the exalted reputation he has enjoyed: this, indeed, provided the dispositions were his own, and that he was left untramelled, of which there seems to be no doubt.

To retain two armies on two widely-separated lines of operation, each confronted by a superior force—to hold them thus until Grant and Buell had completed their portentous preparations and were ready to move,—was, indeed, the way to invite disaster. Beauregard's plan of uniting everything at Bowling Green and overwhelming Buell was correct, and Johnston assented to it. But it was too late; he had waited too long: Grant moved, and Johnston, baulked in his offensive intent, had to turn his efforts to the defence of his menaced left flank. He resolved to defend Nashville at Donelson. Yet, here again his dispositions had the character of a weak division of force. He made everything contingent on the issue on the Cumberland, and at the same time retained on the Nashville line, where he intended to do nothing but fall back, as great a force as he assigned to the defence of the position that was to decide his fortunes. The fourteen thousand men with which he fell back from Bowling Green he did not regard as available for any serious opposition to the advance of Buell; yet it was certainly too large to do nothing *but* fall back with. Moreover, he committed a great error in shutting up the army for the defence of his water flank within the works at Donelson. As a position for an army, Fort Donelson was nothing; Fort Henry was nothing. The specific intent of these works was to bar the

Tennessee and the Cumberland to the advance of a fleet. The event proved that had they been properly constructed, both would have been equal to this object; for in a conflict of an hour and a half the batteries at Donelson inflicted on the gun-boats a decisive repulse without themselves suffering any damage. With the garrisons of these works foot-loose and united with the force forwarded from Bowling Green, a field-army could have been formed that would have covered these works indirectly, and which, being free to roam in all directions, might have made itself very formidable. As for the "Gibraltar" of Columbus, it was a mere *bete noir*. The works were so constructed as to require at least fifty thousand men for their defence — five times the force the Confederates had at hand.

These lessons were indeed not lost on General Johnston. In the shipwreck of his army he read the prodigious mistake he had committed; he saw that the only hope of salvation lay in concentration and a vigorous offensive, and in a remarkable letter addressed from Murfreesboro' to Mr. Davis he foreshadowed the new policy and the expectations he based thereon in this significant utterance: "If I join this corps to the forces of General Beauregard, *then those who are now declaiming against me will be without an argument.*"

How these forces *were* joined, and what befell thereon, will form the subject-matter of the story of that chequered campaign that culminated at SHILOH.

III.

SHILOH.

I.

PRELUDE TO SHILOH.

On the westerly bank of the Tennessee, 219 miles from its mouth, is the historic spot of Pittsburg Landing. Its site is just below that great bend in the river, where, having trended many miles along the boundary-line of Alabama, it sweeps northerly in a majestic curve, and thence flowing past Fort Henry, pours its waters into the Ohio. The neighboring country is undulating, broken into hills and ravines, and wooded for the most part with tall oak-trees and occasional patches of undergrowth. Fens and swamps, too, intervene, and, at the spring freshets, the back-water swells the creeks, inundating the roads near the river's margin. It is, in general, a rough and unprepossessing region, wherein cultivated clearings seldom break the continuity of forest. Pittsburg Landing, scarcely laying claim, with its two log cabins, even to the dignity of a hamlet, is distant a dozen miles north-easterly from the crossing of the three State lines of Alabama, Mississippi, and Tennessee — a mere point of steamboat freighting and debarkation for Corinth, eighteen miles south-west, for Purdy, about as far north-west, and for similar towns on the adjoining railroads. The river banks at the Landing rise quite eighty feet, but are cloven by a series of ravines, through one of which runs the main road thence to Corinth, forking to Purdy. Beyond the crest of the acclivity stretches back a kind of table-land, rolling and ridgy, cleared near the shores, but wooded and rough further from the river. A rude log chapel, three miles out, is called Shiloh Church; and, just beyond, rise not far from each other two petty streams, Owl Creek and Lick Creek, which, thence diverging, run windingly into the Tennessee, five miles apart, on either side of the landing.

On this rugged, elevated plateau, encompassed by the river and its little tributaries like a picture in its frame, lay encamped on the night of the 5th of April, 1862, five divisions of General Grant's Army of West Tennessee; with a sixth, five miles down the bank, at Crump's Landing. Thrust though it was far out into the enemy's domain, yet the very scene of its encampment told more strongly than any language how absolutely secure this army felt from any hostile visit, and how unsuspicious it was of any shock of battle. The camps had been fixed on the bank nearest the enemy, while the other was equally available. The five divisions, irregularly grouped between the creeks and river, were palpably positioned without any regard to order of battle or to possible attack. Behind, rolled a broad and deep river, without fords, without bridges, without transportation. Before, not a single spadeful of earth had been thrown up for intrenchment during the month's sojourn, whether in front of the advance divisions, or across the roads leading into the camp, or at the fords on the flanks. Not a single cavalryman patrolled the outer walks; the scanty infantry outposts lay within a mile of the main line, and their unconcealed camp-fires flared high and cheerily into the damp April air. The few sentinels were wont to chat and laugh aloud, and, whenever morning came, their pieces were irregularly discharged, merely to clear them of their loads. Within the noiseless rows of white tents lining and dotting the rough plateau, the slumberous army now dreamt peacefully of home, or of that day yet distant when it would march on the enemy's stronghold at Corinth, joined by the column of Buell. At that moment, the leading division of Buell's army of the Ohio lay at Savannah, nine miles down the river on the other bank. Wearied that night with their four days' march from Columbia, Nelson's men slept heavily. A long rest had been promised to them, to be broken only the next day by a formal Sunday inspection, and leisurely during the week ensuing it would join the associate army of West Tennessee; for transportation had not yet been made ready for its passage of the river, nor had General Halleck yet come down from St. Louis to direct the movement on Corinth, for which it had marched. Behind Nelson, the rest of Buell's army trailed that night its line of bivouac fires full thirty miles backward on the road to Columbia.

Silent in Shiloh woods yonder, within sight of Grant's camp-fires and within sound of his noisy pickets, lay grimly awaiting the dawn, 40,000 Confederate soldiers. It was the third of the three great armies drawn together that night towards Pittsburg Landing, — an army supposed by its fourscore thousand dormant foes, from Commanding-General to drummer-boy, to be lying *perdu* behind its Corinth fieldworks, twenty miles away. It had crept close to the Union lines, three fourths of a mile from the pickets, less than two from the main camp — so close that, throughout the night, the bivouac hum and stir and the noisy random shots of untrained sentinels on the opposing lines indistinguishably mingled. This stealthily-moved host lay on its arms, weary after a hard day's march over miry roads on the 4th, a day's forming on the 5th, and a bivouac in the drenching rain of the night intervening. No fires were lighted on the advanced lines, and, farther back, the few embers, glowing here and there, were hidden in holes dug in the ground. Most of the men lay awake, prone in their blankets, or chatted in low tones, grouped around the stacked arms, awaiting the supplies which commissaries and staff-officers were hurrying from the rear ; for, with the improvidence of raw troops, they had already spent their five days' rations at the end of three, and were ill-prepared to give battle. But others oppressed with sleep, had for the time forgotten both cold and hunger.

Sheltered in the gloom of tall trees, and under the watch and ward of chosen sentinels, patrolling and challenging with low, steady voice, a council of Confederate generals gathered in the cleared spot which, at converging paths, formed the head-quarters. A small fire of logs crackling and sputtering in the centre threw a strange light on the surrounding figures. A drum served for writing-desk near the firelight, and a few camp-stools for furniture, eked out by blankets spread upon the ground.

Foremost in the group stood Albert Sydney Johnston, the Commander-in-Chief. Tall, erect, well-knit, and powerful, his dignified and martial figure gained effect by the gray military cloak which protected it from the chilly evening. His face, bronzed and set by the campaigns of two and forty years in the Black Hawk war, in the Texan struggle for independence, in the war with Mexico, and for many years past in Indian outpost service through Utah and California, was a trustworthy index to the man. The firm mouth and chin and the steadfast, sunken eyes, showed a soldier resolute, self-controlled, thoughtful, and fearless. Grave, modest, and reticent always, he seemed at this council even more abstracted than his wont. Often he moved from the fire to the edge of the group as if walking away to ruminate his own thoughts, and anon returned to take part in the discussion. He was, indeed, greatly impressed with his responsibility ; and in his supreme devotion to his cause, had no moment to spare for personal forebodings. Before another sunset, this soldier was fated to have fought his last battle.

In marked contrast to the Scotch features and bearing of Johnston, was his associate, Beauregard. Walking rapidly to and fro, with his lithe and slender figure divested of its outer cloak, he spoke tersely and spiritedly with a tinge of French accent, on the prospects of the morrow. His face, with its small, regular features, pointed beard, and keen eyes, showed somewhat the effect of the illness under which he was still laboring; but his bearing was entirely soldierly, his short step was energetic and firm, his voice clear and strong. Obviously vexed at the day's mishaps of manœuvre, he only awaited anxiously for success in the coming battle, in which he had a personal as well as a patriotic stake. For already the brilliant promise of his youthful Mexican career had come to fruition, and with the laurels of Fort Sumter and Manassas still fresh upon him, he had come to restore the Confederate fortunes in the West.

Near by was Hardee, whose corps lay closest to the Union outposts, a Georgian, but matching the inherited foreign air of Beauregard, by one acquired by long military education in France. As compiler of the Infantry Tactics, and Commandant of Cadets at West Point, and as a fine theoretical soldier, his opinions received due weight. Physically, he appeared tall, broad-shouldered, and muscular, and from his good-humored face did not seem to take amiss a little rallying, which even the grave occasion did not forbid a brother officer from indulging, on his gallantry in other fields than those of war.

Breckinridge, commander of the reserves, and rather of forensic than of martial renown, a man of fine features and imposing appearance, lay silent upon his blanket, and did not obtrude his views upon older soldiers. In truth, his general opinions were well-known to be like Beauregard's, strongly aggressive. Vice-President, and almost President of the Union, little more than a twelvemonth gone, he was still quite as much Kentuckian as Confederate; and to "redeem" Kentucky he had urged, long before the fall of Fort Henry, an offensive campaign against Louisville.

Bragg, proud of his well-drilled Pensacola corps, and vaunting in general the power of discipline, was, neverthe-less, in marked physical contrast to the uniform military bearing of the others. His face was wan and haggard, its features being rude and irregular, and his body stooping. His beard was iron-gray, and growing together over the bridge of his nose were a pair of bushy black eyebrows, under which his sharp and restless eyes seemed befitting to his character as a thorough disciplinarian, and to his well-known tartness of temper. Even before the war his fame was national, and his name, and that of his battery, as insep-arably linked as Taylor's with the historic field of Buena Vista.

Lieutenant General Polk, whilom Bishop of Louisiana who, — a West Pointer by education, — had exchanged the crosier for the sword, was the last of the main figures of the group. He was above the middle height, and broad-chested, and his open face denoted courtesy and courage as well as a fine intelligence.

The council was long and animated. Beauregard and Bragg, the chief speakers, talked often and earnestly, while Polk and Breckinridge said little, in the presence of these more famous soldiers. There was much that was vexatious. The weather had been contrary from the start, the country was hostile to campaigning, the raw troops were unused to march-ing and manœuvre, their officers not less so. Already a day had been lost; for the night before, the rain descending in torrents, had drenched the men in bivouac and made the nar-row and tortuous roads, always bad at best, next to impassa-ble. The artillery and trains and even the infantry columns struggled painfully through the mire, so that what with raw troops and raw officers, with carelessly examined ground and roads twisting confusingly through brake and swamp, joined to some misapprehensions on the part of corps commanders, two days had been expended in getting hither from Corinth.

Instead of attacking at dawn of the 5th, dusk found the troops wet, hungry, and exhausted, and just brought into position. The whole move had been based on striking a blow before Buell should come up, and every minute was golden.

The wretched organization of the army was another subject of discussion, and of ill-boding. Two days' experience had shown its lamentable defects. Bragg openly declared that many officers in the army were not equal to the men whom they were expected to command; Beauregard regretted the want of engineers to inform him of the *terrain* of the morrow's battle-field; and all the generals found much to apprehend from the imperfect staff organization, while the responsibility for these and other failings, was by more than one speaker laid directly at the door of the Richmond authorities, where unquestionably it belonged.

As the discussion, however, went on, and the encouraging omens were in turn reviewed, the tone of the council became firm and confident. The enemy had been secretly approached and the surprise would be complete. He was found most lamentably unprepared — the general absent at his head-quarters, nine miles down the river, and on the other shore at that, with his camp unintrenched, not one cavalry picket out, with his outposts near his main line, with his troops badly placed, and finally, with no pontoons or transportation on the river, to which it was proposed to drive him. Anxious inquiry was made, indeed, concerning the whereabouts of Buell; but on this all important point, Beauregard, from the last report of the spies, who had brought him fresh news of each day's march of Buell, and each night's bivouac, was able to declare him at least one day's march from the battle-field, and with no boats ready to cross him. Moreover, the Confederate troops, despite their hard initiation, were full of fire and confident of victory. In numbers, they were nearly equal to Grant's forces, who were, also, for the most part raw and indifferently organized; while against the conquerors at Donelson, could be matched Bragg's fine corps from Pensacola.

Ten o'clock came and passed before the officers had all separated, but at length the early start arranged for the morrow, provoked the suggestion of retirement. All parted with high hopes. Of the associate commanders, Johnston was clearly resolved to wipe out the hasty and unjust reproach cast on him after Donelson, while Beauregard, forgetting alike his sickness and his disappointment at the ill-omened delay, pointing the departing officers towards the Tennessee, said, with a confident smile, " Gentlemen, *to-morrow* night we sleep in the enemy's camp."

It was the eve of Shiloh.

The situation just portrayed had followed upon a noteworthy chain of events. With the fall of Fort Donelson, crumbled forever the entire first line of Tennessee defence — the line of the Cumberland, as it may be called — stretching due east from Columbus, through Fort Henry, Fort Donelson, and Nashville, to Mill Spring, and onward to the Alleghanics. But the recoil was slight, for a secondary line had already been stretched out and was a-fortifying. General Polk, in receiving orders to evacuate Columbus, was also directed to " select a defensive position below ; " and the point chosen was forty miles down the Mississippi, embracing Island No. 10, the main land in Madrid Bend, and the village there. This, being rapidly intrenched, became the *point d'appui* for the left of what was hastily pencilled as the second grand Confederate line for the defence of the easterly slope of the Mississippi Valley. From Island No. 10 it was at first popularly believed the cordon would strike easterly through Jackson, the head-quarters of one Confederate army, to Murfreesboro', the head-quarters of another, and thence to Cumberland Gap, thus retiring the Confederate right and centre

through a vast segment, and abandoning all East Kentucky
and much of Tennessee, but keeping the left strong and fast
as with the death-clutch on the Mississippi, and fairly pro-
truding the line at Island No. 10.   But great events forced
the abandonment of this line before it had acquired consist-
ency.   The fall of Donelson had developed a new problem
for the Union commanders, since two lines of advance into
the Confederacy were now presented by the physical geography of the region.   One runs south-easterly through Nashville to the rocky eyrie of Chattanooga, the future route of
Rosecrans — thence onward to the ocean, the future path of
Sherman : the other is the line of the Mississippi.   It was
needful to fight them both out in conquering the Confederacy,
and, accordingly, the absolute importance of neither could be
overrated.   But, it having been wisely resolved no longer, as
at the outset, to move over both at once, it remained to give
to one or other the priority in time.   The choice fell upon
the Mississippi route, for many potent reasons.   The repossession of the Mississippi was one of those grand national
ideas which are so powerful in moving a people to patriotic
effort.   It was to reopen the Mississippi to navigation, that
the West had risen *en masse*, recognizing in its obstruction
by insurgent batteries an act quite as astounding as the men
on the other flank of the Alleghanies had discovered in the
menaced siege of Washington.   Such a success would be more
palpable and grander than the mere penetration of half a
dozen States in any other direction — and proportionally add
prestige to the Union arms, dishearten the Confederates, and
challenge the applause of the world.   These were general
considerations : there were special ones more important.
The campaign on the Mississippi allowed naval co-operation ;
not so that towards Chattanooga.   The latter required grand
preparations of supplies and reinforcement, and the opening
and holding of long lines of railroad communication.   All
that was conquered of the river could be easily held — not

so, as Buell found, with the road to Chattanooga; for a move to the south-east, besides exposing the flanks and rear of the column itself, would leave all Western Kentucky and Tennessee to the returning enemy, and unravel the victorious campaign as far back as Louisville or Cairo. Finally, it ran the hazard of a series of battles deep in the recesses of the Confederacy.

There was still another class of weighty and special circumstances. The Confederates were holding points all along the Mississippi — at Columbus, Island 10, Fort Pillow, Memphis, — and a column moving down the left bank would cut them all off, with their garrisons, armaments, and strategic positions. It might even interpose between Johnston's Tennessee army at Murfreesboro', and Beauregard's Mississippi army at Corinth, and attack one before the other could come up. Now the second line of Confederate defence chosen by Johnston was that of the Memphis and Charleston Railroad — too obvious an one for a doubt of its selection to rest in the minds of either of the contestants. It is true that, as we shall presently see, Beauregard was undermining all these schemes and reducing this second line to one of little moment, his primary thought being a new offensive campaign, which should provide its own parry in its reeling stroke. But this conception the Union generals did not know; and never, indeed, discovered it till its consummation on the battle-ground of Shiloh. What they did learn, after their plans were formed, was that Johnston had joined Beauregard, and hence so much of the scheme as contemplated the separation of these officers, had come too tardy off. But there was, then, of course, only the more urgency for the original plan, that of concentrating everything on the Mississippi line, so as to cut off Memphis and the river forts, to seize another section of the river, and, above all, to sever the Memphis and Charleston Railroad. The importance of this great Southern central line of transportation between

East and West proclaims itself, without need of description, along its whole length, from the Mississippi to the sea. All the leading Union generals urged a snapping of that railroad chain — Buell urged it, Halleck urged it, Grant urged it. Indeed, the two latter officers at first moved without waiting for a concentration of force, and only Johnston's junction with Beauregard warned them of its necessity : then, Buell's army, which had already been pressingly tendered several times, was at last joined in the grand campaign.

The great railroad line which Halleck was now bent on permanently securing, as the main object of the campaign, could have been tapped at any one of several points. But everything pointed to an advance up the Tennessee as the most practicable. It was the shortest route thitherward ; and, besides, being so largely accomplished in transports, and with a water line of communication kept open by the navy, it would not consume the spring with vast preparations of troops and trains for a land advance. Moreover, it threatened the rear of all the enemy's positions on the Mississippi — Memphis, Randolph, New Madrid, Island No. 10 — and directly co-operated with Pope and Foote, who were hammering and tunnelling their way down the river, first at and around Columbus, and afterwards at Island 10. But, above all, it was as if, straight from Fort Henry, there lay a direct highway, patent, possible, even now opened up through Tennessee to Alabama, and directly beckoning to conquest — a broad highway whereon the gun-boats — those terrors of the Confederates, and inestimable Union allies — could carry their flag unchallenged fourscore miles into the enemy's domain.

Up the broad stream, accordingly, Halleck promptly pushed the conquerors of Donelson. This fort surrendered on the 16th day of February ; and five divisions of Grant's army were made ready, and embarked on transports early in March. On the 4th of March (for reasons it is needless to exhume)

General Grant was ordered to turn over his forces to General C. F. Smith. Halleck's original design was to establish the expedition as far up the river as Florence, to which point Phelps's gun-boat reconnoissance with the Tyler and Lexington had penetrated on the 8th of February preceding. But a reconnoissance of the same boats on the 1st of March, was checked by a hostile battery at Pittsburgh Landing, and had disclosed the enemy in a formidable position at Corinth; so that it became out of the question to go higher up. Indeed, the first point of landing and depot of supplies was very wisely fixed on the right or easterly bank of the Tennessee, at Savannah. Thence it was resolved to cross the army to Pittsburgh Landing, in support of two columns to be despatched to cut the railroad, one above and the other below Corinth; and if these were successful, to move at once against the enemy's position. Accordingly, the Tyler steamed to Danville Bridge, twenty-one miles above Fort Henry, to await the transports; and these, arriving on the 9th, with General Smith and a large portion of his army, and Sherman's division in advance, were conveyed without molestation to Savannah, where they debarked during the 11th. The next night Wallace's division was put ashore at Crump's Landing, five miles below Pittsburgh Landing; on the 14th, at the latter point, they were quickly joined by Smith's own division and those of McClernand and Prentiss, and the movement was then complete. Instantly on landing, General Wallace was sent out on the direct road from Crumps's to Purdy, and, without opposition, tore up, a few miles north of that village, half a mile of the Mobile and Ohio Railroad, which runs from Corinth to Columbus. But the Memphis and Charleston Railroad was too far beyond for him to attack; and Sherman's column, sent against the latter road, south of Corinth, proved unsuccessful, because the river rising rapidly had overflowed in deep back water between him and his objective. At this time, unhappily, General Smith fell sick of a mortal illness.

7

"That elegant soldier," said McClellan; that "gallant and elegant officer!" said Sherman admiringly, four years later, adding: "Had he lived, probably some of us younger fellows would not have attained our present positions." Smith's own division was turned over to General W. H. L. Wallace; and, meanwhile, the command of the whole expedition had again devolved upon General Grant, who, emerging from his brief cloud, was restored to command on the 14th, and arrived at the head-quarters at Savannah on the 17th of March. Thereupon three weeks of inactivity elapsed, broken only by the battle-thunders of Shiloh.

Meanwhile, a second army was faring forth to the field. March had found Buell and Halleck in parallel commands, the one at St. Louis, in the Department of the Missouri, the other at Nashville, in the Department of the Ohio. Buell, first to detect the clandestine withdrawal of Johnston from his front to the Memphis and Charleston Railroad, urgently suggested a movement up the Tennessee in force, which movement, however, General Halleck had already thought of. Finding their views in unison, Buell next repeatedly tendered, by telegram, his own forces for co-operation; and at length an excellent opportunity for accepting this proposal came on the 12th of March, when the two departments were united as the Department of the Mississippi, under General Halleck. The latter officer then telegraphed Buell to move, and Buell on the very same night, the 15th, put in motion his cavalry, followed next morning by McCook's division of infantry. McCook reached Columbia on the 17th, but found that, while all the other bridges on the route had been saved by the promptness of Buell's march, those over Duck River had been destroyed by the enemy. The river was then forty feet deep, and though gradually receding, it would not do to wait till it became fordable; and the engineer corps worked strenuously at building a bridge, which, however, was not finished till the 31st, when all five divisions again moved forward briskly and handsomely to Savannah, the point of rendezvous fixed by General Halleck. There, Buell was led to expect, according to his instructions, that he would find General Grant and his army. On the 28th, General Halleck informed General Buell that Grant would attack the enemy "as soon as the roads are passable," and that the latter was receiving reinforcements for that purpose. Buell had assigned the 5th day of April for the arrival of his advance division, Nelson's at Savannah. But, on the 4th, General Grant sent Nelson a despatch, stating that he need not hurry, as the transportation for taking him across to the left bank was not yet ready, and would not be ready till the 8th; the day, by the way, after the closing battle of Shiloh. The next day, in response to a suggestion from Buell, that perhaps it would be well to strike the river twenty miles higher up than Savannah, by the Waynesboro' road, which would have brought him opposite Hamburg, — Halleck telegraphed "You are right about concentrating at Waynesboro'; future movements must depend on those of the enemy." A hundred such indications show, like that of the position of Grant's army, already spoken of, how all the Union generals supposed their task was to be one of attack, not of defence, — a deliberate forward movement on Corinth, to be undertaken some days later. But, as good fortune would have it, Halleck's despatch did not reach Buell till he had pushed beyond Waynesboro' in his hasty strides, and Nelson also pressed on to Savannah at Buell's originally appointed time, instead of making the delay which the despatch from Grant had authorized. Despite the rains and the bad roads (which, at this same time, lost the Confederates the fatal twenty-four hours in their march from Corinth), the eighty-two miles from Columbia to Savannah were made by Nelson in four days, and his division lay at Savannah on the eve of Shiloh. Behind, at convenient distances, were the divisions of Crittenden, McCook, Wood, and Thomas.

While the Union Generals were thus eager with their plot, their antagonists had secretly dressed a counterplot, the master-spirit in whose devising was Beauregard. This was, in a word, to rapidly gather an army at Corinth, and fling it upon the reckless camp at Pittsburg Landing before Buell's arrival, and, that succeeding, to march northward in aggressive campaign. The plan was as prompt of adoption as it was bold in conception, and to Corinth quickly flowed from all directions, troops for the army of invasion. The Gulf States were dredged of their garrisons from Memphis to Apalachicola, and the trans-Mississippi states, from Missouri to Texas, poured their troops out at Beauregard's command. Supplies and material, forage and subsistence, were brought on all railroads, while, ordnance lacking, Beauregard begged their bells of churches and families, and many batteries were cast from the metal so collected.

The concentration of troops began on the first of March. The first process was to strip the great forts of all their foolish accumulations of troops; for on arriving West, Beauregard had found Columbus full of troops, and its works built for 14,000. His comment was pointed; " with such a force shut up within a fort, how many troops do you plan to have outside? Fort Donelson, indefensible, and badly defended, has fallen, as well it might, its works being nothing. Unless you have strong works, and troops capable of defending them to the last, it is better not to have forts." His plan, accordingly, was to withdraw their garrisons from the neighboring forts, leave 2,000 men at one strong point on the river above Memphis, with provisions enough for sixty days, spread torpedoes, and, with the aid of gun-boats, set these men to hold the river. All the other works should set free their troops to join in an aggressive movement, and having concentrated everything, he would take the initiative, and seize a victory. Accordingly, he had ordered Polk to withdraw from Columbus to Island 10, which

had been prepared for his reception. The latter point he designed to hold only till he could prepare Fort Pillow, still
further down, which he had selected as the real river defence
of Memphis; and, in fact, it was finished on the very day
when Island 10 was evacuated. Polk's corps of two divisions soon joined Beauregard from Columbus, and Bragg's
fine corps, also of two divisions, came up from Mobile and
Pensacola. The latter had been well drilled by that disciplinarian, and were pronounced the best troops in the
Confederacy; though in reality, they were not the superiors
of the Virginian army of Joe Johnston; but those were the
early days of the war, when the skirmishes and picket duty
around Santa Rosa and Ship Island, and the threatening of
Fort Pickens were supposed to season recruits into veterans.
The Governors of Tennessee, Mississippi, Alabama, and
Louisiana were called on for volunteers, and issued at once
strenuous alarum-cries, so that in speedy response their people flocked towards Corinth by regiments, companies, squads,
or unarmed and singly. All these were slowly crystallized
into the Army of the Mississippi, and to these Johnston added
all his forces, forming Hardee's corps, himself assuming supreme command, with Beauregard as second.

The march of Buell hastened preparations, but most of the
troops were entirely raw, and hence the army took its shape
slowly. Above all, it lacked the appliances of organization;
for the Richmond authorities, usually self-sufficient, narrow-
minded, and wrong-headed past all belief, in their conduct of
affairs, yet went to no such inconceivable lengths of folly and
stupidity, as in their reluctance to organize their armies, and
in their jealousy of conferring such ordinary military rank
and such latitude of power as is necessary for the assembling
of an army, and the gradation of its component parts. The
first condition Beauregard had made in going West, was a
fixed number of troops to fight with, but these, of course, he
did not get, nor any approximation thereto. The second

condition was the detail to him of a staff corps, and some such officers of a higher grade as could aid him in his task of remodelling the Western army. He got that no more than the other, though both were promised with equal distinctness : his fixed number of colonels and lieutenant-colonels, which were to have been sent, never came. These necessities were doubly felt when the problem was to assort and mould the fragmentary bodies of volunteers pouring into Corinth. However, by laying the shoulder to the wheel in steady work, the 1st of April arrived with some approximation — though a vexatiously imperfect one — to the task undertaken, for the troops were at last in good condition and very confident. Johnston's forces lay chiefly along the railroad easterly from Corinth to Iuka, northerly from Corinth to Bethel. Spies and officious people in the region had brought daily and nightly news of the progress of Buell, and the position of each division's bivouac, and equally minute and positive details were known of Grant's army. When Buell's bridge over Duck River was built, it was felt that the blow must be struck at once ; and when, just before midnight of the 2d of April, a courier brought news of Buell's rapid stride from Columbia, the advance was instantly ordered. It was already a day later than originally intended, and then the dispositions for guarding the depots of supplies and the roads around Corinth and Purdy had to be made. But on the 3d, the remainder of the army, about 40,000 strong, moved straight forward over the practicable roads towards the river, where, sixteen miles distant, lay Grant's army at Pittsburg Landing. The advance was to march "till within sight of the enemy's outposts."

Immediately on starting the roads were found in wretched condition, — an evil augmented by the rawness of the troops in marching. By the night of the 4th, however, the main interval had been passed, and the troops ordered to attack at dawn of the 5th. The advance cavalry

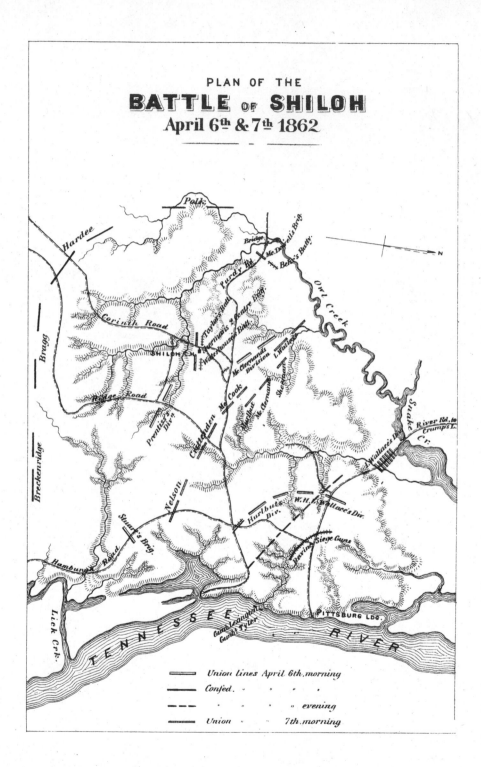

PLAN OF THE
BATTLE OF SHILOH
April 6th & 7th 1862

flushed and eager, had already got upon the Union outposts, and been repulsed by Sherman's advance, for their
pains. But, about 2 o'clock on the 5th, a furious rain-storm
fell, and continuing for hours, drenched the whole army as it
lay in bivouac, filled the creeks, spoiled the roads, and rendered attack impossible. In addition, the bad organization
delayed the troops from getting into position. Intolerably
vexatious as was this loss of a whole day, it only remained to
endure it. The lines were moved up still nearer, till the
advance was but three fourths of a mile from the Union
pickets, and but two miles from the main camp. The troops
were in three lines, according to the order of attack. Hardee's corps of two divisions covered the intersection of the
Pittsburg and Hamburg roads, with half its cavalry on either
flank, between Owl and Lick creeks; Gladden's brigade
of Withers' division of Bragg's corps filling up the space to
the latter stream. Eight hundred yards behind him lay the
rest of Bragg's two divisions in the second line. With a
little wider interval, Polk's corps formed the third, and reserve line, with Breckinridge's reserve divisions upon its
right and rear. The roads were cleared, and the attack ordered betimes in the morning; and so passed the eve of
Shiloh.

II.

THE BATTLE OF SHILOH.

The morning of Sunday, April 6th, broke clear and
pleasant after the rains of the days preceding, and found the
Union army still peacefully sleeping in its camps along the
Tennessee. The general topography of the rugged plateau,
which, seamed with ravines, but mainly ninety or a hundred
feet above the road-bottom, contained the encampment, has
already been drawn: it was at once camp and battle-ground.
Its southerly limit is Lick Creek, which, rising a few miles
in the interior, runs between very high banks easterly to

the Tennessee, at right angles with the latter, three miles above the landing. Near its source, Owl Creek, bending like an arm around the camping-ground, forms the westerly and northerly boundary of the plateau, and emptying into Snake Creek, joins the Tennessee at right angles, two miles below the Landing. The drift or slope of the land is, in general, from the bluffs of Lick Creek across to the banks of Owl Creek; but the enclosure is uneven, and lesser rivulets, of course, swell those already mentioned. The battle-ground is from three to five miles wide, and as much in length. The troops were posted with reference to the roads from the Landing. The main road winding up the top of the hill, there branches, and the right hand one leads along the river across Snake Creek to Crump's Landing. Further on, a mile from the Landing, the main road sends out another branch, this time to the south, up the shore across Lick Creek to Hamburg. Continuing inland, it once more divides, this time into two roads, both leading to Corinth, of which the one nearest the Hamburg road is called the Ridge road, from its elevation. Shiloh Church is three miles out from the Landing, on the further road to Corinth, near Owl Creek, and thence a road runs north-westerly to Purdy. The many cross-roads and interlacing paths need not be described.

The divisions of McClernand, Prentiss, and Sherman, formed the advance line of Grant's army; those of Hurlburt and W. H. L. Wallace the forces at the Landing. Sherman's division, facing south, covered the Corinth road at Shiloh Church, with one brigade on each side of the road, and one on the extreme right guarding the bridge on the Purdy road over Owl Creek; while, detached to the extreme left of the whole army, Sherman had a brigade, under Colonel Stuart, guarding the Hamburg road at Lick Creek Ford, near the Tennessee. Prentiss, on Sherman's left, was guarding the Ridge road, facing southerly and south-westerly. McClernand was on Sherman's left and rear, on the Purdy road — his line and Sherman's forming an acute angle, by the extension of their left wings. Hurlburt and W. H. L. Wallace were back at the bluff near the Landing, where were all the supplies, — the forage, subsistence, stores, and trains. Lew Wallace lay at Crump's Landing, with his brigades posted conveniently on the road running thence to Purdy.

Ere the gray of dawn, the advanced line of Johnston's army, composed of Hardee's corps, strengthened on its right by Gladden's brigade from Bragg's, stealthily crept through the narrow belt of woods, beyond which all night they had seen their innocent enemy's camp-fires blazing. No fife or drum was allowed; the cavalry bugles sounded no reveille; but with suppressed voices, the subordinate officers roused their men, for many of whom, indeed, the knowledge of what was to come, had proved too exciting for sound slumber. Bragg's line as quickly followed, and, in suit, the line of Polk and Breckinridge.

By one of those undefinable impulses or misgivings which detect the approach of catastrophe without physical warning of it, it happened that Colonel Peabody, of the 25th Missouri, commanding the first brigade of Prentiss's division, became convinced that all was not right in front. Very early Sunday morning, therefore, he sent out three companies of his own regiment and two of Major Powell's 12th Michigan, under Powell's command, to reconnoitre, and to seize on some advance squads of the enemy, who had been reported flitting about, one and a half miles distant from camp on the main Corinth road. It was the gray of dawn when they reached the spot indicated; and almost immediately, from long dense lines of men, coming swiftly through the tall trees, opened a rattling fire of musketry. It was the enemy in force. The little band fell back in haste, firing as best they might. Close on their heels pressed the whole of Hardee's line, and enveloping the left of Prentiss's camp, stretched in a broad swathe across to the gap between his division and Sherman's, and thence onward across Sherman's. Instantly the woods were alive with the rattle of musketry right and left, on front and flank. The Confederate batteries, galloping up on every practicable road and path, unlimbered in hot haste, and poured their shot over the head of the infantry in the direction of the tents now faintly gleaming ahead. The startled infantry outposts, mechanically returning a straggling fire, yielded overborne by the mighty rush of their enemy, and then streamed straight back to the main camps. The divisions of Sherman, Prentiss, and McClernand started from their peaceful slumbers amid the roar and smoke of battle. The exultant Confederates, creeping so long with painful reticence, now woke the forests with their fierce, long-pent yells. The flying pickets served, like avant-couriers to point the way for their pursuers. And thus, with the breaking light of day, over-hung by sulphurous battle-clouds, through which darted the cannon-flash, while the dim smoke curled forward through every ravine and road, and enveloped the camps, Grant's army woke to the battle of Shiloh.

So rude an awakening might well unnerve veterans, and much more these raw troops thus thrust invitingly out for attack, many of whom were unused even to loading their own muskets. But instantly, from all the tents, amid the long-roll of drums, the quick cries of "turn out," and "fall in," from company-officers and sergeants, the rapid roll-calls of the orderlies, the clink of rammer and gunstock, the orders mingling everywhere, in all tones, from officers of all grades, the astounded troops of Sherman, Prentiss, and McClernand hurried half dressed into line; while command-ers were hastily fastening on swords, or mounting horses, and aids were flying back to rouse the men of Hurlbut and Wallace in the rear.

At the height of the shouting, the forming of the troops, the spurring hither and thither of the aids, the fastening of belts and boxes, and the dressing of the laggards,

the enemy's advance with loud yells swept through the intervening forest, and burst upon the camps.

It was now about 7 o'clock, and the resistance of the
Union picket line, feeble as it necessarily was, had been of
priceless service in gaining time, while the rough and impracticable interval over which the Confederates had to pass
served to break up somewhat as well as to extend and thin
their lines. There seems to have been no special tactical
formation, nor any massing of men on a key-point — the
key-point, if any there was, had not been discovered. The
movement in short, was predicated on a surprise, and the
method, to fling the three corps-deep lines of the Army of the
Mississippi straight against the Union army from creek to creek;
to " drive it back into the Tennessee." As for the Union
generals, overwhelmed with surprise and chagrin, they could
only strike back where the enemy struck, seeking above all
to save the camps. Such was the nature of the confused,
irregular, but bloody series of conflicts, which now raged for
three hours, during which time the Union troops succumbed,
and yielded the first breadth of debatable ground.

Prentiss' division occupied the Union left (except for the
detached brigade of Stuart), and covered the Corinth ridge
road. Against him rushed Hardee's right and Gladden's
brigade, but it was a full hour before the outposts of Peabody's
brigade had been driven back into Prentiss' camps. By
that time Prentiss had his line hastily formed. About 7
o'clock, Gladden moved upon Prentiss' centre, and soon the
roar of artillery and musketry on both sides proclaimed
general battle. Meanwhile, Hardee's line having been protracted and divided all along the Union front, Bragg threw
the second line by detachments, into the gaps, to reinforce
it. Before half past seven o'clock, therefore, Bragg's line
had moved up, and was fighting, intermingled with Hardee's.
Now the right of Bragg's two divisions was the division of
Withers, one brigade of which, Gladden's, had the night

before been put into the first line, on Hardee's right. The whole three brigades were now fighting together against Prentiss' division. Chalmers' brigade swept around to Prentiss' left flank; Gladden's pushed at his centre, and Jackson's struck his left, and began to pour through the gap between Prentiss and Sherman. The batteries on both sides being run to the front, plowed through the opposing ranks; Gladden was struck by a cannon shot and mortally wounded, charging at the head of his brigade; Peabody was mortally wounded in the Union lines. The Confederates pressed on, gaining little by little on either flank, till the fire from their three batteries, as well as the infantry fire of their three brigades began to cross in Prentiss' lines. Regiments gave ground here and there, now on the left, now on the right, now in front, and before nine o'clock, the Confederates having driven Prentiss from all his camps, were masters of the field. The camps were quickly despoiled, accoutrements, clothing, rations just cooked, and plunder of all sorts even, seized. With difficulty the officers drew their men together, and Withers's triumphant division was re-formed, to move once more on the new line of the Union left.

Simultaneously, Hardee's centre and left had been attacking the Union right, or the division of Sherman, whose line ran across the other Corinth road. The centre was at Shiloh Church, and Sherman had put two batteries there, those of Taylor and Waterhouse, and two brigades, Hildebrand's on the left of the road, and Buckland's on the right. On the right of Buckland was McDowell's brigade, with Behr's battery on the right and rear, on the Purdy road. McClernand, just in rear of Sherman, had promptly sent three regiments to the support of Hildebrand, on Sherman's left, and three batteries soon after moved over. By seven o'clock, the Confederate advance showed through the woods, and opened a straggling fire.

Half an hour later, the whole Confederate force was up;

the three brigades of Hardee's corps — Hindman's, Cleburne's, and Wood's, formed the right of the line which burst upon Sherman. Bragg's original second line of two divisions had already been separated, as we have seen, and the right one, Withers's, thrown against Prentiss. His left division, that of Ruggles, was formed on Hardee's left, its three brigades being Gibson's, Anderson's, and Pond's.

Before eight o'clock, the battle was raging with fury at all points; for, in dogged determination to drive their foe to the river, the line of Confederate advance was determined simply by what might yield to their onset. For an hour the contest was severe, the Union batteries being well posted and extremely well served, and inflicting grievous punishment upon the Confederates, whenever the latter appeared from the cover. Sherman himself was indefatigable in remedying the misfortunes of the surprise; he moved in every part of the field, attended personally to the fire of batteries, held up raw regiments to their task, and, long before noon, became the central figure on the Union side at Shiloh. Towards his left, when Hindman, Cleburne, and Wood gradually passed in between himself and Prentiss, and swung upon his left flank, the firing was so hot (for Sherman clung to this point with bull-dog tenacity, regarding it as the key-point to his position) that Bragg threw Gibson's brigade of Ruggles's division across to Hindman's support. Sherman's batteries, however, tore this column badly while it marched across by the right flank to its new position; the other two brigades of Ruggles, those of Anderson and Pond, remained and attacked Sherman's right, under McDowell. Polk's third, or reserve line was not long kept from the contest. Three regiments and several batteries from McClernand, and four regiments from Hurlburt had early arrived on Sherman's left, and enabled him to withstand the Confederate attack there. Seeing this heavy reinforcement at an important point, Johnston, who had ridden to the front, and who, according to Polk, at once showed "the ardor and energy of a true soldier," and promised victory in "the vigor with which he pressed forward his troops" — Johnston himself called on Polk for a brigade to support the right. Stewart's brigade of Clark's division was given to him, and he took it in person. Beauregard next demanded a brigade for the left to help Ruggles, and Cheatham led one to that point. Finally, Polk threw his two remaining brigades against Sherman's centre. The Confederate troops, being now all in action, soon served Sherman as they were serving Prentiss. The latter, at nine o'clock, had been driven from his camps, and the brigade of Polk's corps, which Johnston led into the gap between Prentiss and Sherman, completely turned the latter's left flank. The rush which finally broke Prentiss, also broke up Hildebrand, and his two left regiments fell back in great disorder and "disappeared from the field." Instantly the Confederates swooped upon Waterhouse's battery, and Sherman's left was turned. He gallantly clung a little longer to Shiloh Church, and held up McDowell and Buckland, together with the two brigades sent from McClernand's division. Polk's two brigades, however, now moved up, and, with those of Anderson and Pond, attacked the two Union divisions, and carried Behr's battery in an instant. Meanwhile, the Confederates hurried their artillery down along the brook in the gap on Sherman's left and rear, and routed his troops with an enfilading fire. Sherman then fell back, and, before ten o'clock, had surrendered his whole camp. General Polk says that the forces of Sherman and McClernand immediately opposed to him, "fought with determined courage, and contested every inch of ground," and that "the resistance at this point was as stubborn as at any other on the field."

We have now, at ten o'clock, reached a sort of epoch in the battle. The first onset of the Confederates has been successful, and the divisions of Sherman and Prentiss, supported in part by those of Hurlburt and W. H. L. Wallace, have been driven from their camps. There was neither at this time nor later, any positive lull in the battle; but the retreat of the Union forces caused the taking up of a new and concentrated line, and a portion of the Confederates paused in unsoldierly fashion for plundering the captured camps, before they essayed the sequel of their task. Sherman, on losing. his camps and two batteries, had two brigades left to work with, McDowell's and Buckland's, and Taylor's battery. As for Hildebrand's brigade, they had mostly long since fled, and were running towards the Tennessee, on whose banks an immense throng of fugitives from the various divisions, in detachments of all sizes from regiments down to groups of fours, was already collecting, and swelling each hour. Sherman's remaining troops retreated to McClernand's right, where they were halted, and got in hand to renew the contest. The Union line was so confused and irregular thenceforth, and so constantly swaying and shifting, that it would be uninstructive as well as uncandid, to pretend to draw it in detail. In general, however, Sherman's residue of troops was on the right; next, McClernand's division; next, Wallace's; next (after recovering), Prentiss's; next, Hurlburt's; finally, Stuart's detached brigade of Sherman's division. A word will explain how this disposition was reached. The stress of the opening attack on Prentiss and Sherman was very naturally along the two Corinth roads across which they lay. Between the roads was an unguarded interval, into which the Confederates had passed, and by which they had flanked both divisions. McClernand, Hurlburt and Wallace had instantly moved up to relieve the stress on this worst point — which supposing we assign to the first Union positions the dignity of a line, — would be called the centre. There they substantially remained, receiving the shock of battle as they came up—McClernand first, because nearest, and the others quickly after. Sherman, on being driven back, had naturally fallen on the right of McClernand, so as not to impede his fire.

McClernand had moved forward in detachments, as we have seen, to Sherman's left, in instant answer to an urgent call for help.   Now, by the abandonment of the camps of the two advance divisions, he was stoutly holding his own, having swung around so as to face nearly south-east, on the main Corinth road.   Wallace's shortest road up from the landing brought him to the left of McClernand, where he arrived in time to receive the direct impact of the dense column pouring down the Corinth road after turning Prentiss out of his tents. Hurlburt, at 7½ o'clock, had received a message from Sherman that " he was already attacked in force, heavily upon his left." We have seen that the main battle began about seven.   Hurlburt within ten minutes had Veatch's brigade on the march to Sherman's left, where it soon arrived, and went into action, together with the column from McClernand.   In the new alignment it became separated, half being formed on Mc-Clernand's right, and half on his left.   A few minutes later, came similar tidings from Prentiss, and Hurlburt then took forward his two remaining brigades, those of Williams and Laumann.   He marched to the rear and left of Prentiss, and met an appalling sight.   "His regiments drifted through my advance," Prentiss gallantly striving, but in vain, to rally them.   Fortunately, Hurlburt's men were not broken up by this perforation of their columns, and their line was rapidly formed.   Behind Hurlburt, Prentiss "succeeded in rallying a considerable portion of his command," and then, says the former, "I permitted him to pass to the front of the right of my third brigade, when they redeemed their honor."

Stuart's brigade, or what was left of it, for he had suffered like Sherman and Prentiss from the independent volition of some subordinates, in moving their commands to the rear — was on. Hurlburt's left.   Weeks before, when this whole camping-ground had been occupied with a view to moving on Corinth, Sherman had stretched his command over the front, along Owl and Lick creeks, — a space of three or four miles, the other divisions being placed as already indicated, in quasi support. Stuart, accordingly, was off on the left on the Hamburg road, which crosses Lick Creek near the Tennessee. At $7\frac{1}{2}$ o'clock he had received from Prentiss a verbal message like that sent to Hurlburt. "In a very short time," he adds, "I discovered the pelican flag advancing in the rear of General Prentiss's head-quarters." So quickly was the latter officer's camp turned on the left. Stuart formed his three regiments, and, in answer to a request, Hurlburt in fifteen minutes had a battery and a regiment in the long interval between Stuart and Prentiss. Half an hour elapsed, during which the enemy got a battery in a commanding position, and opened a fire of shells on Stuart's camp. Before long, the Confederates began to move across upon him from Prentiss's left and against his other flank. The ground is the highest on the whole field, and defensible by a small force. Riding to the right, Stuart found that "the battery had left without firing a gun, and the battalion on its right had disappeared." Riding to the left, he found his own regiment there had also departed, as he was told, to "a ridge of ground very defensible for infantry" in the rear. "But," he expressively adds, "I could not find them, and had no intimation as to where they had gone." Several hours later, it is pleasant to know, that his search was rewarded, by discovering "seventeen or eighteen men" of this force, who, under the adjutant, joined him.

For five hours, now, the battle went confusedly on. Its general tenor was the forcing back of the Union troops more or less slowly to the landing. Had the *terrain* been other than it was, the result might have been more quickly accomplished. But rolling and wooded, cleft and cut up by ravines, with here and there a commanding and defensible ridge but no salient positions, it afforded opportunity for protracted, irregular, and severe fighting. Both in attack and defence it threw upon subordinate officers the care of their own commands. It prevented also the decision of the day by a stroke on either side, and neither a blow nor a counter-blow was of necessity fatal. In this irregular and fragmentary fighting, however, the chief brunt fell upon Wallace, McClernand, and Hurlburt, — not only because the divisions of the two former had had the experience of Donelson, while the other three divisions were mostly raw, but also because the troops of Sherman and Prentiss had become disorganized and used up by the morning's surprise. General Grant came upon the field as soon as he could arrive from Savannah, where he had heard the roar of battle. It took a considerable time to reach the Landing, but not long afterwards to ride to the point to which his troops had been driven from their camps.

The Confederate lines had, meanwhile, been not much less confused than those of their enemy. They had advanced with three lines of battle and a reserve; in two hours they had thrown everything in, by divisions, brigades, or even regiments, just where it happened to be wanted. As some of the Union divisions had at times portions of three or four divisions under their control in the confused disorganization, so it was precisely with the Confederate corps commanders. Polk's corps was divided from one end of the line to the other. At length, he sought out General Bragg, and it was arranged that Bragg henceforth should take charge of the right, Polk of the centre, and Hardee of the left, independent of former dispositions. This was at half past ten o'clock, and the commands so continued thenceforth through the day. From that time till three the conflict went on with vigor. The Confederate leaders now positioned troops, now encouraged them, now personally led them. The right of the Confederate line under Breckinridge had for several hours a long and obstinate contest with Hurlburt, aided by Prentiss. But the Union centre, held by Wallace, and the left by McClernand, were especially aimed at by the

Confederates, in order to cut their way through to the Landing. Here was the Confederate centre, which has been described as flanking Sherman on the left and Prentiss on the right, — Hardee's line, with the brigades of Hindman, Cleburne, and Wood, three brigades of Polk's corps, under Cheatham, and Gibson's brigade of Ruggles's division. Bragg and Polk again and again tried to force this position. Wallace had the three batteries of Cavender's battalion well posted on commanding ridges and well served, and his infantry behaved well. McClernand did the same for his three batteries, those of Schwartz, Dresser, and McAllister. Under Wallace's vigorous command, Bragg's efforts long failed. On the left, however, Polk and Hardee, attacking with the brigades of Pond and Anderson, and a portion of the centre, had already found easier work. Sherman's disordered line in that quarter could with difficulty be recovered from the shock of the morning. It was formed of parts of Buckland's and McDowell's brigades. The former officer says that, in forming line again on the Purdy road, "the fleeing mass from the left broke through our lines, and many of our men caught the infection and fled with the crowd." One regiment, Cockerill's, was kept in something like organization; but as to the rest, "we made every effort to rally our men, with but poor success. They had become scattered in every direction." The Confederates accordingly turned the Union right, and possessed themselves of McClernand's camps, and half the guns of his three batteries. McClernand and the rest of Sherman fell back to the right of Wallace, who still held fast to his camp near the Landing.

So far as the Confederates had a tactical plan now, it was to turn the Union left, and, sweeping along the bank, capture their base at the Landing, and drive them down the river. On the Confederate right, opposite Hurlburt and Stuart, were the divisions of Breckinridge, Withers, and Cheatham, under the direction of Johnston himself, who, energetic and determined, was exerting his personal influence with his men.   The Confederate General became frequently exposed to the hot fire of artillery and musketry rolling from Hurlburt's line.   One of the latter's batteries, indeed, had been instantly abandoned by its officers and men, as he says, "with the common impulse of disgraceful cowardice."   The other two, however, had an effective fire from commanding positions, while several of his infantry regiments exhausted their ammunition for a time.   For a time the Confederates made tremendous charges against this position, and, amid the hot fire which was returned, about two o'clock a ball struck Johnston as he sat on his horse, eagerly regarding the movement.   He refused to notice it, and gave orders as before; but it was the death-wound.   Governor Harris, his volunteer aid, riding up, found him reeling in the saddle.   "Are you hurt?"   "Yes, I fear mortally."   And, with these words, stretching out his arms, he fell upon his companion, and a few minutes later expired.

Of the military character of Sydney Johnston, it is difficult to speak with surety.   He has certainly left a great fame; but this probably has its foundation rather in what was anticipated of him than in what he achieved.   He was a man of a high order of character, just, generous, chivalrous, and brave.   He had an eminent administrative faculty, and Davis highly regarded his political talent.   But it is doubtful whether he would have risen to the rank of such men as Lee, Joseph E. Johnston, or Jackson.   His manner of defending the frontier committed to him was very faulty, and the readiness with which he followed the suggestions of Beauregard shows that he had but little power of initiative and but slight appreciation of grand war.

It was now three o'clock, and the battle was at its height. Dissatisfied with his reception by Wallace, on the Corinth road, Bragg, on hearing of Johnston's fall, on the right, determined to move round thither and try his success anew.

He gathered up the three divisions already spoken of, and, with specific orders of attack, flung them against Hurlburt, Stuart, and Prentiss. The assault was irresistible, and the whole left of the Union position giving way, Bragg's column drove Stuart and Hurlburt to the Landing, swept through Hurlburt's camp, pillaging it like those of Prentiss, Sherman, Stuart, and McClernand. Simultaneously, Polk and Hardee, rolling in from the Confederate left, forced back the Union right, and drove all Wallace's division, with what was left of Sherman, back to the Landing, — the brave W. H. L. Wallace falling in breasting this whelming flood. Swooping over the field, right and left, the Confederates gathered up entire the remainder of Prentiss's division — about 3000 in number — with that officer himself, and hurried them triumphantly to Corinth.

At five o'clock the fate of the Union army was extremely critical. Its enemy had driven it by persistent fighting out of five camps, and for miles over every ridge and across every road, stream, and ravine, in its chosen camping-ground. Fully 3000 prisoners and many wounded were left in his hands, and a great part of the artillery with much other spoils, to grace his triumph. Bragg's order, "Forward, let every order be forward;" Beauregard's order, "Foward boys, and drive them into the Tennessee," had been filled almost to the letter, since near at hand rolled the river, with no transportation for reinforcements or for retreat. Before, an enemy flushed with conquest, called on their leaders for the *coup de grace.* What can be done with the Union troops? Surely the being at bay will give desperation. Unhappily the whole army greatly disorganized all day, was now an absolute wreck; and such broken regiments and disordered battalions as attempted to rally at the Landing, often found the officers gone on whom they were wont to rely. Not the divisions alone but the brigades, the regiments, the companies, were mixed up in hopeless confusion, and it was only a heterogeneous mass of hot and exhausted men, with or without guns as might be, that converged on the river-bank. The fugitives covered the shore down as far as Crump's, where guards were at length posted to try to catch some of them and drive them back. The constant "disappearance," as the generals have it, of regiments and parts of regiments since morning, added to thousands of individual movements to the rear, had swarmed the Landing with troops enough — enough in numbers — to have driven the enemy back to Corinth. Their words were singularly uniform — " We are all cut to pieces." General Grant says he had a dozen officers arrested for cowardice on the first day's battle. General Rousseau speaks of " 10,000 fugitives, who lined the banks of the river and filled the woods adjacent to the Landing." General Buell, before the final disaster, found at the Landing, stragglers by "whole companies and almost regiments ; and at the Landing the bank swarmed with a confused mass of men of various regiments. There could not have been less than 4000 or 5000. Late in the day it became much greater." At five o'clock "the throng of disorganized and demoralized troops increased continually by fresh fugitives," and intermingled "were great numbers of teams, all striving to get as near as possible to the river. With few exceptions, all efforts to form the troops and move them forward to the fight utterly failed." Nelson says, " I found cowering under the river-bank, when I crossed, from 7000 to 10,000 men, frantic with fright, and utterly demoralized." Of the troops lately driven back, he expressed the want of organization by saying the last position "formed a semicircle of artillery totally unsupported by infantry, whose fire was the only check to the audacious approach of the enemy." Even this was not all. The Confederates sweeping the whole field down to the bluff above the Landing, were already almost upon the latter point. Such was the outlook for the gallant fragments of the Union army at 5 o'clock on Sunday.

But Grant's star was fixed in the ascendant. It chanced that the Confederates, by sweeping away Prentiss on the Union left, had been thrown chiefly towards the southerly side of the Landing. Now, at that point, as has been described, intervenes a precipitous wooded ravine, "deep, and impassable for artillery or cavalry," says General Grant, "and very difficult for infantry." And it was precisely here, that, as that commander explains, "a desperate effort was made by the enemy to turn our left and get possession of the landing, transports, etc." A hard task, therefore, was set the Confederates at the end of their day's toil. In addition, the Union gun-boats now reinforced the troops, and at half past five furiously raked the hostile lines which had drawn towards the Landing. The moral effect of these shells on both the armies, was even greater, as so often at that stage of the war, than the physical. A third piece of fortune favored the Union armies. It chanced that, on the bluff, had been deposited and parked many siege guns, with heavy ordnance of various sorts, designed as a part of the train for that future move upon Corinth, which to-day had been so unexpectedly barred. No artillerists, of course, had yet been prepared for the guns; but Colonel Webster, of General Grant's staff, energetically called for volunteers to get these pieces into position and essay work with them; and plenty of cannoneers he found whose field artillery had been captured during the day.

As the fragments of light batteries came galloping in, these were ranged with the heavy guns, and, in short, a formidable semicircle of forty or fifty guns, or more, of all sizes, soon girdled the Landing, along the brow of the ravine, which formed an excellent defence. This latter, indeed, stretched far beyond the bluff, and winding around, continued its protection quite to the Corinth road, the guns dotting its edge, all along. On the right of the guns an effort was made to disentangle the army that had rushed pell-mell in that direction, while, on the left, the gun-boats partly covered the artillery position.

At this crisis, also, and to assure the fortune of the army so lately trembling in the balance, Buell's advance rushed with loud cheers upon the scene. It was Nelson's division, which had arrived thirty hours before at General Grant's head-quarters, but, finding no transportation ready, had been kept all day from the battle. But, stimulated by the ever-nearing roar of battle, Nelson's men had hurried along the overflowed roads of the west bank, and Buell, finding the artillery-wheels sticking hub-deep in mire, had authorized Nelson to drop his trains and push on. So, by effort and expedient, Nelson got up the river, was ferried across, and his well-drilled men, disregarding what they saw and heard, rushed spiritedly to the front, and Ammen's brigade deployed in support of the artillery at the point of danger. The glad news of reinforcement spread like wildfire in the driven army.

Already now, the Confederates were surging and recoiling in a desperate series of final charges. Warned by the descending sun to do quickly what remained to be done, they threw forward everything to the attempt. Their batteries, run to the front, crowned the inferior crest of the ravine, and opened a defiant fire from ridge to ridge, and threw shells even across the river into the woods on the other bank. Their infantry, wasted by the day's slaughter, had become almost disorganized by the plunder of the last two Union camps, and a fatal loss of time ensued while their officers pulled them out from the spoils. The men, still spirited, gazed somewhat aghast at the gun-crowned slope above them, whence Webster's artillery thundered across the ravine, while their right flank was swept by broadsides of 8-inch shells from the Lexington and Tyler. "Forward" was the word throughout the Confederate line. Bragg held the right, on the southerly slope of the ravine, extending near the river, but prevented from reaching it by the gun-boat fire; Polk the centre, nearer the head of the ravine; while Hardee carried the left beyond the Corinth road. At the latter point, the line was half a mile from the water, and four hundred yards from the artillery on the bluffs. There were few organizations even of regiments, on the Union side, but a straggling line from Wallace's and other commands, voluntarily rallying near the guns, was already opening an independent but annoying fire: and these resolute soldiers were as safe as the torrent of fugitives incessantly pouring down to the Landing, among whom the Confederate shells were bursting. Again and again, through the fire of the artillery, the gun-boats and Ammen's fresh brigade and the severe flanking fire of troops rallying on the Union right, the Confederates streamed down the ravine and clambered up the dense thickets on the other slope. Again and again they were repulsed with perfect ease, and amid great loss; for besides their natural exhaustion, the commands had been so broken up by the victory of the day and by the scramble for the spoils, that while some brigades were forming others were charging, and there was no concerted attack, but only spontaneous rushes by subdivisions, speedily checked by flank fire. And, when once some of Breckenridge's troops, on the right, did nearly turn the artillery position, so that some of the gunners abandoned their pieces, Ammen, who had just deployed, again and finally drove the assailants down the slope.

Confident still, flushed with past success, and observing the Union *débâcle* behind the artillery, Bragg and Polk urged a fresh and more compact assault, on the ground that the nearer they drew to the Union position, the less perilous were the siege guns and gun-boats. But the commander-in-chief had been struck down, and Beauregard, succeeding to supreme responsibility, decided otherwise. Bitterly then he recalled the lack of discipline and organization in his army, entailed by the jealousy and ill-timed punctiliousness of Rich-

mond.   Victory itself had fatally disordered his lines, and
the last hard task of assault had thrown them back in confusion from the almost impregnable position.   Better to withdraw with victory than hazard final defeat; for already the
sun was in the horizon, and the musket-flashes lit up the
woods.   The troops were all intermingled, and several brigade commanders had been encountered by the general, who
did not know where their brigades were.   Since darkness
already threatened to leave the army in dense thickets under
the enemy's murderous fire, all that was left of the day would
be required in withdrawing so disorganized a force.   Buell
could not have got more than one division along those miry
roads to the river.   It was a day's work well done: to-morrow should be sealed what had auspiciously begun.   Thus
reasoning, Beauregard called off the troops just as they were
starting on another charge, and ordered them out of range.
Then night and rain fell on the field of Shiloh.

Next morning, the astounded Confederates beheld a fresh
enemy in the lines whence they had expelled a former the
day preceding.   Surely the Union host was hydra-like, with
a new and deadlier crest springing on the trunk from which
the other had been shorn: or like the mystic wrestler who
rose refreshed from mother-earth, whenever he was flung
there, spent and bleeding.   The new foe was the army of
Buell; and as Beauregard caught sight of its handsomely-
deployed columns, he instantly felt that in counting on possible tardiness or want of skill in its commander, he had
reckoned without his host.   Buell, so soon as his restless
troops could be thrown across Duck river, had (though unsuspicious of the need) driven them on with such soldierly
celerity to Savannah that, had the attack of Beauregard been
expected and prepared for, Nelson's division was in season to
have been posted far out in the woods at Shiloh Church; for
they were at Grant's head-quarters eighteen hours before the

battle. With like energy, Buell at the first roar of battle had despatched couriers to all his other divisions to drop their trains and move up by forced marches; so that, on Monday morning, three divisions and three batteries were present to redeem the lost laurels of Sunday. Lew Wallace's division, too, was up from Crump's Landing. Hearing the guns on Sunday at Shiloh, he drew up his troops to march, and impatiently awaited the orders, which, in effect, came at $11\frac{1}{2}$ o'clock, bidding him push over to Snake Creek, cross it, and form on the Union right. Quickly his troops were off, but on the road they met three officers of Grant's staff, who were travelling that way. For Wallace they brought no orders, but they did bring such vivid tidings of the day's disaster and gloom, that Wallace learned that what was once the Union right was now in the Confederate rear. Instantly halting, he retraced his steps, crossed Snake Creek by the river road, nearer the Landing, and arrived at nightfall, after the battle was over.

What with the arrival of Buell's troops and Lew Wallace's, and the untying from its almost Gordian knot of the army of Grant, there was a busy stir on Monday morning. Of Grant's forces, after eliminating the dead who lay on the field, the wounded who all night lay there, still more pitiable, and the hopelessly fugitive, there was still a respectable remainder; and the batteries were assorted and patched, and the artillerists rallied, for of these there were more than enough for the guns. As for the Confederate army, it rose from bivouac in sorry plight, and the day's work obvious before them was not of a sort to freshen their spirits. At least, however, Beauregard had fulfilled his promise to "sleep in the enemy's camp," for his lines were in those of Prentiss, McClernand, and Sherman, and the latter's head-quarters had been usurped by Beauregard. But it was an uneasy slumber they had seized, in camps hardly worth the winning; for throughout the night the gun-boats had thrown eight-inch shells towards the camps at intervals of ten and fifteen minutes, which, as Beauregard reports, "had broken the rest of the men." At midnight, too, a drenching rain had fallen upon them; and so, tired, wet, faint with hunger, and with no rations for the coming day, at dawn they rose again for battle with a new army.

Monday was Buell's opportunity; and he proposed to drive the enemy across Owl Creek, to whence he came. Having thrown heavy pickets well out, and formed Nelson's and Crittenden's divisions in advance of Grant's line, he gave orders to attack at dawn. Four fresh divisions could be counted on—Nelson's, Crittenden's, and McCook's, of Buell's army, and Lew Wallace's, of Grant's—about 27,000 strong; while a large force of Grant's troops were gradually brought up as supports, and, indeed, subsequently took part in the battle. While many of Buell's troops were unaccustomed to battle, they were all well drilled and well managed, and, accordingly, were sure of a better fortune than that of their comrades of yesterday. Whatever, indeed, the amount of disorganization and disaster on the day before, as at Bull Run, nothing could be said against the courage or manliness of the troops; for the fault was chiefly in the negligence and inexperience of their officers: it was fine material, but it had not been finely used, and many of the same regiments which then behaved badly, afterwards, when better disciplined and directed, made themselves an honorable name. The troops of Buell and Wallace were somewhat exhausted by the previous day's marches and a restless night; for Wallace, like Beauregard, noted that "it stormed all night terribly"; and that the gun-boat fire made "sleep almost impossible"; but they were in good condition and confident. Behind them formed the troops engaged before, and moved up as the former advanced, and, as Buell writes, "rendered willing and efficient service during the day." Against nearly 50,000, the Confederates could now oppose less than 30,000 jaded men.

Beauregard, too, had suffered, though not as much as Grant, from straggling, for his troops were raw, and his troops had broken by hundreds from the ranks and strayed back towards Corinth, till a provost-guard drove them back. The killed and wounded on Monday had amounted to 6000 or 8000, and the exhausted and stragglers swelled the troops *hors du combat* to 10,000, to be subtracted from the original 40,000. There was trouble, too, from the want of ammunition and rations.

By half-past five, Nelson and Crittenden were both moving their main lines, with soldierly precision, upon the Confederate position. As the troops passed the interval, the profuse battle-wrecks, the plundered camps, the dead and wounded friend and foe, instructed, as says Rousseau, "the most ignorant soldier that the army had been driven in by the enemy till within a few hundred yards of the river." While, on the march, it could be seen how the gun-boat shells had fired the underbrush wherein the maimed and dying of both sides lay, and how the rain from heaven had at length mercifully quenched the flames when help from man there was none. Nelson quickly flushed the covey of Confederate pickets, and at six developed the main line. In the ensuing halt, Crittenden got up on Nelson's right and the division lines were dressed, while the batteries of Mendenhall and Bartlett woke up and amused the Confederate artillery. The formation made, McCook's advance brigade, Rousseau's, appeared and drew up on Crittenden's right, soon followed by Kirk's, on Rousseau's right, and later, after a rapid march, by Gibson's, on the right of Kirk. On the opposite side of the plateau, near Owl Creek, Lew Wallace was forming his full division, composing the Union right, while between Wallace and Buell the forces engaged on Sunday were brought up. McClernand very promptly rallied his men, and moved them forward so far as to be engaged even in the early skirmishes. Later, at ten o'clock, Sherman put what was left of his two remaining brigades, Buckland's and Stuart's, and of his batteries, between McClernand's right and Wallace's left, while, half an hour earlier, Hurlburt supported McClernand on the left by Williams's brigade and a battery, and on the right by Veatch's and Laumann's.   But all these troops were chiefly relied upon for support; and, though the gallantry of the men got them hotly engaged during the day, they were not pushed beyond endurance : the stress fell upon Buell and Wallace.   The former, arranging his line between six and seven o'clock, "found upon the ground parts of two regiments, perhaps 1000 men, and subsequently a similar fragment came up of General Grant's force."   He put the first on McCook's right, and the second on his left, and afterwards "sent other straggling troops of General Grant's force" to McCook's right.   These dispositions made, skirmishers thrown out, and reserves to each brigade provided, the whole of Buell's three divisions went forward.   For a short interval the line progressed rapidly.   Then, at seven o'clock, it reached Beauregard's main front, and met a determined resistance.

The ground on which the Confederates stood was substantially that of the camps of Prentiss, Sherman, and McClernand, which having been occupied in bivouac the night preceding, now lay a little in rear of the line of battle.   This line stretched in front of Lick and Owl Creeks, and across all the roads so often described.   The dawn of day found the Confederates very much disorganized.   No time, however, was lost.   The early advance of Nelson caused a rapid gathering and assorting of the disordered and shattered fragments of Beauregard, who met the onset with so firm a front that Nelson found himself checked.   At length Crittenden's division came up to Nelson's right, and Mendenhall's battery, hurrying across, engaged the Confederate batteries, and stayed the infantry advance.   Despite their fatigue, Beauregard was already hurling his concentrated columns to an attack on his right : he had engaged all of Nelson and Crittenden, and before eight o'clock had also fallen upon Rousseau's brigade of McCook's division, which had just then completed its formation on Crittenden's right. At eight o'clock, Cheatham's division, which had been posted hitherto, awaiting orders, in the rear of Shiloh church, was thrown in, in front of Buell, on Breckinridge's line. The fire on the Confederate right which had before been hot, was now redoubled, and rolled across all three of Buell's divisions. So severe was the artillery fire that Hazen's brigade was thrown across the open field into the fringe of woods where two batteries were posted, in order to dislodge them. Buell was then at Hazen's position, and in person gave the command " forward ! " which ran echoing along the line, and was obeyed with a cheer. These troops had never before been in battle, but were in splendid drill and discipline, and moved forward in the best possible order. They soon caught the enemy's volleys, but did not slacken their pace ; for it was a novel experience, and they did not resort, like veterans, to trees or cover. Driving in some outlying infantry supports, of whom not a few were sent as prisoners to the rear, Hazen, after half a mile of advance, got upon the batteries themselves. But at this moment the gallant brigade received a cross fire from both flanks from the rallied enemy, and being without support on either hand, was forced to fall back, with a loss of one third of its men. The sally had been a little too impetuous, so much so as to break up the organization ; but it was one quite natural at so early a day in the war, and was a mistake in the right direction.

Meanwhile, the Confederates had fiercely engaged, by nine o'clock, all Nelson's line, and despite the rough ground on his left, succeeded in turning that flank, it being unprotected by artillery. But Ammen's brigade held on stubbornly, till Terrill's guns, not long before landed, dashing down the Hamburg road, went into battery on Nelson's left, silenced the Confederate pieces, and relieved the position. Angry at being baffled, the Confederates quickly charged Terrill and dislodged and drove in his battery with the loss of a caisson. But the effort was amongst the last which the Confederates could endure in this corner of the field. Moreover, Lew Wallace and Grant's other forces on the right had so pressed upon the Confederate left, endangering the line of retreat, that Beauregard moved Cheatham's entire division by the left flank back past Shiloh Church, to form on his left, where Bragg was briskly engaged. About ten o'clock, accordingly, Nelson found the pressure in his front relaxed, and no longer at a halt or receding as before, he began to gain ground. Beatty's regiment from Boyle's brigade, hitherto held in reserve behind Crittenden, was quickly thrown in by Buell to turn the scale; while the Union batteries and men ran to the front, and at length successively silenced the battery which had annoyed Buell's left, and then those playing upon his centre. At the same time Crittenden's left got to the woods in its front and drove out the Confederates. In a word, Buell at length rolling heavily upon the Confederate right, Beauregard abandoned his ground in that direction, and shortened and concentrated his line across the two Corinth roads. Eight hundred yards in rear of his first position, Breckenridge halted on a new line and opened artillery fire; but Crittenden, emerging from the woods, fell on the battery, and seized a part of it before it could be run off. However, the ground beyond was subsequently so hotly contested, that the Confederates recovered their lost guns in an advance which swept back all of Buell's line; but again they they were captured. As for Nelson, by one o'clock his left had swung easily around the Confederate right, moved at trail arms in the double quick over the ridges, and took possession of that part of the field.

Let us turn now to McCook. On Crittenden's right Rousseau's brigade was early engaged sustaining the attack of 8 o'clock, and the heavier succeeding ones. Meanwhile, Kirk's brigade and a part of Gibson's, had been ferried across from

Savannah, hurried to the ground, and were deployed by Mc-
Cook in short supporting distance to the right and rear of
Rousseau. Willich's regiment he held in reserve behind his
second line. McCook shared the varying fortunes of the
morning, till the gradual giving way of the Confederate right
by 10 o'clock. Then Rousseau, finding his advance no
longer checked, moved onward till he encountered the troops
withdrawn to the Corinth road from Nelson's front. Here a
fierce and long contested engagement took place, the Confederates forming in McClernand's camp to which they clung
with desperation; but which at length they were forced to
abandon to Rousseau, together with a battery captured the
day before, of which one section had been playing on Rousseau's advance. But as the Union line swept forward,
McCook and Crittenden had become separated, and a coun-
ter-attack on McCook's left threatened to turn it, and
was the signal for a fierce struggle. There then came a
lull, and at one o'clock the battle began with fresh fury.
McCook had reached a key-point in the Confederate line,
a green wood about five hundred yards east of the church.
Two batteries, one next the church and the other nearer
the Hamburg road, swept the open space with grape and
canister in front of the green wood, and the musketry
fire was very severe. Grant hurried forward what aid he
could to McClernand, Hurlburt putting in the remainder
of his division, and Sherman appearing with his brigades.
"Here," says Sherman, "at the point where the Corinth road
crosses the line of General McClernand's camp, I saw for the
first time, the well-ordered and compact Kentucky forces of
General Buell, whose soldierly movement at once gave confidence to our newer and less-disciplined forces. Here, I saw
Willich's regiment advance upon a point of water-oaks and
thicket, behind which I knew the enemy was in great strength,
and enter it in beautiful style. Then arose the severest mus-
ketry-fire I ever heard, and lasted some twenty minutes,

9

when this splendid regiment had to fall back." Indeed, the conflict, arising on McCook's left, had spread all along his front and over that of Crittenden. Willich's regiment having passed through Kirk's brigade, to the front, was thrown across to the green wood, in double column on the centre, with the flank companies skirmishing in advance. Then it received the overpowering attack which Sherman witnessed. At this juncture, Kirk's brigade got into position on McCook's left, and Rousseau, who had expended all his ammunition in the morning's battle, retired through it to the rear for a fresh supply. Gibson was next thrown in on Kirk's left. For an hour a terrific contest went on, the Confederates holding their position tenaciously, and sometimes even taking the offensive. Finally, at two o'clock, Rousseau's brigade again moved to the front, supported by one of Hurlburt's brigades on the left, and by McClernand on the right. McCook had no artillery; but the three uncaptured guns of Wood's battery and two of McAllister's were turned by McClernand and Sherman against the enemy. Finding the Confederates at last giving way before him, McCook ordered a general advance, and Rousseau's brigade "beautifully deployed," says Sherman, "entered this dreaded wood, and moved in splendid order steadily to the front, sweeping everything before it." Indeed, the battle was already decided. At 1½ o'clock, Beauregard had issued orders to withdraw from the field. The last desperate fighting covered the attempt, and the final Union advance at two o'clock was comparatively unresisted. The withdrawal commenced on the Confederate right, in front of Nelson, and was transmitted to the left. At the latter point, Lew Wallace had steadily swung forward, participating in the varying fortunes of the day. His division also, at two o'clock, finding the obstinate enemy giving way, burst through the woods, easily carrying all before them. The Confederate retreat was conducted with perfect order and precision. Half a mile distant from Shiloh Church, on a commanding ridge, a reserve, selected for that purpose, was drawn up in line of battle for the expected attack.

It did not come. Having waited half an hour, the line was withdrawn a mile further. Here the artillery played for a time upon a small Union column advanced in pursuit; but no engagement took place, and even this desultory firing ceased by four o'clock. The Battle of Shiloh was over.

III.

RESULTS OF SHILOH.

The story of the Southern war is filled with the records of great battles, whose immediate fortunes were divided with such equal hand that both sides claimed the victory — each protesting itself perfectly satisfied with the result. And certes, it must be conceded that an obvious indecisiveness stamps many grand battles of the war, whose duration therefore they did not affect. In many cases, what were account-ed great victories by either antagonist did not alter the fight-ing power of the vanquished, and merely led up to a really decisive action, which happening a little later, furnished in itself the best proof possible that the earlier struggle was but preliminary and preparatory, and not therefore the decisive action of the campaign. Such, for a single example, were the battles of Chantilly and second Bull Run, in a campaign which culminated on the decisive plains of Antietam; such Burnside's assault on Fredericksburg, and Hooker's en-gagement at Chancellorsville, which preceded the decisive struggle at Gettysburg. Neither the fury of the contest nor the mournful catalogue of losses, nor the mere overrunning of territory, in such cases, is the question at issue, which turns, rather, upon the success or the failure of the attempt to permanently change the conditions of the war. In like manner, a great victory may be but the legitimate conse-quence of a decisive triumph preceding, as when Port Hud-·

son followed the fall of Vicksburg; and here, too, it is not
the mere corollary which must be pronounced the decisive
action, since, though the fruit dropped, the bough had first
to be shaken.

Our present concern, however, is chiefly with that class of
actions which, regarded at the time as drawn at best, came to
show themselves at length so thoroughly decisive on the subsequent course of the contest, that we cannot figure to ourselves what the war might have been had these battles
matured to opposite issues.

Pre-eminent among such contests looms up the battle of
Shiloh.   In this famous action — the most terrific and deadly
of the war up to that time — both parties claimed to be
satisfied with the result.   The Confederates, on the one hand,
pointed to the fact that they had completely surprised the
Union camps, had captured and possessed them, together with
many guns and flags and trophies, and in an even fight from
dawn till dusk had driven their enemy in demoralized mass
to the shelter of his gun-boats, his siege-train, and his reinforcements.   And, though it was true that on the second day
the fortune of battle was reversed, yet it was a credit rather
than a disgrace — a victory of *morale* — to fall back stubbornly and in good order before 25,000 fresh troops; and,
finally, while the Confederate loss had been by official
account 10,699, the Union loss on both days, including prisoners, was nearly 15,000.

The Union forces, on their part, without seeking to conceal
their chagrin over the first day's battle, justly claimed victory in the second.   Accordingly, thanksgivings went up all
over the North for the timely arrival of Buell, and his final
repulse of the Confederate army; and never was gratitude,
for what seemed a providential interposition, more fittingly
rendered.

It was not, however, until much later that the true import
of the battle of Shiloh was discovered; and it was found that

the immediate revelations of the battle-field were of small consequence compared with subsequent developments. In order to comprehend the full significance of Shiloh, we must know, on the one hand, the great Confederate possibilities which were forever buried on that field, and, on the other hand, the great Union actualities which thence took rise and grew to maturity.

It is difficult to picture the keen disappointment with which, on Monday afternoon, Beauregard having given the reluctant orders to withdraw from Shiloh, turned his horse's head towards Corinth and rode through the gloomy forest aisles. His hopes were entirely dashed to the ground; and a well-founded expectation of carrying the war into the North was for him entirely gone. Called from Virginia to the West by a deputation of its despairing citizens, headed by Colonel Pryor, who fancied that in the hero of Sumter and Manassas, they saw their deliverer from the perils that compassed them, he had promptly accepted the summons, and went to Tennessee with the purpose of setting afoot an aggressive campaign. Before he could accomplish this intent, fort Henry and fort Donelson fell, with all the superincumbent defensive line. Annoyed, but not in despair, he commenced afresh; and, discovering that he had been shamefully deceived as to the force he would find ready to take the field in the West, he bent himself to creating those numbers which in Virginia he had demanded as a prerequisite for starting. The disaster at Donelson he accounted severe, but not irreparable. His original plan was to concentrate all available forces between Humboldt and Bowling Green, and fall on Buell, whose advance he then regarded as much more dangerous than Grant's. The fall of Donelson and the prompt Union demonstrations up the Tennessee and Cumberland, left no doubt of the course to be adopted thereafter. It was clear that Grant was determined to push on to the Memphis and Charleston Railroad — a line of supply important to be kept

intact.   Beauregard therefore resolved that everything should
be abandoned in Central Tennessee for the moment, and all
concentrated on some point near the western terminus of
the Memphis road.   These forces, while 'gathering, would
naturally defend the road (though that, in his plan, was of
secondary importance), and, at the earliest moment should
be hurled forward in an offensive movement through Tennessee and Kentucky, falling on each of the Union armies in
turn, and crushing them both.   This plan he suggested at
once to General Johnston, proposing at the same time to
serve as second in command.   Beauregard's courier met
Johnston before the latter had got to Murfreesboro', on his
way from Nashville, and that officer, accordingly, continued
his retreat south-easterly towards the Tennessee, to join
Beauregard, with the view to march " onward to the Ohio."

Thus weighty was the purport of the battle delivered at
Pittsburg Landing.   The genius of Beauregard had effected
a double change in Confederate policy, making concentration
take the place of distribution, and the campaign no longer
defensive, but offensive.   Before his day the Confederate
popular idea of military defence had been primitive and
juvenile.   It was to ridge and stripe the broad valley with
numberless lines of parallel earthworks, behind which forces
were to be deployed from flank to flank ; when one line should
be carried, retreat would be had to another and another, even
to the last row of parapets.   Both parties indeed began by
planning campaigns in metaphor ; and if the one had its
dream of an "anaconda coil," the other clung not less closely
to its whimsical fancy of a "last ditch."   But when Beauregard arrived, what he found marked out for a second offensive
line, he cut short, strengthened and assumed as the base of
an aggressive campaign.   His inspiration was the true one ;
and, with proper support, it had met success.   As it was, it
barely failed.   So complete was the surprise, that General
Grant himself writes that he had not thought an attack possi-

ble until several days later, and, when the assault began, "did not believe that they intended to make a determined attack but simply to make a reconnoissance in force." Sherman, too, avers that he did not discover the enemy were attacking in force until long after he had sent back for reinforcements.

Such, then, was the dangerous movement, which, but for an unexpected turn of fortune, might have carried, in the words of Buel, "the remnant of Grant's army prisoners into the enemy's camps." What limit to its onward roll might have been opposed thereafter, it is hard to say. Being frustrated at the start, the Confederate leaders concealed, as far as possible, the true intent of the campaign, and Beauregard, by adroit phrases, covered up the depth of his disappointment; but Bragg, less reticent, declared it, in his official report, a movement "which would have changed the entire complexion of the war." Such it indeed was. I symbolize Shiloh to myself as the representation of the South rampant and flaming in the house of Mars. It was a fierce massing and hurling forward of everything to gain a supreme object — the conquest of the Mississippi Valley. But it spent its fury and its force in vain; and it is a notable fact, that never again in the Valley of the Mississippi were the Confederates able to take the offensive.

I presume that my opinion of this action on the Union side will already have been disclosed in the recital of the battle; but lest there should be any doubt touching this, I shall state in precise terms what judgments seem to be warranted by the facts. The retaining the troops on the left bank of the Tennessee River (unless for immediate advance, which was the object General C. F. Smith had in view when he placed the army there weeks before), and that, too, without any appliances of defence, was undeniably a great error on the part of General Grant. Nor can this verdict be regarded as traversed by a pungent statement made by General Sherman: "It was necessary," says he, "that a combat fierce and bitter, to test the manhood of the two armies, should come off, and that was as good a place as any. It was not then a question of military skill and strategy, but of courage and pluck." Now, with the deference due the opinion of a soldier so eminent as General Sherman, I submit that this declaration is specious rather than sound ; for precisely in proportion to the importance of the result of this primal "test of the manhood of the two armies," was it incumbent on the Union commander to make such dispositions as would gain for his army the advantage in this "test." Of the tactics of the battle-field there is nothing to be said. The subordinate commanders acted on their own motion, according to the extent of their ability. The men fought stubbornly, and with no lack of solid pluck ; but nothing could repair the original faults of disposition and the effect of the surprise. It is impossible to overrate the importance of Buell's arrival on the field at the close of the first day. And, as partizan malignity has tried to make it appear that Buell's oncoming was tardy, it is a simple act of justice to add that, on the contrary, his zeal in the previous marches caused him greatly to outstrip his orders. Moreover, not only did the weight he threw into the scale on the 7th redeem the field ; but his proximity on the 6th — a proximity known to the Confederate commanders — relaxed the nerve of Beauregard's attack during the latter part of that well-nigh fatal day.

It now remains to speak of the territorial results of this battle. As the fall of fort Donelson was the signal for a general abandonment of the first Confederate valley line of defence, so the repulse of Shiloh was followed by the abandonment of the second. In order to concentrate troops at Corinth, Beauregard had been compelled to arrange the evacuation of Island No. Ten. On the morning after the battle of Shiloh, Gen. Mackall surrendered this famous but overrated position, with its remaining garrison, its magazines, artillery, camps, and camp equipages — everything in short which had not been previously transferred to fort Pillow. Immediately thereafter, the Union fleets passed down the Mississippi towards the latter point, and simultaneously General Halleck moved cautiously upon Corinth, with the three columns of Buell, Grant, and Pope. But Beauregard was already convinced that the campaign was lost in the West, and only sought to delay his opponent by a show of resistance, compelling him to lose time in making siege approaches. The theatre of war, therefore, presented at either wing the spectacle of a Union army laboriously spading its way towards the fortified position of its enemy, McClellan before Yorktown, and Halleck before Corinth. At length, however, the pantomime was over, and Beauregard, having held Corinth from the 7th of April to the 29th of May, evacuated it on the night of the latter day. The retreat had been made leisurely, and, under the cover of strong picket lines, Beauregard had sent south every possible thing that could be of value to him in Corinth. The remaining material he blew up in a tremendous explosion, which served as a signal that the Union troops might enter In the capture of Corinth, which Beauregard himself declared "the strategic point of the campaign," the success of Shiloh was now rounded out and complete.

Even here, however, the results of that battle-field had not ceased. The fall of Corinth rendered fort Randolph and fort Pillow, river positions of great strength, and which had justified Beauregard's selection by the repulse of the Union fleet, exposed to a land attack in the rear. Both these positions accordingly were surrendered to the triumphant Union columns. Deprived of its river defences on the one hand, and the army which covered it on the other, Memphis, the most important city yet unconquered on the Mississippi, was forced to capitulate, and thus, in fine, the mighty tide of Union triumph rolled adown the shores of the great river.

The operations around Corinth and Memphis had been, more-over, of very great assistance to the magnificent stroke of Farragut at New Orleans. The gathering of troops from all the Gulf States to Corinth, the accumulation of gun-boats, naval supplies, artillery and handicraft-men to Memphis and its forts, had been loudly complained of at New Orleans ; and it had been with too much justice apprehended that the at-tention paid to barring the river at the north would result in leaving it unbarred at the south.

Inland, however, as well as on the river banks, the results of Shiloh were of portentous magnitude. The concentration and defeat at Shiloh and Corinth had uncovered all Central and Eastern Tennessee to the Union columns. The latter, raiding in every direction, found their progress comparatively unopposed, and began for the first time to make acquaintance with the interior of the Confederacy. As for the Memphis and Charleston road, that great object of the campaign had long since been secured, and was penetrated and broken in many places. With great facility, Mitchell's column, pro-jected by Buell from Nashville long before Shiloh, reached and permanently broke up the railroad at Huntsville, five days after that battle. This energetic officer and others now marched boldly hither and thither in Tennessee, Mississippi and Alabama. It was felt on all hands that vast as was the area to be reduced to the dominion of the Union, a great segment had already been overrun, and patience and stout hearts were all that the conquest of the remainder demanded.

Eng.ᵈ by J.B. Forrest.

Photo. by Gurney

Dick & Fitzgerald, New York.

IV.

ANTIETAM.

____

I.

PRELUDE TO ANTIETAM.

At Chantilly, Lee sat alone in his tent, revolving in his mind the events of that astonishing campaign which had witnessed the defeat of two Union armies whose broken fragments lay on the Potomac like the stranded wreck of a noble fleet. While thus the Confederate commander meditated, there dawned upon him the conception of a stroke more bold than all the deeds yet done — a stroke which seemed to make past performance tame by the plenitude of its promise. That for which he had assumed the offensive was already attained — the armies of McClellan and Pope had been hurled back to the point whence they set out in the campaign of the spring and summer, the siege of Richmond was raised, the war was transferred from the banks of the James and Rapidan to the borders of the Potomac. Why should he not now pass the borders, raise the standard of revolt on Northern soil, overwhelm the demoralized remnants of his adversary and dictate a peace in the capital of the Union? The thought, assuming shape in his mind determined itself in a resolve, and hastily penning a despatch, Lee, from Chantilly on the night of the 2d September, 1862, announced to the Chief of the Confederacy in Richmond his purpose to move on the morrow into Maryland.

Such was the origin of that first Confederate invasion which culminated in the battle of Antietam — the memorable combat which forms the subject-matter of the present chapter. Let us review in rapid retrospect those antecedent operations in Virginia that allured the Confederate commander to this seductive but fatal adventure.

The Spring campaign in Virginia opened with a bold stroke and high promise. The Union army, by a vigorous initiative, at once reduced the Confederates to an attitude of defence. Johnston fell back from Manassas behind the Rapidan. McClellan moved to Fortress Monroe.

But, from the moment the Army of the Potomac landed on the Peninsula, there arose in the minds of those who controlled the military councils at Washington a sense of insecurity touching the safety of the National capital, from the defence of which they had seen the noble army that had been created under its walls taken away in ships to a far distant base. This sentiment, entertained in all honesty but in ignorance of the true principles of war, by the President, by his Cabinet, and by Congress, gave the first blow to the success of the Peninsular campaign. The powerful corps of McDowell, thirty thousand strong, when on the point of embarking at Alexandria to follow its comrades to Fortress Monroe, was arrested and retained in front of Washington. The measure added no real security to the capital, the safety of which rested less in the presence of a covering force than in the vigor with which Richmond should be assailed. But it greatly weakened the Army of the Potomac.

The second blow was still more fatal. The hope of the Peninsular campaign lay in the expectation of rapidly launching forward the Union army against Richmond. It was in its conception essentially an offensive manœuvre, wherein, by a quick advance, McClellan might fall upon the enemy's army before it could be strengthened, and on his capital ere yet it showed any bulwarks of defence. Should he be brought to a pause on the Peninsula, the movement, ceasing to be an offensive *manœuvre*, would become a mere transfer of base, followed by a long and laborious process of forced efforts — the enemy having on his side all the advantage of time. When the army of Napoleon, in 1800, debouched by the pass of Saint Bernard into the plains of Italy, it suddenly found its progress checked by the cannon of Fort Bard, guarding the valley of the Doria, through which the army must pass : so that at the very moment when it was fancied every difficulty was overcome, an obstacle presented itself that threatened to utterly defeat Napoleon's bold campaign. A like obstruction now arose before the Army of the Potomac. It found itself brought to a halt in front of the works of Yorktown — works the existence of which was indeed well known to McClellan, but the real nature of which proved to be different from all anticipation. Unhappily McClellan was not capable of the kind of stroke by which Napoleon overcame Fort Bard. The rivers on either flank were closed to the fleet; the line of fortification was adjudged inassailable by a direct attack; and the Union general deemed it necessary to undertake a siege. It was a great misfortune; for though Johnston, seeing the formidable offensive preparations of his antagonist, at length abandoned the lines of Yorktown, yet their tenure gained for the Confederates a month of precious time that was employed in preparations which doubled the difficulties the Army of the Potomac was doomed to encounter.

From Yorktown the Army of the Potomac advanced on the heels of the Confederates, who retired up the Peninsula towards Richmond. Accident precipitated, on the way, the battle of Williamsburg (May 5), a combat which, though characterized by little of generalship, served to illustrate the superb fighting qualities of the troops. Johnston was forced to withdraw in consequence of a flank movement by Hancock ;

and the army, continuing its advance, reached the Chickahominy, astride of which the corps were established late in
the month of May.

In retiring his army to Richmond, the astute strategist then
in command of the Confederate forces acted in the predetermined purpose of passing from the defensive to a vigorous
offensive as soon as circumstances should indicate a favorable
moment to strike. Such an opportunity now presented itself.
By a most fatuitous partition of strength, the Union force in
Virginia had been divided into no less than three independent
armies, in addition to the main Army of the Potomac. The
"Mountain Department," of Western Virginia, had been
carved out for General Fremont; the "Department of the
Shenandoah" had been constituted for General Banks; and
to General McDowell had been assigned the "Department of
the Rappahannock," at the time his corps was detached from
the Army of the Potomac. The army under command of
McDowell had been raised to an effective of 40,000 men, and
was thrown forward to Fredericksburg. When the Army of
the Potomac reached the Chickahominy it was proposed to
send forward McDowell's column to co-operate with it in the
attack of Richmond. Discerning the menacing position of
this force, Johnston determined on a plan of operations that
would prevent McDowell's junction with McClellan, and at
the same time neutralize all the remaining Union forces in
Northern and Western Virginia. The execution of this plan
was committed to Stonewall Jackson who, after the retirement of the main Confederate army to Richmond, had been
retained in the valley of the Shenandoah.

  The point of attack was skilfully chosen. Instead of assailing the force of McDowell, with whom, having but 15,000
under his command, he was too weak to cope, Jackson, after
dealing a blow at Fremont's force, fell upon Banks, who held
post at Harrisonburg in the lower part of the Shenandoah
valley. Banks retreated up the valley, followed by Jack-

son, as far as Harper's Ferry, where he remained till May 30th.

The tidings of Jackson's apparition in the Shenandoah valley caused the wildest excitement at Washington and prompted measures that jumped exactly with the intent of the Confederate commander. McDowell was stopped in his march to join McClellan, and hurried off to the Shenandoah valley, there to unite with the forces of Banks and Fremont in an attempt to "bag" Jackson. But that wily officer, having already accomplished all that was desired, having neutralized forces that made an aggregate of 60,000 men, slipped through between his pursuers and escaped to his mountain lair in the lower part of the valley. The chaos that ensued presented to Johnston precisely the opportunity he desired, and he hastened to take advantage of it.

At this time two corps of the Army of the Potomac were on the right bank or Richmond side of the Chickahominy and three corps on the left bank. The means of communication were very imperfect. "It was," said General Johnston afterwards to the writer, "a situation in which, by bringing the mass of my force against two fifths of that of my adversary, I might confidently hope to overwhelm that fraction." The experiment, tried on the last day of May, in the battle of Fair Oaks, did not, however, realize the expectations of the Confederate commander. The front attack was, indeed, successful in overwhelming the Union force; but a turning column, which, under Huger, had been assigned the duty of reaching the bridges of the Chickahominy and fatally severing communication between the two wings, failed in its purpose; and Sumner, having, with admirable soldierly promptitude, crossed the Chickahominy, braced up the shattered fragments of the two corps and saved the day. During the action, General Johnston was severely wounded, and compelled to retire from the field for many months. The command then passed into the hands of

General Robert E. Lee, by whom it was retained until the close of the war.

Of the officer into whose hands were thus committed the fortunes of the Army of Northern Virginia little was known of a nature to mark him out for the remarkable career that awaited him. His military experience had been of no more extended scope than those of his brother officers of the regular army of the United States. He had never fought a battle; and in his one campaign in Western Virginia he had been signally outgeneraled by Rosecrans. After this he was reduced to engineer-duty and sent to a kind of military Coventry — to supervise the construction of defences on the South Carolina coast. Yet there was in this grave, high-minded, and respected son of Virginia that which inspired his fellow-citizens with the belief that he was fitted for the greatest commands; and the Virginia Legislature brought to bear on the Richmond Executive so weighty a pressure that Mr. Davis was compelled to recall Lee in March, 1862, and appoint him to the office of General-in-chief — an office which, in fact, was created expressly for him. The hurt received by Johnston brought Lee to the front as commander in the field.

In the Army of the Potomac the month of June passed in elaborate preparations for the grand assault on Richmond. But meanwhile Lee also was resolved on taking the initiative, for the purpose of raising the siege of the Confederate capital. "The intention of the enemy," says Lee, "seemed to be to attack Richmond by regular approaches. The strength of his left wing rendered a direct assault injudicious, if not impracticable. It was therefore determined to construct defensive lines, so as to enable a part of the army to defend the city, and leave the other part free to cross the Chickahominy and operate on the north bank. By sweeping down the river on that side, and threatening his communications with York River, it was thought that the enemy would

be compelled to retreat or give battle out of his entrenchments. The plan was submitted to his Excellency the President, who was repeatedly on the field in the course of its
execution.".

In carrying out this plan of operations, Lee determined to
unite Jackson's force with the main body. As, however, it
was necessary to effect this with great secresy, he masked
Jackson's withdrawal by ostentatiously sending a division
from Richmond to reinforce that officer, and caused it to be
given out that he designed a renewal of operations in the
Shenandoah valley. This *ruse* had the desired effect, and
Jackson, marching rapidly in the direction of Richmond,
reached Cold Harbor on the Chickahominy, on the 27th of
June. This stroke instantly threw McClellan on the defensive, and that at the very moment when he was "advancing
his picket lines, preparatory to an attack." At this time the
right of McClellan's line rested on Beaver Dam Creek, where
a part of the corps of Porter held an entrenched position.
This force, after inflicting a severe repulse on the troops of
Longstreet and Hill that had moved from the south bank
of the Chickahominy, found its right flank turned by Jackson,
and withdrew to the vicinity of Gaines's Mill, where Porter
with his corps took up a position covering the bridges of the
Chickahominy. Here Lee delivered battle on the afternoon
of the 27th, and compelled the retirement of Porter's command to the right bank.

It is easy to see how thoroughly compromised McClellan's
position had now become. Lee already laid hold of his communications with White House. McClellan therefore determined to transfer his army, by a change of base, to the James
River. In what manner and with what entire success this
difficult manœuvre was conducted, is known to all the world.
Stoutly holding his adversary in check by a rear-guard, he
withdrew his immense trains and material safely to the
James, and then forming the army on the slopes of Malvern,
10

gave the Confederates so bloody a repulse that Lee was fain next day to retire towards Richmond. The result of the campaign was no material gain to Lee, for his losses surpassed those of McClellan, and when the army reached the James River, it was in a position that was in fact more menacing to Richmond than that it held on the Chickahominy. Nevertheless, the moral advantage remained with the Confederates.

From the chequered experiences of the Army of the Potomac we must now look away to another field.

After the retirement of Jackson to join Lee, the rumps of armies that had been scattered over Northern Virginia, under Banks and Fremont and McDowell, were united into one body, with the title of the " Army of Virginia," and placed under the command of General J. Pope. With this force, that officer advanced along the line of the Orange and Alexandria Railroad, and took position in the vicinity of Culpepper, where he threatened Gordonsville and Charlottsville and the westward communications of the army at Richmond. Lee could not fail to see the great advantage which his central position between the armies of McClellan and Pope gave him for a stroke against the latter. Howbeit, so long as the Army of the Potomac remained on the Peninsula, its presence was too threatening to permit the Confederate general to move against Pope. He therefore contented himself with sending the corps of Jackson to hold the Army of Virginia in check. Jackson, moving to Gordonsville, advanced against Pope, and on the 9th of August assailed his advanced corps under General Banks, who held post near Cedar Mountain. Although Jackson was compelled to retreat to Gordonsville, such was the alarm for the safety of Washington which his presence awakened in the breast of General Halleck, now General-in-Chief of the Union forces, that he ordered McClellan to embark his army and transport it back to Alexandria. This movement was no sooner disclosed by the shipment of the sick, than Lee, discerning the turn of affairs, resolved to advance with his whole force against Pope. " A part of General McClellan's army," says he, " was believed to have left Harrison's Landing. It therefore seemed that active operations on the James were no longer contemplated, and that the most effectual way to relieve Richmond from any danger of attack from that quarter would be to reinforce General Jackson and advance against General Pope." The execution of this plan was begun on the 13th August, when Longstreet was put in motion for Gordonsville. The remaining divisions of Lee's army followed a few days after.

So soon as Longstreet joined Jackson, the two advanced towards the Rapidan, with the view of attacking Pope; but the latter avoided an encounter by retreating behind the Rappahannock, where he was joined by Burnside's command, that had moved from the James River to unite via Fredericksburg with the army of Pope. The Confederates then pressed northward to the Rappahannock, on the opposing banks of which several days were passed in manœuvres, while Stuart, with fifteen hundred troopers, was sent on an expedition to cut the railroad in Pope's rear. Then, on the 25th of August, Lee, masking his front along the Rappahannock with Longstreet's force, directed Jackson to make a turning movement on his adversary's right, and place himself on the Orange and Alexandria Railroad between Pope's army and Washington. Jackson by forced marches had accomplished this purpose by the following night, striking the railroad at Bristoe Station and Manassas Junction.

It is manifest that Lee did not regard his opponent as a man to be feared; for in detaching Jackson he severed his army in twain and presented Pope an excellent opportunity to make a decisive stroke. The means at the disposal of that officer would certainly have warranted vigorous action. He had already been joined by three corps of the Army of the Potomac and the remaining two were *en route* from Alexandria.   But Pope showed himself incapable of appreciating his advantage, and after a series of shiftings and turnings that were very *mal apropos*, he found himself, on the 29th, confronting Jackson on the battle-field of Bull Run.   Unhappily the opportunity had passed : Lee had gained time to hasten forward with the remainder of his army and had joined his lieutenant during the forenoon of the 29th.   Pope acted on the offensive on the 29th, but was repulsed. Next day, Lee took the initiative.   After a warm engagement he turned his antagonist's left, and by night had carried the field of battle and swept Pope's whole force, with great loss, across Bull Run. The pursuit was continued during the two following days as far as Chantilly, where an engagement took place on the afternoon of the 2d September.   It was unimportant in its results, but cost the sacrifice of two of the ablest officers of the service — General Stevens and Phil. Kearney, that bright ideal of a soldier, who was wont, grasping the sword with his single hand and placing the reins between his teeth, to lead his men in charges that were irresistible, and whom his division loved as the soldiers of the Tenth Legion loved Cæsar. At Chantilly Lee cried a halt, while the broken battalions of the once proud Union army reeled and staggered back to the fortifications of Washington.

Such, then, were the circumstances under which Lee, sitting alone in his tent at Chantilly the night of the 2d September, formed the audacious resolve of invasion.   It must be confessed there was much to prompt this course. The astonishing success that had crowned his first campaign had given Lee a sense of confidence in his own powers and his army a contempt for its adversary. The Union army, shattered physically, but still more shaken in *morale*, he might well conclude could offer but a feeble resistance, while Maryland, in passionate songs, had invoked deliverance from what, with an overstretch of poetic license, was called the "tyrant's foot." How these facts, working together in the mind of Lee, determined themselves in a resolve, let that General himself state. "The armies of Generals McClellan and Pope had now been brought back to the point from which they set out on the campaigns of the spring and summer, and the objects of their campaigns had been frustrated. The war was thus transferred from the interior to the frontier, and the supplies of rich and productive districts made accessible to our army. To prolong a state of affairs in every way desirable, and not to permit the season for active operations to pass without endeavoring to inflict further injury upon the enemy, the best course appeared to be the transfer of the army into Maryland. The condition of Maryland encouraged the belief that the presence of our army, however inferior to that of the enemy, would induce the Washington government to retain all its available force to provide against contingencies which its course towards the people of that State gave it reason to apprehend. At the same time it was hoped that military success might afford us an opportunity to aid the citizens of Maryland in any efforts they might be disposed to make to recover their liberty. Influenced by these considerations, the army was put in motion."

It must be left to the imagination of the reader to conceive what disorder and alarm meanwhile reigned in Washington. With dismay those who controlled the military councils saw the legitimate fruit of their own devisings come back upon them; for, in removing the army from the Peninsula, they had, of their own accord, unloosed Lee and invited the destruction of the forces in Northern Virginia. They had sown the wind: they now reaped the whirlwind. The structure of the army was completely dislocated: half the men had abandoned their colors, not through fear, but from the knowledge that they were without a head. And only these broken battalions lay between Lee and Washington! Never before had the national capital been in such peril — not even when, the year before, the fugitive mob of McDowell rushed in panic under its walls. That was before the Confederates had developed a definite military policy; this was after a campaign which, having commenced with the raising of the siege of their own capital, naturally inflamed their minds with the desire of capturing the capital of their adversary.

In this dark hour the President turned for help to that officer who, during the last disastrous days of the campaign, had been reduced to the duty of playing quartermaster to Pope. He turned to General McClellan as the only man who could bring order out of the chaos into which affairs had fallen. And it is certain that whatever may have been the estimate the Government put upon his ability, it knew at least that he alone had the power to restore cohesion and confidence to the Army of the Potomac. On that same 2d of September, when Lee from Chantilly was telegraphing to Richmond his purpose of moving into Maryland, Mr. Lincoln, accompanied by General Halleck, went to beg McClellan to go out, meet, and take command of the retreating army for the defence of the capital. Getting at once into the saddle, he hastened forth to seek the disorganized forces, applied himself with vigor to his task, and soon wrought an astonishing moral transformation in the army. The troops who had learnt by experience the difference between generalship and military incapacity, hailed with joy his restoration to command. Thousands of absentees rallied to their standards, discipline recovered its sway, and the shapeless mass became the Army of the Potomac once more.

The rehabilitation of the army was for the time the paramount consideration, excluding all others; but this happily being soon accomplished, McClellan turned his attention to the duties imposed upon him by the presence of the enemy. Lee did not long leave his opponent in doubt touching his intentions; for, turning aside from the "high upreared and abutting fronts" that defended Washington, the

Confederate commander passed the Potomac by the fords near Leesburg, and concentrated his columns at Frederick, Maryland. Thither McClellan immediately directed the Army of the Potomac, on routes covering Washington and Baltimore. The right wing was under Burnside, the centre under Sumner, and the left under Franklin.

The Confederate van, composed of Jackson's divisions, made its entry into Frederick on the 6th of September. The "liberating army" was now on Northern soil, and confidently awaited the expected rising on the part of the citizens of Maryland, who were admonished, in a proclamation issued by General Lee, to "throw off the foreign yoke." But the Confederates soon discovered they were doomed to disappointment in this expectation. There was found to be not only little secessionist sentiment in Western Maryland, but it proved that those who were willing to join the revolt dared not do so until Lee should show his ability to maintain himself in the State. The spectacle of Jackson's unkempt and unclean soldiers, shoeless, and clad in tattered butternut or gray, awakened no enthusiasm; loyal women dared to throw out the flag of the Union from their windows, and the recruiting offices established by Lee stood empty. In fact the invasion, so far as it was based on the hope of exciting insurrection, was, from the start, a failure. In addition, McClellan was approaching. Lee, therefore, evacuated Frederick on the 10th and 11th, moving westward beyond the mountains. The van of the Union army entered the town the next day amid the hearty plaudits of the people.

What now was Lee's design? what his plan of operations? Let him tell us in his own words: "It was proposed to move the army into Western Maryland, establish our communications with Richmond through the valley of the Shenandoah, and, by threatening Pennsylvania, induce the enemy to follow, and draw him from his base. Now it had been supposed that the advance upon Frederick would lead to the evacuation of

Martinsburg and Harper's Ferry, thus opening the line of communications through the valley. But this not having occured, it became necessary to dislodge the enemy from these positions before concentrating the army west of the mountains. To accomplish this with the least delay, General Jackson was directed to proceed with his command to Martinsburg, and, after driving the enemy from that place, to move down the south side of the Potomac upon Harper's Ferry. General McLaws, with his own and R. H. Anderson's divisions, was ordered to besiege Maryland Heights, on the north side of the Potomac, opposite Harper's Ferry, and Brigadier-General Walker to take possession of Loudon Heights, on the east side of the Shenandoah, where it unites with the Potomac. These several commands were directed, after reducing Harper's Ferry and clearing the valley of the enemy, to join the rest of the army at Boonsboro' or Hagerstown."

This plan of operations was embodied in an order of march, of which copies were distributed to the several division commanders; but, by accident, one of these fell into the hands of the very man whom of all others in the world it was to Lee most important it should not reach. It appears that through some negligence the copy of this order sent to General D. H. Hill was left behind at Frederick when the Confederates moved westward; and when McClellan reached that city on the 13th, the paper was placed in his hands. Certainly one's adversary is not the person a General most desires to take into his confidence when executing such an enterprise as that upon which Lee was now bent!

The advantage which the possession of this order gave McClellan was, of course, immense. Nor did he delay availing himself of his opportunity: the army was immediately pressed forward in vigorous pursuit. From Frederick the Union columns wended their way through the picturesque region of Western Maryland, over the Catoctin Mountains, and across the lovely Middleton valley, then arrayed in the glory of a golden harvest, till they confronted the massive buttress of the South Mountain range. Where, meanwhile, was Lee?

Respecting his hopes and purposes at this time, the Confederate commander in his official report, makes a very frank statement. "The advance of the Federal army," says he, "was so slow, at the time we left Frederick [no wonder, considering General Halleck's constant remonstrances that McClellan was moving too far from Washington], as to justify the belief that the reduction of Harper's Ferry would be accomplished and our troops concentrated before they would be called on to meet it. In that event it had not been intended to oppose its passage through the South Mountains, as it was desired to engage it as far from its base as possible." Accordingly, while Jackson and McLaws and Walker had proceeded towards Harper's Ferry, Lee's remaining divisions under Longstreet and D. H. Hill had passed quite west of the South Mountains, the former to Hagerstown, the latter to Boonsboro', there to await the reduction of Harper's Ferry, when the divisions engaged in that enterprise were to unite with them. Stuart, with his troopers and a couple of batteries of horse artillery alone remained to cover the rear. Now, on the afternoon of the 13th, Lee was surprised by a message from Stuart informing him that the Union column was approaching the South Mountain on the great road from Frederick to Boonsboro', which traversed the ridge by a gorge named Turner's Gap. This information was the more alarming, seeing that the operations against Harper's Ferry had not been conducted as rapidly as had been expected. If now in this state of facts the Union force should penetrate the South Mountain, it would find itself in Pleasant Valley, directly in the rear of the Confederate force that under McLaws was co-operating with Jackson in the reduction of Harper's Ferry from the side of Maryland Heights. The consequence could not fail to be disastrous to Lee. It would in fact break up his whole plan of campaign.

To prevent this result it only remained for Lee to make such dispositions as would cover the siege of Harper's Ferry. In this nature greatly favored him, for the South Mountain range running northward from the Potomac, played the part of a natural curtain and furnished an excellent line of defence. As it could be penetrated only by Turner's Gap and by another pass, five miles nearer the Potomac named Crampton's Gap, it was simply requisite to firmly guard these *débouchés*, and the whole Union army would be held off at arm's length, as it were, with one hand, while with the other the Confederate commander was securing the rich prize of Harper's Ferry. Accordingly McLaws was directed to divert part of his force from the operations against Maryland Heights in order to guard Crampton's Gap in his rear while D. H. Hill was instructed to hasten back from Boonsboro' to look after Turner's Pass, and Longstreet was commanded to countermarch from Hagerstown to the latter's support.   It happened that the left wing of the Union army under Franklin was moving on the road leading to the former pass, while the right wing under Burnside followed by the centre under Sumner was advancing by the Boonsboro' road towards the latter pass ; but both McLaws and Hill had time to dispose their troops for the defence of the gaps, for the force that Stuart had met nearing the South Mountain on the afternoon of the 13th, was but the van guard of cavalry under Pleasonton : the infantry, being yet considerably behind, did not arrive before the passes until the morning of the 14th, and then only with the heads of columns.

It needs not go beyond the facts of the situation already presented to apprehend the course of conduct which duty now imposed on McClellan.   He knew that behind that mountain wall, at Harper's Ferry, twelve thousand men were helplessly environed by the enemy, and he was bound if possible to relieve them.   It is true their presence there was no fault of his ; for he had urged on General Halleck, as soon as he learned Lee had crossed the Potomac, the necessity of withdrawing the garrison from Harper's Ferry as a point at once useless and untenable from the moment the Confederates were in Maryland. It matters not that official pedantry, disregarding this sage counsel, had retained those men in a trap until every avenue of escape was cut off. McClellan was bound by every consideration of honor and duty to do his utmost to succor them.

McClellan certainly appreciated the weight of the obligation imposed upon him; but it will be always a matter of regret that more impetuosity could not have been thrown into the execution of the task. It required a considerable part of the day to bring up the troops, to reconnoitre and to make dispositions: so that it was not till late in the afternoon that after many tentatives, the crests of the mountain were carried by Franklin's charge at Crampton's Gap, and by that of Burnside at Turner's. Finding their positions thus compromised, Longstreet and D. H. Hill, during the night retired ten miles westward to Sharpsburg near the Potomac. Next morning the Union troops debouched by the passes into Pleasant Valley. Would they still be in time to relieve Harper's Ferry? It was so hoped, and for two days past McClellan, by frequent discharges of artillery had endeavored to convey to Colonel Miles tidings of his approach. Now that the South Mountain was passed it was a march of no more than six miles for the force that issued through Crampton's Pass to reach Harper's Ferry, whence the booming of guns announced that it still held out. But by a tragic conjuncture, just as the army had burst the barrier that separated it from the beleagured garrison, an ominous cessation of firing announced that Harper's Ferry had fallen! Let us now see in what manner this untoward event fell out.

Ere yet the Union army had reached South Mountain, Jackson on the 13th, having passed the Potomac at Williamsport, had approached Harper's Ferry from the south, and drew up his force fronting Bolivar Heights on which the main body of the garrison had taken post. While Jackson was to attack Harper's Ferry from that direction, McLaws's division was to occupy Maryland Heights, and Walker's Loudon Heights. As the Potomac separated him from the former and the Shenandoah from the latter, it was a matter of vital importance to establish communication and co-operation between the different bodies of the investing force.   Jackson therefore signaled the heights opposite him in order to ascertain if the forces had yet come up. No reply was received. McLaws had not been able to gain possession of Maryland Heights, and the reason of this is now to be given. While Colonel Miles retained the bulk of his force in Harper's Ferry, he assigned a part of the garrison under Colonel Ford to the defence of the heights on the Maryland side. In this disposition of his troops, the vital error was that he did not withdraw everything from Harper's Ferry, and concentrate all on Maryland Heights — an extremely defensible position, and completely commanding Harper's Ferry, which lies in the bottom of a funnel formed of the three mountains named respectively Bolivar, Maryland, and Loudon Heights.   The presence of Ford's force on Maryland Heights, and the natural difficulties of the ground, obliged McLaws to consume the greater part of the 13th in preparations for the attack ; but when in the afternoon his troops moved forward to scale the heights, Ford, after a brief and unskilful resistance, abandoned the mountain and fled across the Potomac to Harper's Ferry. The Confederates during the night dragged more artillery up the rocky sides of Maryland Heights and crowned the crest.

On the morning of the 14th, McLaws, from his eyrie, was able to send response to Jackson's renewed and eager signals ; Walker, on Loudon Heights, gave the like sign : the investment was complete — the garrison was at the mercy of the besiegers. Jackson himself shall tell us the sequel :

" At dawn, September 15th, Lieutenant-Colonel Walker

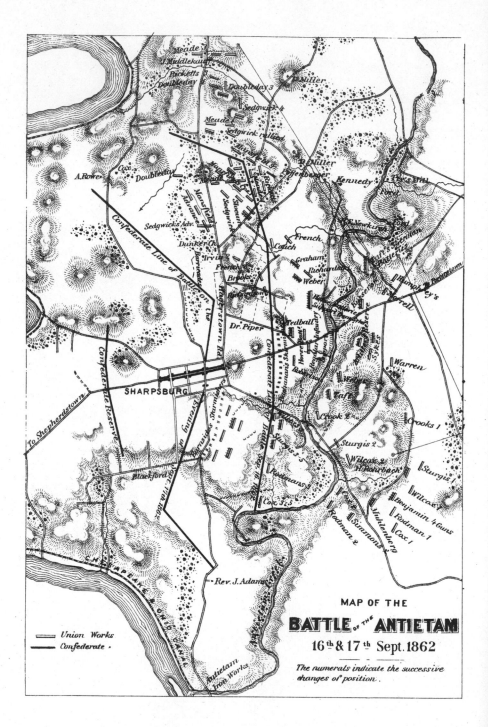

MAP OF THE

BATTLE OF THE **ANTIETAM**

16th & 17th Sept. 1862

The numerals indicate the successive changes of position.

Union Works
Confederate ·

SHARPSBURG

To Shepherdstown

Rev. J. Adams

Antietam Iron Works

C. & O. CHESAPEAKE & OHIO CANAL

opened a rapid enfilade fire from all his batteries at about one thousand yards range. The batteries on School-house Hill attacked the enemy's lines in front. In a short time the guns of Colonel Crutchfield opened from the rear. Those of Pegram and Carpenter opened fire upon the enemy's right; the artillery on Loudon Heights again opened on Harper's Ferry, and also some guns of General McLaws from Maryland Heights. In an hour, the enemy's fire seemed to be silenced, and the batteries were ordered to cease their fire, which was the signal for storming the works. General Pender had commenced his advance, when the enemy again opening, Pegram and Crenshaw moved forward their batteries and poured in a rapid fire. The white flag was now displayed, and shortly afterwards Brigadier-General White (the commanding officer, Colonel D. S. Miles, having been mortally wounded), with a garrison of about eleven thousand men, surrendered as prisoners of war. Under this capitulation, we took possession of seventy-three pieces of artillery, some thirteen thousand small arms, and other stores. Leaving General A. P. Hill to receive the surrender of the Federal troops and take the requisite steps for securing the captured stores, I moved, in obedience to orders from the commanding general, to rejoin him in Maryland, with the remaining divisions of my command."

The denouement at Harper's Ferry restored Lee's fortunes; for up to the time that he received tidings of its fall, it seemed probable that he would be compelled to re-cross into Virginia and abandon the campaign.

II.

THE BATTLE OF ANTIETAM.

Descending the western slope of the South Mountain, one suddenly emerges into a lovely valley, spreading out in many graceful undulations and picturesque forms of field and forest,

to the Potomac.   This stream, turning sharply to the north
at Harper's Ferry, forms the westward limit of the valley,
whose breadth from the mountain to the river may be from
eight to twelve miles.   But before reaching the Potomac, at
a distance of six or eight miles from the passes of the South
Mountain, one comes upon the stream Antietam, which,
flowing from the north in drowsy, winding course, empties
into the Potomac a few miles above Harper's Ferry.   As this
brook makes with the Potomac an acute angle, and the Potomac forms a reentrant angle on itself, there is thus left between the two streams an enclosed space of two or three
miles broad and twice or thrice that length.   From the western margin of the Antietam the ground rises in a slope of
woods and cultivated fields to a bold crest, and then falls back
in rough outlines of rock and scaur to the Potomac.   The
town of Sharpsburg nestles just behind the ridge, above
which the steeples of its churches are visible from the east
side of the Antietam, and in the rear of Sharpsburg is the
Shepherdstown ford of the Potomac.

It was upon this coign of vantage, his back towards the
Potomac, his front covered by the Antietam, that Lee, on the
morning of the 15th of September, drew up his force, or
rather what of his force was with him — to wit: the divisions
of Longstreet and Hill that during the night had been compelled to abandon the defence of the South Mountain passes.
Jackson and McLaws and Walker were still at Harper's Ferry,
which did not surrender till the morning of the 15th, and
from which Lee had yet no reports.   In taking post behind
the Antietam, therefore, Lee was in position either to repass
the Potomac by the Shepherdstown ford, if he should be
pressed too hard by McClellan, or to stand and receive battle
if the conclusion of operations at Harper's should set Jackson and his companions free to unite with him at Sharpsburg.   While there anxiously awaiting the turn of events,
Lee, during the forenoon of the 15th, received from Jackson

tidings of the surrender of Harper's Ferry — tidings which
he says "reanimated the courage of the troops." Forth-
with he instructed his lieutenant to march with all haste by
way of Shepherdstown ford and join him at Sharpsburg. His
arrival was hardly to be looked for that day, but it was certain next morning; and in the interim Lee judged he could
readily hold McClellan in check.

Howbeit, it was now manifest to Lee that the terms on
which he would be compelled to meet his antagonist were
very different from those he had hoped to establish for himself ere he should be brought to battle. In the revelation
already made of his intent, it will be remembered that he had
expected — the words are his own — "to move the army into
Western Maryland, establish our communications with Richmond through the valley of the Shenandoah, and, by threatening Pennsylvania, induce the enemy to follow, and draw him
away from his base of supplies." Now if we may translate
this very general statement into specific terms, it probably
means that Lee designed to take position in the Cumberland
valley as far north as Hagerstown, where, masking his movement by the mountains he would be able to send forward a
raiding column towards the Susquehanna, and if this manœuvre should prompt the Union commander to follow his
impulse by an advance northward, east of the South Mountain
range (as a like movement induced Meade to do during the
campaign of the following year), an opening would then be
afforded him of moving upon Washington. It was otherwise
decreed. The retention of the Union armies at Harper's
Ferry obliged Lee to detach two thirds of his force to secure
its capture, and by its capture his communications with
Richmond. The unwonted rapidity with which his opponent
moved forward from Frederick made it necessary for him to
use the remaining third of his strength in covering the siege of
Harper's Ferry. Finally, the expulsion of this force from the
South Mountain before yet Harper's Ferry had fallen, com-

pelled him to retire towards the Potomac. Henceforth his movements were controlled by the prime and imperious necessity of effecting a concentration of his troops, rather than by his original purpose of manœuvring the Union army away from its base. He was no longer offensive but defensive. Strategically, he was already foiled. Why, then, did he resolve still to remain in Maryland? The answer is obvious. To have re-crossed the Potomac without a battle would have weakened him morally, investing the whole enterprise with the aspect of an aimless and Quixotic adventure. Besides, he believed himself to be able to worst his antagonist in a trial of strength, for he was elated by many successes, and he counted much on the supposed demoralization of the army of the Potomac. In taking his stand, therefore, in that south-western corner of Maryland, he challenged combat that must in its very nature be decisive. If beaten, he would be compelled to seek safety in flight across the Potomac; if victorious, Washington and Baltimore would lie open to him.

While Lee, awaiting anxiously the arrival of Jackson, occupied his mind with these grave speculations, the Union army which, on the morning of the 15th, had defiled from the South Mountains and moved in long shining columns athwart the valley, reached the heights on the east side of the Antietam, across which, defined on the rim of the opposite crest, the hostile infantry and artillery were plainly visible. Unhappily, if McClellan, as is averred, had designed to assail Lee immediately on meeting, and thus take advantage of the yet divided condition of the Confederate force, he lost the opportunity. In spite of his efforts to launch forward the army in rapid pursuit, much time had been lost; Burnside delayed several hours beyond his appointed time of starting in the morning; there was considerable confusion and cross purpose in the marches, and when, well on in the afternoon, McClellan reached the Antietam, no more than two divisions

— Richardson's division of Sumner's corps, and Sykes' division of Porter's corps — had yet come up : so that, by the time a sufficient force was in hand to authorize his seizing the offensive, the day had passed by, and with it the opportunity to take Lee in his sin. During the morning of the 16th, the whole of the Union army had arrived, saving Franklin's command, which was still in Pleasant Valley ; the corps were then posted behind the ridge on the east side of Antietam Creek — Burnside's corps on the left, Porter's in the centre Hooker's corps and the two corps under Sumner on the right. The crest was crowned with batteries so placed as to deliver a very effective fire. Let us now see the position of Lee's forces.

From the town of Sharpsburg two main roads lead out — the one running eastward across the Antietam to Boonsboro' ; the other northward on the west side of the Antietam to Hagerstown. The distance from Sharpsburg to the stream is as near as may be a mile. Lee posted his troops between the town and the Antietam — Longstreet's command to the right (south), and D. H. Hill's division to the left (north) of the Boonsboro' road. Their line was nearly parallel to the Antietam. Hood's division of Longstreet's command was, however, placed on the left of Hill's line, where it was somewhat "refused" and stretched across to the Hagerstown road. When Jackson came up with two divisions on the 16th, he was placed to the left of the Hagerstown road ; and as this part of the field was the scene of the most deadly encounters of the 17th, it will require a little speciality of description.

If leaving the town of Sharpsburg the pedestrian walks out northward by the Hagerstown road, he will, at the distance of a mile, reach a small edifice, known as the "Dunker Church," situate on the road, hard by a body of woods. This wood, which has a depth of about a quarter of a mile, runs along the Hagerstown road for several hundred yards, entirely on the left hand side as you proceed from Sharps-

11

burg. Then there is a field, the edge of which runs at right angles to the road for about two hundred yards, thus making an elbow in the woods. The field then turns to the right, and runs along the woods parallel to the Hagerstown road for a quarter of a mile, when the wood again turns square to the left and extends back about half a mile, making at this point again an elbow with the strip of woods running along the road from the church. The timber-ground is full of ledges of limestone and small ridges, affording excellent cover for troops. It was here that Jackson's troops were posted. The field from the timber to the Hagerstown road forms a plateau nearly level, and in higher ground than the woods which slope down abruptly from the edges of the plateau. The field, however, extends not only *to* the Hagerstown road, but for a considerable distance to the east side of it, when it is again circumscribed by another body of timber, which we may call the "east woods." The woods around the Dunker Church, the "east woods," and the open field between them formed the arena whereon the terrible wrestle between the Union right and Confederate left took place—a fierce flame of battle which, beginning in the "east woods," swept back and forth across the field, burst forth for a time in the woods around the Dunker Church, and which left its marks everywhere, but in most visible horror on the open plain.

Lee stood on the defensive. In order, therefore, to assume the offensive it was necessary for McClellan to pass the Antietam. That stream is in this vicinity crossed by several stone bridges, of which one is at the crossing of the Keadysville and Williamsport road; a second, two and a half miles below on the Boonsboro' road; a third, about a mile below the second on the Rohrersville and Sharpsburg road. It has a few fords, but they are difficult. The last of these bridges, which was opposite the Union left, under Burnside, was found to be covered by marksmen protected by rifle trenches. The second, opposite the Union centre, under Porter, was unobstructed save by the fire of the hostile batteries on the crest. The first, or upper bridge, beyond the Union right, was entirely unguarded, and a ford hard by was also available. The plan formed by McClellan was to cross at the upper bridge, assail the enemy's left with the corps of Hooker and Mansfield, supported by Sumner's, and, if necessary, by Franklin's, and as soon as matters should look favorably there to move the corps of General Burnside across the lower bridge against Lee's extreme right, upon the ridge running to the south and rear of Sharpsburg, and having carried his position to pierce along the crest towards their right; finally whenever either of these flank movements should be successful to advance the centre with all the forces then disposable.

The execution of this plan was begun on the afternoon of the 16th, when Hooker's corps was ordered to cross the Antietam by the upper bridge and ford. The passage was effected without opposition, and Hooker, moving to the west and south penetrated, amid slight skirmishing, as far as the woods on the east of the Hagerstown road. Thus far he advanced, but no farther that night; for Hood's two brigades which had lain in the edge of the timber near the Dunker Church, were, on the approach of Hooker, marched across the open fields to the east woods, and there joined combat. As, however, it was dark when the encounter took place, no result was reached. Each party occupied the woods; but, before midnight Hood's brigades were relieved by two of Jackson's command. During the night Mansfield's corps made the passage of the Antietam, and lay a mile in rear of Hooker. Sumner held his corps in readiness to cross at daylight. McClellan had now plainly revealed his intent; it was manifest that morning must precipitate decisive action — an unwelcome reflection to Lee, for four divisions of the Confederate forces had not yet returned from Harper's Ferry.

The light of day, the 17th of September, broke with tender beauty over the lovely valley of the Antietam, and dawned upon the mighty hosts that there confronted each other in battle array, conscious that the issue not only of a campaign but of the War itself hung on what should that day be done.   The collision was not delayed, and with early light the morning stillness was broken by the rattle of musketry and the hoarse clamor of two hundred guns.

McClellan opened the conflict by seizing the initiative and hurling his right (the corps of Hooker) against the left of his antagonist.   It will be remembered that in the east woods Hood's division had the night before been relieved by two brigades of Ewell's division of Jackson's corps.   These were early in the morning strengthened by another brigade. In addition to this division, there was at this time present with Jackson only the Stonewall division, under General Jones, for the division of A. P. Hill had not yet returned from Harper's Ferry.   But while Ewell's division was thus thrown forward in advance, the Stonewall division was held in hand behind out-cropping ledges of limestone in the wood near the Dunker Church : so that the attack at first fell alone upon the three brigades in the east wood.   The assault was made by Hooker's centre division, which, as it happened, was the division of Pennsylvania Reserves under Meade — Doubleday's division being on its right, Ricketts' on its left. It was marked by wonderful impetuosity on the Union side, and by stubborn resistance on the part of the Confederates. However, after an hour's fighting, such was the vigor with which the attack was pressed, and so destructive to Jackson's troops was the fire of the numerous batteries on the east side of the Antietam (placed, says Jackson, so as to enfilade his line), that the Confederate brigades gave back with great loss across the open field and over the Hagerstown road to the woods beyond — the woods around the Dunker Church, where Jackson's reserves lay.   If it had occurred to General Hooker at this time to bring up the corps of Mansfield, form it on his right, and with this well-developed front assail the

Confederate left, there is no doubt that the whole of that wing might have been swept away. There is a commanding eminence, to the right of where Hooker's flank rested, which would thus have been occupied, and as it is the key of the field, taking *en revers*, the woods with the out-cropping ledges of limestone where Jackson's reserves lay, its possession would, in all likelihood, have been decisive of the field. Hooker failed to perceive this; but he advanced his line to reap the fruit of his first advantage — thrusting forward his centre and left over the open field towards the woods west of the Hagerstown road. No sooner, however, had the troops approached the crest of the plateau than Jackson's reserves, with the re-formed battalions of Ewell's division, emerged from the woods and joined issue with the advancing line in a combat of extraordinary ferocity. Equal in mettle, the combatants faced each other on the open plain within short range, neither side yielding, and both plying their deadly work with such desperate ardor, such inflexible determination as few battle-fields have witnessed. The mortal struggle was only ended when at length the opposing fronts had torn each other to shreds. Then both sides retired; but even when the broken fragments went back, the spectators from the distant stand-point of the east side of the Antietam could trace in the dead that covered the ground where lines had stood — dreadful witness of a struggle whose character may be gathered from the followiug statement of the mortality it entailed:

Of the Confederate losses, Jackson thus writes in his official report: "The carnage on both sides was terrific. At an early hour General Starke (commanding the Stonewall division) was killed, and Colonel Douglas (commanding Lawton's brigade) was also killed. General Lawton, commanding division and Colonel Walker, commanding brigade, were severely wounded. More than half of the brigades of Lawton and Hays were either killed or wounded, and more than a third of Trimble's and all the regimental commanders in those brigades except two, were either killed or wounded. Thinned in their ranks, and exhausted of their ammunition, Jackson's division and, the brigades of Lawton, Hays and Trimble, retired to the rear, and Hood, of Longstreet's command, took their place." On the Union side, Hooker's corps had been completely shattered, and indeed the men even when withdrawn from under fire were so shaken in *morale* that the corps may be said to have been completely broken up: so much so that General Sumner testifies that when he soon afterwards came upon the field, he "saw nothing of Hooker's corps at all."

When the stress had become heaviest upon him, but before yet he had been compelled to give way, Hooker summoned up the corps of Mansfield, which was in the rear, and which, arriving about half past seven A. M., was formed with the division of Williams on the right and that of Green on the left. This force, brought into action later than it should have been, was immediately met by the division of D. H. Hill, which had meanwhile been called up from the position in which it had lain behind the Dunker Church, to brace up the shattered corps of Jackson. The events that succeeded are thus recounted by Hood's two brigade commanders. Says Colonel Law: "On reaching the Hagerstown road, I found but few of our troops on the field, and these seemed to be in much confusion, but still opposing the advance of the enemy's dense masses with determination. Throwing the brigade at once into line of battle, facing northward, I gave the order to advance. The Texas brigade, Colonel Wofford, had in the meantime come into line on my left, and the two brigades had now moved forward together. The enemy, who had by this time advanced half way across the field, and had planted a heavy battery at the north end of it, began to give way before us, though in vastly superior force. The fifth Texas regiment, which had been sent over to my right, and the fourth Alabama, pushed into the wood in which the skirmishing had taken place the evening previous, and drove the enemy through and beyond it. The other regiments of my command continued steadily to advance in the open ground, driving the enemy in great confusion from and beyond his guns. So far we had been successful, and everything promised a decisive victory." Says Colonel Wofford: "Moving forward in line of battle, the brigade proceeded through the woods into the open field towards the cornfield, where the left encountered the first line of the enemy. . . By this time, the enemy on our left having commenced falling back, the first Texas pressed them rapidly to their guns, which now poured into them a fire on their right flank, centre and left, from three different batteries, before which their well-formed line was cut down and scattered. Being two hundred yards in front of our line, their situation was most critical. Riding back to the left of our line, I found the fragment of the eighteenth Georgia regiment in front of the extreme right battery of the enemy, located on the pike running by the church, which now opened upon our thinned ranks a most destructive fire; the men and officers were gallantly shooting down the gunners, and for a moment silenced them. At this time the enemy's fire was most terrific, their first line of infantry having been driven back to their guns, which now opened a furious fire together with their second line of infantry, upon our thinned and almost annihilated ranks."

These extracts detail with sufficient accuracy what may be called the second round in the combat between the Union right and Confederate left. It resulted in driving back both the remnants of Hooker's corps and the divisions of Mansfield's command from the open field to the woods in which the contest opened in the morning. So complete indeed was the repulse that for a time the hostile camp was only held in check by a single battery, which unsupported, maintained its ground on the Hagerstown road. The brave veteran, General

Mansfield had been killed while examining the ground in his front; Hooker, severely wounded in the foot, had to be carried from the field, and only disaster seemed imminent, when most opportunely, at nine o'clock, Sumner came upon the field with his corps.   Let us now see in the narratives of Hood's brigade commanders how sudden a change now fell on their thus far victorious advance.   Says Colonel Law : "So far we had been entirely successful, and everything promised a decisive victory. It is true that strong support was needed to follow up our success, but this I expected every moment.   At this stage of the battle, a powerful Federal force, ten times our number, of fresh troops was thrown in our front.   Our losses up to this time had been very heavy ; the troops now confronting the enemy were insufficient to cover properly one fourth of the line of battle ; our ammunition was expended, the men had been fighting long and desperately, and were exhausted from want of food and rest.   It was evident this state of affairs could not long continue.   No support was at hand.   To remain stationary or advance without it would have caused a useless butchery, and I adopted the only alternative — that of falling back to the wood from which I had first advanced." Says Colonel Wofford : "By this time, one brigade had suffered so greatly that I was satisfied they could neither advance nor hold their position.   Presently our line commenced to give way, when I ordered it back, under cover of the woods to the left of the church, when we halted and waited for support.   None arriving, after some time, the enemy commenced advancing in full force.   Seeing the hopelessness and folly of making a stand with our shattered brigade, and a remnant from other commands, the men being greatly exhausted, and many of them out of ammunition, I determined to fall back to a fence in our rear, where we met the long-looked for reinforcements."

Such was the result of Sumner's attack, and it was made solely by his right division under Sedgwick — French's division being disposed to hold the ground where before Hooker's left had been, and Richardson's division being thrown still further to the left, confronting the Confederate centre under D. H. Hill. Sedgwick, by his impetuous attack, not only cleared the open field, but following up his success, seized and held possession of the woods west of the Dunker Church. It was the farthest advance yet made, and bade fair to secure victory to the Union arms, when fortune once more gave the preponderance of force to the enemy. Just as Hood's troops, thoroughly beaten in the encounter with Sumner's command, were retiring from the field, and Sedgwick's division had gained the woods around the Dunker Church, the Confederate divisions of McLaws and Walker, which had that morning arrived, assailed Sedgwick, whose position, by reason of the very success that had rewarded his attack was a critical one, being separated by a wide, unguarded interval from all support on the left. The story of the onset of McLaws, and what thereby resulted to the Union force, is thus told by that officer himself: "Just in front of the line was a large body of woods, from which parties of our troops, of whose command I do not know, were seen retiring [the body of woods was that already so frequently noted as the wood around Dunker Church, and the Confederate troops seen retiring by McLaws were those of Hood, driven back by Sedgwick's attack], and the enemy I could see, were advancing rapidly, occupying the place. My advance was ordered before the entire line of General Kershaw could be formed. As the enemy were filling the woods so rapidly, I wished my troops to cross the open space between us and the woods [the open space *in rear of the woods* near the Dunker Church, not the open space between the body of woods and the "east woods"], before they were entirely occupied. It was made steadily and in perfect order, and the troops were immediately engaged, driving the enemy before them in magnificent style, at all points, sweeping the woods with perfect ease, and inflicting great loss on the enemy. They were driven not only through the woods, but over the field in front of the woods, and over two high fences beyond and into another body of woods over half a mile distant from the commencement of the fight." In a word, the Union force was compelled to fall back to the same woods in which the battle had begun in the morning; but the Confederates were unable to push their advantage any further, and finding themselves exposed to a biting fire on the open plain, they also withdrew to their vantage ground in the woodland west of the Dunker Church.

Such was the course of the eventful action between the Confederate left and Union right — an action into which half of each army had been drawn in successive installments, and which, marked by a series of fierce encounters, ended at eleven o'clock by leaving the combatants in the secure positions they had occupied in the morning. Both sides were greatly exhausted, and showed little disposition to resume the offensive, at least over ground that had proved so fatal to each. The Confederates, however, descrying the great interval remaining between Sumner's right division, under Sedgwick, and his centre division, under French, sought to work their way through the woods, and penetrated this interval, which was protected only by one or two batteries, that had been left without infantry support. At this critical moment Franklin, with the divisions of Smith and Slocum, reached the ground, and under the direction of Colonel Taylor of the staff of General Sumner, formed his troops so as to cover the threatened point: then, throwing forward the brigade of Colonel Irvin in a vigorous sally, he forced the Confederates back to their own place. General Sumner, however, did not esteem it prudent to hazard full attack with the divisions of Franklin, judging that the repulse of these, the only available reserves, would imperil the safety of the whole army.

While yet the combat raged between Sumner's right and the forces of McLaws, the former instructed his left divisions, under French and Richardson, to attack as a diversion in favor of Sedgwick. This purpose was vigorously executed by both commanders — the former driving Hill from his first position to the cover of a sunken road, where he was assailed by the divisions of Richardson, and thrown back to the Hagerstown road. Unfortunately, however, the success was not pushed to a conclusion — Richardson contenting himself with taking up a position to hold what he had won. On the left of Richardson, Pleasonton's division of cavalry and horse artillery held the centre of the Union line, and repulsed several assaults. During the whole afternoon, however, comparative quiet reigned both at the right and in the centre.

If, now, we recur to the original plan of battle, it may be asked with some surprise, "Where, meanwhile, was Burnside?" It has been seen that McClellan designed to attack with his left in support of his right; and at eight A. M. he ordered Burnside to carry the lower stone bridge, near which his corps was massed, and then gain possession of the Sharpsburg heights. A glance at the map will serve to reveal the supreme importance of the duty entrusted to Burnside; for a successful assault of the Sharpsburg crest must not only have relieved the excessive pressure brought to bear against Hooker and Sumner on the right, but must have menaced Lee's line of retreat to the Shepherdstown ford of the Potomac. The progress of Burnside's movement was accordingly awaited with much anxiety; but after some time had elapsed the commander, not hearing from him, dispatched an aid to ascertain what had been done. The aid returned with the information that but little progress had been made. McClellan then sent him back with an order to General Burnside to assault the bridge at once, and carry it at all hazards. The aid returned a second time with the report that the bridge was still in possession of the enemy; whereupon McClellan commanded Burnside to carry the bridge at the point of the bayonet. But by hesitation and uncertain efforts that officer

allowed himself to be held in check during the entire forenoon by a few hundred riflemen : so that Lee was free to
concentrate nearly his whole force at the decisive point on
the left ; and in fact the main action was decided on the right
before Burnside succeeded in forcing a passage.   This was
effected at one P. M. — five hours after the bridge should have
been carried by a *coup de main*.   A halt was then made by
General Burnside until 3 P. M. ; upon hearing which,
McClellan dispatched a message, desiring him — I use the
General's own words — to " push forward his troops with the
utmost vigor, and carry the enemy's position on the heights ;
that the movement was vital to our success ; that this was a
time when we must not stop for loss of life if a great object
could thereby be accomplished ; that if, in his judgment, his
attack would fail, to inform me so at once, that his troops
might be withdrawn and used elsewhere on the field." Urged
by such imperative messages, Burnside pressed forward to the
attack of the heights, and meeting but little opposition to his
advance, he succeeded in gaining them and crowning the crest.

Two hours earlier this success would have been decisive of the whole field.   But one of the results of the fatal
delay was, that it gave A. P. Hill, who had that day been
marching from Harper's Ferry, time to reach the field.
Approaching Sharpsburg from Shepherdstown, he arrived
just as the heights had been carried, and forming his division so as to apply it on the left flank of Burnside's line, he,
in a few minutes, swept the Union force back to the protection of the bluffs at the bridge of the Antietam.   But the
Confederates did not pursue. As all the reserve corps of
Porter had been brought into action on the west side of the
Antietam, with the exception of a force of less than four
thousand men held to protect the centre, McClellan, fearful
of an attack against that important part of his line, was
unable to comply with General Burnside's request for
reinforcements, and contented himself with charging that

officer to hold the bridge at least. The Confederates, however, were in no condition to take the offensive, and night soon ended this bloody but thus far indecisive battle.

The morning of the 18th, found both commanders standing at bay — each thinking more of making his own position secure than of assailing his adversary. During the day, however, McClellan received an accession to his strength of two divisions under Couch and Humphreys, and he then determined to resume the attack on the following day. General Lee also received a reinforcement of one division, the last of those that had been operating against Harper's Ferry. But as, on the previous day, he had not been able to bring into action more than 40,000 men, and as the fresh force was far from making up for his losses, he resolved to retreat — a purpose that he carried into execution the night of the 18th, passing the Potomac into Virginia by the Shepherdstown ford. An attempt at pursuit, which was made on the 19th, failed — part of Porter's corps that crossed the Potomac suffering a considerable loss. After this, both armies remained for several weeks quiescent — the Confederates in the Shenandoah Valley near Winchester, and the Union army in South western Maryland in the vicinity of Sharpsburg.

III.

RESULTS OF ANTIETAM.

In entering upon the historical interpretation of the battle of Antietam we are constrained, more perhaps than in the case of any other action in the war, to look away from the mere phenomena of the field itself to those larger considerations in which its true significance is to be sought.

Had a battle marked by the characteristics and attended with a result similar to those of Antietam been fought between the armies of North and South on the Rappahannock or the

Peninsula, it would certainly have differed in no respect from the many indecisive actions in Virginia. Indeed in respect of that important test of success — the comparative material loss and gain — the advantage was with the Confederates ; for McClellan's losses exceeded 12,000, while those of Lee were not above 9000. But we are all conscious that the memorable combat in that corner of South-western Maryland would be ill judged by any such comparison ; and assuredly to those who remember how oppressive a load of doubt and fear was lifted from the public mind by the intelligence that Lee had been forced across the Potomac, it needs no argument to prove that a logic, larger and more liberal is needed for the right measure of the value of the victory of Antietam.

This measure is to be sought in the extraordinary train of events already narrated as the antecedents of the Maryland campaign. We must recall the overwhelming disasters that befel Pope, the blows under which he reeled back from the Rapidan to the Potomac. We must conceive the utter demoralization into which the Union army had fallen in consequence of these untoward experiences of bad generalship, and reflect that only this panic-stricken mob stood between Washington and Lee's victorious legions. We must form to ourselves an image of the terror and dismay that overcame the Government, and the inexpressible humiliation brought home to the heart of the people of the North. We must take into account what fearful augment these sentiments received when it was known that Lee had actually passed the barrier of the Potomac and stood on the soil of the loyal States. We must estimate, not in the light of subsequent events but in the light of existing probabilities, how strong was the likelihood of a secessionist uprising in Maryland, should Lee be able to maintain himself north of the Potomac. We must remember the boldness and vigor of the Confederate movements in Maryland, and the prestige acquired by the capture of Harper's Ferry, with its twelve thousand men. Finally, we must add to all the images of dread and fear (vague indeed, and indefinable, but from that very circumstance, all the more powerful) raised in the public mind by the very thought of *invasion*. With these considerations as the data of a judgment, let the reader say of what and of how much was that sanguinary field decisive which saw the insurgent army, after being shattered in the conflict, compelled to abandon the invasion of the North, and with its arrogant assumptions of superior valor brought low, seek refuge behind the barrier of the Potomac.

Nor would it be beyond the warranty of sound reason if we should enlarge the scope of our induction by the reflection of what would have been the result upon the issue of the war, had McClellan suffered defeat at Antietam. It is very certain that had that fate befallen the Union army, there was nothing between Lee and Washington and Baltimore. And even had the national capital not fallen a prey to the Confederate advance, who shall say how different a reception Lee's ragged, hatless, and shoeless soldiers might have met in Eastern Maryland from that they experienced in the loyal section within which their manoeuvres were circumscribed. It is not worth while now to discuss how far the mistakes of the national government gave a tinge of plausibility and a flavor of force to the Confederate commander's lofty recitation of the wrongs inflicted upon "down-trodden" Maryland. But imagine the language of Lee's proclamation, held not in the little city of Frederick, before the ordeal of battle, but in the great city of Baltimore, after a defeat of the Union army, and who would venture to forecast what under the circumstances might have been the ultimate upshot of the audacious foray? If the country was spared the experience of whatever of reality might have lain behind the curtain of contingency, it was because Antietam intervened to thrust aside that horror. And under whatever category the pedantry of military classification may range that action, it is very

certain that to the present generation of men it can never
appear otherwise than as a signal deliverance and a crowning
victory.

Nor can we overlook the association which is known to
have subsisted between this great battle and that decisive
political stroke, the promulgation of the policy of Emancipation by the Executive of the United States. Of this association an interesting memorial in Mr. Lincoln's own words
has lately been made public. "It had got to be," said he,
"mid-summer, 1862. Things had gone on from bad to worse,
until I felt that we had reached the end of our rope on the
plan of operations we were pursuing; that we had about
played our last card, and must change our tactics, or lose the
game. I now determined upon the emancipation policy;
and without consulting with or the knowledge of the Cabinet,
I prepared the original draft of the proclamation, and, after
much anxious thought, called a Cabinet meeting on the subject. This was the last of July or the first part of the month
of August, 1862. This Cabinet meeting took place I think
upon a Saturday. . . Nothing was offered that I had not
already fully anticipated and settled in my mind, until Secretary Seward spoke. He said, in substance : 'Mr. President,
I approve of the proclamation, but I question the expediency
of its issue at this juncture. The depression of the public
mind consequent upon our repeated reverses, is so great that
I fear the effect of so important a step. It may be viewed
as the last measure of an exhausted government, a cry for
help; the government stretching forth its hands to Ethiopia,
instead of Ethiopia stretching forth her hands to the government.' His idea," said the President, "was that it would be
considered our last shriek on the retreat. 'Now,' continued
Mr. Seward, 'while I approve the measure, I suggest, sir,
that you postpone its issue, until you can give it to the country supported by military success, instead of issuing it, as
would be the case now, upon the greatest disasters of the

war.'" Mr. Lincoln continued : "The wisdom of the view of the Secretary of State struck me with great force. The result was that I put the draft of the proclamation aside, waiting for a victory. Well, the next news we had was of Pope's disaster at Bull Run. Things looked darker than ever. Finally came the week of the battle of Antietam. I determined to wait no longer. The news came, I think, on Wednesday, that the advantage was on our side. I was then staying at the Soldiers' Home. Here I finished writing the second draft of the proclamation; came up on Saturday; called the Cabinet together to hear it, and it was published the following Monday. I MADE A SOLEMN VOW BEFORE GOD, THAT IF GENERAL LEE WAS DRIVEN BACK FROM MARYLAND, I WOULD CROWN THE RESULT BY THE DECLARATION OF FREEDOM TO THE SLAVES." [Carpenter's Six Months in the White House.]

If the Army of the Potomac, instead of retaining the ascendancy it acquired over its enemy in this great action, was afterwards doomed to many defeats; if the victory was very far from being made to fulfil the conditions it should have fulfilled; if Antietam was a name "writ in water," it was on account of causes that are only too well known. Too well known for this result ever to be ascribed to the fault of the noble Army of the Potomac; too well known for it not to be laid to the door of that evil policy which, by committing the army to incompetent hands, left it to pour out its blood in unavailing efforts in two disastrous campaigns on the Rappahannock.

12

V.

MURFREESBORO'.

I.

PRELUDE TO MURFREESBORO'.

In the cedar-brakes that border the sluggish stream of Stone River, in Northern Tennessee, was fought on the last day of 1862 an action that must always be memorable in the history of the war. When first its story was flashed over the land, men only saw that a battle, fierce and terrible beyond all previous example in the West, had been delivered; and the North rejoiced with exceeding great joy that in the mighty wrestle the enemy had been hurled discomfited from the field. But when the true relations of this contest came to be apprehended, it was perceived to have a weight and meaning beyond that which attaches to any mere passage at arms — it was seen that it bore upon the whole life of the rebellion. And now that, in the light of history, we can contemplate this victory as it stands related to all that went before and all that came after it, we readily discern that it is one of those few pivotal actions upon which, in very truth, turned the whole issue of the war. This fierce, far-reaching fight in the cedar-brakes of Stone River is known as the battle of Murfreesboro'.

To gain a point of view from which we may justly estimate the place of Murfreesboro' in the history of the Western

Eng^d by W. Wellstood.   Photo. by Bogardus

W S Rosecrans

Dick & Fitzgerald, New York.

campaigns, let us regard Chattanooga as the key of the mountain region of the centre zone. Thus regarding it, we shall see that the battle of Murfreesboro' is at once the summation of the whole series of military events that succeeded Shiloh and the condition precedent of the possession of Chattanooga.

When the campaign in the Mississippi Valley that commenced with Fort Donelson and rose to a climax in Shiloh was brought to a close in the occupation of Corinth, the massive concentration of strength which both belligerents had formed on that theatre fell asunder, and each turned his efforts towards a campaign on the Chattanooga line.

To this common aim diverse motives prompted the opposing parties.

The possession of Corinth put into the hands of the Union commander the Memphis and Charleston Railroad as a direct line of advance towards Chattanooga, which is some two hundred miles to the eastward of Corinth; and so soon as he had established himself at the latter place, General Halleck commanding the united armies of Buell and Grant, determined to throw one of these armies into East Tennessee, the possession of which had long been coveted both for military and political reasons. Retaining, therefore, the army of Grant to operate in the Valley of the Mississippi, he detached the Army of Ohio, under Buell, to move by the Memphis and Charleston Railroad against Chattanooga, which, as the citadel of the mountain fastness of Tennessee and the *point d'appui* for operations towards Atlanta, was a strategic point of the first importance. Corinth was occupied by the Union army May 30th, 1862; on the 11th of June Buell's force was put in motion from that place towards Chattanooga.

But while the Union commander thus planned, the Confederate commander also had turned his thoughts towards Chattanooga as a base of operations for an offensive campaign through Tennessee and Kentucky; and at the same time that Buell began to move eastward, Bragg who had superseded Beauregard in command of the army of the Mississippi, commenced to withdraw the mass of his force from Tupelo, where the Confederates had taken position after the evacuation of Corinth, and concentrated it upon Chattanooga, leaving the commands of Price and Van Dorn to confront Grant in the valley of the Mississippi. The Union commander aimed to take advantage of the concentration of the Confederate forces on the Mississippi line by seizing Chattanooga; the Confederate commander aimed to take advantage of the concentration of the Union forces on the same theatre by an advance towards the Ohio. Out of this mutual resolve arose an extraordinary series of movements which it behooves as to sketch in outline, as the background of the canvas on which the mighty combat of Murfreesboro' is drawn.

Buell, as already stated, began his march from Corinth to Chattanooga on the 11th of June, 1862. The movement was initiated by McCook's division, which reached Florence the 15th. It was followed closely by Crittenden's division; while Wood's division was advanced to and beyond Tuscumbia to repair and guard the road, and Nelson's division took its place between Iuka and Tuscumbia. The divisions moved forward in close succession by marches of fourteen miles a day — Nelson's and Wood's as soon as they were relieved from the road by other troops. Wood's division finished crossing the Tennessee at Decatur the 6th of July; the other three divisions, having made the passage at Florence, were positioned in the vicinity of Athens and Decatur by the end of June. If this advance has the appearance of tardiness it is to be explained by the conditions under which it was made.

The line of operations against Chattanooga prescribed to Buell by General Halleck was the direct route through North

Alabama by way of the Memphis and Charleston Railroad, which he was to repair as he advanced, with the view of receiving his supplies thereby.

The distance from Corinth to Chattanooga by this railroad is two hundred miles; and for eighty miles, that is from Corinth to where it crosses to the north bank of the Tennessee at Decatur, this line runs parallel with the enemy's front. The design of using this road as a line of communications for an army advancing upon Chattanooga, was therefore chimerical, unless indeed we suppose the enemy capable of passively permitting it. Nevertheless General Halleck made it a condition of the movement that this road should be employed; so that until the end of June Buell's troops were engaged in opening it and Thomas's division was detained a month longer in guarding it. The inexpediency of attempting to keep open this line then became so manifest that it was abandoned; and Buell began repairing the railroads that run northward from the Tennessee River to Nashville and Louisville.

When Buell had crossed the Tennessee, he added to his army the force under General Mitchell, whom he had left behind to guard Middle Tennessee at the time he moved westward to make a junction with the army of Grant previous to the battle of Shiloh. Mitchell, during this time had taken advantage of the absence of the Confederates in the Mississippi Valley to advance into North Alabama, and had occupied Florence and Decatur. Another Union column under General Morgan had seized possession of Cumberland Gap. These commands numbered about 16,000 men, and, united with the four divisions of 25,000 men that Buell had brought from Corinth, raised his force to above 40,000 men.

The problem of an advance on Chattanooga was now fairly before Buell — a problem beset with difficulties, and requiring many complicated conditions for its solution. Of these the most important was the opening of an assured line of communications, by means of the Nashville and Decatur

and Nashville and Chattanooga Railroads, with his base on the
Ohio, a base distant from his front of operations by three
hundred miles. East of Huntsville to Chattanooga, the roads
for the whole distance (above a hundred miles) traverse the
Alpine region of the Cumberland Mountain, the spurs of
which run down nearly to the Tennessee River, leaving only
here and there a narrow valley or "cove" of arable land.
The whole country is rough and barren, and east of Stevenson
as far as Chattanooga it is almost destitute both of population and supplies. For subsistence, therefore, it was necessary to look solely to the far distant base on the Ohio. But
the work of opening the railroads proved much more formidable than had been anticipated : it required the whole month
of July to put them in running order. In the mean time
Buell had thrown forward two divisions under McCook and
Crittenden to Battle Creek, within twenty-five miles of Chattanooga ; and by the end of July, 1862, all the preparations
for an advance against that place were complete.

But while Buell was thus establishing his communications
for the movement upon Chattanooga, Bragg had been rapidly
transferring his army from Mississippi to East Tennessee.
He arrived in person at Chattanooga on the 28th of July, by
which time he had his whole force well in hand, and held the
mountain line from that point eastward. Covering his right
at Knoxville was a Confederate force of 13,000 men, named the
"Army of East Tennessee," under Kirby Smith. This, with
his own command, gave Bragg an army of about 50,000 men
for the bold offensive movement he was soon to initiate.
Meanwhile, he employed a very effectual means of gaining
time for his own preparations and obstructing those of his
antagonist, by a series of persistent and destructive raids on
Buell's long line of railroad communication. This service was
entrusted to two enterprising partizan leaders, Forrest and
Morgan, who with bodies each of one or two thousand troopers, were let loose into Tennessee and Kentucky. Morgan

had already begun his operations early in July. He threatened Bowling Green and Munfordsville about the 8th; he then defeated three companies of cavalry at Barkeville, destroyed the depot at Lebanon, proceeded north through Lexington as far as Paris, and finally, toward the close of July, recrossed the Cumberland near Mill Spring, and made his way to Knoxville. Morgan had not yet disappeared from Kentucky when Forrest made a foray into Tennessee. The 13th of July he suddenly appeared at Murfreesboro', where he surprised and captured the garrison, consisting of some fourteen hundred men, and did such serious damage to the railroad, that Buell was compelled to send back Nelson's division to Murfreesboro' for its protection. Forrest then threw himself between Murfreesboro' and Nashville, destroying several important bridges, and effected a safe retreat. He was immediately succeeded by Morgan, who once more appeared on the scene in August, and gave the finishing touches to the work of destruction.

Everything was now in readiness for an offensive movement on the part of the Confederates, and this was begun about the middle of August by the column under Kirby Smith. From Knoxville this force moved northward, debouching from the Cumberland Mountains by passes to the west of Cumberland Gap. By this movement Smith laid hold of the connections of the Union columns at the latter place, and compelled it, after it had remained until its supplies were exhausted, to retreat on an eccentric line towards the Ohio. He then advanced into Central Kentucky, defeated and routed the Union force of General Nelson, at Richmond, on the last day of August, and pushed towards the Ohio in the direction of Cincinnati, which he threatened, thus drawing all the Union levies to that point for its protection, and clearing the way for the advance of the main army. This Bragg initiated the 21st of August. Crossing the Tennessee at Chattanooga and Harrison, he debouched from Waldron

Ridge into the Valley of the Sequatchy, turned Buell's left, and menaced his line of communications.

If we examine the direction of the great Cumberland range in its strategic relations to the theatre on which the opposing armies were operating, we shall see at a glance the extraordinary facilities it gave the Confederates for such a movement as Bragg now set on foot. The communications of an army occupying, as did the army of Buell, Southern Tennessee and Northern Alabama, are the Louisville and Decatur and Louisville and Chattanooga Railroads, which run due north and south. But to these lines the Cumberland Mountains, which trend but slightly to the east of north, are throughout their whole length nearly parallel. It is clear, therefore, that an army holding, as did the army of Bragg, this mountain fastness as a base of operations could act at will against the communications of the Union army. The positions occupied by Buell were in fact mere points in space, of no military importance whatever, and quite at the mercy of the enemy. Indeed, even had Buell had possession of Chattanooga at this time, he could not, under the circumstances, have maintained himself there. Experience has shown that the tenure of that position is only possible with an army large enough to guard the *débouchés* of the Cumberland range, to hold both banks of the Tennessee as far west as Stevenson, where the Chattanooga Railroad crosses that river, and to secure its railroad communications with the Ohio by means of fortified depots well garrisoned, and a movable column to check the operations of raiders. Now, for this service the resources of Buell were entirely inadequate. Less in all than 40,000 men, it required more than half this force to hold his depots, while necessity obliged him to cover the whole front, several hundred miles in extent, from Decatur to Cumberland Gap. His communications were in depth from two to three hundred miles, and entirely exposed to disturbance by even insignificant bodies of hostile cavalry — an arm in which he was almost wholly deficient. But it must be remembered that Buell did

not hold Chattanooga — that point, already in possession of
a hostile force superior in numbers to his own, was made the
objective of an offensive operation under circumstances in which
it has been seen that even a defensive attitude was difficult of
maintenance. In fact, the whole scheme of campaign against
Chattanooga, projected without the means of insuring the
conditions essential for its tenure, was chimerical, and manifested on the part of General Halleck, who planned it, a gross
lack of appreciation of the theatre of war. Of the truth of
the principles here laid down, Bragg gave a palpable demonstration the moment he crossed the Tennessee.

We have seen how, up to the time the Confederate commander seized the initiative, Buell, still looking to the capture of Chattanooga, was engaged in busily pushing forward
his preparations to that end by insuring his communications,
accumulating supplies, and getting in readiness the means
of crossing the Tennessee. But on the first motion of his
antagonist he was thrown on the defensive, and the moment
he learnt Bragg had debouched through the mountains, Buell,
seeing his left turned and his communications menaced, was
compelled to retreat. Accordingly, on the 30th of August,
he issued orders to the various commands and guards distributed over about one hundred and fifty by one hundred miles
of territory and some three hundred miles of railroad, to
concentrate at Murfreesboro' on the 5th of September. The
Confederate force, however, by moving to the eastward of
that place, by way of McMinnville and Sparta, compelled
the Union army to retreat on the 10th of September to
Nashville. Bragg, masking his purpose by threatening Nashville with a small column, passed the Cumberland with his
main body at Carthage and Gainesboro', from sixty to eighty
miles east of that place, and marched straight upon the Nashville and Louisville road. This compelled Buell to evacuate Nashville for the purpose of covering Louisville, though
he left at the former place a garrison under General Negley,

who successfully resisted the force, under Breckinridge, sent against it.

In the relative situations of the opposing armies, the Union force retreating upon Louisville had to describe an arc, whereas the Confederate force marching to lay hold of the former's line of communications, moved upon the chord. The point at which Bragg resolved to strike this line was at Munfordsville, Kentucky, where the Nashville and Louisville Railroad crosses Green River. The distance to this place by the route on which the Confederates advanced is sixty-eight miles; from Nashville it is one hundred and five miles. Bragg's division on the 14th September reached Munfordsville, the surrender of which was demanded but refused by Col. Wilder, commanding the Union garrison. The enemy then attacked the place, but met a severe repulse. The main body, however, arrived before the place on the 16th, and Colonel Wilder then surrendered with four thousand men.

When the Confederates had reached Munfordsville, the Union army had only been able to attain Bowling Green on the Louisville and Nashville Railroad, fifty miles *south* of that place. Bragg, therefore, was now between Buell and the Ohio, and planted directly upon his line of retreat. The goal was immediately in view. Louisville lay open.

Howbeit, in the hour of his triumph he grew timid, and turned away from the prize.

That Louisville was the objective of Bragg's movement is sufficiently indicated by the direction of his march, and by the great intrinsic importance, morally as well as military, of the capture of that city. At Munfordsville he was, on the 16th, within sixty miles, or three marches, of that place, while his opponent was three marches behind. Yet he delayed till the 20th at Munfordsville, and then, in place of advancing upon Louisville, he diverged eastward to Bardstown. Next day his rear guard was driven out of Munfordsville by the van of Buell's army, which, the way to Louisville being now open, marched immediately on that place — the head of the column reaching it on the 25th and the last division on the 29th of September. Bragg reached Bardstown the 26th, and thence moved to Frankfort, where he joined Smith's column. This marks the termination of the campaign, so far as regard the enemy's offensive movement. It will be in place now to briefly consider it as a whole.

The choice of the line of manœuvre was skilful on the part of the Confederates. Without striking a blow, but by simply launching forward against the communications of the Union army, Bragg compelled it to abandon North Alabama, the whole of Tennessee, and the whole of Kentucky. It is evident also that he so combined the marches of his columns that they could not be attacked in detail by his antagonist. Finally, by grasping Buell's line of retreat at Munfordsville, he was in position to force the Union commander to fight a battle facing northward. But, just at this point, Bragg, abandoning his advantage, drifted eastward. We are left to surmise his motive, but there are, probably, facts enough known to lead conjecture up to the door of truth.

Bragg knew that there had been assembled at Louisville a considerable force of newly-raised troops. These numbered about 20,000 men, but they were perfectly raw, undisciplined, and, in a measure, unarmed. General Buell testifies that they could not have withstood the veteran army of the enemy for two hours. It is probable, however, that the Confederate commander greatly exaggerated both their strength and efficiency, and this will supply one reason for his conduct. Another was that his own rations were nearly exhausted, and to quickly replenish his store he judged it best to move into Central Kentucky, where Kirby Smith, who preceded him in the invasive movement, had collected at Bardstown, and other points large depots of supply. Moreover, in marching on these, he marched straight towards reinforcements. It may also be considered that he was apprehensive of the peril in which he would place his own rear, if in marching against Louisville he should fail to take the town by *coup de main;* and from what he learnt of the force that had been gathered there he probably feared it could not be taken by a *coup de main.* Such, in all likelihood, are the considerations that controlled the conduct of the Confederate commander. They were certainly not without weight. Nevertheless, that he was in position to crown his campaign by a decisive blow, and, at the same time was unable to take advantage of his opportunity, proves that there was somewhere a fatal error either in the conception or the execution of his movement. This error it will not be difficult to discover.

Two ideas prompted the Confederates in this campaign of invasion — the one, the reconquest by arms of the territory of Tennessee and Kentucky ; the other, the political reconstruction of those States in the Confederate system. If it be conceded that the latter design was in its very nature conditioned upon the achievement of the former purpose, we shall touch at once the root of the mistake that baulked this ambitious scheme. Bragg confounding cause and effect, seems to have acted on the supposition that the end could be accomplished without the means. Hence, in place of first crushing the Union army, he contented himself with manœuvring it back upon its base on the Ohio, and then fell off into Central Kentucky, where he and Kirby Smith began to issue absurd proclamations, and amused themselves with the comedy of setting up a Confederate governor in the capital of the State. As, at the same time, Lee, under the same circumstances, was doing the same thing in Maryland, it is probable that both acted in accordance with a predetermined policy — a policy, however, that indicates very little practical wisdom on the part of its framers. To believe that the inhabitants of border states, like Maryland and Kentucky, pressed upon by the massive power of the North, would link their fortunes with the revolt before the formidable Union armies on their soil had been beaten, and before the so-styled "liberating" armies had given any proof of their ability to maintain themselves, was to suppose human nature very different from what it is in actual experience ; and the utter failure of both invasions demonstrated the futility of the scheme upon which they were based.

It would involve considerations too purely military to attempt to say where Bragg could or should have struck the Union army : enough to establish the principle that until that army was beaten there was no surety for the possession of any of the territory gained. It may indeed be said that Bragg's force was not sufficient to risk a decisive battle ; but it is certain that it equalled, if it did not exceed, that of his opponent. Moreover, if Bragg's army was inadequate to a real offensive, the Confederates showed a misuse of their forces in the centre zone : for they undertook to act offensively at the same time upon two lines in the same theatre of operations. While Bragg was moving into Kentucky the armies of Price and Van Dorn took the initiative against Grant in Mississippi. This was contrary to correct principle : the main body of the Mississippi army should have been united to the Chattanooga force while Grant was merely confronted by a small corps. The result was that the Confederates were on both lines too weak. Price and Van Dorn were beaten both at Corinth and Iuka ; and they did not even prevent Grant from forwarding to Buell, a reinforcement of two divisions, of which one reached him the 1st, and the other the 12th of September.

Buell's conduct of the retrograde movement from the Tennessee to the Ohio was marked by great skill. It does not appear that any opportunity was afforded of attacking the enemy in detail. Consequently in withdrawing to Louisville where he united with the army there, and was in position to assume a vigorous offensive, he did what was best under the circumstances. It is true, he was bitterly reproached for "allowing" the enemy to invade Kentucky; but it is not by the excited clamor of a panic-stricken population that great military movements are to be adjudged in history.

And now there devolved upon General Buell the weighty duty of marching forth to overthrow Bragg and drive the Confederates from Kentucky, where they had established themselves seemingly with the intent of remaining *en permanence*. This he hastened to do; but first of all it was necessary to effect a reorganization of the army, which after its arduous campaign and long marches was much worn, though the matchless discipline established by Buell, a master in that science, had wonderfully preserved the integrity of the army. The last division reached Louisville the 29th of September. On the same day the incorporation of the new troops under General Nelson was completed, and on the morning of the 30th the consolidated army was prepared to march against the Confederate forces which occupied the principal part of Kentucky. The columns would have been put in motion that day, but in the mean time an order arrived from Washington relieving General Buell from the command of the army, and appointing General G. H. Thomas in his stead. Thomas, however, refused to supersede Buell, for whose military talent he cherished the highest respect, and the command was therefore restored to the latter officer. The army marched on the 1st of September in five columns. The left moved towards Frankfort to hold in check the force of the enemy, which still remained at or near that place. The other columns, marching by different routes, fell respectively into the roads leading from Shepherdsville, Mt. Washington, Fairfield, and Bloomfield to Bardstown, where the main force of the Confederates under General Bragg was known to be. On reaching that point, however, it was found that the rear of the enemy's infantry had retired eight hours before, and all the information indicated that Bragg would concentrate either at Harrods-

burg or Perryville. The centre under Gilbert, and the left
under McCook, were therefore directed on the latter place, and
the right under Crittenden, was sent by the Lebanon road, which
passes four miles to the south of Perryville. The afternoon of
the 7th the centre corps had arrived within three miles of Perryville, and was drawn up in order of battle. As the enemy
was apparently in the act of concentration for battle at that
point, orders were sent to Crittenden and McCook respectively to move forward early in the morning into position on
the right and left of the centre. Buell had expected an
attack early in the morning on the centre corps while it was
isolated, but as it did not take place, no formidable attack
was apprehended after the arrival of the left corps, which
took place about 10 A. M. Considerable cannonading had
been going on during the morning between the centre corps,
and the firing extended thence to the left, and became brisker
as the day advanced, but it was not supposed to proceed from
any serious engagement. At four o'clock, however, an aid
from McCook arrived and reported to Buell, who was with
the centre, that the general was sustaining a severe attack,
which had been going on for several hours, and which he would
not be able to withstand unless reinforced! This action, thus
precipitated, is known as the battle of Perryville, or Champion
Hills. It was fought on the part of the Confederates by two
divisions against the left corps under McCook, and as the
enemy caught that corps isolated and in the act of formation,
he was able to inflict heavy damage upon it, the casualties
numbering about four thousand. Though the corps was much
shaken in the first event, it afterwards recovered itself, and
maintained its ground so stubbornly that at nightfall the
Confederates were compelled to draw off without any material
advantage.

No doubt was entertained that Bragg would endeavor to
hold his position at Perryville, and accordingly Buell issued
orders to the commanders to join battle next morning. Day-

light, however, revealed the fact that he had retired towards
Camp Dick Robinson.   Buell then advanced in pursuit; but
Bragg, constantly refusing battle, retired southward in the
direction of Cumberland Gap.   The pursuit was pushed as
far as Loudon, where Buell called a halt, not being minded
at that season of the year to attempt a campaign in the rough,
barren, and difficult mountain region of East Tennessee.
When, therefore, it was clear that the enemy had abandoned
the invasion, Buell turned his columns south-westward into
Middle Tennessee, with the purpose of removing the line of
the Louisville and Nashville Railroad.   By the end of October the army reached Bowling Green and Glasgow, whence
Buell designed pushing forward immediately to Murfreesboro.'
But, on the 30th of October, he was superseded by Rosecrans.

The circumstances under which General Rosecrans assumed
command of the Army of the Ohio committed him to an immediate offensive, as well for moral as for material reasons.
The events of the extraordinary summer campaign, whereof I
have presented the outline in the preceding chapter, were
thought to have been highly favorable to the Confederates,
who had been able to throw back the Union army from the
Tennessee to the Ohio, and had, after ravaging Kentucky,
succeeded in making good their escape to whence they
came.   Now, though these events were in no wise out of the
ordinary tenor of war, and may now be studied with a perfectly philosophic composure, they must be estimated, not in
the " dry light " of history, but in the effect they, at the time,
produced on an excitable, patriotic, and unreasoning public.
The invasion itself created profound alarm — a sentiment
which, by one of those rapid transitions that come over masses
of men in time of war, changed into deep disgust and humiliation when it was seen that the enemy " escaped " with impunity.   This feeling found official expression in the removal
of General Buell from the command of the army.   Judging

this act in the catholic spirit that should be brought to the interpretation of the war, we may not be disposed to censure the Administration for a measure that undoubtedly was prompted by a well-meaning motive; but it is at the same time incumbent on us to render equal justice to one who has been the object of most unmerited obloquy.

Buell, like McClellan, was unfortunate in attaining a great command at a time when the country's experience of war made it certain that many victims must fall. But he was an eminent soldier, of a grave, high order of mind, distinguished for the breadth of his military views, the soundness of his combinations, and the vigor, but not brilliancy of his execution. His theory was to fight only for important objects, to manœuvre so as to gain strategic advantages, and to make success as certain as possible. He would do nothing for popular effect, and had not that pliability and those arts that are so useful for a commander in the early stages of a popular war, and that often enable mediocre men who possess this talent to attain success. He was a good disciplinarian, and the army was never at any subsequent period in such condition of efficiency as it was under his command. Also, it must be remarked, that he never lost the confidence of his army, which always cherished unbounded respect for his ability.

It will thus have sufficiently appeared that the very circumstances under which the command fell to General Rosecrans implied that he should speedily assume the offensive, and the enemy very soon took such a course as made the Government tenfold more urgent that he should do so. When Rosecrans assumed command the army was in the vicinity of Bowling Green and Glasgow; and the garrison which General Buell had left at Nashville, under Negley, was closely beleaguered by Forrest's cavalry, and Breckenridge's division of infantry. Rosecrans, therefore, determined first of all to relieve Nashville, which he did by sending forward McCook's corps to that place. But, before he could throw for-

ward the remaining corps, it was absolutely essential to repair the Louisville and Nashville Railroad, which was badly
broken.   This work consumed the greater part of November,
by the end of which month the railroad was put in repair,
and the whole army concentrated at Nashville.

Now, while Rosecrans was engaged in this necessary preliminary duty, Bragg, who, on his retirement from Kentucky,
had passed by Cumberland Gap to Knoxville, and thence to
Chattanooga, put his army again in motion northward.
Passing up the railroad to within forty miles of Nashville, he
assumed an intrenched position at Murfreesboro', whence
he began to demonstrate in many motions of offence.   It was
plain, therefore, that the campaign which had been left indecisive was about to be forced to an issue in a battle that
must decide the fate of Kentucky and central Tennessee.
Both sides energetically pushed forward preparations for
aggressive action; but Rosecrans was beforehand with his
antagonist, and having, by the last week in December,
succeeded in accumulating sufficient supplies for a campaign,
he began the manœuvres that resulted in the battle of Murfreesboro'.   The events of this great action now remain to be
told.

II.

THE BATTLE OF MURFREESBORO'.

CHRISTMAS-DAY of the year 1862 passed amid festivities
that smoothed the wrinkled face of war and lent a wholly
peaceful air to the rival camps at Nashville and Murfreesboro'.
But before daybreak next morning Rosecrans, having completed all his preparations, put his army in motion amid a
drenching rain.   It advanced in three columns, and skirmishing began almost from the start, for Bragg's superiority
in cavalry enabled him to confine his adversary almost within
his infantry lines.   By the night of the 30th Rosecrans had

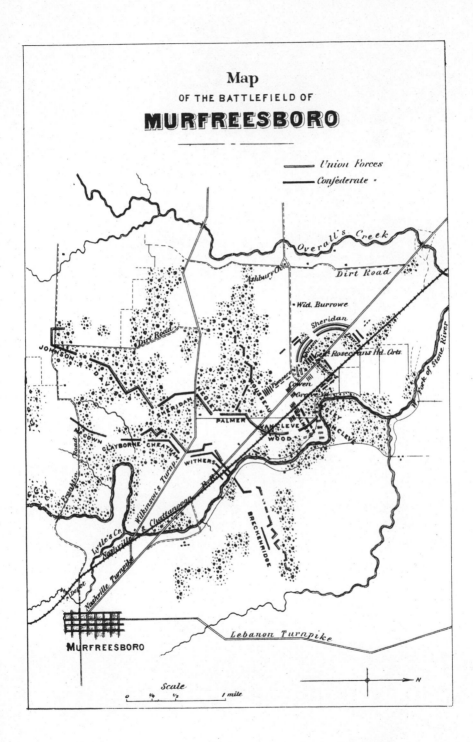

Map
OF THE BATTLEFIELD OF
MURFREESBORO

Union Forces
Confederate

Overall's Creek

Ashbury Ch.

Dirt Road

Wid. Burrowe

Sheridan

Dirt Road

Rosecrans Hd. Qrts.

JOHNSON

DAVIS

SHERIDAN

Cowen
Grove

NEGLEY

ROUSSEAU

PALMER

CLAYBORNE

CHEATHAM

VAN CLEVE

WOOD

CLEVE

PAGUIN Road

WITHERS

Wilkinson's Turnp.

Nashville & Chattanooga

BRECKENRIDGE

Lytle's Cr.

Nashville Turnpike

Depot

West Fork of Stone River

MURFREESBORO

Lebanon Turnpike

Scale

0   ¼   ½   1 mile

N

fought his way into position, facing the army of Bragg, which was posted in front of Murfreesboro'. The manner in which the opposing lines were drawn will be readily apprehended from a study of the accompanying map.

Stone River, rising in the high country south of Murfreesboro', runs nearly north, passes that town a mile to the west, and empties into the Cumberland a few miles above Nashville. Bragg placed his force on the west side of that stream, with his line running nearly west and south, but he prolonged his right flank across the river to the east bank, where one division (that of Breckinridge) held the approaches to Murfreesboro' from that side. All the rest of the Confederate force, embracing four divisions, was placed on the west side of Stone River.

The Union army was disposed entirely on the west side of Stone River — the left wing consisting of three divisions under General Crittenden, the centre of two divisions under General Thomas, and the right of three divisions under General McCook. The left wing rested on the river, and the line then stretched nearly south for a distance of four miles, the right flank being thrown across the turnpike that runs westward from Murfreesboro' to Franklin, and is known as the Franklin Pike. The Nashville turnpike and the Nashville Railroad, which formed Rosecrans's communications, approach in this vicinity very close to Stone River, which, indeed, they cross a short mile above Murfreesboro', into which they conduct. In the narrow interval between the Nashville road and the river were placed the divisions of Wood and Van Cleve of the left wing — the latter in reserve in rear of the former. Palmer's division of the left wing was deployed on the right of the Nashville road; and the line was continued southward by the two divisions of the centre under Thomas, of which two divisions that of Negley held the front line, and that of Rousseau was in reserve in rear of the left centre. The three divisions of the right wing, respectively under Sheridan, Davis, and Johnson, were deployed and continued the line southward across the Franklin turnpike, where the right flank was refused in a crotchet. The cavalry, two brigades, was equally divided upon the flanks.

If this disposition of the Union forces be noted, it will appear that there was a heavy concentration of troops on the left; for a line cutting the Union front in two equal parts would place the right wing, under McCook, alone on the one side, while the centre and left, under Thomas and Crittenden, would appear on the other. This disposition was made for attack, and Rosecrans's plan was as follows:—Two divisions of the left wing—those of Wood and Van Cleve—were at dawn to cross Stone River and overthrow Bragg's right, consisting of the division of Breckenridge, which was discovered to be alone on that side of the stream. On the east side of the river are commanding heights which, when taken possession of and crowned with artillery, would enable the left to see in reverse the enemy's works fronting the centre of the Union line. It was expected that the artillery fire would so shake the Confederates that the Union centre under Thomas and the remaining division of the left wing under Palmer, would be able to carry their front, while the left wing, continuing its movement, would swing into Murfreesboro', and then moving westward by the Franklin road attain the flank and rear of the Confederates and drive them westward off their line of retreat. To the right wing, meanwhile, was assigned the duty of holding the hostile left in check.

The plan was bold, brilliant, and in many respects calculated to inspire sanguine hopes. For the assurance of success in the essential feature, the offensive movement by the left wing, ample provision was made in the great preponderance of force there brought to bear on the enemy; but the entire operation was conditioned on the ability of the Union right meanwhile to buffet hostile assault. With such a procedure no fault can be found, for if a commander cannot rely on holding the enemy with one arm, while he strikes with the other, bold combinations of battle and decisive results are out of the question. Nevertheless, in proportion as ulterior results depend on the conduct of a force to which is assigned a special duty must be the adequacy of the provision looking to that end. Now if we examine critically the disposition of the Union right, it is easy to see that there was some ground for apprehension touching its ability to perform the task given it to do. That wing, consisting of the corps of McCook, was disposed from right to left in the order of the divisions of Johnson, Davis, Sheridan, and first of all it is to be remarked that as each division presented two brigades deployed in front and one in reserve, the line was unduly long, and therefore somewhat thin and weak. Secondly, it was rather too much advanced, that is, faced too much eastward; whereas it would have been more secure in being more refused and facing more southward. Thirdly, it exposed an almost naked flank, the right division having but one brigade thrown back in a crotchet.

That Rosecrans could fail to appreciate the danger to his right is not likely, for as he knew that his antagonist held all his divisions save one on the west bank of Stone River, the contingency of Bragg's acting offensively against the Union right was not to be overlooked. In point of fact, Rosecrans appreciated the danger, and was solicitous regarding his right. When informed by General McCook, at the time the troops were placed in position, that his corps was facing strongly to the east, he told that officer that such a direction to his line did not appear to him a proper one, and that it ought with the exception of his left to face much more nearly south, with the right division en- tirely in reserve. " Still," the commander added, "this must be confided to you, who know the ground better." However, when the corps commanders had assembled that night, Rose-

crans having set forth his plan of battle as above given, recurred once more to the question of the right wing; and,
addressing General McCook, said; "To-morrow there will
be a battle. You know the ground. You have fought over
it. You know its difficulties. Can you hold your present
position for three hours?" "Yes, I think I can," replied
McCook." The commander then added: "I don't like the
facing so much to the east. If you don't think your present
the best position change it. It is only necessary for you to
make things sure." No change was made however: the
officers separated, and the troops lay on their arms awaiting
the morrow.

While Rosecrans thus planned, Bragg, too, had formed his
resolution; and it is worthy of note that the Confederate
general also had not only determined to act offensively, but
he had determined to act with his left against the Union
right, in the same manner as the Union general had resolved
to act with his left against the Confederate right. On the
west side of the river, the left of the Confederate line was
held by two divisions under Hardee, and the centre, with its
right resting on the stream, by two divisions under Polk; on
the east side the division of Breckinridge held post. Breckinridge's duty was to cover the approaches to Murfreesboro'
against menace of the Union force, while the offensive was
to be taken up by the extreme left, continued by the whole
line in succession to the right — the move to be made by a
constant wheel to the right on Polk's right as a pivot. The
aim of Bragg was to force the Union right and centre back
against its left and Stone River, and lay hold of its line of
communications with Nashville. The plan was not less
daring than that of Rosecrans. Both forces lay on their
arms that night, conscious of the mighty struggle that the
dawn must bring. The Union army numbered forty-seven
thousand; and the Confederate army thirty-five thousand
men of all arms.

Morning of the last day of the year, dawned in unwonted mildness, and with early light each army began the execution of the plans formed by the opposing chiefs. Rosecrans had established his head-quarters in rear of the left which, as already seen, was to cross Stone River and swing into Murfreesboro'. This, the initial movement, being ordered by the commander, was immediately begun. Van Cleve's division took the lead. Two brigades made the passage without interruption. Wood, filing his division down to the river brink, prepared to follow.

The movement commenced auspiciously. It is true that from the right some sounds of fight had been heard, but they indicated nothing of moment and they excited only satisfaction, for if the enemy's attention was fixed on the right, the way would be all the more open for the decisive stroke on the left — McCook, meanwhile, holding his opponents over there for " three hours." The troops accordingly continued to pass the stream with joyful haste, when suddenly from the far-off right there came an outburst of battle that gave pause to the moving column, for it was of such volume and fierceness as betrayed a crisis risen at the very outset of the fight. It was, in fact, the enemy's initiative.

It has been noted that Bragg also had resolved to attack with his left, and while the Union troops were crossing Stone River to swing into Murfreesboro', he too was preparing his stroke. It was found that the left Confederate division under McCown exactly fronted the right Union division under Johnson, but as it was discovered that this flank was somewhat thrown back, McCown moved still further to the left so that he might quite overlap the Union right before moving forward, the space vacated being filled up by the division of Cleburne which had been in reserve. He then advanced and carried the position of the Union right by an impetuous rush, Johnson's division being swept in a few minutes from the field. It is claimed in the reports of the Confederates that

the initial movement was a surprise.   But wrongly, for the
advance was observed for half a mile, being in great part
over open ground.   Yet the affair reflected no credit on the
officers of the Union division, among whom there appears to
have been great want of vigilance.   Indeed, one of the brigade commanders, General Willich, who had gone to the head-
quarters of his divisional general, Johnson, was captured before he could rejoin his command ; and when Johnson moved
forward his remaining brigade, it speedily shared the fate of
the other two.   The division lost eight guns.   Then the Confederates, surging round their left, poured down upon the uncovered flank of the next division, that of Davis, which was at
the same time assailed by Cleburne in front.   Davis made
better resistance, and stubbornly repelled several attacks ; but
his position had become already too thoroughly compromised ;
he also retired after a mournful loss of life and abandoning
several pieces of artillery.   The enemy then pouring in, began to surge against the remaining divisions of the right wing,
and the two divisions of Polk, which had thus far been silent,
also opened in savage volleys against that division and
against the Union centre, and against the right of the left wing.

Such was the dread meaning of the clamor that checked
the movement of the left, and held the filing column in breath-
less suspense — such the result achieved in less than an hour.
It was long, however, before the full extent of the disaster
was known at head-quarters.   The first message from Mc-
Cook said only that he was pressed and needed assistance ;
it did not tell of the rout of Johnston's division, nor yet of the
consequent withdrawal of that of Davis. Rosecrans determined,
therefore, to continue his own offensive movement ; and he
dispatched word to McCook to make stubborn fight.   He
was loth to give up his own well-considered plan ; loth to be
compelled to follow the enemy's initiation.   Nor did there
seem to be any need.   He still held a mighty force in his left
hand ; if McCook would only maintain his ground, or contest

it with such stubborn resistance as to afford "three hours" of time, he would hurl forward that wing, lay hold of his enemy's communications, and take in flank the enemy that was flanking him. So to McCook he returned this message : "Tell him," said he, flaming out vehemently, "to contest every inch of the ground. If he holds them we will swing into Murfreesboro' with our left, and cut them off." Then to his staff — for there was in this commander that highest array, that courage that can coolly bear to risk partial loss for greater gain — "It is working right."

But how far it was from "working right" soon became known. A second message arrived from McCook, announcing that the right wing was being driven — a fact that was only too manifest, for from the thickets that bound the open plain west of the Nashville road, the debris of the broken divisions began to pour forth in alarming volume. Then, bitter as it was to abandon his own movement, Rosecrans saw plainly that necessity so obliged him to do. To throw forward his left was now impossible : that was predicated on McCook's ability to hold the enemy for "three hours." But the issue was now entirely changed : it was not a question of fighting to lose with the right for the purpose of fighting to gain with the left — it was a question of saving the right, now breaking in pieces, of covering his vital lines, menaced by the enemy, of guarding them in such a manner that hostile effort should not prevail against them at least. His resolution was instantly formed. He drew back his left from across the river, ordered all of Wood's division, saving the regiments guarding the ford, to the support of the right wing, and then calling on his staff to mount, hurried to the right to prepare a new line, to hold together the dissolving masses of his forces, to maintain a stout defensive front, since after the disaster to his right he might no longer hope to execute his bold offensive stroke.

Happily an event occurred to second this purpose, and

give the commander the needed time to establish his new lines.

The difference between troops is great : the difference between officers is immensely greater. While the two right divisions of McCook were being assailed and brushed away, an equal hostile pressure fell upon his left division. But here a quite other result attended the enemy's efforts ; for not only were the direct attacks repulsed with great slaughter, but when the flank of the division was uncovered by the withdrawal of the troops on its right, its commander effecting a skilful change of front, threw his men into position at right angles with his former line, and having thus made for himself a new flank, buffeted with such determined vigor and such rapid turns of offence, that for two hours he held the Confederates at bay — hours precious, priceless, wrenched from fate and an exultant foe by the skill and courage of this officer, and bought by the blood of his valiant men. This officer was Brigadier-General P. H. Sheridan : the details of his splendid exploit are of too much moment to be overpassed in the recital of the eventful struggle of Stone River.

When the Confederate divisions of McCown and Cleburne had fully engaged Johnson and Davis, the division next towards the Confederate right, which was the division of Withers, assailed Sheridan, whose front was held by the brigade of Sill and Roberts, with the brigade of Shaeffer in reserve. The hostile approach was over an open cotton-field, and as the Confederates advanced in column closed in mass with a depth of several regiments, they received a heavy fire from three batteries advantageously posted along Sheridan's line. This, though destructive in its effects, did not, however, stay the enemy's onset, and the mass steadily approached to within fifty yards of the edge of timber in which lay Sheridan's troops. Then upstarting, the infantry poured in the faces of the Confederates a fire before which they paused, and then new volleys, before which they wavered, broke, and

ran. Sill, seizing the opportunity, advanced with his brigade, charged home· on the assailants, and drove them in
confusion across the open field and behind their intrenchments. The discomfiture of the enemy was complete; but
it was not purchased without heavy cost. The young and
chivalrous Sill fell while leading this charge. Such was the
first act of Sheridan's fight.

The time consumed in the occurrences here narrated had
sufficed to accomplish the rout of the divisions on Sheridan's
right, which caused that officer's position to be completely
turned, and exposed his line to a fire from the rear. The
conventional procedure would have been for Sheridan to
have then retired, justifying the motive on the ground that
his flank was uncovered. He did much better. Hastily
retiring his right and reserve brigades, he caused the left
brigade, under Colonel Roberts, to charge with the bayonet
into the woods from which he had withdrawn the two former
brigades. This caused the enemy to recoil and gave Sheridan
time to form his right and reserve brigades on a new line, to
which, drawing back the left brigade from its charge, he joined
it also. Sheridan's new front was at right angles with his
former line. That had been faced east, this faced south;
that had been at right angles with the Nashville road, this
was parallel to it, and advanced, perhaps, a mile in front of
it. Parallel to it, and yet how little of this vital line he
could cover, for when the two Confederate divisions that had
swept Johnson and Davis from the field, had wheeled to the
right and faced westward, looking towards the Nashville road,
these divisions overlapped, by nearly their whole length, the
right of Sheridan! But points on a battle-field are not protected merely by the direct presence of troops. Whatever
upon a flank causes the assailant to break there, and obliges
him to overcome that obstacle, covers that flank. It may be
a height, stream, or morass. It may be the breasts of valiant
men. Sheridan's division was such an obstacle. The Con-

federate divisions to his right were free to pass on beyond
him; but in doing so they fatally severed themselves from
that part of their line he held in his front, and exposed themselves to be taken in flank and rear.   It was clear, therefore,
that Sheridan must be driven off before they could safely
advance.   So they doubled in towards their right, and he,
gathering his troops and batteries about him like a sheaf of
spears, prepared to receive the shock of the mighty mass,
and make time for the new dispositions the commander was
pressing forward.   All to his right had gone like sea-weeds
torn by waves from jutting crags; but the swelling surges
dashed in vain against the rock-like resistance of this division.   Such was the second act in Sheridan's fight.

The resistance offered by Sheridan's division in his second
position gained an hour's respite.   At the end of that time
the enemy had accumulated so heavily on his flank that he
was compelled again to make new dispositions.   Once more
he effected a change of front.   Throwing forward his left to
support it on the right of Negley's division of the centre,
under Thomas, he drew back his two right brigades so as to
face westward, covering the rear of Negley's line, and planted
his batteries on the salient of his front.   In this position, in
the thicket of cedars, he was again savagely assailed, and the
most terrible and sanguinary conflict of the day occurred.
The full weight of the four divisions of Hardee and Polk
was hurled against the two divisions of Sheridan and Negley.   Three times they moved forward in impetuous assaults,
and thrice they received such a biting fire that they reeled
and recoiled.   Another hour of infinite price was thus gained.
But then there came an end to the power of resistance of
the Union line — Sheridan's men had spent all their ammunition, and no fresh supply could be obtained, for the discomfiture of the troops of the right wing had allowed the
enemy's cavalry to break through to the rear and capture its
ammunition-train.   Nor was this all: he had lost Sill in the

first onset; he now lost Roberts, soon afterwards Shaeffer —
all his brigade commanders killed. It only remained to use
the steel in order to gain time to retire his line: so the
reserve brigade charged forward, and under cover of this
audacious sally, Sheridan retired the fragments of his division
through the cedar thicket, and out into the open plain west
of the Nashville road. No sooner had this withdrawal taken
place than Negley, whose men had hitherto been covered by
Sheridan, found himself enveloped by the enemy, and he was
compelled to cut his way through their swarming ranks back
to the open space. The right was gone, the centre gone, the
army hung by a single point on the left. Happily, this point
was of a diamond quality, and, as will presently appear, gave
time to bring order out of the wreck of a stranded army.
It was eleven o'clock when Sheridan's division, with compact
ranks and empty cartridge-boxes, debouched from the cedar
thickets to the open plain, stretching along the Murfreesboro'
turnpike. He had lost seventeen hundred and ninety-six
men; and with the cost of their heroic lives had won three
hours, which Rosecrans, to whom he now reported, had been
using to the best advantage. "Here is all that are left," said
he, sadly, as he joined his chief. It is now time to look at
what had been the procedure of that commander.

When at length Rosecrans comprehended the full extent
of the calamity, he hastened to suspend the movement of the
left wing, and then, followed by his staff, galloped to the
scene of conflict. Two things were immediately to be done:
one, to sustain the division of the right wing that solitarily
stood at bay to hold back the enemy; the other, to form a
new front covering his line of communications. It was,
indeed, a moment of terrible trial, for it seemed that the
army was going all to staves. But the moral courage of the
commander was equal to the occasion. "It was now," says
an eye-witness, "a series of commands too often delivered in
person to superior or subordinate, it mattered not, while his

staff galloped at his heels in mute anxiety lest he should fall." He heard of the rout of the right wing : he said, "We shall beat them yet." The report of the death of General Sill was confirmed. "We cannot help it," replied he; "brave men must be killed in battle." Of the capture of General Willich, and the hurt that had befallen General Kirk. "Never mind," he exclaimed, "we must win this battle." On another occasion, when about to dash forward under the enemy's fire, a young aid expostulated with him; " Ah, my boy," said the commander, who is a devout Catholic, " make the sign of the true cross, and let us go in."

Rosecrans's first impulse was to support Sheridan ; but the troops with which to do this? At length he found Thomas the lion-hearted, calm amid the fury of battle. One of his divisions under Negley was stoutly sustaining Sheridan's left ; but he had another one in reserve, that of Rousseau. " Push that into the cedar brake in rear of Sheridan," said the chief, and Thomas, in person, went to see it done. Rousseau, advancing into the cedar brake, disappeared as completely in the thick brush as if a wall had been built around him. He went in by the right flank, and had partially deployed his leading brigade (the brigade of regulars), when he was struck by the enemy, and in ten minutes the division came out again a cloud of broken battalions.

Meanwhile, to establish a new line along the Murfreesboro pike, towards which the enemy was working his way, Rosecrans withdrew two thirds of the left wing under Crittenden. Upon a commanding knoll overlooking the open plain west of the Murfreesboro' road — a plain which the enemy would have to traverse when they should debouch for the cedar thicket — he massed his batteries as Napoleon at Austerlitz. Thus a firm *point d'appui* was gained, and when Rousseau withdrew from the cedars he was formed in the open plain along the railroad as a nucleus on which the new formation of the army was established. Yet notwithstanding the vigor of the resistance presented by Sheridan and Negley, it is doubtful if this could have been effected, such was the necessarily unjointed condition of the army in the process of passing from one formation to another, had it not been for the extraordinary tenacity with which the left clung to its position. In order to grasp clearly the situation, let it be understood that the entire right and centre have gone out and are confusedly striving to get into position on the new line ; and that two divisions of the left wing have also been taken to patch it out. It will result that there remained on the original front only the right division of the left wing — the division of Palmer ; and that the shape of the army was that of a crotchet, the short side being Palmer's division facing southward ; the long side being the rest of the army facing westward — indeed not yet facing any whither, but getting into position to face westwards, if only the short side hold on long enough to afford time, and do not give way, thus exposing the army to fire in front, flank, and rear before its formation is completed. Of the division of Palmer, the left brigade under Colonel W. B. Hazen, now the left of the army, was to the east, and at right angles, with the Nashville pike in a scanty grove of oaks covering an inconsiderable crest between the pike and the railroad, which intersect at an acute angle about four hundred yards in front ; the other two brigades (those of Cruft and Gross) were posted on the west side of the pike in the skirt of a cedar wood. The ground was open in front of the division. During the earlier events of the day, Palmer had already sustained successfully a severe attack ; but now that everything was gone except this force, the enemy began to assail it with a ferocity that showed he fully understood the advantage which success would there give him. The Confederates forming in the position which will be found marked in the accompanying map, as " Cowan's burnt house," poured like an avalanche on the front of Palmer, carrying away the two right brigades, and leaving only Hazen with his brigade of twelve hundred men to foil the enemy's ardent efforts against this vital point. Less skilfully manœuvred this force would have been an insignificant obstacle to the hostile masses that surged against it; but Hazen proved himself, like Sheridan, equal to theemergency. The two right brigades having been partially reformed, were sent to him, and these Hazen formed in the grove to the left of the turnpike known as the "Round Forest," where with his left flank well screened by Stone River, he repulsed a series of repeated and desperate attacks. In the final assault, the Confederates met a fire so destructive, that when within three hundred yards they broke to the rear. One of the enemy's battalions alone adventured a nearer approach, but that with every mounted officer and half its men shot down, threw itself flat upon the ground within one hundred and fifty yards, unable to advance and not daring to retreat. So the vital point was held, though it cost the sacrifice of one third of Hazen's heroic brigade. The service rendered by that gallant officer was of the most extraordinary character, for there were many times during the forenoon when a momentary slackening of his efforts would have lost the field. While thus Hazen rebuffed the enemy, the army drifted into its new position; and scarcely was the fresh formation completed when the Confederates, with that shrill slogan in which the men of the South were wont to utter their passion in battle, debouched from the cedar thicket and faced the Union array, drawn on the side along the Nashville and Murfreesboro' road.

Marvellous as had been the success that had thus far attended Bragg's efforts, it was yet of no effect until it should be crowned by a decisive stroke against the Union force now standing at bay. The Confederate chieftain, full well aware of this, and unwilling to see his advantage melt away in an incomplete achievement, made his dispositions for a renewed assault. However, his army was in very unfit condition for the task before it : the mixed fight and pursuit through several miles of dense forest had greatly disorganized the commands, and no time was afforded to adjust the alignments, since the orders were imperative to press on without halting : so that the supporting and advancing lines had become inextricably mingled. Moreover, Bragg's losses already counted by thousands, and he had no reserves.

When the enemy broke from under cover, Rosecrans's line presented a scene of portentous grandeur. For instantly the massive concentration of artillery opened a prodigious clamor, and the figures of the cannoneers, defined on the rim of the hill, were seen through a pall of fire and smoke to labor and leap in frantic energy, while from the long lines of infantry such volleys of musketry went forth as smote the hostile front, and caused it to bend and break in confusion into the depths of the woods. If charge was designed by the enemy, it was quenched in the first volley, for none was made ; and it needs only to cite this unwilling testimony of General Cleburne, the ablest of Bragg's division commanders, to show how thorough and decisive was the check that befel this last effort against the centre and right : "Following up the success," says Cleburne, "our men gained the edge of the cedars, and were almost on the Nashville turnpike, in rear of the original centre of Rosecrans's army, sweeping with their fire his only line of communication with Nashville ; but at this critical moment the enemy met my thinned ranks with another fresh line of battle, supported by a heavier and closer artillery fire than I had yet encountered. A report also spread, which I believe was true, that we were flanked on the right. This was more than the men could stand. Smith's brigade was driven back in great confusion ; Polk and Johnson's followed. As our broken ranks went back over the fields, before the fire of their fresh line, the enemy opened fire on our right flank, from several batteries which they had concentrated on an eminence near the railroad, inflicting a

14

heavier loss on Polk's brigade than it had suffered in all the previous fighting of the day. The division was rallied on the edge of the opposite woods, about four hundred yards in rear of the scene of the disaster, though some of the men could not be stopped until they reached the Wilkinson pike." Like evidence is given by the officers of all the Confederate corps. Such a change had come over the *morale* of the men who had fought so determinedly in the morning, and such a renewed outburst of spirit was displayed by the Union army when it found itself advantageously placed, and its energies directed in person by its skilful commander!

Foiled in his efforts to further prevail against the new and powerful front of his adversary, Bragg determined upon a renewed effort against the left flank. In order to give assurance of success in this design, he recalled from the east side of Stone River the division of Breckinridge, which, as it had been relieved of all menace by the withdrawal of the whole Union force to the west side, and had not been engaged during all the action, was during the afternoon transferred across the river, and united with the right of Polk's line — a reinforcement of four brigades, seven thousand fresh men. The key and salient point of this flank was still held by stout Hazen, though his own command was now well braced up, both on the left and the right. When at four o'clock the Confederate attack was commenced, it developed in such determined ferocity, that Rosecrans himself, solicitous touching this vital point of his line, hastened hither to sustain it with his own magnetic presence. Colonel Garesché, his chief of staff, was at his side; and, as the two careened across the fiery field, a shell grazing the person of Rosecrans, carried off the head of his lieutenant, the devoted and chivalrous Garesché, model of all that is pure and lovely and of good report.

But not for grief over nearest or dearest was there then time — the fate of a mighty conflict hung trembling in the balance; and the captain, hastening to the front, addressed the soldiers with that kind of plain and savage Saxon, which comes first to the lips of men in battle, " Men," said he, " do you wish to know how to be safe? Shoot low. Give them a blizzard at their shins! But do you wish to know how to be safest of all? Give them a blizzard, and then charge with cold steel! Forward, now, and show what you are made of!" The injunction was obeyed with a will, and after meeting a repulse in his first ordered attack, Breckenridge advanced his second line; it broke to the rear at the first volley. Thus the action ended, and the two hosts lay on their arms. That night the moon shed its lustre into the dark depths of the cedar brake, where the debris of battle and many thousand bodies of valiant men, dead or moaning in agony worse than death, attested the bloody work done on that last day of 1862.

The action of the 31st of December was in every respect a drawn battle. Both sides failed to make good their tactical plan. It was, therefore, thus far, decisive of nothing, the issue must depend on the sequel.

That Bragg expected to make it decisive for the Confederates, ultimately forcing the retreat of the Union army, is not doubtful. He had quite driven it from the field with a loss of twenty-eight pieces of artillery, more than one third its entire force in that arm, and a very large part of its train; he had practically severed its communications with Nashville by an active cavalry, and he was in position by thrusting forward his left to lay hold of its line of retreat. But Bragg, in this surmise, misjudged the temper of his antagonist. Rosecrans had planted himself there to stay, and when in an assemblage of his officers that night, some offered the kind of timid counsels so readily engendered among small bodies of men, the commander declared his purpose in one shining sentence, " Gentlemen, we fight or die right here! "

When dawn of the 1st of January, 1863, came, both armies were found in position; but the Union army so far from discovering any sign of a purpose to retreat, was seen preparing its vantage ground by improvised defences as if for a permanent stay. The day was passed by Bragg in mute expectancy, in an attitude which seemed to say, "Why don't you retreat? Do you not know that you were beaten yesterday?" Rosecrans knew no such thing. He only knew that "we must win this battle"; his only resolve was "we shall fight or die right here." It was found that there was ammunition enough for another battle. "The only question," says Rosecrans, "was where it was to be fought."

In his original plan of offensive action, it had been Rosecrans's design to swing with his left into Murfreesboro' and upon the rear of the enemy. It would appear that he still held to this purpose; for having now established his position so securely as to be in condition to invite rather than fear attack, he, on the 1st, threw a force again to the east side of Stone River; and followed up the movement by transferring the division of Van Cleve and a brigade of Palmer's division to crown the heights on that bank. His manœuvre was so obviously menacing to Bragg's position that he hastily returned Breckinridge's division to its original position on the eastern side of the stream, and on the afternoon of the 2d, he ordered that officer to dislodge the Union force. To this end, a spirited attack was begun by Breckenridge at 3 P. M. Van Cleve's division manifested a great want of steadiness, and retired across the river after an insignificant resistance. Grosse's brigade of Palmer's division, however, maintained its ground; and when Hazen's brigade was sent across in support, the enemy fled precipitately, a result that was due less to the resistance the Confederates encountered from the Union infantry, than to the fearful havoc made in their ranks by the artillery fire from the opposite bank of Stone River, by which in half an hour, Breckinridge lost seventeen hundred men, or one-third of what remained of his division.

This was the last offensive effort of Bragg, and after remaining another day in a kind of dazed expectation that his opponent would retire, he resolved to do so himself. He accordingly withdrew his army during the night of the 3d, and passing through Murfreesboro', betook himself southward into Central Tennessee, establishing his shattered forces at Shelbyville and Tullahoma. Murfreesboro' was at once occupied by Rosecrans; but his army was in no condition to undertake an immediate pursuit.

This was the issue of the famous battle in the cedar brakes of Stone River, wherein were put *hors de combat* near twenty-five thousand men, of which appalling aggregate the sum of above ten thousand was from the Confederate, and of about fourteen thousand from the Union army.

III.

RESULTS OF MURFREESBORO'.

If there be any force in the exposition I have already made of the circumstances attending the battle of Murfreesboro', it will not be difficult to determine the degree of decisiveness that belongs to that action. The Union army had been thrown back from the front of Chattanooga to the Ohio River. Bragg, with much booty, had retired unmolested to Northern Tennessee, where he took up a position which at once covered the great grain-growing belt of that State, and threatened Nashville. Moreover, not only did he confine the Union army almost within the limits of that city, but he made its tenure very doubtful by the damage which, by means of a cloud of enterprising cavalry, he was constantly able to inflict on the single line of railway upon which the army was dependent for its subsistence. It was necessary therefore that a battle should be fought that would decide the possession of Middle Tennessee. Whether or not the battle of Murfreesboro' had this effect, let the sequel show.

Had General Bragg succeeded in making good his intent, the action of the 31st of December would have been decisive for the Confederates — as decisive as Frederick's battle of Prague, which it closely resembled in its conception. Had General Rosecrans succeeded in making good his intent, it would have been decisive for the Union army, since it would have forced the enemy from his line of retreat. But both parties having failed in their tactical plans, and the position of Murfreesboro' being *per se* of no strategic importance, the advantage would obviously rest with the side which longest maintained its ground. This advantage, with all the moral prestige attending it, was at length surrendered to Rosecrans.

Such to all appearance was the sum of what Murfreesboro' determined. Men indeed rejoiced at the result, and with justice; for if we consider the train of evils that came upon the army in consequence of the first day's fortune to the right wing, if we consider how nearly the day was lost, we shall see how much it was to have even saved the army from amid such perilous environment — how much more it was to have, in addition, inflicted a repulse upon an exultant enemy, and finally compelled him to leave the field.

It behooves us, in the estimate of results in war, to take into account, not merely the ills that actually befall us, but the worse ills that might have befallen us, had they not been averted (and which are therefore to be esteemed a positive good) ; and thus judging, it is plain that the victory at Murfreesboro' takes additional lustre from the dangers out of which it was plucked, and the enemy's discomfiture, additional completeness from the triumph so confidently anticipated, and so nearly attained. Moreover, the result was doubly grateful to the country, coming at the time it did. The summer campaign had shown the enemy everywhere on

the offensive, both east and west, and though the Confederates had been compelled to retire both from Virginia and
Kentucky, yet the impunity with which they escaped in each
case left a deep sting in the minds of the people of the North.
To these events succeeded in the army of Grant a series of
unfortunate checks, and in the army of the Potomac the
bloody repulse of Fredericksburg. It was while the heart
of the North was lacerated with the story of that frightful
slaughter, that the tidings of Murfreesboro' were flashed over
the land. What a relief those tidings brought! Men saw
indeed how costly was the sacrifice; but they saw also that
the sacrifice was not in vain. They saw an army which,
receiving a terrible blow, yet not only did not retreat, but
was able to give so weighty a counter-stroke as to force the
enemy from the field; and they saw the steadiness of the
troops matched by the most inspiring qualities of generalship
on the part of the commander. It was a dayspring of hope
and courage; and when President Lincoln, on receiving the
news of the battle, telegraphed to General Rosecrans, "God
bless you and all of you — please tender to all, and accept
for yourself, the nation's gratitude for your and their skill,
endurance, and dauntless courage," and when the General-in-
chief, in words of unwonted warmth, thus greeted him:
"The victory was well earned, and one of the most brilliant
of the war; you and your brave army have won the gratitude
of the army and the admiration of the world,"—they only
expressed a sentiment which all the North felt in its heart of
hearts.

But it is not alone or even chiefly in what were the patent
and ostensible results of Murfreesboro', that we discern the
true degree of decisiveness that marks that action. Rather
is it in those larger consequences which it prepared and made
possible. The blow there dealt Bragg's army proved to be
one of those deep-seated hurts that disclose themselves and
develop their full effect only after a certain lapse of time.

The gravity of the damage lay not in the material loss of ten thousand men (the Union loss was fully as great), but in the shock which the Confederate army received in its vital part. For the Union army never lost the ascendancy which at Stone River it acquired over its antagonist; and when a few months after that action Rosecrans initiated his grand movement on Chattanooga, the feebleness of the resistance he encountered gave the best evidence of how thoroughly the *morale* of Bragg's army was shaken. This movement, the worthy sequel of Murfreesboro', and a signal epoch in the history of the war, I now proceed to sketch in outline.

The advance from Murfreesboro' was begun the 24th of June, 1863 — as early a period as the necessity of awaiting the season of favorable weather, the formation of an adequate cavalry force, the accumulation of supplies, and a due regard for operations in other parts of the theatre of war, would permit. Bragg's army at this time occupied a strongly fortified position north of Duck River — his infantry extending from Shelbyville to Wartrace, and his cavalry on the right to McMinnville : the line was covered by a range of high, rough and rocky hills, that ran east and west between Murfreesboro' and Shelbyville, and were only practicable by a few passes held by the Confederates. Rosecrans determined to dislodge the Confederates from this stronghold on the Duck River, by threatening their line of retreat. This manœuvre was successfully executed, though with immense difficulty, owing to a storm of great severity, which, continuing for many days, rendered the roads almost impassable. Having first threatened direct attack on Shelbyville, Rosecrans, by a rapid manœuvre of concentration, massed his corps at Manchester, when Bragg, seeing his line of retreat compromised, withdrew to Tullahoma, eighteen miles further south, on the Nashville and Chattanooga Railroad. Here the Confederates had a stronghold that they had been long and elaborately fortifying. But Rosecrans, by a second turning movement on Bragg's right, forced him to fall back, and the Confederates, having crossed the mountains and the Tennessee River, returned to Chattanooga, whither also he drew Buckner's force from East Tennessee. This enabled the column of Burnside, which was acting in concert with the army of the Cumberland, to seize possession of Knoxville. Rosecrans followed in pursuit across the Elk River to the base of the Cumberland range, which he proposed to cross as soon as the railroad should be repaired and supplies accumulated. The conduct of this preliminary act of the campaign was, in the highest degree, brilliant and completely successful. In nine days the enemy was driven from two fortified positions, and compelled to give up the possession of the whole of Middle Tennessee. The operation was accomplished in the midst of the most extraordinary rains ever known in that part of the country, and the result was achieved with a loss of five hundred and sixty men killed, wounded, and prisoners. The Confederate army showed great demoralization, and manifested the strong ascendancy which the Union army had gained over it in the battles of Murfreesboro.'

The railroad having been put in repair by the middle of August, and opened forward to the Tennessee River, it next remained to undertake the arduous operation of crossing the Cumberland Mountains, a lofty mass of rocks separating the waters which flow into the Cumberland from those which flow into the Tennessee.

The movement was begun August 16th, and completed 20th, when the column had reached the Tennessee River, which it was necessary to cross in order to attain Chattanooga, where the main body of Bragg's army was encamped. As this was an operation of great delicacy, and as it was therefore very important to conceal to the last moment the point of crossing, Rosecrans disposed his corps so as to cover a very extended front, stretching from Harrison's, ten miles above Chattanooga, to Bellefonte, fifty miles below. While Hazen made dexterous feints in the former direction, Rosecrans caused bridges to be prepared at Bridgeport and Caperton's; and upon these, between the 29th of August, and 4th of September, he threw the whole army across the Tennessee. The distance from Bridgeport to Chattanooga is twenty-eight miles, and from Caperton's Ferry to Chattanooga about forty miles; but the country is one of excessive difficulty, as the following description will show.

On the south side of the Tennessee River a series of Alpine ridges run southward from the river in a direction parallel with each other, leaving between each mountain vale a valley or cove. The first of these, and the one next the Tennessee, is Sand Mountain, the sides of which are very precipitous, and over which a few, and these very difficult roads, lead into Lookout Valley, which is shut in between Sand Mountain and Lookout Mountain, the next ridge to the eastward. Lookout Mountain is a vast palisade of rock, rising two thousand four hundred feet above the level of the sea, in abrupt rocky cliffs, from a steep, wooded base. It is practicable for a distance of forty-two miles by only three roads. East of Lookout Mountain runs Mission Ridge, and between the two is Chattanooga Valley, a valley which follows the course of Chattanooga Creek. Finally, to the east of Mission Ridge, and running parallel with it, is another valley — Chickamauga Valley, following the course of Chickamauga Creek — which has, with Chattanooga Valley, a common head in McLemore's Cove, enclosed between Lookout Mountain on the west, and Pigeon Mountain to the east. At the mouth of.this valley, upon the south bank of the Tennessee, stands Chattanooga, which, shut in by these well-nigh impassable mountain barriers, fully merits the appellation of "Hawk's Nest," which the word signifies in the aboriginal Indian.

To force his way through these barriers was the task undertaken by Rosecrans. And first in order was the crossing of

Sand Mountain — an enterprise that was successfully effected.
Thomas crossed to Trenton and occupied Frick's and Stevens's
Gaps on Lookout Mountain; Crittenden followed, and took
post at Wauhatchie, while McCook (with the exception of
Sheridan's division, which was to cross at Bridgeport and
move *via* Trenton to Winston) was put on march to Valley
Head and Winston Gap. These movements were completed
by Crittenden's and McCook's corps on the 6th, and by
Thomas's corps on the 8th of September. The enemy was
found occupying the Point of Lookout Mountain, and in
order to dislodge him from Chattanooga it was necessary
either to carry Lookout Mountain, or manœuvre so as to
compel him to quit his position. The latter plan was chosen,
and its execution set on foot by sending a body of cavalry
and a division of McCook's corps south-eastward to the
vicinity of Alpine, thus threatening the railroad in Bragg's
rear. Meantime, Thomas was to cross Lookout Mountain by
Frick's and Stevens's Gaps, to McLemore's Cove, and Crittenden was to move by roads near the Tennessee into Chattanooga, in case the enemy should evacuate it. These movements were begun on the 8th; but next day Crittenden discovered that the enemy, fearing for his communications, had
abandoned Chattanooga, which was immediately occupied by
Crittenden.

Up to this time nothing could be more admirable than the
strategy by which Rosecrans effected his purpose. We shall
now have to follow him in a procedure to which the same
praise cannot be given. Two courses were now open to
Rosecrans — either to concentrate his forces at Chattanooga,
ending the campaign there; or to follow up Bragg with the
view of first dealing him a damaging blow, and then establish
himself in Chattanooga. That the former course was feasible
will readily be perceived, from a statement of the positions of
the several corps. On the 9th, when Crittenden threw his
force into Chattanooga, Thomas's corps was in Lookout Val-

ley, near Stevens's Gap, twenty miles to the south, and Mc-
Cook's corps in the same valley, about twenty miles further
south. Between the Union army, thus positioned, and the
Confederate force in McLemore's Cove, was the rocky barrier
of Lookout Mountain, "a perpendicular wall of limestone."
This could only be forced by an enemy seeking to penetrate
between Thomas and Crittenden, by the single pass of
Stevens's Gap, which was held by Thomas. It was, therefore,
perfectly feasible to direct two of Thomas's divisions to
follow Crittenden into Chattanooga, while the remaining
division was held at Stevens's Gap, until McCook's corps
could be called up and marched past that point, when the
whole army could have been concentrated at Chattanooga,
without its being in the power of Bragg to have prevented, or
even molested the movement. This would have been a judicious course.

The second course was not only judicious — it was brilliant;
for it is manifest that much greater security would be given
to the possession of Chattanooga by first beating Bragg in the
plain, and crippling his strength before establishing the army
in the mountain fastness. This plan Rosecrans determined
to adopt. It must be stated, however, that the method of its
execution violated military principles, and that although he
escaped with impunity, it was purely owing to the imbecility
of his adversary.

When on the night of the 9th of September, it was discovered that Chattanooga had been abandoned by the Confederates, the weight of testimony led Rosecrans to believe
that Bragg was retreating to Rome, sixty-five miles south of
Chattanooga. The Union commander immediately took
measures for pursuit. He directed Crittenden to hold Chattanooga with one brigade, to recall Hazen's forces from the
north side of the Tennessee, and with his corps follow up
Bragg by way of Ringold and Dalton; Thomas to move across
to the east side of Lookout Mountain, and occupy the head

of McLemore's Cove; McCook to march his whole corps upon Alpine and Summerville, for the purpose of interrupting Bragg's retreat and taking him in flank. These movements were predicated on the hypothesis that Bragg was retreating on Rome, and with that view, were well devised to make a decisive stroke. But in point of fact he had only fallen back a few miles from Chattanooga, and taken position with his main body at Lafayette, and his right at Gordon's Mills, on Chickamauga Creek. Therefore, the farther the movements ordered by the Union commander progressed, the more did each column become compromised, and the more was the safety of the whole army put in jeopardy. The real situation of the Confederate force was not discovered until the 12th; and it then became with Rosecrans a matter of life and death to effect a concentration of his army.

It would be difficult to conceive a situation of greater peril than that in which the Union columns were now placed. Crittenden's corps was on the east side of Chickamauga Creek; Thomas was at Stevens's Gap; McCook was at Alpine — a distance of fifty-seven miles from flank to flank. Concentration could not possibly be effected in less than three days. Bragg held position opposite 'the centre of the Union army, with his adversary, whose isolated fractions he was free to strike at pleasure, quite at his mercy. It was only necessary that he should fall upon Thomas with such a force as would crush him; then turn down Chattanooga Valley and throw himself between the town and Crittenden, overwhelming him; then pass back between Lookout Mountain and the Tennessee River into Lookout Valley, and cut of McCook's retreat to Bridgeport. In fact, Rosecrans voluntarily lent his opponent the same opportunity which, only after infinite manœuvring, Napoleon obtained over the Austrians when debouching from the Alps, he burst upon the plains of Italy in the campaign of Marengo.

Bragg could not fail to *see* so obvious an opportunity.

But he was incapable of availing himself of it. He passed the succeeding six days — all of which time was required to bring about a junction of the Union corps — in a series of feeble tentatives; and on the 18th of September, Rosecrans, by great good fortune, had effected a concentration of his army in McLemore's Cove, on the west side of Chickamauga Creek. In this position he covered Chattanooga, which, if the Confederates wished to repossess, they must first fight for it.

If the exposition of this conduct of the Confederate commander has shown that, in point of generalship, Bragg was not a man to be greatly feared, it is now due to state that, since the Union army crossed the Tennessee, circumstances had been materially changed. The Confederates had meanwhile received three considerable accessions to their strength — the East Tennessee force of Buckner, the remnants of the Mississippi army, and, above all, two highly disciplined divisions of Lee's army, brought by Longstreet from Virginia. These reinforcements gave a considerable preponderance to Bragg, who, assuming the offensive, precipitated the bloody combat of two days, known as the battle of Chickamauga.

It does not come within the scope of this work to enter into any detailed recital of the events of this action, which indeed are well known. The issue of the 19th September was a drawn battle; that of the 20th was a grave defeat to the Union army — a defeat only saved from being utter disaster by the rock-like firmness of Thomas who, with portions of all the corps, checked the enemy's victorious advance, and permitted the withdrawal of the army to Chattanooga. Bragg's purpose was to compel the retreat of the Union army across the Tennessee; but the result did not at all realize this intent, for the falling back was only into Chattanooga, which was the original objective of the campaign. Although, therefore, Chickamauga was tactically a defeat to the Union army, yet the strategic result of the campaign, as a whole, was a most substantial and crowning victory — the secure occupation of the fastness of East Tennessee, and of Chattanooga, the citadel of that great mountain system which ran like a wedge into the heart of the South. This possession was never afterwards relinquished : it became the scene of new triumphs for Grant, and the base whence Sherman moved to Atlanta.

As General Rosecrans was deposed from command soon after the close of this campaign, I cannot terminate this sketch without a brief analysis of his capabilities as a commander. While I shall have no difficulty in avoiding those cruel slanders that have been heaped upon this officer, it may not be so easy for me, who, during two months at Murfreesboro', enjoyed an intimate converse with that brilliant and highly cultivated mind, and afterwards accompanied him on the triumphal campaign to Chattanooga, to escape some prepossessions in his favor. Nevertheless, I shall endeavor to judge him with that impartiality and candor which it is my habit to bring to the estimate of military men.

Rosecrans's connection with the Army of the Cumberland, as its chief, lasted just a year. His great field engagements during that period were two — Murfreesboro' and Chickamauga : the one fought two months after he took command, and the other in the eleventh month of his commandership — the one being offensive, a drawn battle tactically, and a victory in its results ; the other defensive, and technically a defeat, though under circumstances that did not allow it to baulk a great strategic success previously won. But "pitched battles are the last resort of a good general," and if Rosecrans had few battles, he had many triumphs, and a sure title to fame in that great series of operations by which he forced the powerful army of the Confederates to abandon the whole State of Tennessee, and by which he advanced the Union standard from the Cumberland to the Tennessee River, planting it upon the rocky bulwark of Chattanooga. This campaign bears an analogy to that of Sherman from Chattanooga to Atlanta — the distance traversed being the same, and the result in each case being largely due to a system of well-combined manœuvres. But the means at the disposal of Rosecrans were greatly inferior to those of Sherman, and it must be borne in mind that as Rosecrans's march was prior to Sherman's, the difficulty was enhanced by the novelty of the operation. Indeed, Rosecrans's campaign from Murfreesboro' to Chattanooga furnishes the type of those great movements over large spaces that were made with such success at a later period of the war.

This fact will, perhaps, enable us to fix upon the salient quality of Rosecrans's military talent. It is as a strategist that he chiefly distinguished himself; for in the fashion of his mind there were some peculiarities that would often mar his success. He was, for example, always too weak to dismiss from command a number of very incompetent subordinates. In the conduct of battle, though extremely brilliant, he lacked calm, and was capable of measures that were egregiously bad. Of this his conduct at Chickamauga will afford an illustion, and it will at the same time give me an opportunity of explaining an act which at the time was by some cruelly attributed to a want of courage — a quality which might as well be denied Julius Cæsar as Rosecrans.

When at Chickamauga the enemy pierced the right wing, Rosecrans and staff were forced back in the rout, and by the intervention of the Confederates separated from the centre and left of the army. In order to reach the centre and left, Rosecrans had to climb Mission Ridge, and make a detour of seven or eight miles. When he had gotten as far as Rossville, the point at which he might either turn southward and make towards the centre and left, or northward, and make to Chattanooga, word was brought him that Negley's division was routed. Now Negley held the extreme left. Unfortunately, there was at the same time a lull along the whole

battle-front: so that to Rosecrans's apprehension, every circumstance conspired to raise the conviction that the whole
army had been routed, and that the best thing he could do
was to return to Chattanooga, reorganize its shattered masses,
and prepare for a defensive battle. He did so, and on-reach-
ing Chattanooga telegraphed to Washington his belief that
the army had been beaten and routed.

Now, the question as to how we are to judge this conduct,
is so intimately connected with the peculiarities of Rosecrans's
mind, that it may be said to turn on a point of metaphysics.
Rosecrans is a man, who, in his mental powers, is incapable
of staying at those half-way houses of impression and belief,
in which men ordinarily rest when they have not the means
of judging with certainty. He is by constitution an absolutist
in thought. He knows only *convictions*, and when he has
made up his mind to a conclusion, he cannot be moved from
it. Hence, he is either tremendously right, or tremendously
wrong. Unhappily, it was the latter at Chickamauga. If
he had been correct in his theory as to the fortune of the day,
he did the best thing that could possibly be done in returning
to Chattanooga. He was not right in his theory, and his
action in accordance with that theory was a great error.

But, whatever deduction may be made in consideration of
such things from Rosecrans's title to complete commandership, no candid mind who shall review the course of the
war can forget that it was he who, in the "winter of our
discontent," brought an outburst of summer hope in the triumph of Murfreesboro', and who, by a giant leap, clutched
the crown of victory in the mountain fastness of Chattanooga.

15

VI.

THE MONITOR AND MERRIMAC.

I.

PRELUDE TO HAMPTON ROADS.

COULD we fancy some ancient monarch of the quarter-deck, some Blake, DuQuesne, Tromp, Ruyter, nay, even a Jervis or a Nelson of our own century, risen from his bed of fame and escorted to a modern ship of war, what would not be his bewilderment at the scene! Amazed at his surroundings, he would accuse his own eyes of treachery, and declare himself delirious or dreaming: and when, after infinite wonder, the truth became clear to him, he would no longer recognize his profession, and would confess that he was but a novice in naval combat. In place of that majestic structure of oak and canvas, perfected by the elaboration of centuries, and beautiful in the form and finish of its multitudinous details, over which his admiral's pennant once floated, he beholds under his feet a long, low, iron-bound raft, rising but a few inches out of the water, and, fixed thereon, a stumpy iron cylinder. No cunningly-carved stern or quarter-gallery, no magnificent figure-head, no solid bulwarks surmounted with snowy hammocks, no polished and shining capstan, no neatly-coiled cables, nothing of all the paraphernalia of that holy-stoned deck he was wont to pace in great glory, now meets his eye: there is only a rusty, greasy, iron planking, stript of all adornment, and indeed of everything once familiar. At each larger swell the ocean rushes over the deck, a result which his astonished gaze finds to be a matter of design. Instead of those clouds of canvas he was wont to see stretching far up into the sky, with all their attendant complexity of rope and spar, there is not only no sail visible, but no yard for a sail, nor a single mast for a yard. That vast apparatus of timber and rigging which marked the sailing-craft of less than twoscore years ago, is shorn clean to the hull, so that for this modern nondescript the whole art of navigation seems to be useless. Yet, since the structure moves, and with steady rapidity, our spectator searches, but in vain, for the motive power. When instructed that it is buried deep under water, safe from the reach of hostile shot, that it consists of a new agent, steam, operating a new instrument, the screw-propeller, his mystery redoubles: but when he extends his glance beneath the deck, and for himself descries the wondrous machinery collected there, toiling with its awe-inspiring strength and precision, his astonishment passes all bounds.

Nevertheless, a greater shock of surprise is in store. This uncouth marvel steams straight into the centre of a vast fleet of those enormous, three-decked wooden floating gun-boxes, such as might have won or lost the fight off Trafalgar, and instantly opens fire. Thunderstruck at her audacity, our resurrected admiral finds every one of her numerous opponents greater in bulk, with thrice her complement of men, and twenty or fifty times her number of guns. But the miracle is soon explained: the missiles of the whole fleet, pattering against the iron fortress-walls, break with the impact, or glance off, leaving a shallow dent in proof of their harmlessness. He misses the familiar music of battle, with shot flying through port-hole or crashing through hull, tearing rigging and bringing down masts, with guns dismounted and gunners slain by scores, with cockpit full and scuppers running with blood : the crew are as safe behind an impregnable rampart as if on their pillows at home ; and indeed most of them, no longer sailors but stokers, in lieu of manning the tops or standing at the deck batteries, are assigned the humble functions of tranquilly shovelling coal, far down below the water-line !   Meanwhile, from within the ugly cylinder, a pair of monstrous guns, which to our astounded on-looker appear even more fabulous by their gigantic dimensions than aught else he has witnessed, hurl forth huge spheres, as the machinery of their wondrous gun-shield revolves them to every quarter of the compass.   Each shot crashes a yawning cavern through the sides of some adversary, into which the waves pour in torrents ; while, by another modern device, that of "horizontal shell-firing," such of the ill-starred wooden navy as are not sunk outright, are blown up, or clothed in flames.   Confounded beyond measure at each moment's revelations, "what engine of destruction," at length he exclaims, "can this be, at once invulnerable itself, and annihilating to all around it? and what is this type of the war-ship of the nineteenth century?"   The answer is quickly returned, — "It is the American Monitor."

It is chiefly within the last quarter of a century that naval warfare has been revolutionized by new inventions and devices, and the crowning act of progress, the introduction of the monitor iron-clad, dates from the War of the Rebellion. Under our own eyes have been consummated innovations which make all previous naval history merely the object of antiquarian research, and previous naval science profitless knowledge.   The early annals of naval warfare have now little that is practically worthy of record.   At a bound, the science of ship-fighting leaps to the heroic battles of immortal Greece.   In two regards, at least, the naval contests of Greece and Rome are more worthy of our notice now than the ship-fighting of nearly twenty centuries thereafter ; for those ancient people give us in their galley-beaks the exemplars and models of the ram, revived in our day, after so long disuse : they, too, were wise enough to protect from hostile missiles the motive-power of their war-ships, namely, the banks of oars and the slaves who sat and worked them. When sails came into vogue on war ships, the motive-power, especially after the introduction of gunpowder, was always exposed to the enemy's shot, and only the screw-propeller accomplished, in this respect, what the fleets of classic ages had achieved ; so it happens that, for us, two thousand years of experience dwindle to a span, and Cape St. Vincent and Trafalgar are as old and as far off as Salamis and Actium.

With the introduction of gunpowder, five hundred years ago, came the arming of war vessels with artillery, and therewith the first noticeable epoch in maritime warfare. It immediately wrought a change in the form of vessels, and in the art of ship-building ; for, whereas, during the centuries preceding, the hulls bore up wondrous superstructures, including pent-houses and protections for the knights and archers who thence flung their spears and put in flight their arrows, now, being swept by the fire of cannon, the decks were stripped by degrees of these extra shields and adornments. The masts, the sails, the rigging, as well as the hulls, were thenceforth gradually modified, in view of the destructive weapons to which they were exposed. Nevertheless, war vessels were vulnerable, and not only as floating forts for combatants, but in their own motive-power. However, nearly five centuries passed without adding much either to the science of naval construction or to that of naval manœuvring in battle. Then, at length, in our time, a grand discovery was made in the use of steam as a motor, which opened a new era in shipbuilding, and wrought wonders in the navigation of the globe. But it was long after this novel locomotive had been tamed to the uses of commerce, and famous progress had been made in steam machinery, that the new agent was applied to naval warfare.   This tardiness may have been somewhat due to the peace then reigning over the greater part of the civilized world, which accordingly distracted inventive genius from the arts of destruction to those of traffic and national wealth ; but it chiefly sprang from an intrinsic mechanical difficulty of application.   The cumbrous paddle-wheels on the one hand interfered with the battery-power of the ship, and also with the employment of her sails, which for economy's sake it was desirable to use, whenever no emergency required steam ; on the other hand, the steam machinery itself, and the whole motive-power, presented a fair target to the enemy, and the ship might lie a helpless log on the water from receiving a single hostile shot.   This difficulty was overcome by the genius of Ericsson, who made the screw-propeller an instrument of practical utility.   Then crossing from the old world to the new, that engineer built for America, in the year 1842, the first screw-propeller war vessel ever constructed, the admirable U. S. steamer Princeton.   It was the forerunner of a mighty change in the armaments of maritime nations, and was the model on which all the screw navies have been constructed ; all the great naval powers, the world over, destroying or revamping their sailing vessels, substituted the new motor.   In England, this work was officially reported as complete only two years before the Southern insurrection. Thus, under our eyes, and as if but yesterday, modern warfare on the seas was thoroughly revolutionized, and, history repeating itself, once more as in the elder days, the motive-power of war vessels was shielded from the weapons of the enemy.   It yet remained, however, for two screw-propelled vessels to manœuvre in actual combat ; and that memorable spectacle took place for the first time in the battle of Hampton Roads.

Meanwhile another great change had occurred in naval warfare, of which this same matchless contest whereof I write, furnished, if not the very earliest, at least the fullest and most instructive example. This was the practice of horizontal shell-firing, whose terrible destructiveness in wooden ships was instantly apparent from the time of its proposed introduction. In this, the American Colonel Bomford successfully disputes with Paixhan, to whom the honor is generally ascribed, the merit of priority of invention. But we come down to very recent days for the practical use of shell-guns in hostile combat. The Russians first demonstrated their value by firing with them the Turkish fleet at Sinope during the Crimean war. But it was the shell-firing of the Merrimac in Hampton Roads against the ill-fated Cumberland and Congress, as contrasted with the harmless discharges of the same guns next day against the impregnable Monitor, that first pointed the great moral taught by horizontal shell-firing from the batteries of war-vessels. That battle rang the knell of wooden navies the world over, and all maritime nations bent themselves to building armored ships.

At the outbreak of the Rebellion, an enormous disparity was visible between the naval strength of the Union and that of the Confederacy. The regular war-steamers of the United States, though scanty in numbers, contained some of the finest ships in the world. But on this navy was imposed the task, Herculean in proportion, of maintaining a stringent blockade along a sea-line of three thousand miles of American coast, stretching from Cape Henry to the harbor of Galveston; and the Navy Department went busily to work, hooted meanwhile by the people, who, too excited then to see the enormous difficulties in the way, chafed at the open coast, and groaned afresh over each story of successful blockade running. The department bought up, right and left, in every port, and wherever it could find them, the vessels of the mercantile marine, and every floating object propelled by steam which could by hook or crook be turned into a war-vessel, was purchased at an inflated price; so that peaceful transports and ferry-boats were soon swarming the Western waters and the Atlantic coast, armed and equipped as gun-boats. Meanwhile, of course, the keels of many new war-vessels were laid. The first essay at construction embraced twenty-three gun-boats of the Wissahickon class ; and the next, at least in the wooden navy, were ten sloops of the Lackawanna class — but the steam machinery of most of these was generally considered as defective : four of them, however, the Kearsage, Oneida, Wachusett, and Tuscarora, were favored with machinery like that of the excellent vessels of the Iroquois and Wyoming class, and accordingly proved successful.

Meanwhile, the Confederates had their naval problem also before them, but with scantier means of solution. Their object was to break up the blockade, to repel naval forays on their rivers and coasts, and to send out ocean guerillas to cripple the vast commerce of the Union. For this latter purpose, as indeed for most of the blockade-runners, they relied on friendly aid from transatlantic dock-yards, and received it in the Alabamas, the Shenandoahs, the Sumters, and all the famous English cruisers which, built, furnished, armed, equipped, and manned in English ports, were rather Cosmopolitan than Confederate, since they rarely or never touched on Southern shores. To pause, however, in naval operations with the exploits of these English ships would have been to render the "Confederate States Navy" a misnomer, and the office of its Secretary a sinecure. There was work enough to do in breaking the blockade and meeting the incursions of Union gun-boats. Desperate as was the outlook, the Confederate Navy Department made such efforts as it could : it promptly seized all luckless crafts which could be snapped up in its rivers and harbors ; and it began to build many new gun-boats at various points in the South, though such was the lack of material and of trained mechanics, that the work dragged, and even when complete made but a sorry show. Two agents were sent from Montgomery to New York, in

March, 1861, to purchase steamers for war vessels, and a third, in May, to Europe.

Recovered from the first excitement, the navy departments, both at Montgomery and Washington, looking across the ocean saw that iron-clad ships were to play the leading part henceforth in naval warfare. It was in July, 1861, that Secretary Welles recommended Congress to appoint a board to study into this matter. The Secretary's words were cautious, for he believed that it was "a subject full of difficulty and doubt," and that both the English and French experiments, if not "absolute failures," were of questionable success. The Confederate Navy Department had arrived at an earlier and profounder faith in armed vessels. On the 8th of May, 1861, it addressed a letter to the Congressional Naval Committee, reviewing the whole history of armored ships, and adding, with no little prescience that " such a vessel at this time could traverse the entire coast of the United States, prevent all blockades, and encounter, with a fair prospect of success, their entire navy. If to cope with them upon the sea, we follow their example, and build wooden ships, we shall have to construct several at one time, for one or two ships would fall an easy prey to their comparatively numerous steam frigates. But inequality of numbers may be compensated by invulnerability, and thus not only does economy but naval success dictate the wisdom and expediency of fighting with iron against wood without regard to first cost." This letter, like the Union Secretary's recommendation, was doubtless inspired by some officer who felt the significance of the iron-clad question as few men in America, north or south, then felt it, and what is still more creditable, grasped the naval situation of the hour. Whatever its origin, this letter, instead of keeping on in the commonplace rut which both the combatants were pursuing, proposed to strike out in a new path, and by one brilliant stroke level the enormous naval disparity between the Union and the Confederacy. Indeed, it would have been hopeless to build wooden ships against those of the North, since in addition to the start the latter already had, she was flowing with materials and skilled labor, of which, on the other hand, the South was wofully destitute. This plan aimed to introduce a new engine of warfare which at its apparition would, as with a magician's wand, wave the accumulated navies of the enemy into nothingness.

Such was the origin of the iron-clad Virginia, or, as she is known in history, the Merrimac; for, while the Confederate Congress hastily dispatched an agent to Europe to buy or build an iron-clad, the Navy Department, eager to lose no time, and fearful of a failure in the European project (as fail it did), set itself to building iron-clads at home. As might have been expected, this endeavor ran counter to the opinions of nearly all the leading officers of the Confederate navy, as well as of such unprofessional people as gave the subject a thought. Indeed there were few persons not wedded to the commonplace idea of the shallow Commander Maury, which was to build small wooden gun-boats to match those of the Union. In June, Commander Brooke (formerly Lieutenant Brooke, of the U. S. Navy) drew a plan of an armored vessel, which was doubtless suggested by the well-known plan which R. L. Stevens had offered to the United States government as early as 1842.

Thus far all was well: but, now, no suitable engines could be had anywhere, even from the Tredegar works. In this dilemma, resort was had to the Merrimac, which lay abandoned in the Norfolk Navy Yard. It was at once seen that there, ready to hand, were a hull and engines complete, and that it was only needed to razee the famous frigate to the water-line, and to build thereon an iron casement for the protection of the battery to be put in her. Indeed, in the frigate Merrimac was already complete what the Confederates with their scanty resources could not hope to match, it being the vessel which had astonished English ship-

wrights by her magnificence, and by the tremendous power
of her battery. She had been but partially burned and
scuttled, and, it being resolved to make her substantially like
the original Stevens battery, the order was, on the 23d day
of June, 1861, given to commence the work. The Merrimac
was soon raised and docked, at trifling cost, and was immediately cut down to her second streak of copper, about twenty
feet from the under side of the keel. The hull was now two
hundred and eighty feet long and fifty-six feet wide, and obviously buoyant enough to allow a heavily-armored casemate
to be built upon her deck. This casemate was estimated, by
observers in the subsequent battle, to be from one hundred
and thirty-five to one hundred and fifty feet long. The iron
plates designed for it were rolled in Richmond, and over
seven hundred tons were thence sent down to Norfolk for her
construction. The projection beyond the submerged shield
was designed to act as a ram; but, when the shield was on,
a cast-iron beak was added.

The foundation of the shield or casemate consisted of
heavy timbers, resting on the sides of the hull, and rising
therefrom in the shape of a roof: it corresponded to the
wooden backing of broadside ships. One thickness of iron
plates, each six inches broad and and one and a half inches
thick, was then laid diagonally upon this frame, and bolted
thereto; to this was, in like manner, fastened a second thickness of plates, two and a half inches thick, but laid diagonally
in the opposite direction, the whole iron armor consisting of
four inches. The casemate was in the form of a roof whose
sides rose at an angle of but thirty-five degrees from the horizon; they did not meet in a ridge, but on the top was a flat
platform which acted as a convenient deck. The beams of
the old Merrimac extended some distance beyond the sides,
and from the ends of these beams to a considerable distance
below the water line, heavy timber was bolted in so as to form
massive guards for the protection of the hull. Both the ends

of the vessel and the eaves of the casemate were submerged two feet, and a light false bow was put on to prevent the water from banking upon the casement, when the vessel was in motion : the submerged ends were to serve also as tanks into which the water would be admitted to regulate the draft ; a large smoke pipe rose from the peak.

It only remained now to put in her battery, which was of a formidable character. It consisted of eight 9-inch Dahlgren guns, with four heavy 7½-inch rifles, of Commander Brooke's pattern, in which latter the service charge was twenty-one pounds of powder. The rifled guns were designed either for solid bolts or shells, but in the actual combat it so happened that, not expecting an iron-clad for an antagonist, the Merrimac was furnished, for her rifled guns, with shells only. She was pierced with six ports on each side, so arranged that six guns could be used in each broadside, of which one could be pointed ahead, and one astern, and two others diagonally : the ports were provided with suitable port-stoppers and closing-gear. However, since the ports were but five feet above the level of the water, the battery could operate only when the sea was very nearly smooth. Like all broadside iron-clads, she had a great draft of water, it being twenty-two and a half feet, and this made her liable to get aground whenever manoeuvring in the limited space to which her career was restricted. The work upon her was hurried as much as the scanty Confederate resources would allow, but it was not till the 5th day of March, 1862, two days before she sallied out, that she was completed. Meanwhile, for this deadly bane to Northern navies, there had been found an antidote.

The not-over-confident suggestion of Secretary Welles concerning iron-clad steamers, already quoted, was immediately taken up by Congress, and the Secretary was authorized to appoint a board of three naval officers to receive and report upon proposals for such vessels, a million and a half dollars being appropriated for the instant construction of such as might be approved. The proper advertisement was issued, specifying, among other things, as one is amused to see, that the vessels must "carry an armament of from eighty to one hundred tons weight," and must "be rigged with two masts." The board consisted of Commodores Smith and Paulding, and Commander Davis. Their report was modest even to diffidence, and confessed their "scanty knowledge in this branch of naval architecture." They declared that "opinions differ amongst naval and scientific men as to the policy of adopting the iron armature for ships of war;" but upon the whole they recommended it for coast and harbor defence, "but not for cruising vessels": and they assert confidently, "that no ship or floating battery, however heavily she may be plated, can cope successfully with a properly constructed fortification of masonry." They also announce that "it is assumed that $4\frac{1}{2}$-inch plates are the heaviest armor which a sea-going vessel can carry." In fine, of seventeen propositions, for one reason or another but three were accepted. One of these turned out to be that of the Galena; another, that of the New Ironsides; while the third was the plan of one J. Ericsson, an engineer not altogether obscure, since the time when, with the Princeton, he revolutionized the navies of the world: it seems that he now proposed once more to reconstruct them by his iron-clad Monitor.

"This plan of a floating battery is novel," say the board, rather dubiously, but upon the whole, they "recommend that an experiment be made with one battery," and, reminded afresh of that element of "novelty," they add, "with a guarantee and forfeiture in case of failure in any of the properties and points of the vessel as proposed." Looking further into the contract, we find the inventor contemplating a vessel one hundred and seventy-two feet long, forty-one feet beam, eleven and a half feet depth of hold, ten feet draft, twelve hundred and fifty-five tons displacement: her speed shall be nine statute miles per hour, her price $275,000, her time of construction one hundred days.   The plan was indeed novel, but such, perhaps, as might be expected from one who, having in early days been a rival and competitor of Stephenson in steam locomotion, had afterwards achieved many valuable triumphs, both in steam and in caloric, which, during a career of forty years, had proved him one of the most accomplished engineers of his age, and that not only by reason of his originative genius, but also by his extraordinary executive ability and a perfect mastery of details which guaranteed success in practical working, even to his initial experiments.   But, not to pause upon the professional minutiæ of his busy life, in the science of naval construction America had had cause for confidence in him; since it was he who had first successfully introduced the screw-propeller; he who had built for the United States, twenty years before, the Princeton, the first war steamer with her motive power protected, ever launched; he who constructed for it the first of the direct-acting engines now in general use; he who built the first wrought-iron twelve-inch gun; he who invented the valuable compressor-gear for taking up the recoil of heavy guns.   Nor was America alone indebted to the genius of Ericsson, since he built for England the war steamer Amphion, into which he put direct-acting horizontal engines of his own invention, of a style not even yet surpassed.   For France, Ericsson's agent built the Pomone, the first screw war steamer ever constructed in Europe; and, let us add, the very device of a Monitor which he was now giving to America, he had offered to the Emperor Napoleon, just seven years previously, in September, 1854, for the Crimean War.   Such was the man, who now proposed an invention to his government, which, little comprehended, luckily was not on that account set aside.

Immediately upon the report of the board, the Secretary of the Navy directed Captain Ericsson to go on with his work, so that, to use the latter's language, "while the clerks of the department were engaged in drawing up the formal contract, the iron which now forms the keel plate of the Monitor was drawn through the rolling mill." When the problem of an impregnable vessel presented itself to the mind of Ericsson, instead of taking the track of his predecessors, and loading down a vessel of the conventional type with an enormous iron cuirass, he resolved, as his grand aim, upon a concentration of armor, — a matter impossible with a high-sided vessel. With a ship of given size, in order to carry the thickest armor possible, which was the point desired, the parts above water must obviously be made to present the least possible area requiring protection; hence, Ericsson first contrived a hull which retained the proper buoyancy, and yet exposed the minimum surface above the water; and this was the famous monitor hull. Nor did this hull possess a single advantage only, but a combination of many. It offered to the enemy a target so small as to make his hitting it once in many times a mere piece of good fortune; it allowed a thickness of iron and timber to be concentrated there absolutely impregnable to the heaviest modern artillery, making the rare shot which should strike it of no avail, so that it would be a matter of perfect indifference to those within whether the ship were struck or not; by dismissing all superfluities, it reduced the expense of construction to a small fraction of that of broadside iron-clads of inferior power; and finally, being low in the water, the waves, instead of dashing against her sides, or rising upon her as on the Merrimac's casemate, could glide over her, doing no harm. The great question of buoyancy with impregnability, thus settled, the next problem was to furnish a battery-power which would render impregnability impossible in any adversary of a different type. Here, again, since the greatest things are the simplest, Ericsson resorted to concentration in guns, or the offensive power, as he had to concentration in armor, or the defensive power; and indeed the use of armor in naval warfare forced the employment of very heavy artillery to pierce it. Accordingly, in the centre of his raft-like vessel, Ericsson fixed a revolving cylinder of wrought iron, just large enough in diameter to contain a pair of heavy guns, and just high enough for the gunners to stand up in it without discomfort. Within this turret he purposed to place guns of a calibre never before dreamed of; so that even those carried by the first Monitor by no means approached his standard. Simple and single as the present Monitor appears to the unprofessional eye, it is a perfect cluster of inventions, including hull, turret, revolving machinery, the turret supports, the rings on which it turns, the gun-carriages, the devices for aiming and moving the guns, the compressor-gear, the port-stopper, the construction of the side armor, the contrivance for perfect ·ventilation, the anchor-well, the rudder and steerage contrivance, the details connected with the engines and propeller, and many other things, all beyond our province to describe.

The urgency of the times spurred the executive ability of Ericsson into full play. With his own hand he made all the working drawings of the Monitor, though it was, in popular phrase, wholly " cut from new cloth." He so arranged the details as to achieve the greatest dispatch in their construction, giving out first the parts which required the longest time in building; and he employed various constructors for this purpose. The hull was built at Greenpoint, the turret-engines and their gearings at Schenectady, the turret itself at one New York shop, the motive machinery and propeller at another, and all from the inventor's own drawings. All the parts, being collected and put together, fitted with the nicety of a dissecting map, and they formed the iron-clad Monitor. The origination of the idea was not less marvellous than the thorough engineering capacity which elaborated the minute details, on whose perfection the success even of the most brilliant invention depends. The Monitor's keel was laid on

the 25th of October, 1861 ; steam was applied to her engines
on the 30th of December ; she was launched on the 30th of
January, 1862 ; and was practically completed on the 15th
of February : it was the most remarkable feat of naval construction on record.   When finished, her total length, over
armor and " overhang," was 172 feet, and the length of the
hull proper, 124 feet ; her total beam, over armor and backing, was 41½ feet, the beam of the hull proper being 34 feet ;
her depth, 11 feet ; her draught, 10 feet ; her total weight,
with everything on board, 900 tons : the diameter of her
turret, inside, 20 feet ; its height, 9 feet ; its thickness, 8
inches ; the vessel's armor, 5 inches of iron and 3 feet of oak.
It only remains to say that, both at the inception and during
the progress of the Monitor, the project was jeered at as
chimerical.   How prejudice and slavery to conventionalities
may warp the judgment even of practical men, was seen
when eminent ship-builders attended the launch, expecting to
see the little craft, destined to an immortality of fame, go to
the bottom as soon as she should slide from mother earth.
But Ericsson only smiled at the ignorant ridicule cast upon
his new nondescript.   A few weeks later was to be fought a
battle, not only the first between iron-clads, but the first
between screw-propelled ships, embracing two revolutionary
naval agents, the product of the brain of one man.

II.

THE BATTLE OF HAMPTON ROADS.

An hour after noon of the 8th of March, 1862, a fleet of
steamers was discovered by the Union lookout in Hampton
Roads, descending the Elizabeth River, rounding Sewall's
Point, and standing up towards Newport News.   The signals
were promptly made to the blockading squadron in that
neighborhood, whereof two sailing vessels, the frigate Congress and the sloop-of-war Cumberland, were anchored off

Newport News, and the remainder of the fleet near and about Fort Monroe, six miles distant. So soon as the tidings spread, the fine frigates Minnesota, Roanoke, and St. Lawrence got under way, slipped their cables, and, with the aid of tugs, moved up towards the approaching enemy. The gale of the previous day had abated, and there was but little wind or sea. As the Confederate fleet steamed steadily into view its character became apparant; the central figure was the long-expected Merrimac, whose advent had been the theme of speculation through days and nights for many weeks, not only in the squadron which waited to receive her, but throughout the country. The cry of "the Merrimac! the Merrimac!" speedily ran from ship to fort, and from fort to shore. To the curious eyes of the thousand spectators gazing intently from near, or peering through telescopes from afar, she seemed a grim-looking structure enough — like the roof of an immense building sunk to the eaves. Playing around her, and apparently guiding her on, were two well-armed gun-boats, the Jamestown and Yorktown, formerly New York and Richmond packets, which seemed to act like pilot-fish to the sea-monster they attended. Smaller tugs and gun-boats followed in her wake, some of which had emerged from the James River. On she came, the Cumberland and Congress meanwhile bravely standing their ground; and, as the Merrimac approached the latter vessel she opened the battle with the angry roar of a few heavy guns. The Congress answered with a full broadside, and when the Merrimac, passing her, bore down upon the Cumberland, the latter, too, brought to bear upon her every available gun, in a well-delivered fire. To the chagrin of both vessels, their heaviest shot glanced as idly from the flanks of their antagonist as peas blown at the hide of a rhinoceros. Hot and terrific as was the firing that now took place, the contest could only be of short duration. With fell intent, the huge kraken, unharmed by the missiles rained upon her, bore down upon the Cumberland, and, striking that ill-fated vessel with her iron beak, under terrific momentum, rent a great gaping cavern in her side. In an instant it was seen that all was over with the Cumberland. But, while the waters rushed into the yawning chasm, and while the ship sank lower and lower, her gallant crew, led by their heroic commander, Lieut. Morris, refused to quit their posts, and with loud cheers continued to pour their broadsides upon the gigantic enemy. As the guns touched the water they delivered a last volley : then down to her glorious grave went the good Cumberland and her crew, with her flag still proudly waving at the mast-head.

Meanwhile, the consorts of the Merrimac had furiously engaged the Congress with their heavy guns. Warned by the horrible fate of the Cumberland, she had been run aground in an effort to avoid being rammed by the Merrimac. But the latter, at half past two, coming up from the destruction of the Cumberland, took deliberate position astern of the Congress, and raked her with a horrible fire of heavy shells. Another steamer attacked her briskly on the starboard quarter, and at length two more, an unneeded reinforcement, came up and poured in a fresh and constant fire. Nevertheless, until four o'clock the unequal, hopeless contest was maintained ; and with each horrible crash of shell, the splinters flew out, and the dead fell to the deck of the dauntless Congress. She could bring to bear but five guns on her adversaries, and of these the shot skipped harmlessly from the iron hump of the dread monster who chiefly engaged her. At last, not a single gun was available ; the ship was encircled by enemies ; her decks were covered with dead and dying, for the slaughter had been terrible ; her commander had fallen ; she was on fire in several places ; every one of the approaching Union vessels had grounded ; no relief was possible ; then, and then only, was the stubborn contest ended, and the flag of the Congress hauled down.

And now, with the waters rolling over the Cumberland and with the Congress in flames, the Confederate dragon, still belching her fiery, sulphurous breath, turned greedy and grim to the rest of the Union Squadron. Arrived within a mile and a half of Newport News, the Minnesota grounded while the tide was running ebb, and there remained a helpless spectator of the sinking of the Cumberland and the burning of the Congress. The Roanoke, following after, grounded in her turn; more fortunate, with the aid of tugs, she got off again, and, her propeller being useless, withdrew down the harbor. In fine, the St. Lawrence grounded near the Minnesota. At four o'clock, the Merrimac, Jamestown, and Yorktown, bore down upon the latter vessel; but the huge couching monster, which in a twinkling would have visited upon her the fate of the Cumberland, could not, from her great draft, approach within a mile of the stranded prey. She took position on the starboard bow of the Minnesota, and opened with her ponderous battery; yet with so little accuracy, that only one shot was effective, that passing through the Union steamer's bow. As for her consorts, they took position on the port bow and stern of the Minnesota, and with their heavy rifled ordnance played severely upon the vessel, and killed and wounded many men. The Merrimac, meanwhile, gave a share of her favors to the St. Lawrence, which had just grounded near the Minnesota, and had opened an ineffectual fire. One huge shell penetrated the starboard quarter of the St. Lawrence, passed through the ship to the port side, completely demolished a bulk-head, struck against a strong iron bar, and returned unexploded into the wardroom; such were the projectiles which the Merrimac was flinging into wooden frigates. Very soon the St. Lawrence got afloat by the aid of a tug, and was ordered back to Fort Monroe. The grounding of the Minnesota had prevented the use of her battery, but at length a heavy gun was brought to bear upon the two smaller Confederate steamers, with marked effect. As for the 10-inch pivot gun, its heavy shot were harmless against the Merrimac. Thus the afternoon wore on, till with the parting day died the fury of battle ; at length at seven o'clock, to the great relief of the Union Squadron, all three Confederate vessels hauled off and steamed back to Norfolk.

So ended the first day's battle in Hampton Roads. What wild excitement, what grief, what anxiety, what terrible foreboding for the morrow possessed the Union Squadron when night fell, cannot be described. All was panic, confusion, and consternation. That the Merrimac would renew the battle in the morning was too evident, and the result must be the destruction of a part of the fleet, the dispersion of the rest, and the loss of the harbor of Hampton Roads. Her first victim would be the Minnesota, now helplessly aground off Newport News ; next, whatever vessel might be brave or rash enough to put itself in her way ; whether she would then pause to reduce Fort Monroe ; or, passing it by, would run along the Northern coast, carrying terror to the national capital, or making her dread apparition in the harbor of New York, was uncertain. The commander of the Fort, General Wool, telegraphed to Washington that probably both the Minnesota and the St. Lawrence would be captured, and that "it was thought that the Merrimac, Jamestown, and Yorktown will pass the fort to-night." Meanwhile, that officer admitted that, should the Merrimac prefer to attack the fort, it would be only a question of a few days when it must be abandoned.

It was upon such a scene that the little Monitor quietly made her appearance at eight o'clock in the evening, having left the harbor of New York two days before. Long before her arrival at the anchorage in Hampton Roads the sound of heavy guns was distinctly heard on board, and shells were seen to burst in the air. The chagrined officers of the Monitor conceived it to be an attack upon Norfolk, for which they were too late, and the ship was urged more swiftly along.

At length a pilot boarded her, and, half terror-stricken, gave a confused account of the Merrimac's foray. The response was a demand upon him to put the Monitor alongside the Merrimac; terrified at which, the moment the Roanoke was reached he jumped into his boat and ran away. The appearance of the Monitor did little to abate the consternation prevailing. That so insignificant a structure could cope with the giant Merrimac was not credited; and those who had anxiously watched for her arrival, for she had been telegraphed as having left New York, gazed with blank astonishment, maturing to despair, at the puny affair before them Her total weight was but nine hundred tons, while that of the Merrimac was five thousand; — what had yonder giant to fear from this dwarf? A telegram from Washington had ordered the Monitor to be sent thither the moment she arrived; but this of course was now disregarded, and the senior officer of the Squadron, Captain Marston, of the Roanoke, authorized Lieutenant Worden to take the Monitor up to the luckless Minnesota and protect her.

It was a memorable night. In fort, on shipboard and on shore, Federals and Confederates alike could not sleep from excitement: these were flushed with triumph and wild with anticipation, those were oppressed with anxiety or touched the depths of despair. Norfolk was ablaze with the victory, and the sailors of the Merrimac and her consorts caroused with its grateful citizens. In Hampton Roads, amidst the bustle of the hour, some hopeless preparations were made for the morrow. The Monitor, on reaching the Roanoke, found the decks of the flagship sanded and all hands at quarters, resolved, though destruction stared them in the face, to go down in a hard fight. Her sister-ship still lay aground off Newport News, tugs toiling all night painfully but uselessly to set her afloat again: meanwhile, a fresh supply of ammunition was sent to her. As for the officers and crew of the Monitor, though worn out by their voyage from New York, they had little mind for sleep, and passed much of the night in forecasting the issue of the coming day. The stories poured into their ears respecting the armor and battery of the Merrimac had not dismayed them, or weakened their confidence in their own vessel; yet, as the officers had not been long enough on her to learn her qualities, nor the men to be drilled at the guns and at quarters, the guns, the turrets, the engines, the gear, and everything else, were carefully examined, and proved to be in working order.

While thus in toil and expectation the night-hours passed, an entrancing spectacle illumined the waters around. The landscape, a short distance off, in the direction of Newport News, was brilliantly lighted by the flames of the burning Congress. Ever and anon a shotted gun, booming like a signal of distress, startled the air around the ill-fated ship, when its charge had been ignited by the slowly-spreading flames. Ten hours now, the ship had been burning; and at one o'clock in the night, the fire reached the magazine, which blew up with an explosion heard more than fifty miles away. At once, in a gorgeous pyrotechny, huge masses of burning timber rose and floated in the air, and strewed the waters far and wide with the glowing debris of the wreck: then succeeded a sullen and ominous darkness, in which the flickering of the embers told that the course of the Congress was nearly run. Meanwhile, the dark outline of the mast and yards of the Cumberland was projected in bold relief on the illumined sky. Her ensign, never hauled down to the foe, still floated in its accustomed place, and there swayed slowly and solemnly to and fro, with a requiem-gesture all but human, over the corpses of the hundreds of brave fellows who went down with their ship.

At six o'clock on the morning of March 9th, the officer on watch on the Minnesota made out the Merrimac through the morning mist, as she approached from Sewall's Point. She was up betimes for her second raid, in order to have a long day for the work.   Quickly the Monitor was notified, and got up her anchor; the iron hatches were then battened down, and those below depended on candles for their light.   It was a moment of anxiety on the little craft, for there had been no time for drilling the men, except in firing a few rounds to test the compressors and the concussion, and all that the officers themselves, who were now to fight the ship, knew of the operation of the turret and guns, they learned from the two engineers who were attached to the vessel, and who had superintended her construction.   When the great smoke-pipe and sloping casemate of the Confederate came clearly into view, it was evident that the latter had been smeared with tallow to assist in glancing off the shot.   As she came down from Craney Island, the Minnesota beat to quarters; but the Merrimac passed her and ran down near to the Rip Raps, when she turned into the channel by which the Minnesota had come.   Her aim was to capture the latter vessel, and take her to Norfolk, where crowds of people lined the wharves, elated with success, and waiting to see the Minnesota led back as a prize.   When the Merrimac had approached within a mile, the little Monitor came out from under the Minnesota's quarter, ran down in her wake to within short range of the Merrimac, " completely covering my ship," says Captain Van Brunt, " as far as was possible with her diminutive dimensions, and, much to my astonishment, laid herself right alongside of the Merrimac."   Astounded as the Merrimac was at the miraculous appearance of so odd a fish, the gallantry with which the Monitor had dashed into the very teeth of its guns was not less surprising.   It was Goliath to David; and with something of the coat-of-mailed Philistine's disdain, the Merrimac looked down upon the pigmy which had thus undertaken to champion the Minnesota.   A moment more and the contest began.   The Merrimac let fly against the turret of her opponent two or three such broadsides as had finished the Cumberland and Congress, and would have finished the Minnesota; but her heavy shot, rattling against the iron cylinder, rolled off even as the volleys of her own victims had glanced from the casemate of the Merrimac : then it was that the word of astonishment was passed, " the Yankee cheese-box is made of iron!"

The duel commenced at eight o'clock on Sunday morning, and was waged with ferocity till noon. So eager and so confident was each antagonist, that often the vessels touched each other, iron rasping against iron, and through most of the battle they were distant but a few yards. Several times, while thus close alongside, the Merrimac let loose her full broadside of six guns, and the armor and turret of the little Monitor were soon covered with dents. The Merrimac had, for those days, a very formidable battery, consisting of two $7\frac{1}{2}$-inch rifles, employing twenty-one pound charges, and four 9-inch Dahlgrens, in each broadside. Yet often her shot, striking, broke and were scattered about the Monitor's decks in fragments, afterwards to be picked up as trophies. The Monitor was struck in pilot-house, in turret, in side armor, in deck. But, with their five inches of iron, backed by three feet of oak, the crew were safe in a perfect panoply ; while from the impregnable turret the 11-inch guns answered back the broadsides of the Merrimac.

However, on both sides, armor gained the victory over guns; for, unprecedented as was the artillery employed, it was for the first time called upon to meet iron, and was unequal to the task. Even the Monitor's 11-inch ordnance, though it told heavily against the casemate of the Merrimac, often driving in splinters, could not penetrate it. So excited were the combatants at first, and so little used to their guns, that the latter were elevated too much, and most of the missiles were wasted in the air; but, later in the fight, they began to depress their guns; and then it was that one of the Monitor's shot, hitting the junction of the casemate with the side of the ship, caused a leak. A shot, also, flying wide, passed through the boiler of one of the Merrimac's tenders, enveloping her in steam, and scalding many of her crew, so that she was towed off by her consort. But, in general, on both ships the armor defied the artillery. It is this fact which contains the key to the prolonged contest of that famous morning. The chief engineer of the Monitor, Mr. Newton, questioned afterwards by the War Committee of Congress, why the battle was not more promptly decided against the Merrimac, answered : — "It was due to the fact that the power and endurance of the 11-inch Dahlgren guns, with which the Monitor was armed, were not known at the time of the battle ; hence the commander would scarcely have been justified in increasing the charge of powder above that authorized in the Ordnance Manual. Subsequent experiments developed the important fact that these guns could be fired with thirty pounds of cannon powder, with solid shot. If this had been known at the time of the action, I am clearly of opinion that, from the close quarters at which Lieutenant Worden fought his vessel, the enemy would have been forced to surrender. It will, of course, be admitted by every one, that if but a single 15-inch gun could possibly have been mounted within the Monitor's turret (it was planned to carry the heaviest ordnance), the action would have been as short and decisive as the combat between the monitor Weehawken, Captain John Rodgers, and the rebel iron-clad Atlanta, which, in several respects, was superior to the Merrimac." He added that, as it was, but for the injury received by Lieut. Worden (of which hereafter), that vigorous officer would very likely have " badgered " the Merrimac to a surrender.

The Minnesota lay at a distance, viewing the contest with undisguised wonder. "Gun after gun," says Captain Van Brunt, "was fired by the Monitor, which was returned with whole broadsides from the rebels, with no more effect, apparently, than so many pebble stones thrown by a child. . . clearly establishing the fact that wooden vessels cannot contend with iron-clad ones; for never before was anything like it dreamed of by the greatest enthusiast in maritime warfare." Despairing of doing anything with the impregnable little Monitor, the Merrimac now sought to avoid her, and threw a shell at the Minnesota which tore four rooms into one in its passage, and set the ship on fire. A second shell exploded the boiler of the tug-boat Dragon. But by the time she had fired the third shell, the little Monitor had come down upon her, placing herself between them. Angry at this interruption, the Merrimac turned fiercely on her antagonist, and bore down swiftly against the Monitor with intent to visit upon her the fate of the Cumberland. The shock was tremendous, nearly upsetting the crew of the Monitor from their feet; but it only left a trifling dent in her side armor and some splinters of the Merrimac to be added to the visitors' trophies.

It was now that a shell from the Merrimac, striking the Monitor's pilot-house, which was built of solid wrought-iron bars, nine by twelve inches thick, actually broke one of these great logs, and pressed it inward an inch and an half. The gun which fired this shell was not more than thirty feet off, as the Merrimac then lay across the Monitor's bow. At that moment Lieut. Worden, the commander, and his quartermaster, were both looking through a sight-aperture or conning-hole, which consisted of a slit between two of the bars, and the quartermaster, seeing the gunners in the Merrimac training their piece on the pilot-house, dropped his head, calling out a sudden warning, but at that instant the shot struck the aperture level with the face of the gallant Worden, and inflicted upon him a severe wound. His eyesight for the time and for long after was gone, his face badly disfigured, and he was forced to turn over his command to Lieut. Greene, who hitherto had been firing the guns. Chief Engineer Stimers, who had been conspicuously efficient and valuable all day by his skilful operation of the turret and by the encouragement and advice he gave to the gunners, thereby increasing the effective service of the guns, now personally took charge of the latter, and commenced a well-directed fire.

However, with the wounding of Worden, the contest was substantially over, a few well-depressed shots rang against the cuirass of the Merrimac, and the latter despairing of subduing her eager and obstinate antagonist, after four hours of fierce effort, abandoned the fight, and with her two consorts, steamed away for Norfolk, to tell her vexation to the disappointed throng of spectators, and then to go into dock for repairs.

The great misfortune the Monitor had experienced in the loss of her determined commander prevented her from pursuing, and forcing the battle to a surrender. But, left in possession of the field, the little vessel could hardly believe at first that her enemy had beat a retreat; but greater were the surprise and relief of the Minnesota, which, unable to expect a successful issue to the contest, had made all the usual preparations for abandoning the ship, and had laid a train to her magazine. The rest of the squadron in whose cause this timely champion had flung down the gauntlet and entered the lists, together with the troops in the forts, found equal cause for gratitude. Cheers and congratulations rose up on all hands, and the enthusiasm was as great as had been the depression of the previous day. The joyous news was flashed through the North, and now from Congress, now from Chambers of Commerce and Boards of Trade, now from public meetings and societies convened for the purpose, thanks and laudations were poured upon the Monitor, Ericsson, her inventor, Worden, her commander, Greene, her executive officer, Newton, her chief engineer, Stimers, the engineer detailed to accompany and report on her, and who worked the turret, all the officers in short, and the crew shared the honors. The President, members of his cabinet, many of the diplomatic corps, officers of both services and many ladies too, crowded to see the new engine of warfare and to view

with their own eyes the place of the conflict of Hampton
Roads.

III.

RESULTS OF HAMPTON ROADS.

The Monitor and the Merrimac have long since run their
course, and shared the fate of the Cumberland and Congress;
but the influence of their desperate struggle in Hampton
Roads, ever-widening from that day onward, has extended all
over the globe. The results of this battle were both national
and international, belonging on the one hand to the Southern
insurrection, but on the other hand to the naval science of all
nations, the ratio of whose maritime supremacies it readjusted.

Had the Merrimac continued the triumphant career which
she began, it is difficult to compute her possible devastation.
During the present generation at least, the emotions which
thrilled America, north and south, at the receipt of the tidings
of Hampton Roads cannot be forgotten; the surprise, the joy,
the triumph, the measureless hopes which filled the South,
the anxiety, the consternation, the dread forebodings which
swept over the North. Beginning with the Minnesota, which
she would quickly overcome, the Merrimac, let loose among
the Union fleet in Hampton Roads, would have burst through
it like an avenging fury, destroying everything in its course,
and scattering all that it did not destroy. How powerless
indeed the wooden fleet would have been against this one
mailed monster, the story of the first day's battle tells. With
the Union fleet dispersed or led captive to grace its triumphs,
the Merrimac would have remained the monarch of Hampton
Roads. The blockade would have been raised, and a great
ocean highway thrown open at the very threshhold of the
Confederate capital. The tenure of Fort Monroe would have
been insecure; for it was generally declared that, at that
time, with the whole Union fleet, transports and all, driven

off, the reduction of the fort by the Merrimac and her various consorts, armed as they were with very heavy ordnance, would be but a question of days.   What loss of men and material, what loss of strategic position, and above all prestige, would have ensued to the Union arms from such a disaster, it is easy to appreciate.   Moreover, the possession of Hampton Roads and by consequence of the James and York Rivers would have ruined the campaign set afoot by General McClellan for the capture of Richmond, and by forcing the choice of a different line of operations, would have changed the whole military as well as the whole naval history of the war.   Nor is it McClellan's campaign alone which would have been thwarted, but all subsequent campaigns, requiring a base on the James, or the York, or the Appomattox, as long as those waters were in Confederate keeping.   In other words, it would have blocked up the chief or the only practicable line of operations against the Confederate capital; for as to overland campaigns, their errors were illustrated by a series of experiments growing more sanguinary and more fatal, from first to last, until they were forever abandoned: what, then, if the water approaches to Richmond had been kept open to its use?

Such would have been the possibilities had the Merrimac found no Monitor to dispute the mastery of Hampton Roads, even had she been content to stay within the confines of the watery realm she had conquered.   Suppose, however, that, after achieving her other conquests, she had run out to sea?   In a northerly course, what had prevented her from steaming up the Potomac, to the terror of the National Capital, or barred her from the harbor of New York itself, there to sweep through the shipping, capturing or destroying at her fancy, and laying under contribution the chief commercial city of the Union?   Or, turning southward, what had hindered her from breaking the blockade of other ports, as she had broken that of Norfolk, and in such a stroke what decisive triumph was there not for the South, what depth of disaster for the North?

The circle of possible results again enlarges ; for, with such Confederate naval successes, foreign nations must have ultimately inclined to recognition and support of the Confederacy. The Merrimac's operations would, as their least result, have supplied the Confederacy with whatever arms or munitions of war or other products or fabrics she might require ; but, beyond that, the blockade itself would have been so compromised, as no longer to command the respect of nations which, hostile from national policy to the Union, waited no aggravated pretext for turning the scale against it. Never were the prospects of the Confederacy for foreign aid brighter than in the spring of 1862 ; and so strongly was this truth felt at the North, as well as at the South, that the mere presence of Admiral Milne's British fleet in the St. Lawrence was looked upon with distrust and trepidation, and with many prophecies that it was stationed there to take advantage of the first successful breaking of the blockade. Angry words must have been exchanged with France and England, words would have been followed by blows, the Confederacy would have received the alliance of one or both of those countries, and the republic have been forever rent in twain.

Thus much of what might have been the issue of the battle of Hampton Roads but for the Monitor. This aspect seems the graver on reflecting that, had the North resorted to the broadside system of iron-clads, of which the New Ironsides was an example, then, not to speak of draft, or thickness of armor, or calibre of battery, or expense of construction, or any other of those respects in which the Monitor system proclaims its excellence, the mere time required in their building would have been fatal to the cause of the Union. Not only would the Merrimac have accomplished all that was expected of her, but she would have been reinforced by other iron-clads, to double or treble her work of destruction ; for the

Confederate Government started in advance of the National Government in iron-clad construction, and the success of the Merrimac would have caused the hurrying to completion of the other similar craft already begun. Thus, long before a fleet of broadside iron-clads, long before a single one even could have been made ready, the sceptre of naval supremacy, and therewith National Independence, would have passed into the hands of the South. But now we must turn to the actual issue of the battle of Hampton Roads.

The immediate result of the conflict between the Monitor and the Merrimac was obviously enough the overthrow of the great projects conceived by the latter vessel, the salvation of the Union squadron, and the preservation of the blockade and of Fort Monroe. Its wider result was to furnish to the Union a new engine of warfare, which, rapidly and cheaply constructed, proved impregnable in defence and irresistible in attack. The Confederate vessels, ingenious, formidable, and fatal to any but the monitors, were yet hopelessly inferior to these. While the principle on which the original monitor was constructed, remained fixed, and was reproduced in her successors, her defects in details were easily noted and avoided in the subsequent copies, and such larger experiments on a more generous scale were made, as the country, grateful for the services rendered on the 9th of March, was willing to authorize. Soon, therefore, the Union navy possessed a full fleet of Monitors. With these it maintained a blockade which otherwise could not have been maintained, as at Charleston and Savannah ; with them it conquered again and again powerful Confederate casemated iron-clads, like the Atlanta and the Tennessee ; with them it withstood the fire of some of the heaviest artillery known to modern warfare, and in return, silenced the enormous earthworks in which that artillery was planted, as at Fort Fisher. In fine, the Monitor met to the full all the requirements of the war, whether in the passive duty of blockade, or in the active one of sinking hostile ships and capturing hostile citadels.

There was another office, too, besides the overthrow of its immediate enemies, which the Monitor performed for the Union. The 15-inch gun in the impregnable Monitor turret, mutters with its deep voice, "hands off," to whatever transatlantic nation might before have meditated an interference in the American War. Before the rapidity of the achievement was comprehended, a squadron of monitors patrolled the Atlantic seaboard, capable of destroying any fleet that might challenge entrance to its harbors. The lesson was not lost upon foreign ministers, who inclined to think twice before encountering this new and terrible engine of defence.

The story of the battle in Hampton Roads created the profoundest sensation in the court of every maritime nation. For months, not only the scientific but the popular journals were filled with the discussion of its merits and its meaning; the professional naval world was profoundly agitated; Admiralty Boards and Ministers of Marine conned its details; in fine, Russia and Sweden promptly accepted the Monitor as the solution of the naval problem of the age, and followed the lead of America in reconstructing their navies on that system. France and England had, unfortunately for themselves, been committed to the broadside iron-clad before the introduction of the Monitor, and the enormous sums already laid out, (enough to build many squadrons of Monitors), joined to some national pride, and, in the case of England at least, re-enforced by a wondrous obstinacy of depreciation only to be understood when one reads such histories as that of the screw-propeller — these causes prevented the renunciation in France and England of their iron-clad navies already built, and the substitution of the turreted Monitor. However, in both countries, the combat of the 9th of March was received with the profoundest study, and was regarded as the death-stroke to wooden war-vessels. In England, on hearing the news of

17

the battle, the House of Commons, in obedience to general sentiment, stopped at once the great military project of building forts at Spithead for the defence of Portsmouth. The Defence Commission, too, was hastily reassembled for the special purpose of considering the effect of the "recent engagement that has taken place in the Chesapeake between the naval forces of the United States and the Confederates," on the erection of these forts. The Royal Commission found "the expression of opinion which followed the action of the Merrimac and Monitor," and the "doubts that took possession of the public mind" thereupon to be "not unreasonable." But when, notwithstanding these doubts, the Commission had the hardihood to recommend the construction of the forts, the government, again menaced by the House of Commons, was forced to abandon this position, and the proposed Spithead forts were given up, reliance being had for defence, in the future, upon iron-clad vessels.

The War of the Rebellion ended, America found that in her Monitor system she had gained an advantage over every other nation on the globe. While the enormous outlays of Great Britain and France had produced a series of vessels which, according to simple scientific calculation, could not attempt to withstand a first-class Monitor, she, at trifling cost, had secured an iron fleet, which, having performed inestimable service in quelling the insurrection, now furnished an impregnable defence to her coast from hostile invasion. The heavy rolling of broadside iron-clads, even in comparatively smooth seas, exposes their hulls below the armor to a hostile shot in a vital point; and, in addition, not only subjects the gun-ports to a liability of water rushing into them, but obviously renders accurate gunnery impossible. Again, it is impossible to build a broadside iron-clad of any practicable size which can be covered with armor sufficient to resist modern artillery, and the result is the adoption of the "central fort system," which covers the vessel with iron only amidships, and leaves the rest to be shot through and through : yet, even the thickest parts can be penetrated by the Monitor's guns. Finally, there comes the difficulty of working in broadside anything like the heavy guns used in the Monitor. In a word, to say nothing of the monstrous size and unwieldiness, of the enormous cost, of the impracticable draft, of the English broadside ships, the very best of them could be shot through in their most heavily-armored parts by the tremendous ordnance of the Monitors, whilst a great part of them is not protected at all. On the other hand, their heaviest missiles would rattle idly from the impregnable Puritan or Dictator as if they were but pebble-stones.

The Monitor is, in its nature, one of those radical expressions of a scientific idea which do not admit further change in principle, though, of course, permitting improvements in detail. It was not the result of a ship-builder's experiment, no lucky guess or happy accident, but a calculated product, wrought out in the endeavor to solve a problem then engaging the mind of the chief naval powers of the world. The transatlantic methods employed on that intricate question do not complete the requirements of the problem. We have already seen how, in order to produce the maximum impregnability, the hull of the Monitor was permitted to protrude but a few inches above water, and her decks were stripped of bulwarks and all other unnecessary appendages. Thus, while the Warrior, a vessel of 10,000 tons total displacement, can only support about four and a half inches of armor, and that for only about half her length, the little harbor-monitors of the Passaic class, designed simply for coast defence, though only about one-fifth the Warrior's size, carry armor nearly twice as thick from stem to stern. As for the heavy Dictators and Puritans, though but half as large as the Warrior, their armor is more than thrice as thick as that of the English ship in its thickest part, and that throughout their entire lengths. Then, on the other hand, it was desirable to mount heavier guns in the new vessel than had ever before been carried, or had ever before been provided against, or could be provided against except on the Monitor system. Thence sprang the device of the cylindrical turret which, being revolved on its periphery by steam-power, could adroitly turn its port-holes to any point in the horizon. Nor was this turret complete in its operation till so built that it formed a water-tight joint with its deck. Within this impregnable floating castle the power of the enclosed artillery is only limited by the genius of the gun-maker; for the turret is an impervious gun-carriage, which, operated by mechanism, can carry ordnance of any size, and only awaits for the limit to which the art of gunsmithery shall go.

Should it happen that, while the United States adopts the monitor war-vessels, her maritime rivals remain content with those of the broadside pattern, the successful initiation of the former in the battle of Hampton Roads will have resulted in giving to America the supremacy of the seas. But should it happen, as is far more likely, that sooner or later, and by gradual steps, England and France shall be forced to copy the Monitor, with such petty modifications as may soothe national pride, then, as iron-clad vessels have revolutionized naval warfare, so monitors in turn will revolutionize the warfare of iron-clads; and the pigmy warrior of Hampton Roads will have dictated reconstruction to the navies of the world.

In these modern days of ours, mechanism has made vast inroads on the domain of *morale*, and nations which once ruled the seas by virtue of the courage and skill of their sailors, and by national pride and training in marine enterprise, have found their prestige swept away. Mechanism usurps the offices once performed by men. In this era of mechanical warfare, it is idle to expect moral excellence to supply the lack of material strength. With equal advantages, indeed, the former will pluck victory from any battle, but

material superiority itself supplies confidence, and however
brave the assailant, he may find he is dashing his head against
a rock.   Naval war still more than war on the land is a question of science, and we cannot expect bravery to accomplish
miracles or to reverse the conclusions of natural laws.   So
found the Niagara, when off Lisbon she encountered the
Stonewall.   Nor is it always enough to have iron hearts in
wooden walls.   It is a curious speculation what might have
been the result of the Southern insurrection, had the Confederacy possessed, and the Union lacked, mechanical geni-
uses who would have furnished her novel implements and
engines of destruction.   Had some skillful brain armed her
troops with a cheap breech-loading rifle ; had some Ericsson
equipped her with a fleet of monitors, while the North was
laboring at tardily-constructed broadside iron-clads ; or supplied her with batteries not the less terrible in power because
they avoided the use of expensive engines ; or protected her
rivers and so the great cities lying thereon ; or given her
some perfect torpedo capable of clearing all her blockaded
harbors : in short, had scientific devices made up for want of
resources, by inventions suited to the humble capacities of the
South, what might not have been the issue?   War grows to
be each day an exacter science.   A nation, arming itself with
a needle-gun, confidently rushes upon its neighbor twice as
strong in numbers and resources, and, at a thought, brings
the great rival's knee to the dust.   Nations can be made or
undone at the desk of an engineer.

VII.

VICKSBURG.

I.

PRELUDE TO VICKSBURG.

In the minds of the hardy freemen who dwell upon the hundred tributaries of the Father of Waters, there arose, at the very beginning of the war, a grandiose aspiration, that at once determined the objective of military operations in the West, and supplied, as from an unfailing reservoir, the inspiration and moral stimulus to make their bright ideal an actuality. This aspiration was the opening up of the Mississippi. For the streams on which the men of the West dwelt, did not more surely go to swell the tide of the great river, than did the current of their interests and affections flow adown its course to the Gulf: and they would not brook hostile jurisdiction over that continental highway of commerce and inter-communication. They resolved that the Mississippi should run "unvexed to the sea."

The colossal conception of the conquest of the Mississippi valley shaped the earliest military efforts of the West, and associated itself with the most brilliant triumphs in that theatre of war. It was for this express work that the first army and fleet of Grant and Foote were formed at Cairo. Now, when in the early months of 1862, this army and fleet were prepared to move, the insurgents held control of nearly the whole of the great river. By means of the forts below New Orleans, they commanded its outlet in the Gulf of Mexico. By means of the fortifications of Columbus, they closed navigation from the North up to within twenty miles of where, at Cairo, the Ohio and Missouri coming together, form the main artery of the Mississippi.

The Confederate defence of the Mississippi included a double problem. It was necessary, first of all, to obstruct navigation to the Union fleet, which could best be done by fortified batteries erected at chosen points where the river's banks swell into bluffs. But in order to make such intrenched camps secure against capture from the land side, it was requisite that they should be covered by a force powerful enough to meet the Union army in the field. Unless the latter purpose could be realized, it was vain to suppose that any point could be held; for while such fortified strongholds might readily avail to bar the advance of a fleet, they must, unless protected by an army, fall an easy prey to a force in condition to invest them from the rear. This the Confederates, after one rude lesson, learnt; and if we briefly review the course of Union conquest in the basin of the Mississippi, we shall see that the fate of the great river was nearly always dependent, not on the attack or defence of specific fortified points, but on the issue of actions waged between the rival armies in the field.

The first position taken up by the Confederates on the Upper Mississippi, was Columbus. It completely realized that part of the problem that concerned the obstruction of the river to navigation. No efforts were made against it; but it is certain that it could have effectually resisted all naval attacks. When, however, Fort Donelson fell, Columbus was entirely uncovered; and being without the protection of an army, it was exposed to certain capture from the rear. Beauregard, into whose hands the defence of the Mississippi Valley then fell, undoubtedly did the best that was to be done, when he ordered its evacuation, thus saving the garrison and the siege guns, which were removed to Island No. Ten, forty-five miles below Cairo, and twenty-five miles below Columbus.

The theory of action formed by Beauregard, showed an appreciation of the correct method of defending the Mississippi. This was to accumulate a force large enough to assume the offensive against the Union army in the field. If successful, Columbus would be easily regained; but as he might be unsuccessful, he resolved to prepare a powerful system of river-works at Fort Pillow, one hundred and thirty miles below Island No. Ten — obstructing the river meanwhile at the latter place, until the fortifications of Fort Pillow should be completed. Against Island No. Ten, the flotilla of Foote and the army of Pope proceeded immediately after the reduction of Donelson, the army of Grant meanwhile moving to Pittsburg Landing on the Tennessee. But neither the army nor navy made any impression against the defences of Island No. Ten, which successfully withstood a three weeks' bombardment, and gave the Confederate engineers ample time to construct the works of Fort Pillow. This being accomplished, the island was evacuated the 7th of April, the date of the battle of Shiloh.

After the disastrous upshot of Shiloh, Beauregard retired to Corinth. He there covered Fort Pillow; and until the Confederates should be forced from Corinth, Fort Pillow could not be assailed save by the navy. Foote, immediately after the evacuation of Island No. Ten, steamed down to assail the new stronghold, and began a bombardment which was kept up six or seven weeks without any effect whatever. But, when at the end of May, Beauregard's army was compelled to retire from Corinth, Fort Pillow, entangled in the evil fortunes of that army, had to be abandoned also. This left the Mississippi open to Memphis, sixty-five miles below. The Union fleet immediately proceeded against that place, and after a decisive engagement with the Confederate gun-boats, secured its capture. Thus, in four months from the opening of the campaign in the West, by virtue mainly of the two decisive victories at Donelson and Shiloh, the Mississippi was loosed of hostile jurisdiction through all the stretch from Cairo to Memphis — a distance of two hundred and forty miles, comprising the whole shore of Kentucky and Tennessee on the left bank, and the whole shore of Missouri, and nearly one half of that of Arkansas on the right bank.

While thus the flotilla of Foote was steadily advancing down the course of the Mississippi, the brilliant victory of Farragut, who carrying his fleet through the inferno of hostile craft, fire rafts, obstructions and forts, laid his ship alongside the wharfs of New Orleans, wrested from the enemy the Mississippi's outlet in the Gulf. Shortly after the surrender of New Orleans, Farragut dispatched a part of his squadron, under Commander Lee, to ascend the Mississippi. The expedition was of the nature of a reconnoissance; for it was unknown what batteries or obstructions the enemy might have above in the long stretch of many hundred miles between the lower fleet, and that of Foote which at the time was still bombarding Island No. Ten. For many days the fleet steamed up stream without interruption, taking possession of Baton Rouge, Natchez, etc.; and at length, on the 18th of May, 1862, arrived before that town whose name, then first leaping to light in the history of the war, was destined to associate itself with one of the most memorable sieges on record. The fleet, in fact, arrived before Vicksburg.

It was at this time unknown what defensive preparations the Confederates might have at Vicksburg. Indeed, however, they were slight, and had but recently been initiated by General M. L. Smith who, under directions of Beauregard, began the erection of batteries on the high bluffs that overlook the Mississippi. When Smith took command on the 12th of May, three batteries had been nearly completed; and he energetically prosecuted the erection of others: so that, when the Union vessels arrived on the 18th, and demanded the surrender of Vicksburg, the Confederate officer felt able to reply that, "having been ordered here to hold these defences, his intention was to do so as long as it was in his power." Commander Lee, judging his naval force too feeble to cope with the batteries, awaited the arrival of additional vessels, which soon began to reach him from New Orleans, and by the 28th of May, ten gun-boats lay before Vicksburg, and a bombardment was begun. But meanwhile the Confederates had not been idle. "These ten days," says General Smith, in his official report, "I consider the most critical period of the defence of Vicksburg. Batteries incomplete, guns not mounted, troops few, and both officers and men entirely new to service. Had a prompt and vigorous attack been made by the enemy, while, I think, the dispositions made would have insured their repulse, still the issue would have been less certain than at any time afterwards. It was not long before they apparently came to the conclusion that no impression could be made on our works by their gun-boats, nor the erection of new batteries prevented, wherever attempted; and the remaining six batteries, of the ten first mentioned, were constructed under their eyes. From the 28th of May to the middle of June the firing was kept up at intervals, and more or less heavy the latter part of the time, directed mainly at the town, and at localities where they apparently thought troops were encamped."

While the Confederates labored at their defences, new accessions of strength came to the fleet, till finally, towards the close of June, Farragut, with his entire squadron of gun-boats, and the mortar-fleet of Porter, lay off Vicksburg. An infantry force of four regiments, under General F. Williams, had also come up in transports, and begun to cut a navigable canal accross the sharp bend which the Mississippi here makes. Finally, for in the mean time Fort Pillow and Memphis had fallen, the upper squadron, under flag-officer Davis, Foote's successor, was able to descend the river to Vicksburg,

whose batteries alone divided the two fleets. With the portentous armament thus gathered against Vicksburg from above
and below, it was resolved to make a determined effort for its
reduction. A furious bombardment was begun on the afternoon of the 27th of June, and renewed at daylight of the 28th,
when the lower fleet was put in motion. Steaming up stream
in front of the city, the gun-boats delivered broadside after
broadside at the batteries, while the mortar-ketches from below filled the air with bombs. The cannonade was kept up
with prodigious firing for two hours; but, though seven of
the gun-boats succeeded in running the gauntlet and joining
the upper fleet, yet no damage whatever was inflicted upon
the defences. The vessels, however, continued to pour their
fire into the batteries until the 15th of July, when the Arkansas, a powerful iron-plated ram which the Confederates had
just completed, descended from the mouth of the Yazoo,
twelve miles above Vicksburg, and, after disabling two of the
Union gun-boats, escaped under protection of the Vicksburg
works. As the passage of this craft threatened the destruction of the mortar-fleet below, Farragut was compelled to
descend with such of his vessels as he had taken above Vicksburg. This he did by running the guantlet of the batteries
on the night of the 15th; and finally, on the 27th of July,
after several days of continued firing, both the upper and
fleets disappeared from in front of Vicksburg.

The canal also proved a total failure; and, at the end of
July, General Williams returned with his force to Baton
Rouge. Thus ended what may be called the first siege of
Vicksburg. It had continued for seventy days — from the
18th of May to the 27th of July, 1862 — during a considerable part of which time Vicksburg was under a bombardment, the severity of which may be judged from the
fact that 25,000 shot and shell were, from first to last,
thrown into that place by the fleet. No impression whatever was made on the defences: not a single gun was dis-

mounted, and the Confederate casualties numbered but seven killed and fifteen wounded.

If it required any demonstration of the impotence of floating armaments in the reduction of well-constructed and adequately-defended water batteries, such demonstration was certainly given by the seventy days' bombardment of Vicksburg. But it needed no such proof. The fleet had already failed in its efforts against each of the strongholds on the Mississippi; and these in succession, from Columbus down, had fallen only in consequence of the defeat of the army covering them on the land side. Columbus fell when it was uncovered by the capitulation of the army at Donelson; Island No. Ten fell when Beauregard lost Shiloh; Fort Pillow and Memphis fell when the evacuation of Corinth left them without protection. Vicksburg, which had laughed to scorn the persistent efforts of two mighty fleets, was manifestly safe so long as the Confederate army, that stood between it and the Union force, was able to maintain itself in the field. Let us now see what was the situation in this regard.

It will be remembered that in a previous chapter we have seen how, after the occupation of Corinth by the armies under General Halleck, the Army of the Ohio, under General Buell, was directed upon Chattanooga, and how the main body of the Confederate "Army of Shiloh" was, under Bragg, transferred to that mountain fastness, and from there initiated the strategic moves that, during the month of September, 1862, threw Buell's army back to the Ohio River. This mutual reduction of the rival forces operating in the basin of the Mississippi left on both sides comparatively small armies to act in that region. The Union force remained under General Grant; the Confederate force under Price and Van Dorn. But as it had been arranged by Bragg that these officers should, as a diversion in favor of his campaign in Kentucky, assume the offensive against the Union force, Grant was, by their enterprising operations, diverted entirely from a proper offensive, and, until the month of October, was kept too busily engaged in foiling their designs to give any heed to ulterior plans of campaign. These, however, so soon as he was relieved a little from pressure, came again prominently into the foreground of his purpose.

Of the objective now to be aimed at in the theatre of operations controlled by General Grant there could be no possible doubt. It was obviously that river stronghold that had arrested the progress of the ascending and descending Union fleets, and against which these fleets had, during the previous months of May and June and July, in vain expended all their fury. Manifestly, it was Vicksburg which, with its outpost at Port Hudson, formed the sole remaining barrier to the free navigation of the Mississippi.

The line at this time held by General Grant was substantially the line of the Memphis and Charleston Railroad between Memphis and Corinth — his right flank on the Mississippi at the former place, his left at Corinth. But in front still lay the forces of Price and Van Dorn, which, in November, 1862, were consolidated under the control of Lieutenant-General Pemberton. This army, occupying the line of the Tallahatchie, two hundred miles to the north of Vicksburg, was Vicksburg's real defence — the real barrier to Grant's advance against that place. Till this force should be eliminated, the solution of the problem could not even be begun. And that it was a problem in other regards beset with difficulties, a brief exposition will easily show.

In the debatable strip of territory between the two rival armies, whereof that of Grant held the southern border of West Tennessee, and that of Pemberton the northern border of West Mississippi, there flow southward from the transverse ridge that crosses this zone many small streams, which, form the Tallahatchie and the Yalabusha: and these rivers, in turn commingling, constitute the Yazoo, which, flowing nearly parallel with the Mississippi for two hundred and ninety miles, at length empties into the great river six miles above Vicksburg.   This stream, with its numerous estuaries making into it from east and west, gives its character to the country through which Grant was to attempt an advance towards Vicksburg from Memphis and Corinth — a country intricate, amphibious, and cut up by numberless bayous and swamps.   From Memphis to Vicksburg the distance, to follow the turnings and windings of the sinuous Mississippi is 390 miles.   By land, as the crow might fly, from Memphis, or say from Grand Junction on the Memphis and Charleston Railroad, where Grant's centre lay, it is not much above 200 miles ; or, if we follow the course of the Mississippi Central Railroad, which is about as direct as the path of the crow, and which was to be Grant's line of advance, the distance from Grand Junction to Jackson is 205 miles, and at Jackson it is but "one side-step to the right" — or forty-six miles due westward — to Vicksburg.   Now, Pemberton held the line of the Tallahatchie, and covered all the country in his rear to Vicksburg, with which point also he had direct railway communication by the Mississippi Central Railroad. Holly Springs on that same railroad, a few miles south of Grand Junction, he held as an advance post.   To force Pemberton from the line of the Tallahatchie, and then to throw him back over all the intervening country to Vicksburg, was the task undertaken by Grant.   Let us signalize this as the first of his numerous attempts against the Mississippi stronghold.   We shall now see how, opening brilliantly at the end of November, the campaign in a month closed in most total failure.

The plan of operations devised by General Grant for the purpose of forcing Pemberton from the line of the Tallahatchie, embraced a double or rather a triple combination of moves — the main force to press upon the Confederate front, Sherman to march from Memphis to threaten their left flank on the Tallahatchie, while a cavalry force was to cross from the west side of the Mississippi below that line, and threaten their railway communications. The execution was begun the 27th of November. The force destined to make the demonstration on the enemy's rear, consisting of a body of about seven thousand cavalry from the Union army of the trans-Mississippi, under Generals Washburne and Hovey, crossed the Mississippi from Helena, and advanced towards the Tallahatchie, destroying the railroad behind Pemberton's front. This menace immediately caused the Confederate commander to fall back from his advanced positions and from the line of the Tallahatchie to Grenada, 100 miles south of Grand Junction, where the railroad from Memphis southward (the Mississippi and Tennessee) strikes the Mississippi Central road. The effect of this move made it unnecessary long to continue the development of Sherman's sally from Memphis, for Grant, with the main body of the army was immediately able to press on over the path cleared for him by Pemberton's retreat. The advance was pushed steadily southward through Holly Springs, along the railroad line, beyond the Tallahatchie, till the 3d of December when the head-quarters were established at Oxford, and the cavalry thrown well forward towards Grenada, where Pemberton had taken post. The success thus far had been brilliant, had cost next to nothing, and had resulted in carrying forward the Union front fifty miles nearer Vicksburg. To repeat the leap, it was only necessary for Grant to secure his line of supplies by repairing the railroad back to his great depot at Holly Springs. This work was pushed forward with such energy, that by the middle of December the army was ready for a new advance; and for this advance a plan more bold than that already wrought out was elaborated.

It was an obvious inconvenience attaching to the line of operations chosen against Vicksburg, that the army must depend for its supplies on the single thread of railway connecting it with its depot at Holly Springs — a line which must become more and more lengthened and precarious as the army penetrated deeper and deeper into the hostile country, and which, if Grant at length should be able to plant himself in the rear of Vicksburg, would have a depth of above two hundred miles. There was, however, one mode in which this difficulty might be entirely overcome. If, instead of attempting to repair and hold the railroad in the long and difficult advance, a force descending the Mississippi to the mouth of the Yazoo, six miles above Vicksburg, could open up this water line, it was evident that not only would the Confederate force opposing Grant be constrained to fall back, but that the Union army might cut itself entirely loose from the railroad, in the assurance that by the Yazoo supplies would await it to the very gates of Vicksburg. Such was the conception of Grant, and the execution of the plan was intrusted to General Sherman, who, at Memphis, commanded his right wing. It was arranged, that while Sherman was thus operating on the Yazoo, Grant was to press forward the left to Jackson, when the two, uniting, would invest Vicksburg from the rear.

Sherman having embarked his divisions in transports, steamed down the Mississippi from Memphis the 20th December, 1862.   On Christmas day, he was off the mouth of the Yazoo ; on the 26th, the transports, convoyed by a fleet of gun-boats under Acting Rear Admiral D. D. Porter, ascended the Yazoo to the distance of about twelve miles, where the troops disembarked on the south bank of the river, near the mouth of Chickasaw Bayou. Here, on a range of bluffs, the Confederates showed batteries defending the river and a line of defence covering the approaches to Vicksburg, which lay seven miles to the south.

If we now recur to the relative situation of the opposing forces, the reflection will spontaneously suggest itself that the condition of Pemberton at Grenada could not fail to be very critical, what with Grant pressing his front and now Sherman a hundred miles in his rear and at the very door of Vicksburg. The total military strength of the Confederates in the department of Mississippi and East Louisiana was 39,000, and the force with which Pemberton himself confronted Grant was not above 25,000, scarcely more than half that of his opponent, while the garrison of Vicksburg consisted but of a few brigades under General M. L. Smith, opposed to Sherman's forty thousand men. It resulted that even should he take advantage of his interior position, and unite both his detachments against the one or the other Union force (Grant or Sherman), Pemberton would find his aggregate outnumbered by either singly.

But in point of fact Pemberton's condition was not in the least critical, for by a bold initiative he had in the mean while succeeded not only in neutralizing Grant, but had compelled him to beat a rapid retreat: so that by the time Sherman's force disembarked on the bank of the Yazoo Pemberton was able to confront it there with nearly his whole force. This untoward turn of fortune befel the Union arms in this wise.

After Pemberton had been compelled in consequence of Grant's first move to give up without a blow the line of the Tallahatchie, and fall back upon Grenada, he began to consider how he might thwart his adversary's manifest design of pressing his advantage by a renewed advance towards Vicksburg, and with this view he resolved to dispatch a cavalry column to operate against Grant's railroad communications. The whole of the Confederate mounted force under General Van Dorn accordingly moved around the Union flank by a wide detour, and on the 20th of December struck Holly Springs, Grant's main depot of supplies. The dispositions for the security of this place were little proportioned to its vital importance. It was, in fact, wholly destitute of defences, and was merely held by a force of from twelve to fifteen hundred men under an incompetent commandant. Van Dorn seized the place without opposition, made prisoners of the garrison

18

and destroyed the immense accumulations of quartermaster's, commissary and ordnance stores destined to supply Grant's force in its contemplated advance. The blow was decisive. Grant was compelled to fall back to Holly Springs, abandoning all that had been gained in his first initiative.

The surrender of Holly Springs took place on the 20th of December, just as Sherman was dropping down the Mississippi towards Vicksburg; and it was in entire ignorance of the disaster which was to deprive him of the co-operation of Grant, that Sherman on the 26th, having, as we have seen, disembarked on the south bank of the Yazoo, prepared to grapple with the duty that there met him. Let us see what this was.

To the Confederates it had since many a month become obvious that Vicksburg must sooner or later become the object of strenuous attack, and that not merely as before by the fleet, but by the Union army approaching from the rear. To provide against the day when this shonld come, General M. L. Smith, the same energetic officer who had supervised the defence of the place when first assailed by the gun-boats of Farragut, and who still remained in command, had constructed a system of earthworks enveloping Vicksburg from the north and east and south. But as a landing on the Yazoo was a contingency to be apprehended, and a movement which if effected by the Union force would enable it to place Vicksburg immediately under siege, Smith had prepared an outer line of defence to cover the approaches from the Yazoo — a line to which the configuration of the country added great strength.

The heights upon which the "Queen City of the Bluff" is built are the abutment upon the Mississippi of a broken ridge of hills that stretches far into the interior, in nearly a direct line, and in a direction at about right angles with the general flow of the river. The Yazoo in its course southward and eastward finally touches the base of these hills at a point known as Snyder's Mills, or Haynes's Bluff, twelve miles from its debouchure in the Mississippi, and thirteen miles north of Vicksburg. There is thus between the hills and the Yazoo a triangular-shaped area of bottom-land densely wooded, with the exception of one or two plantations on it, and intersected with bayous and low swampy ground. Skirting the hills from Snyder's Mills, down to near the Mississippi, is first a swamp, then an old bed of the Yazoo containing considerable water and only to be crossed without bridging at three points whither torrents from the hills have borne along sufficient matter to fill up the bed, and finally down to the Mississippi a heavy belt of timber which had been felled into abatis. There was thus a continuous obstacle, twelve miles long, formed of abatis and water, skirting the base of the hills and but a short distance from them, terminated at one end by fixed batteries and a fortified position at Snyder's Mills; at the other end by the heavy batteries and field-works above Vicksburg. So long as the works at Snyder's Mills were held, the whole Yazoo Valley was defended. The Confederate commander believed he could hold these works even with a slight force, provided the Union army was compelled to make a direct assault upon them from the river, and was not permitted to disengage itself from the bottom described: so having determined upon the base of the hills as the proper line, he prepared in advance to guard the three natural approaches by throwing up earthworks, felling timber, etc.

It was against this position that Sherman, having effected his landing on the 26th December, found himself compelled to advance. The point of debarkation was in the vicinity of Chickasaw Bayou, which was about the centre of the enemy's line of thirteen miles from Vicksburg on the left to Haynes's Bluff on the right. From this point the troops were in the morning thrown forward in four columns, and pressed back the enemy's pickets to the lagoon or bayou, which, as already mentioned, was passable only at three points. Steele's division on the left, moved out above the mouth of Chickasaw

Bayou; Morgan's below the same bayou; Morgan Smith's on the main road to Vicksburg, and A. J. Smith's still further to the right. The more the ground was examined, the more difficult it was seen to be; and both the 27th and 28th passed in reconnoissances and skirmishes, attended with no great loss. It was then resolved to make on the following day a concentrated attack with the view of passing the bayou, and carrying the intrenched heights beyond. In front of the right, under A. J. Smith, opposite the enemy's left, were the heavy abatis stretching towards Vicksburg: it was determined only to demonstrate there. In front of the right centre, under Morgan Smith, was a passage across the lagoon by a sandbar two hundred yards wide. In front of the left centre, below Chickasaw Bayou, was a good levee or dry part of the lake. In front of the left, above the bayou, where Steele had gone on the 28th, the ground proved so impracticable that his division was brought back and put in support of Morgan's. It resulted that it became necessary for Sherman to try his fortunes in attack at the positions occupied by Morgan and Morgan Smith. The attempt was not a promising one; but it was the best that could be done. The interval of several days that had elapsed since the expeditionary force had appeared on the bayou, had sufficed for Pemberton to reinforce the Confederate officer of Vicksburg with some six or eight brigades; and although the force was much inferior to that of Sherman, it had the advantage of occupying a seemingly impregnable position.

The morning of the 29th the left storming column was formed of Morgan's division, strengthened by the brigades of Blair and Thayer, about noon moved forward to traverse the dry part of the lake, under cover of a furious cannonade. The story is brief and bloody. "When within four hundred yards," says the Confederate General S. D. Lee, who commanded the brigade at this point, "our infantry opened — the enemy coming to within one hundred and fifty yards of my lines. Here our fire was so terrible that they broke, but in a few moments rallied again, sending a force to my left to turn my left flank. This force was soon met, and handsomely repulsed. The force in my front was also repulsed. Our fire was so severe that the enemy laid down to receive it. Seeing their confusion, the twenty-sixth Louisiana, and a part of the seventeenth Louisiana, were marched on the battle-field, and under their cover twenty-one commissioned offi-cers, three hundred and eleven non-commissioned officers and privates, were taken prisoners, four stands of colors, and five hundred stand of arms captured. The enemy left in great confusion, leaving their dead on the field."

The attack of the Union general, Morgan Smith, across the sand-bar on the right, was no more successful than that of Morgan. It was observed that the bank of the bayou op-posite this sand-bar was about fifteen feet high, and it was further increased by an embankment or levee of three feet in height. It was very steep, and, the soil being sandy, the sides had caved in, so that the brow overhung about a foot and a half. To ascend it was utterly impossible without digging a road, and this would have to be done under a deadly fire from the enemy. The path across the sand-bar was about two hundred yards in length, exposed to a double cross-fire, and the only approach to it was over a flat bottom covered with fallen trees. It was, however, resolved to attempt the enterprise, and the sixth Missouri regiment was detailed to lead the van. Of this regiment two companies volunteered for the perilous duty of digging away the bank, so that when the storming-column came, it might be able to pass ahead unobstructed. Rushing forward, these brave fellows reached the shelter of the bank, and set to work at the excavation — the enemy's sharpshooters being over their heads, within a few feet, and so near that when the Confed-erates reached their guns over the bank and depressed them, the Union soldiers below could readily have crossed bayonets

with them.   The remainder of the sixth Missouri then went
forward in aid of their comrades; but for some reason the
assault was long delayed, and after the failure of Morgan's
attack it was too late, and Sherman ordered the regiment
back under cover of darkness.

The failure was conspicuous, and entailed a loss of 1929
killed, wounded, and missing; the Confederate casualties
were 209.   The result left in the mind of General Sherman
no hope of being able to force the Confederate line by a
direct attack; but it was surmised that something might be
gained by another combination.   This was to throw ten
thousand men in transports up the Yazoo, to effect a landing,
under cover of the navy, at the extreme right of the Confederate line, where the range of hills abuts at Haynes's Bluff,
and assail the batteries on that flank, while the rest of the
force preserved its position at Chickasaw Bayou and attacked
to hold the enemy there.   This movement was to have been
made during the night of the 31st December, but a dense
fog rendered it impracticable then, and for other reasons it was
afterwards abandoned.   Sherman, accordingly, re-embarked
his troops on the 2d of January, 1862, dropped down the
Yazoo to the Mississippi, where he was met by General
McClernand, who had been sent down to assume command
of the expedition.   By that officer the force was ordered to
Milliken's Bend, a great elbow made by a curve in the Mississippi, twelve miles above Vicksburg.   The four divisions
were formed into two corps — the Thirteenth under General
Morgan; the Fifteenth under General Sherman.

Not till he had abandoned the Yazoo attempt as hopeless
did Sherman learn the ill fortune that had overtaken Grant,
compelling that officer to renounce his part of the co-operative effort against Vicksburg, and fall back to his old line on
the Memphis and Charleston Railroad.   And now Grant
learnt also the ill fortune that had overtaken Sherman.   The

whole scheme against Vicksburg had failed; and the baffled commander was forced to find out some new device.

The failure of this campaign, by narrowing the circle of possibilities, made one conclusion manifest. It was evidently impracticable for Grant to attempt to move his force overland from the line of the Memphis and Charleston Railroad to the rear of Vicksburg; for even should he, in a renewed effort, succeed in forcing Pemberton back to Vicksburg, an advance by that line would be of no avail, and would not enable him to apply his force in the work of siege, since, until the Yazoo could be opened up, he would be without communication and without supplies. It would be merely to make a laborious and aimless march to the vicinity of Vicksburg, when the same end might be attained by transferring the army by water to Milliken's Bend, there to make a junction with the two corps under McClernand. Perceiving this, Grant resolved to make this transfer by water: so leaving merely sufficient force to hold important points in Southern Tennessee and Northern Mississippi, he, during the month of January, 1863, sent forward the bulk of his force from Memphis in transports down the Mississippi. McClernand advantageously employed the interval in making an expedition, attended by Porter's fleet, up the Arkansas River to Fort Hindman, which he reduced, compelling the surrender of the garrison of several thousand men. By the end of January the whole army found itself on the west bank of the Mississippi, in the vicinity of Milliken's Bend, and at Young's Point, a few miles above Vicksburg. Grant, having arrived at Young's Point the 2d of February, applied himself to see what was next to be done. Let us mark this as the initiation of the second series of efforts against Vicksburg.

When Grant sat down to study thus close at hand the problem of the capture of Vicksburg, it was soon manifest that the circle of possible operations was in reality very restricted. The army was on the west side of the Mississippi: it was necessary to cross to the east side, and then, by swinging round in the rear of Vicksburg, either beat Pemberton in the open field, or (if he should retire within the defences) place that stronghold under siege. This transfer of the army might be made either above Vicksburg or below it; but in both cases the thought of how the operation could be effected was most perplexing. If the army should cross the Mississippi below, it would wholly sever itself from a base, seeing that the Vicksburg batteries barred the navigation of the river. The movement above, by the Yazoo, was an inviting one, for that river presented an excellent line of supplies. But the Yazoo, too, was closed by the batteries at Haynes's Bluff, and the approaches to Vicksburg were — what Sherman had found them! Unless, therefore, the obstruction to the navigation of the Mississippi presented by the Vicksburg batteries, or of the Yazoo by the Haynes's Bluff batteries, could be in some way obviated, it seemed impossible to move a step in any plan of operating against Vicksburg. The months of February and March were spent in a series of experiments to obviate this difficulty. They were protracted and arduous: but as they were also wholly futile, I shall confine this recital to a very brief statement of their nature and object.

Of the five expedients to which Grant resorted during the months of February and March, three were designed to overcome the obstacles to the navigation of the Mississippi presented by the Vicksburg batteries, and two to overcome the obstacle to the navigation of the Yazoo, prevented by the batteries at Haynes's Bluff. The first was the canal expedient. This project was a renewal of the attempt which had been made by General Williams in July of the previous year, when the fleet first went up to Vicksburg from New Orleans, and consisted of a cut-off, a mile across the peninsula, formed by a sharp elbow in the Mississippi, opposite the town. If successful in forming a new channel for the Mississippi, it would isolate Vicksburg, and enable transports to pass safely to the new base of operations below. The work was prosecuted for many weeks with great energy and under many difficulties, the chief of which resulted from a rapid rise in the river, that threatened to inundate the camp and the canal. It seemed likely, however, that success would crown the effort, when finally, on the 8th of March, the rise of the river brought so great a pressure upon the dam across the canal near the upper end, at the main Mississippi levee, that it gave way, and let through the low lands back of where the Union camps were a torrent of water that separated the north and south shores of the peninsula as effectually as if the Mississippi flowed between them. The canal project was abandoned.

The second expedient was the opening a practicable route through the bayous which run from near Milliken's Bend, and through Roundabout Bayou and Tensas River into the Mississippi, near New Carthage, below Vicksburg. This also was tried : dredge boats were put to work clearing a passage, and a few small craft were finally able to pass through. But as the river began to fall in April, and the roads between Milliken's Bend and New Carthage grew passable, it became unnecessary to continue work on this route.

The third project was the Lake Providence route. This lake, situated seventy-five miles north of Vicksburg, on the Louisiana side of the Mississippi, is but a mile west of that river, and this opening a canal between the two would afford a navigable route through the lake, Bayou Boele, Bayou Macone, and the Tensas, Wachita, and Red Rivers, into the Mississippi. This project was not greatly esteemed, and after some time it was abandoned.

The fourth expedient and the one that promised best, had for its object to open a route to the rear of the Haynes's Bluff

batteries, on the Yazoo.   The method in which it was proposed to reach this position, will illustrate the extraordinary
hydrographic characteristics of the region in which the army
was operating.   Far north of Vicksburg, Yazoo Pass, a narrow tortuous channel, runs eastward from the Mississippi
into Moon Lake, whence again issuing eastward, it flows into
Coldwater River which empties into the Tallahatchie, which
debouches into the Yazoo.   This was the course the expeditionary force was to take.   It consisted of one division of
McClernand's corps, with two Missouri regiments of Sherman's corps or sharpshooters — the right kind of transportation could not be obtained for more force — and it started at
the end of February, the transports being preceded by a number of Porter's gun-boats.   With immense labor the fleet succeeded in reaching the Coldwater, the 2d of March, and after
this it was expected the course to the Yazoo would be much
easier.   "But," says General Grant, "while my forces were
opening one end of the Pass the enemy was diligently closing
the other."   The Confederates some time previously had skill-
fully chosen and fortified an excellent position to obstruct such
a movement.   Near where the Tallahatchie empties into the
Yazoo, they had constructed Fort Pemberton, a powerful
work of earth and cotton bales, that perfectly commanded the
angle of junction of both rivers ; and they obstructed the
former stream by a raft and sunken vessel.   The Union expeditionary force arrived before the work on the 11th of March ;
but from the first, difficulties beset it.   It was found that the
low ground around the fort was entirely overflowed ; so that
no movement could be made by the army to reduce the work
until the gun-boats should silence the enemy's guns.   But
this, after protracted trial, they were unable to effect, and
after remaining until March 21st, and being joined by
Quimby's division of McPherson's corps, the expedition
returned.

There was now remaining the fifth and final preliminary

expedition. While this force was still before Fort Pember-ton, Admiral Porter had reconnoitred another route by which it was hoped a descent might be made above the Haynes's Bluff batteries. This route was still more intricate than the other. Seven miles above the mouth of the Yazoo, Steele's bayou empties into that river; thirty miles up Steele's bayou, Black bayou enters it from Deer Creek, six miles dis-tant; and descending the Big Sunflower forty-one miles, one finds himself again in the Yazoo, sixty miles from its mouth. So many difficulties, however, were encountered from over-hanging trees and other causes, that the project also was given up after prodigious labors spent in the endeavor to carry it out. "The expedition," says General Grant, "failed prob-ably more from want of knowledge as to what would be re-quired to open this route than from any impractibility in the navigation of the streams and bayous through which it was proposed to pass. Want of this knowledge led the expe-dition on and difficulties were encountered, and then it would become necessary to send back to Young's Point for the means of removing them. This gave the enemy time to move forces to effectually checkmate further progress, and the expedition was withdrawn when within a few hundred yards of free and open navigation to the Yazoo."

Thus five-fold failure rested on the operations against Vicks-burg. But through these very failures the mind of the com-mander had wrought its way out to clearness of vision, and at that very stage when an intellect of less determined fibre would have been resigning itself to a seemingly implacable fortune, Grant, overleaping fate and failure, rose to the height of that audacious conception on which at length, he vaulted into Vicksburg.

II.

THE SIEGE AND FALL OF VICKSBURG.

It was apparent to General Grant from the moment he went in person to Young's Point that the true line of operations against Vicksburg was from the south; but if he was prompted first to exhaust every other expedient, it was because the difficulties seen to beset that mode of action were in reality appalling. It would be necessary first of all to march the army for thirty or forty miles down the west bank of the Mississippi, so as to gain a point where the passage might be made below the enemy's works. It would be requisite that the gun-boats and transports should run the gauntlet of the batteries, in order to cross the army to the east bank and cover the passage. It would then remain to make the crossing of that great and difficult river in face of all the opposition the enemy could bring against the operation. And when these three conditions should be fulfilled, the perils that in the very nature of things attended the execution of the plan, would only have begun. For it would then be necessary for Grant to cut himself entirely off from his base, and launch into the interior of the land, without a new base secured in advance — with the promise of any base at all contingent upon his beating the enemy in the open field, swinging round in rear of Vicksburg, and so operating with his right as to force open the line of the Yazoo.

These considerations serve to fix the character of the plan of operations. It cannot be called a brilliant strategic inspiration, for the move was an obvious one, and had suggested itself even to the rank and file of the army. But if the conception was easy, the execution involved difficulties that might well affright the stoutest heart. Of this there could be no more striking proof than is presented in the fact that the high-vaulting and audacious mind of Sherman shrank

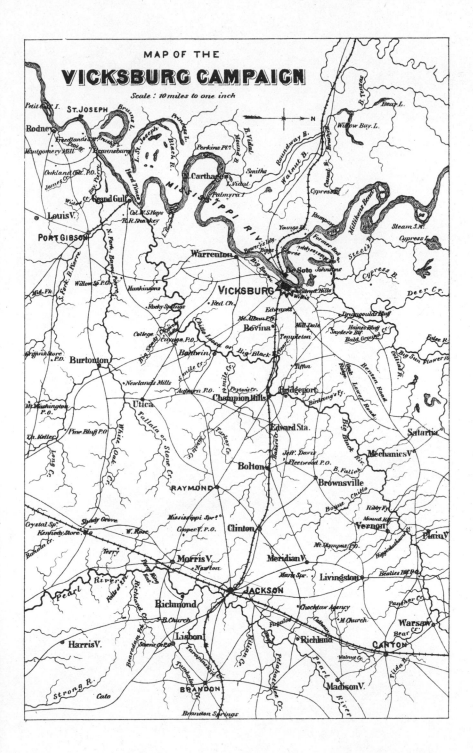

MAP OF THE

VICKSBURG CAMPAIGN

Scale : 10 miles to one inch

from the enterprise ; and on the 8th of April, after the movement below had been initiated, that officer, in a written communication to General Grant, suggested that the army should be transported back to the line of the Tallahatchie and Yallabusha, as a base of operations against Vicksburg. It can only be said that there was that in the composition of General Grant's mind that prompted him to undertake that which no one else would have adventured. Unmoved by all the perils of the operation,. he resolved to go below.

The movement was initiated on the 29th of March, 1863, when the Thirteenth Corps, under General McClernand, was put in motion to cross the peninsula opposite Vicksburg from Milliken's Bend to New Carthage. The march was made with much difficulty, and in face of many obstacles, and finally, when New Carthage was reached, the region was found to have been converted by inundation into an island : so that the advance had to be pushed twelve miles further south, making the distance to be traversed from Milliken's Bend thirty-five miles. McClernand's corps was followed, as fast as supplies and ammunition could be transported over horribly bad roads by the Seventeenth Corps, under McPherson.

This the initial operation being completed, it next fell to Admiral Porter to execute the perilous enterprise of running the gauntlet of the batteries for the purpose of affording the force below the means of passing the Mississippi, and protection in the operation. This exploit was performed in the most brilliant manner, the fleet of gun-boats, together with three transports laden with stores, and protected in their vulnerable parts with hay and cotton, were prepared on the 16th to make the trial trip. The expedition was readily manned by eager volunteers, and under cover of the darkness, the vessels succeeded in passing safely through the fiery ordeal, with the loss of but one of the transports, which was set on fire by a shell. These boats succeeded in getting by

so well, that General Grant ordered six more to be prepared
in like manner for running the batteries; and on the night
of the 22d of April five of them made the passage, one being lost.   The damage suffered by the transports was soon
repaired, and five were found available for service, as were
also six barges out of twelve that had been sent in tow of
the last six boats that ran the blockade.

It now remained to make the passage of the Mississippi.
This operation it was resolved to execute at Grand Gulf,
where the lowest of the Vicksburg system of works was located.   This point is seventy-five miles below Milliken's
Bend, and as the water transportation was insufficient for the
conveyance, they made the march overland to Hard Times,
opposite Grand Gulf.   For the reduction of this latter place,
a combined land and naval force was prepared, and on the
29th of April, Porter, with the fleet and so much of McClernand's corps as could be embarked on the transports, moved
against it.   With his wonted energy, Porter commenced the
attack, which was continued for several hours.   But the
Grand Gulf batteries, erected on high bluffs, proved too
strong for the navy, and Grant, fearing to risk his men in an
attempt at storming the works, determined to turn them by
landing at a point lower down the river.   To carry out this
object, he directed the army to march by the right bank, and
to be prepared to cross opposite Bruinsburg; whilst the transports should, as soon as it became dark, run the fire of the
batteries at Grand Gulf, and so take up positions in readiness
to ferry the army across.   These movements, both by land
and water, were accomplished without loss.   The 30th,
McClernand's corps was safely ferried across and landed on
the east bank of the Mississippi, and started out on the road
to Port Gibson, twelve miles north-east of Bruinsburg, and in
the rear of Grand Gulf.   McPherson's corps followed as
rapidly as it could be put across the river.   The initial
movement was thus in every respect a success — a result due

to the vigor of the execution and the skill with which the enemy's attention was called off to another quarter. The latter operation was entrusted to General Sherman, whose corps, while the others were marching southward, remained at Milliken's Bend. While McClernand and McPherson were crossing at Bruinsburg, Sherman was directed "to make a demonstration on Haynes's Bluff, and to make all the *show* possible." Accordingly on the morning of the 29th, he embarked Blair's division on ten steamers, and, preceded by several iron-clads and gun-boats, the expedition steamed up the Yazoo and lay for the night at the mouth of Chickasaw Bayou, the scene of the repulse the previous December. Next morning the fleet proceeded up within easy range of the enemy's batteries, and for four hours kept up an energetic demonstration. Waiting till towards evening, Sherman caused the troops to disembark in full view of the enemy, and seemingly prepare to assault; "but," says he, "I knew full well that there was no road across the submerged field that lay between the river and the bluff." This produced the desired effect on the Confederates, who could be seen bestirring themselves to meet a forceful attack, which, however, was quite off the purpose of Sherman, who, keeping up appearances till dark, re-embarked his troops. Next day similar movements were made on both sides of the Yazoo, and Sherman then received orders to hasten forward to Grand Gulf.

The *ruse* had succeeded admirably; for while, on the last day of April and the first day of May, Sherman was menacing the approaches to Vicksburg from the Yazoo, the other two corps of the army, seventy-five miles below, had made the passage of the Mississippi, and gained a firm footing on the "high plateau in rear of Vicksburg." Let us now follow the movements of this force.

Having crossed to Bruinsburg during the forenoon of the 30th of April, the van corps under McClernand, after waiting only long enough to draw and distribute four days' rations, was directed by General Grant to move out on the road to Port Gibson, and attain the bluffs some three miles back from the river. The highlands were reached without opposition some time before sunset, and McClernand, deeming it important to surprise the enemy if he should be found in the neighborhood of Port Gibson, pushed on by a forced march that night. An hour after midnight, the vanguard, on arriving within four miles of Port Gibson, was accosted by a light fire of infantry that revealed the presence of the enemy. The troops were then rested on their arms during the short remnant of the night, and at dawn, May 1st, found a Confederate force drawn up to dispute the advance. This proved to be a part of a division which, under General Bowen, had been stationed at Grand Gulf, the left of Pemberton's line. When, on the previous afternoon, Bowen discovered that the Union force was crossing the Mississippi at Bruinsburg, he moved out from Grand Gulf towards Port Gibson, eight miles to the southward, and took position three or four miles in advance of that place to dispute its possession with the Union corps. His division numbered about five thousand men.

The nature of ground in this region makes it extremely defensible, seeing that the roads usually run on narrow, elevated ridges, with deep and impenetrable ravines on either side. Aided by this circumstance, the Confederates made a very stubborn defence, and succeeded in protracting the contest throughout the day, during which, however, they were driven from successive positions with heavy loss, all the four divisions of McClernand's corps and Logan's division of McPherson's corps being brought into action. The Union casualties numbered nearly a thousand; but the success was worth what it cost. During the night Bowen withdrew from Port Gibson, and, having burnt the bridge over the south fork of Bayou Pierre opposite the town, retired across the north fork of Bayou Pierre and took position between that stream and Grand Gulf. Here he was joined the 2d of May by Loring's division from Jackson; but as, during that day, the Union engineers had rebuilt the bridge, and Grant pressed forward to cut off the Confederate force, Bowen and Loring retired northward, crossed the Big Black at Hankinson's Ferry, and thence were ordered by Pemberton to the vicinity of Vicksburg. As, at the same time, the Confederate garrison holding the fortified position of Grand Gulf withdrew, Grant shifted his base of supplies from Bruinsburg to that place. Leaving now the Union army, its banners gilded by the success of the initial operations, to pursue its advance on the rear of Vicksburg, let us review the situation as a whole, and inquire what preparations had been made by the Confederate general to resist the threatened attack.

Towards the close of the year 1862, the Richmond authorities had put into the hands of General J. E. Johnston the military control of the entire western theatre of war — a command embracing both the army of General Bragg in Tennessee, and the army of General Pemberton in Mississippi. At this period he made his head-quarters with General Bragg at Tullahoma, where he was in constant communication with General Pemberton. Now, up to the middle of April, all the dispatches that Johnston received from General Pemberton conveyed the opinion of that officer that Grant would abandon his attempts against Vicksburg — an opinion which, considering the constant failure of the many efforts, was certainly not devoid of plausibility. But he soon found out how greatly he had misinterpreted the purpose of his adversary, for on the 16th of April the fleet passed the batteries, and immediately afterwards the concentration of the army opposite Grand Gulf revealed the real intent of the Union commander. Rudely undeceived by this manifestation, Pemberton, on the 29th telegraphed to Johnston : "The enemy is at Hard Times in large force, with barges and transports, indicating a purpose to attack Grand Gulf with a view to Vicksburg." Scarcely however had this dispatch reached Johnston than Grant, slipping below Grand Gulf, rapidly launched his army across the Mississippi, and before there was time for reply, Pemberton enveloped in the toils of his adversary's bold manœuvres, found it was no longer a question of how to prevent Grant's crossing but how to save Vicksburg. His dispatch of May 1st told the dread story in these words: "A furious battle has been going on since daylight just below Port Gibson . . Enemy can cross all his army from Hard Times to Bruinsburg. I should have large reinforcements. Enemy's movements threaten Jackson, and if successful cut off Vicksburg and Port Hudson." To this Johnston replied immediately, urging Pemberton to "unite all his troops and beat Grant" — excellent advice, no doubt, but of little avail in the actual circumstances of the case.

The situation in which Pemberton found himself when Grant had gained a foothold on the east bank of the Mississippi, was one that demanded a decisive stroke. For the question forced upon him for solution was not one of tactics, but of grand strategy — a question that could be rightly answered only by a mind capable of rising above the letter of war to the spirit of war. This question was, shall Vicksburg be abandoned?

Now, what was Vicksburg? Assuredly nothing but a water-battery for the obstruction of the Mississippi. But when on the night of the 16th of April, the fleet ran the blockade and passed below Vicksburg, that stronghold had ceased to fulfil its functions. In this new shift of affairs, the duty of the Confederate commander changed with it. This did not concern the defence of a post that had become useless: it was his business now to see to the safety of his army, and to foil his antagonist. The communications of the Confederate force at Vicksburg ran eastward by the railroad through Jackson : so that it was only by retiring to that point or beyond, or to a position on the flank that the commander could preserve his interior lines, and the means of being reinforced by Johnston. Grant, the moment he landed on the east bank, menaced to lay hold of this line of retreat, and in fact made Vicksburg untenable. That stronghold might be the tomb of an army, but was of no imaginable utility to the Confederates.

Pemberton was a brave man, and spite of the sinister views of the people of Vicksburg, devoted heart and soul to the insurgent cause, was nevertheless not capable of comprehending such considerations. He had been put to defend Vicksburg, he had gained whatever reputation he had won in its defence, and he had come to regard it in the same manner as General Halleck regarded Harper's Ferry — as a place that could lose its importance by no conceivable change of fortune. He had within its lines supplies for sixty days, he had of troops thirty odd thousand, and he resolved to "hold Vicksburg as long as possible." Accordingly, with this intent, he caused the division of Bowen, after it had been compelled to abandon Port Gibson, and the troops that had been forwarded from Jackson for his reinforcement, to cross the Big Black, and uniting his command, took position behind that river, on the railroad to Jackson, a few miles east of Vicksburg. There he awaited Grant's movements, which were as decided as those of the Confederate were unsure and vascillating.

The region in the rear of Vicksburg, by which Grant was now moving from the south, derives its main military characteristics from the Big Black and its numerous affluents. This stream, rising in Northern Mississippi, flows south-eastward, passes Vicksburg at the distance of ten or twelve miles to the east, and empties into the Mississippi River at Grand Gulf. From Grand Gulf, the temporary base of the army, a line drawn north-east for the length of sixty miles, will strike Jackson, the capital of Mississippi, forty-six miles due east of Vicksburg, with which place it is connected by a line of railroad.

The Confederate force that was driven from Port Gibson had been followed northward to where the direct road from that place to Vicksburg crosses the Big Black at Hankinson's Ferry. Here Grant waited from the 3d to the 8th of May for wagons, supplies, and Sherman's corps. Meantime he sent detachments across the Big Black to make demonstrations of advancing directly upon Vicksburg, which is but about twenty miles north of Hankinson's. But he had no real intention of operating by that line, and only designed to retain Pemberton near Vicksburg while he made a great detour eastward, to guard against any hostile menace to his rear when he should turn westward towards the Mississippi stronghold. Specifically, his purpose was with the left and centre (corps of McClernand and Sherman), to hug close the left or east bank of the Big Black, striking the Vicksburg and Jackson Railroad about midway between these two points, in the vicinity of Edward's Station and Bolton, while he thrust out the right (McPherson's corps) eastward *via* Raymond to Jackson, where it was to destroy the railroad, public stores, etc., and then turning westward, rejoin the main force. The four days from the 8th to the 12th of May were employed in executing these marches. By the latter day Sherman and McClernand had approached nearly to the railroad, at the designated points, which would have been attained in another march. But developments in the region where McPherson was operating caused a slight change of orders. That officer had on the 12th of May, when nearing Raymond, been met by a force of two Confederate brigades, which he overthrew after a two hours' combat. They then retreated upon Jackson, against which McPherson had been directed to march. Now, no solicitude would have been felt touching McPherson's ability to deal with this force; but that same night, General Grant received tidings that reinforcements were daily arriving at Jackson, and that General Johnston was hourly expected there to take command in person. Determining, therefore, to make sure of that place, and leave no force in his rear, Grant altered the previous orders to Sherman and McClernand to strike the railroad at Edward's Station, and directed the whole army upon Jackson. By the morning of the 14th of May Sherman and McPherson had neared Jackson, and McClernand was within supporting distance, at Clinton and Raymond.

On the night of the 13th General Johnston reached Jackson. He found there the brigades of Gregg and Walker that had the day before fallen back before McPherson from Raymond, learnt that Pemberton was at Edward's Station and ascertained that Grant was approaching Jackson. He knew that fragments of Confederate forces were coming towards Jackson from the east and south that would swell the command he would have in hand to eleven thousand, and *hoped* they might arrive in time to enable him to make a stand at Jackson.

It took little time for that acute strategist to discern how false was the situation in which the two Confederate detachments were placed, with the Union army planted between the force under Pemberton and the command he was gathering at Jackson; and instantly comprehending the importance of concentration, he that night directed him to move up to Clifton in rear of the Union force — which, however, he was mistaken in supposing to be a mere detachment. He added: " To beat such a detachment would be of immense value. The troops here could co-operate. All the strength you can quickly assemble should be brought. Time is all-important." But Johnston was doomed to be disappointed in one case and disobeyed in the other. General Pemberton did not heed his instructions to move towards Clinton, and the detachments he was expecting did not reach Jackson : so that when Sherman and McPherson neared that place on the morning of the

14th Johnston had no more than the two brigades of Gregg and Walker. With these he made a rear-guard fight of two hours, in order to gain time for the removal of the public stores, and then retreated six miles northward on the Canton road. The town was then occupied by the Union force, and Grant, leaving Sherman in Jackson to destroy the railroads, bridges, arsenals, etc., about-faced the remainder of the army to march westward, parallel with the railroad, to Edward's Station, Vicksburg-wards.

Let us now see with what fatal certainty Pemberton, by his ill-judged motions, was entangling himself in toils from which at length there was no escape. When on the morning of May 14th he received Johnston's order to march out and attack Grant's rear at Clinton, Pemberton, with his main field force of seventeen thousand men, held position at Edward's Station. Had he obeyed the order, though it is wholly unlikely that he could have carried out the intent of making head against Grant, yet by moving by the left he would, at least have been in position to reach Johnston. But Pemberton had preconceived another plan of action. Incapable of ridding himself of the notion that Vicksburg was his base, he circumscribed all his manœuvres within such limits as would enable him to cover that position. Still it was obviously necessary for him to do something; so he called a council of war. A majority of the officers approved the movement indicated by General Johnston — the others preferred a movement aiming to cut off Grant's supplies from the Mississippi. "My own views," says General Pemberton, "were expressed as unfavorable to any movement which would remove me from my base, which was and is Vicksburg. I did not, however, see fit to place my own judgment and opinions so far in opposition as to prevent the movement altogether; but believing the only possibility of success to be in the plan proposed, of cutting off the enemy's supplies, I directed all my disposable force — say seventeen thousand five hundred — toward Raymond."

Now, what was the nature of the manœuvre which Pemberton thus proposed? In advancing upon Jackson from the Mississippi, the base of the Union army was Grand Gulf, whence it drew its supplies; but when the movement was so completely developed that Grant had reached Clinton (where he was at the time of Johnston's order to Pemberton), he of course exposed his whole line of communications to the Confederate force at Edward's Station. To Pemberton, therefore, it appeared a bold and decisive stroke to march south-eastward from Edward's Station towards Raymond, and thus lay hold of this vital line.

Let us do justice to what of merit there was in this conception: in other circumstances it would have been a correct move. But in the actual facts of the case, the luckless Pemberton was sallying forth to assail a wind-mill, not a real giant. Grant had ceased to have any line of communications. As early as the 11th, five days before this time, he had caused the haversacks of the men to be filled with rations, had telegraphed that he "would communicate no more with Grand Gulf," and having cut his army entirely loose from the Mississippi, marched it forth as a movable column, relying on what supplies were on hand, and what could be obtained from the country, until, having completed his movement, he should burst open the line of Yazoo, and thereby gain a new base on the Mississippi. Little, therefore, recked he of the obsolete depot at Grand Gulf, or any line connecting him therewith — let the enemy swoop down upon it at will — it would only play into his hands!

Big with this doughty purpose, Pemberton — not hastily, but taking thirty hours to ruminate his mighty intent — set his column in motion the afternoon of the 15th south-eastward from Edward's Station towards Raymond. After an advance of four or five miles, night came on, and put a pause to the march. But while he had been dallying, Grant, clear of purpose, had all that day, since early morning, been hastening forward the column by forced marches from Jackson, westward : so that by night the troops lay within a few miles of Edward's Station, the pickets being in contact with those of Pemberton, where he lay on the middle Raymond road. It was now apparent to Pemberton that his march to the south of the railroad, far from harming his adversary, had already compromised his own safety. Next morning, May 16th, this became still more manifest, and as at the same time he received a despatch from Johnston, reiterating anew the order to move north-eastward, so as to make a junction with him, he was willing enough at last to obey. He therefore gave the order to countermarch on Edward's Station, and thence move on Brownsville, fifteen miles to the northeast — an excellent move that would have permitted a Union with Johnston, who was edging constantly westward to be near Pemberton. But this good resolution came too late. Pemberton would have to cross the front of the Union army, already near at hand, and as Grant, on the morning of the 16th launched forward to Edward's Station, Pemberton was caught in his sin, and compelled to form line of battle to meet a collision now become inevitable. The Confederate troops were hastily disposed upon the strong position of Champion Hills, a short distance in the rear, and the rival forces were presently precipitated into an action that decided the fate of Vicksburg.

As the Union force approached, it was with no more than the heads of columns — Hovey's division of McClernand's corps, followed by McPherson's corps of two divisions, being on the direct road from Jackson to Vicksburg, while McClernand with the three remaining divisions of his command, and Blair's division of Sherman's corps was on the roads to the southward, the roads from Raymond to Edward's Station. Sherman's two other divisions were still in the vicinity of

Jackson. But as Grant early in the morning saw that battle was inevitable, he ordered Sherman forward in all haste.

The position of Pemberton was one of great natural strength. His left (Stevenson's division) occupying Champion Hill, a thickly wooded height to the south of the road, on the right of which the timber extends a short distance down the hill and then opens into cultivated fields on a gentle slope and into a valley extending for a considerable distance; his centre (Bowen's division) extended across Baker's Creek, and his right (Loring's division) still farther southward in a thick wood which covered a seeming chaos of abrupt hills and yawning ravines.

Hovey's division brought up against the enemy's left and was disposed for the attack in the wooded ravine and on the hill-side. McPherson's two divisions and Logan and Crocker were thrown to the right of the wood so as to envelop completely the Confederate flank. The four divisions of McClernand were coming into line opposite the enemy's right and centre. While the latter was bringing up and disposing his troops, skirmishing had grown so hot between Hovey's division and the Confederate left that at eleven it swelled into a battle. The commander had not desired to bring on the conflict until the heavy force of McClernand on the left should have come up; but the enemy in front of that officer presented a front of artillery and infantry where it was impossible from the nature of the ground and the density of the front to discover his numbers, so that no headway was made there. Thus Hovey made the attack alone, and though it was executed with great gallantry it was repulsed with severe loss, and two brigades of Crocker's division had to be thrown in to brace up this front. All the time Logan's division was working on the enemy's left flank and the nature of the ground was such as to develop the happiest results from this manœuvre. It was afterwards found that the Vicksburg road, after following the ridge in a southerly direction for about one mile, and to where it intersects one of the Raymond roads, turns almost due west down the hill, and across the valley in which Logan was operating. From this circumstance it came about that Logan's manœuvre threatened directly the enemy's rear — a fact that soon wonderfully weakened the front attacks. Pemberton, however, by drawing troops from his right, restored the equilibrium and was able to take the offensive against Hovey's division, which after struggling bravely against the adverse tide, was overborne, as were also the supports drawn from McPherson's corps. Yet the troops retired stubbornly, and having found partial cover re-formed : an enfilading fire of artillery was then gained upon the enemy, and the hostile line recoiled back to its own place.

Meanwhile Logan, who having worked well round to the enemy's rear, had taken in the full importance of the menacing position he held, rode up to Grant and told him that " if Hovey could make another dash, he would come up from where he was and capture the greater part of the enemy." This was executed as soon as the dispositions could be made ; but as Pemberton had now apprehended how thoroughly his position was compromised, he began to draw off. Hovey and Logan and McClernand then pressed forward and the Confederates, completely broken up, fled in panic rout from the field. Indeed, so rapid was the disintegration and so quickly did the Union force press forward in pursuit, that when the right Confederate division and Loring's came to follow the others from the field, it found the crossing already commanded by Grant and its retreat cut off. It was with difficulty that Loring succeeded under cover of darkness in extricating his force, but being unable to cross the Big Black, he could not join Pemberton and was compelled to make a great detour by the south and east to Jackson, where he reported to Johnston three days afterwards. The Confederates lost many guns in the action of Champion Hill and also heavily in casualities. Nor was the victory purchased without a sacrifice of above two thousand men on the Union side — of which number Hovey's division lost above twelve hundred. The pursuit was continued till after dark — the Union force taking possession of Edward's Station.

The following day, May 17th, McClernand's corps took the advance, with McPherson in support, whilst Sherman, with the pontoon train, was directed to cross the river at Bridgeport. No opposition was encountered until reaching the Big Black, distant six miles. The greater part of Pemberton's army had already been transferred to the west side, but a considerable force had been left on the east bank, and had taken position to dispute the passage of the Big Black, behind a line of intrenchments, both flanks of which rested on the river, and in front of which was a miry slough. After several hours' skirmishing, it was discovered by General Lawler that, by moving under cover of the river from the right flank, a position could be gained from which the line might be successfully assaulted. This was accordingly ordered, and the charge, executed with great spirit, resulted in carrying the whole work, with all its artillery, eighteen guns. Fleeing towards a stream which formed a bridge across the Big Black, many of the Confederates escaped to the west side; but some fifteen hundred were cut off and captured. The enemy, however, succeeded in burning the bridge over which he had passed, two other steamers, and the railroad bridge. This compelled a halt to construct the means of crossing — a task which was accomplished during the night. Sherman, at the same time, passed the Big Black by a pontoon bridge at Bridgeport.

That same Sunday afternoon, the citizens of Vicksburg were startled by the influx of a mob of demoralized fugitives, the wreck of the Confederate army. For two weeks that hapless body had been marched and countermarched in aimless adventure, brought constantly into action in fractions, only to be as constantly overthrown, and now, depressed and disheartened by two weeks of accumulated disaster, it tumbled into the lines that engirdled the city of a hundred hills. Too plainly the citizens saw that evil days awaited them. Their confidence in the commander was completely shaken, and it was with many a sad foreboding that they looked back on all they had suffered during the time since — just a twelve month ago — Farragut had fired his first shot into the town. As for the unfortunate Pemberton, deluded still by his one fixed idea of defending Vicksburg, he threw away the last opportunity presented to him of saving his army. Had he, after the retreat from the Big Black promptly withdrawn the garrison from the town, and directed his column north-westward on the Benton road, he might readily have marched to Vernon, and made a junction with Johnston, who had moved thither. There is not even for him the excuse that the abandonment of Vicksburg would have been an unwarrantable stretch of responsibility on his part; for, as soon as Johnston received tidings of Pemberton's having fallen back to the Big Black, he not only allowed, but ordered him to evacuate Vicksburg. " If Haines's Bluff," wrote he, " be untenable, Vicksburg is of no value, and cannot be held. If, therefore, you are invested in Vicksburg, you must ultimately surrender. Under such circumstances, instead of losing both troops and place, you must, if possible, save the troops. If it is not too late, evacuate Vicksburg and its dependencies, and march to the north-east."

These prescient words — this clear trumpet-sound — came to Pemberton the morning after he had retired within the lines of Vicksburg. There was even yet, perhaps, opportunity to obey the summons, for Grant, having been compelled during the night to bridge the Big Black, was only then putting his columns in motion, and could not arrive before afternoon. Pemberton hesitated, and was lost. He called a council of war: the officers were unanimous for the rejection of Johnston's order; but the reason was a most strange one — " it was decided that it was impossible to withdraw the army with such *morale* and material as to be of further service to the Confederacy." Pemberton, therefore, replied: " I have decided to hold Vicksburg as long as possible, with the firm hope that the Government may yet be able to assist me in keeping this obstruction to the enemy's free navigation of the Mississippi River. I still conceive it to be the most important point in the Confederacy." While yet the debate went on, it was suddenly interrupted by the booming of guns from without the works; and the Union army, spreading out in quick deployment before the lines of Vicksburg, laid the city under siege.

Thus terminated, in eighteen days from the time the army crossed the Mississippi, the remarkable series of manœuvres by which General Grant succeeded in shutting up the Confederates within the defences of Vicksburg, whence they were not to issue save as prisoners of war. If it has been noted that this result was due in part to the extraordinary errors committed by the enemy, it must at the same time be conceded that the conduct of the Union commander was marked by great skill and energy — and that, if his motions were such as might have brought evil consequences under different circumstances, they were justified by the inchoate condition of the enemy's military preparations; for by such rapid strides had the campaign advanced, that Johnston had not time to gather force enough to make even a show of resistance, and Pemberton, by his disregard of his superior's orders, played directly into the hands of Grant in so acting as to insure his being shut up in Vicksburg. ·

By the morning of the 10th of May, Grant had encompassed the Vicksburg defences, which consisted of a system of detached redoubts, connected by rifle-trenches. The ground was difficult, being composed of commanding ridges, with intervening ravines covered with a dense growth of cane and wild grape. The Union lines were drawn within musket range of the works, with Sherman's corps on the right, Mc-Pherson's in the centre, and McClernand's on the left. Whatever peril had overhung the march in a hostile country, without a base, disappeared now that the Union army had attained a position in rear of Vicksburg — for Sherman, on first arriving, had launched forward his column to the Yazoo ; the Confederates abandoned the defences of Haynes's Bluff, and communication with the fleet being secured, the army drew abundant supplies by the Mississippi and Yazoo.

Thus placed, the work that remained for the army to do was not difficult. Vicksburg was doomed. . If the assault of the stronghold obviously promised little, and if the prosecution of siege operations would be long and laborious, there was no need to have recourse either to open attack or the craft of the engineer, seeing that ingress and egress were effectually cut off to the garrison. What remained, therefore, was a mere blockade, and Grant could afford to wait the time when hunger having done its work, Pemberton would be forced to sue for terms of capitulation.

There was, however, a consideration that prompted a different course. It was known that Johnston still hovered between Jackson and Vicksburg, exerting himself to the utmost to gather a relieving force, and as it was incumbent on him to strain every nerve towards bringing relief to Pemberton, it was fairly to be presumed that he would do so. Grant's line of investment was long and consequently everywhere rather weak, and the result of Johnston's coming in on the rear of the army with a force of twenty-five or thirty thousand men, aided by a vigorous *sortie* on the part of the garrison, was not to be contemplated without some apprehension. Grant, therefore, resolved to make an immediate assault — a stroke for which the better result was hoped in consequence of the dispirited and demoralized condition of the garrison. This purpose was carried into execution the afternoon of the 19th ; but it issued in no more than pressing forward the left and centre to a position nearer the enemy's works, for night intervened before a fresh assault could be made. Sherman, on the right, who had secured a position already very close to the hostile line, assaulted with Blair's division, and succeeded in closing up with the Confederate intrenchments. The Thirteenth regulars, the Eighty-third Indiana and the One hundred and twenty-seventh Illinois, even planted their colors on the exterior slope whence they fired upon any head that presented itself above the parapet. But it was found impossible to force an entrance, and after nightfall Sherman withdrew the troops under shelter.

This trial, however, did not cut-off all hope of a better result from a new effort made under more favorable circumstances and with adequate means : so having passed the 20th and 21st in dispositions for a grand assault, the orders therefor were given in the afternoon of the latter day. It was to be made at ten of the following morning, and to be simultaneous, each corps commander set his watch by Grant's. It was to be general along the whole line, and the fleet was at the same time to engage the batteries on the river front as a diversion. At the appointed time, on the morning of the 22d, the three corps moved forward. It was soon found that owing to the nature of the ground, only very narrow fronts could be brought into action. All was quiet in the enemy's lines — not a man being seen until the storming parties, having issued from the shelter of the woods, began to ascend the ridge. Then the Confederate troops, rising up, greeted the assailants with a deadly fire under which many wavered and sought shelter. Yet the bravest, disdaining to retreat, pressed on and portions of each command succeeded in planting their colors on the outer slope of the Confederate bastions — the men burrowing in the earth of the exterior slope to shield themselves from the fire. A handful of men of McClernand's corps, headed by Sergeant Griffith, entered one of the bastions ; but the whole party saving the sergeant, was captured.

On the report of McClernand's success at this point, renewed sallies were made on other parts of the line; but these resulted in nothing save a mournful loss of life, and the demonstration, at a cost of twenty-five hundred killed and wounded, that, in the words of General Grant, "the enemy's position was too strong, both naturally and artificially, to be taken in that way."

It only remained to open a regular siege. Along the entire front batteries, earthworks, and covered-ways were erected, parallels and approaches were constructed, and mines were sunk; but as it is doubtful if these artifices hastened the final *denouement* by a single day, and as the details are of a purely professional nature, these operations are not here to be recounted. For an effective blockade, Grant's position presented great advantages, while his uninterrupted communication by the Mississippi furnished abundant supplies and ample reinforcements. Of the latter, six divisions, including two of the Ninth Corps, under General Parke, arrived during the siege — an increase that enabled the commander to make the investment most complete, to thoroughly protect his flank and rear, and, at the same time, to hold a large reserve force to watch Johnston, of whose motions a word will now be in place.

When General Johnston received tidings of the investment of Vicksburg, he sent word to Pemberton to hold out, and that he was trying to raise a force that might attempt to relieve the garrison. This hope served to restore somewhat the *morale* of the beleaguered troops, and it was constantly kept alive by the arrival of couriers, who succeeded in running the blockade. By early in June Johnston had gotten together a body of four-and-twenty thousand men; but it was deficient in artillery, in ammunition for all arms, in transportation, and could hardly be called an army. At length, towards the end of the month, these deficiencies were partially supplied: so that on the 29th Johnston marched from

Jackson towards the Big Black, and on the 1st of July he had taken position between Brownsville and the river, and begun to reconnoitre where he might best strike a blow in behalf of Pemberton, to whom on the night of the 3d he dispatched a messenger bearing instructions for him to hold out, and that a diversion would be made about 'the 7th to enable him to cut his way out.

But this reassurance never reached Pemberton till long after the catastrophe. Inside the fated lines, despair had succeeded the delusive hope of assistance from without: the long-endured labors, sufferings, and privations, had worn out the bodies and quenched the ardor of the defenders; supplies of food and ammunition, though long carefully husbanded, were both nigh exhausted, and the citizens, living in caves and holes of the earth, passed their days in misery and dread anticipations of what of worse might remain behind.

At length the end came. Early on the morning of Friday, July 2d, a white flag was seen displayed on the parapet in front of the right of the left wing, held by Smith's division of Ord's (late McClernand's) corps; and an officer being sent forward to learn its meaning, it was found that General Bowen, the commander of one of the Confederate divisions, and Colonel Montgomery, of the staff of General Pemberton, were the bearers of a message to General Grant. After being blindfolded, these officers were led over the intervening ridges and ravines to the head-quarters of General Smith, to await the reply of the Union commander. The message proved to be a formal proposition from the Confederate commander for an armistice, and the appointment of three commissioners on each side to arrange terms for the capitulation of Vicksburg. General Grant answered that he did not favor the naming of commissioners, seeing that he had no other terms to offer than the cessation of hostilities by the unconditional surrender of the city and garrison. He stated, however, that if Pemberton should desire it, he would hold

20

an interview with him, between the lines, in McPherson's front, any hour that afternoon. Three o'clock was accordingly fixed as the time of conference, and orders to suspend firing were at once sent along the whole line.

At the hour named, General Grant, attended by several of his lieutenants, reached the ground. Pemberton was somewhat later, but after a few minutes he was seen descending the slope of the opposite ridge, and the commanders, being introduced, began the momentous conference, while thousands of the men of the opposing armies, crowning the surrounding hills, without fear of hostile greeting, looked on, spectators of the scene that had so much of mystery and interest to them.

The colloquy was begun by Pemberton's renewing his proposition for the appointment of commissioners — a proposition which he reinforced by stating that the surrender of Vera Cruz, at which he had been present, was managed in this way. Grant, however, again refused compliance with this request, which came near terminating the parley on the part of Pemberton; but the Confederate, realizing his actual condition, thought better of his half-formed purpose of continuing the struggle. The two commanders then walked off a short distance, to where there stood some small trees and shrubbery, and which is now the site of a monumental stone : there seating themselves on the grass, they remained in consultation for about three quarters of an hour. There was still disagreement in respect of details : and the conference was broken up with the statement from General Grant that he would that night send in his ultimatum in writing. This was accordingly transmitted before midnight, and answered by peep of day on the 4th, in a rejoinder from Pemberton, proposing some modifications. In an immediate replication, General Grant dissented from these modifications. He also stated that if no further communication was received from General Pemberton, he would regard his proposition as rejected, and act accordingly; but should it be accepted, the Confederates were to display white flags along their lines.

After a period of anxious suspense, the symbol of surrender appeared along the length of works. The terms were accepted by the Confederates. The long siege was over. The garrison stacked arms; twenty-seven thousand Confederates received their paroles; and the anniversary of American independence was gilded with a new lustre, for at length, after two years of battle and siege, and such outpouring of blood as did in very deed incarnadine the Father of Waters, the great West made good its vow — the Mississippi went " unvexed to the sea."

III.

RESULTS OF VICKSBURG.

The story of the fall of Vicksburg leaves its effect on the course of the war so plain and palpable as to require little exposition to bring it into clearer light. Most obviously it was one of those strokes the greatest and most decisive in war — the capture of an army. For this was not the surrender of a mere garrison of a post. The thirty-seven thousand men that from the time of the crossing of the. Mississippi by General Grant, fell captives into his hands, were an army — the army defending the valley of the Mississippi, made up of the same battalions that had barred the advance of the Union force from Shiloh down, and augmented by resources in men and material that, drawn from the well-nigh drained reservoir of the Confederacy, left the defence of other important lines weak and inadequate. It was truly a loss irreparable to the South.

Of its direct military bearing, the first in importance was the fall of Port Hudson — a place which, though two hundred miles below Vicksburg, may be regarded as an outwork of that stronghold, destined to cover the flank of it from attack by the Lower Mississippi squadron, and to enclose with Vicksburg a sufficient stretch of the river for free intercom-

munication between the right and centre zones.   This post, as
has already been seen, was invested by General Banks, with a
force from New Orleans, about the same time that Grant
drew his lines around Vicksburg.   The commander of the
post, General Gardner, was, like Pemberton, instructed by
General Johnston to evacuate the place, but the Confederate
officer was already under siege before the order came to hand.
The besieging army was composed of five divisions, and to
this Gardner could only oppose a force of about five thousand
men.   After essaying, on the 27th of May, an assault that
was repulsed, Banks opened the siege in force, and after another unsuccessful attempt, made the 14th of June, to carry
the place by storm, he confined himself to regular approaches.
At length, on the 7th of July, General Gardner having meanwhile heard tidings of the fall of Vicksburg, sent a communication to General Banks asking for " official assurance whether
this is true or not, and if it is, for a cessation of hostilities,
with a view to the consideration of terms for surrendering
this position."   Banks, in reply, transmitted the official dispatch in which General Grant communicated the fact of the
fall of Vicksburg, and on this the Confederate commander
accepted the terms of capitulation offered — the formal surrender being made the 9th of July.

This double victory opened the Mississippi through its
mighty length to the Gulf.   Finger by finger the hand of
iron with which the Confederates had grasped the jurisdiction of the great river had been unloosed, till the last hold,
clutched the more nervously as the tenure became the weaker,
had, with overmastering force, been wrenched from them at
Vicksburg.

If we now take into account that the fate of that
stronghold was not merely the capture of a specific fortified
point of the Mississippi, but the elimination of the entire
army for the defence of the Mississippi Valley, and therefore
the extinction of all possibility of its further defence by the
Confederates, we shall rise to the height of the appreciation

of this colossal achievement. For, what is the possession of the Mississippi? A great soldier shall tell us. "The possession of the Mississippi River is the possession of America, and I say that, had the Southern Confederacy held with a grip sufficiently strong the lower part of the Mississippi River, we would have been a subjugated people; and they would have dictated to us, had we given up the possession of the Lower Mississippi. It was vital to us, and we fought for it, and won it."

This is the language of General Sherman, and it does not overpass the far-reaching reality of this conquest. For the Mississippi plays a greater part than do, ordinarily, rivers. These commonly form only lines of defence; but the Mississippi was the dividing line betwixt two zones of the continental theatre of war. Now, the right zone, comprising the vast territory lying westward of this river, though, in a military point of view less important than the centre and left zone, comprised respectively between the Mississippi and the Allephoures, and the Alleghanies and the Atlantic, was yet the store-house from which the belligerent South obtained a very large part of its supplies, and especially, was the corral whence it drew those great herds of cattle that went to feed the armies in Tennessee and Virginia. It need not be said that when the Confederates lost Vicksburg they lost their last means of communication with the Trans-Mississippi, and military operations in the right zone ceased thenceforward to be of any magnitude or importance.

When in December, 1862, at the time General Grant was preparing to move against Vicksburg, Mr. Davis addressed the citizens of Mississippi at Jackson, he urged them to go to Vicksburg, and "assist in preserving the Mississippi River, that great artery of the country, and thus conduce, more than in any other way, to the perpetuation of the Confederacy, and the success of the cause." To say, therefore, that with such estimate of the importance of this stronghold, its fall must have been to the people of the South the gravest of blows,

would be to state a mere truisim. So that, to its material
effect we must also add its moral effect, accounting it, as we
are bound, one of those disastrous strokes which, rudely
shaking the spirit of the South, threw gloomy doubts upon the
possibility of their ever realizing "the success of the cause."

Whatever work remained to be done in order to make the
conquest of Vicksburg fulfil all the conditions it should in
the process of the war, was soon accomplished. Immediately on the surrender, Sherman, with his own corps,
strengthened by the Fifteenth, was despatched to finish Johnston, who had retired to Jackson. The position taken up by
the Confederate commander proved so strong, that Sherman,
instead of wasting life in assaults, wisely resorted to the
surer operations of the engineers. Appearing in front of
Jackson on the 9th of July, he had by the 12th completely
invested the place, so that both flanks rested on the Pearl
River. Johnston seeing the impossibility of further maintaining himself there, retreated on the night of the 16th, and
soon afterwards his troops were returned to the quarters
whence they had come. Sherman, after destroying the rail-
ways, retraced his steps to the Big Black. Other expeditions
were also sent out in various quarters to give the finishing
touches to the great work, and Grant having a large surplus
of men, sent the division of Steele to Helena to aid Schofield,
then commanding the Department of Missouri, and Ord and
Herron to Banks, to take part in new movements projected
in the Department of the Gulf.

The army now had a long rest from its labors; but when,
in October, it again took the field, there was found in all the
Valley of the Mississippi no foeman worthy of its steel. On
the river line of the West, conquest had been pushed to its
utmost limits, and for grand military operations in the centre
zone, there only remained the mountain line of Tennessee,
where Rosecrans, ensconced in Chattanooga, pointed the way
to Atlanta and the sea.

Engd by H.B.Hall.

Photo. by Gurney

Dick & Fitzgerald New

VIII.

GETTYSBURG.

I.

PRELUDE TO GETTYSBURG.

IF, leaving the burial-place at Gettysburg from the south side, the pedestrian follow the crest of Cemetery Ridge, keeping before him the bold figure of Round Top Mountain as a beacon, he will in a few minutes' walk reach a clump of woods which, so long as a tree thereof stands, must remain the most interesting memorial-spot of the greatest battle of the war. Into this bunch of woods a few — it may be a score or two — of the boldest and bravest that led the van of Pickett's charging column on the 3d of July, 1863, attained. Thus far the swelling surge of invasion threw its spray, dashing itself to pieces on the rocky bulwark of Northern valor. Let us call this the high-water mark of the rebellion.

But in another and larger scope Gettysburg itself is the real high-water mark of the rebellion. For not only was the invasion of Pennsylvania in a geographical sense the most forward and salient leap of the Confederate army, but it was upon that field that the star of the Confederacy, reaching the zenith, turned by swift and headlong plunges toward the nadir of outer darkness and collapse. It is with good reason, therefore, that upon this action, morally if not materially the most decisive of the war, an unexampled interest centres: that its incidents are garnered by the historian; that the fields and roads and woods of Gettysburg are carefully plotted by the map-maker; that its landscape challenges the pencil and canvas of the artist.

There is, first of all, to be noted one characteristic feature that distinguishes this campaign from all other operations undertaken by Lee, whether before it or after it. This is that it was the first, last, and only campaign of invasion, formally designed as such. Anticipating that the reader will mentally traverse this statement by the objection that the Maryland campaign, culminating in Antietam, was also an invasive movement, I answer that it became so not by design but by accidental circumstances. A recurrence to the discussion of that campaign in a previous chapter will show that it was not till Lee had driven Pope within the fortifications of Washington that he conceived the project of moving into Maryland, and that even then the movement was made, not so much with any invasive intent as with the view of holding the Union army on the north side of the Potomac until the season of active operations should have passed by.

The Pennsylvania campaign was planned with far other purpose. This was invasion pure and simple — a flight of the boldest quarry — an audacious enterprise, designed to transfer the seat of war from Virginia to the North country, to pass the Susquehanna, to capture Washington, Baltimore, and Philadelphia: in a word, to conquer a peace on the soil of the loyal States. If there has been hitherto any doubt touching the point, it disappears in the light of official records. The unpublished manuscript report of General Lee, now lying before the writer, sets this matter forever at rest.

Two motives prompted the Confederates to launch out in the daring policy of invasion. Of these the one concerned a matter which is yet involved in great obscurity — to wit, the relations of the Richmond Government with European powers. If some day the secret history of Confederate diplomacy in Europe be laid bare, it will, beyond a doubt, be seen that the Southern agents near the leading governments of the old world, were, at this time, able to announce that, should Lee, after the astonishing successes he had achieved on the soil of Virginia, carry his army into the North, and there make a lodgment promising some degree of permanence, the South would receive the long-coveted boon of foreign recognition.

This was the first motive to the movement, and it happened that it was closely connected with the other inducement to invasion, which was found in the condition of the Confederate force. Never, so runs on all hands the testimony, was Lee's army in such wonderful spirit, or so completely fitted to undertake a bold enterprise, as at the time the Pennsylvania campaign was projected. And this we may well believe, for the result of the entire series of events succeeding Antietam had been such as to raise the *morale* of the army of Northern Virginia to the highest pitch. Since the time when Lee was compelled to abandon Maryland and fall back on the line of the Rappahannock, two great battles had been fought, with most disastrous issue to the Union arms. It needs but to recall the names of Fredericksburg and Chancellorsville, to recall with them the direful history they contain. In the former of these actions, fought in December, 1862, the army of the Potomac, under an incompetent leader, was hurled in reckless slaughter against a fortified position of impregnable strength, and after a fearful carnage was repulsed to the north bank of the Rappahannock, terribly shaken in *morale*. In the latter action, fought in May, 1863, Hooker, after a successful passage of the river, contrived by unskilful combination, to be thoroughly beaten in detail by a greatly inferior force acting on the offensive, and was forced to re-cross the Rappahannock, leaving his reputation as a general behind him. Now, it was not alone that the Confederates in these two encounters were able to kill and spoil nearly thirty thousand men, but their experience in these battles inspired them with a sense of invincibility — they had come to feel that they could not be conquered; while the Union army, distraught by repeated disasters, and changes of commander, had sunk in energy, and lapsed from the faith of victory — a faith which, though long sustained, could not be expected to survive unaffected such accumulated shocks.

These two causes, conspiring together, determined the Richmond authorities to assume the offensive, and the *mot d'ordre* having been given Lee soon after the battle of Chancellorsville, that general immediately applied his mind to the framing a plan of campaign. At this time, the army of the Potomac lay on the Rappahannock, paralyzed by the effects of its late defeats, and rapidly losing its substance by the mustering out of a large body of two years' and nine months' troops, whose term of service expired about this time. The army of Northern Virginia held position behind the impregnable line of earthworks that for thirty miles dotted the south side of the Rappahannock. It also lay in seeming idleness, but in reality portentous preparations for the projected movement were being pushed forward. The two veteran divisions of Longstreet's corps, which had some months before been detached to operate in North Carolina, and which had been absent at the time of Chancellorsville, were recalled to Fredericksburg; the whole body of Confederates' horse was concentrated under Stuart at Culpepper; the equipment, transport service, and *commissariat* were brought up to a high state of efficiency, and by the first days in June Lee was ready to launch forward in his audacious adventure. He found he had a force of almost seventy thousand men, equal in strength to that of his antagonist, and of a mettle that, in the words of Longstreet, made it "capable of anything."

The stragetical procedure devised by the Confederate commander for the accomplishment of the scheme of invasion showed a masterly knowledge of the theatre of war. To dislodge the army of the Potomac from the line of the Rappahannock by a direct passage of the river was far from his thought. Such a project would not only have led to nothing, seeing that even if successful in throwing back the army towards Washington, he would, in advancing upon Washington by the Orange and Alexandria Railroad, have entangled himself in the narrow angle of North-eastern Virginia, with the fortifications of the Capital in his front; but the enterprise would have been so wasteful of his strength as to be fatal to his ultimate purpose, which was to plant his army fresh and entire north of the Potomac. But it was comparatively easy for him to manœuvre Hooker from the Rappahannock by turning his right in the country lying east of the Blue Ridge, and if by this motion he should throw his opponent back upon Washington, he would have the Shenandoah Valley by which to issue upon the soil of Maryland. This line affords extraordinary advantages, in such an operation as that contemplated by Lee, for by guarding the few passes of the Blue Ridge, an army moving northward by the Shenandoah Valley may march entirely free from interruption and at the same time hold its rival in entire uncertainty as to its design. The only Union force in the valley at this time was a corps of a few thousand troops that held position at Winchester under Milroy; but this force Lee calculated on surprising or at least routing.

In execution of his design, Lee during the first days of June, transferred the corps of Longstreet and Ewell by secret marches westward to Culpepper Court House; and to mask the delicate operation, so vital to the success of the movement, he left behind the Hill's corps to occupy the heights of Fredericksburg. This was executed with such success that Hooker knew nothing of it. His aroused suspicions did indeed cause him to throw Sedgwick's corps across the Rappahannock; but the front presented by Hill prevented his penetrating aught of what was going on behind. By the 8th of June Lee had two thirds of his army massed at Culpepper, with the cavalry thrown forward to

Brandy Station, ready to cover the advance. This however was interrupted, for a moment by a movement made by Hooker, who, in order to discover what was passing in the direction of Culpepper, forwarded the main body of the Union cavalry to cross the upper Rappahannock and advance on Culpepper, where he was far from suspecting the presence of Lee's infantry. Pleasonton having crossed the Rappahannock at Kelly's and Beverly's ford, the 9th of June, advanced fighting Confederate detachments of horse to Brandy Station, between the river and Culpepper, where a protracted combat was waged between the two cavalry columns. After gaining some advantage, Pleasonton was compelled to recross the Rappahannock; but he brought back the important intelligence that the main body of the Confederate army was in the vicinity of Culpepper. The disclosure left no doubt in the mind of Hooker that his adversary was meditating an offensive movement, and to the end that he might be in position to meet this, he advanced his right to the upper Rappahannock so as to observe the fords of that stream. But while the Union commander had his attention called in this direction, Lee, by a wide detour westward, had turned his right, and threw out the head of a column into the Shenandoah Valley. Ewell, on the 10th, took the advance, skirting the eastern side of the Blue Ridge through which he passed at Chester Gap: he crossed the Shenandoah River near Front Royal, burst into the valley, and advanced rapidly towards Winchester, before which place he arrived on the evening of the 13th. Next day the Union force at Winchester, under Milroy, was captured or dispersed; four thousand prisoners were taken together with twenty eight pieces of artillery and large stores. The Shenandoah Valley was completely cleared, and Lee was free to pass the Potomac into Maryland.

Startled by this intelligence, Hooker, on the 13th, hastily abandoning his camp on the Rappahannock, began a rapid retrograde movement towards Washington, and Hill, who all this time had remained at Fredericksburg, seeing the Union army disappear, hastened to join the advance corps in the valley. This junction being effected, Lee, on the 22d, threw Ewell's corps across the Potomac to advance into Pennsylvania. Meanwhile, he held Longstreet and Hill in the valley, and Stuart's cavalry scoured the country east of the Blue Ridge.

Hooker, who had drawn back the army to the vicinity of Fairfax and Manassas, was now in a position of distressing uncertainty. Doubtful as to Lee's purpose, he dared not cross the Potomac while yet the bulk of the Confederate army remained in the Shenandoah Valley, and yet his remaining inactive left Ewell free to harry the north country, which was thrown into wildest consternation by the tidings of the invasion. By the 24th of June, the movement of the advanced Confederate corps had become so far developed, that Lee determined to follow to the north side of the Potomac with his remaining force. "The Federal army," says he, "was apparently guarding the approaches to Washington, and manifested no disposition to assume the offensive. In the mean time the progress of Ewell, who was already in Maryland, with Jenkins's cavalry, and had advanced into Pennsylvania as far as Chambersburg, rendered it necessary that the rest of the army should be within supporting distance; and Hill having reached the valley, Longstreet was withdrawn to the west side of the Shenandoah, and the two corps encamped near Berryville. General Stuart was directed to hold the mountain passes, with part of his command, as long as the enemy remained south of the Potomac, and with the remainder to cross into Maryland and place himself on the right of General Ewell. On the 22d General Ewell marched into Pennsylvania with Rodes's and Johnson's divisions, preceded by Jenkins's cavalry, taking the road from Hagerstown through Chambersburg to Carlisle, where he arrived on the 27th. Early's division, which had occupied Boonsboro', moved by a parallel road to Greenwood, and, in pursuance of instructions previously given to General Ewell, marched towards York. On the 24th, Longstreet and Hill were put in motion to follow Ewell, and on the 27th encamped near Chambersburg."

We left Hooker a few miles south-west of Washington, wholly uncertain of the motions of his antagonist, fearful of crossing the Potomac lest he should thus uncover Washington, and fearful also of following the enemy out into the Shenandoah Valley, lest he should expose his right flank to attack from the mountains. However, by the 25th, he learnt that the whole of Lee's column was passing the Potomac far above at Shepherdstown and Williamsport, and he therefore crossed the river, — not to Washington, but forward to Frederick, a stroke that, as I shall show, had an immense effect on the course of the campaign.

The plan of operations devised by General Lee was far from having the character of a roving expedition. It was founded on a thoroughly methodical procedure, and assumed the preservation of his line of communications with Virginia. This line was through the Cumberland Valley, which may be regarded as a continuation of the Shenandoah Valley to the north of the Potomac, and was covered by the South Mountains. Now, owing to the fact that it was so covered, and also to the fact that Lee supposed the Army of the Potomac would manœuvre entirely on the east side of the mountains (being governed in this by the importance of covering Baltimore and Washington), the Confederate commander regarded his line of retreat and communication as quite free from menace. Having therefore on the 27th reached Chambersburg with the corps of Longstreet and Hill, he turned his eyes northward towards the Susquehanna, where Early was operating at York and Carlisle, and he made his preparations to advance and join him. But one consideration gave him pause — namely, the whereabouts of the Army of the Potomac, anent which he was in such ignorance, that, notwithstanding

Hooker had on the 27th, the same day on which Lee with Long-street and Hill reached Chambersburg, concentrated his corps at Frederick, Lee was not even aware that his opponent had crossed the Potomac — far less that from Frederick, where Hooker menaced the Confederate communications, the Union commander had thrown out a force to advance westward through the passes of the South Mountain to Harper's Ferry — a movement that would plant this force directly on Lee's rear and line of retreat.   He knew nothing of all this on the 27th, nothing on the 28th, and still conceiving the Union army to be south of the Potomac, he on the latter day drew out orders for the two corps with him to march the next morning north-ward to join Ewell on the Susquehanna.   But late on the night of the 28th, a scout arrived at the Confederate head-quarters at Chambersburg, bringing tidings that the Army of the Potomac had reached Frederick, and was approaching the South Mountains.

It would be difficult to find in military history a more striking exemplification of the effect produced by " operating on the enemy's communications," than that of this move-ment of Hooker's.   No sooner had Lee received intelligence of the presence of the Army of the Potomac at Frederick, and its menacing movement towards Harper's Ferry, than grave apprehensions touching the safety of his line of retreat, caused him to suspend the forward movement he had ordered. Determined at all hazards to retain the Army of the Potomac on the east side of the South Mountains, he made a manœuvre admirably adapted to accomplish this purpose.   Instead of moving northward from Chambersburg by the Cumberland Valley to the Susquehanna, he resolved to turn eastward, pass the South Mountain range which walls in the Cumber-land Valley on the east side, and by thus directly threatening Baltimore, compel his opponent to draw back from his ad-vance on Harper's Ferry, and hasten in the direction of the

Susquehanna to cover Baltimore.   This movement was begun the morning of the 29th of June.

As it may seem surprising that Lee was so ill informed of his antagonist's movements as to have been unaware until the night of the 28th that the Army of the Potomac had crossed into Maryland (the passage having been made two days before), it will not be unimportant to point out the singular circumstance by which this came about.   It has been seen in the citation already made from General Lee's report that when the Confederate infantry moved into Maryland, Stuart, with the cavalry, was directed to hold the passes of the Blue Ridge leading into the valley of the Shenandoah as long as the Union army should remain south of the Potomac, when he also was to cross and place himself upon the right flank of the Confederate column moving northward.   As, however, Stuart suggested that he could damage Hooker's army and delay the passage of the river by getting in its rear, Lee authorized him to do so, and it was left to his discretion whether to enter Maryland east or west of the Blue Ridge; but he was instructed to lose no time in placing his command on the right of the Confederate column as soon as he should see Hooker moving northward.   In the exercise of this discretion, Stuart determined to pass around the rear of the Union army, and cross the Potomac between it and Washington, believing that he would still be able by that route to place himself on Lee's right in time to keep his chief advised as to his antagonist's movements.   But in order to execute his purpose he was compelled to make a wide detour to the eastward by way of Fairfax Court House.   Reaching the Potomac at the mouth of Seneca Creek, the evening of the 27th, he found the river much swollen by recent rains, and it was only after prodigious exertions that he gained the Maryland shore.   Stuart then ascertained that the Federal army had crossed the Potomac the day before and was marching towards Frederick, thus interposing itself between him and

Lee. He was accordingly forced to march northward through Westminster to Hanover in Pennsylvania, where he arrived on the 30th of June. But as will presently be seen, the army of the Potomac advanced with equal rapidity on his left, thus continuing to obstruct his junction with the Confederate army in the Cumberland Valley : so that Lee, deprived of the services of his cavalry was all this time in comparative ignorance of the motions of the Army of the Potomac. In fact, it was only by accident that on the night of the 28th, he became apprised of the facts that admonished him to desist from his advance towards the Susquehanna, and move to the east side of the South Mountain as a diversion in favor of his menaced communications.

Lest it should be doubted that Lee originally designed crossing the Susquehanna, I add in support of the assertion, the following extract from his unpublished official report : — " It was expected that as soon as the Federal army should cross the Potomac, General Stuart would give notice of its movements ; and nothing having been heard from him since our entrance into Maryland, it was inferred that the enemy had not yet left Virginia. *Orders were therefore issued to move upon Harrisburg.* The expedition of General Early to York was designed in part to prepare for this undertaking, by breaking the railroad between Baltimore and Harrisburg, and seizing the bridge over the Susquehanna at Wrightsville. General Early succeeded in the first object, destroying a number of bridges above and below York ; but on the approach of the troops sent by him to Wrightsville, a body of militia fled across the river and burned the bridge in their retreat. General Early then marched to rejoin his corps. The advance against Harrisburg was arrested by intelligence received from a scout, on the night of the 28th, to the effect that General Hooker had crossed the Potomac and was approaching the South Mountain."

Leaving now the Confederate commander in the execution

21

of his purpose of concentrating his corps from Chambersburg
to the Susquehanna, on the east side of the South Mountains,
with the view of calling off his opponent fram his threatening
motion against his line of communications, we have to note an
important change at the head-quarters of the Army of the
Potomac, which not only (had they but known it) relieved the
Confederates from this menace, but gave an entirely new
complexion to the campaign.   This event was the removal of
General Hooker from the command of the Army of the Potomac.   The cause of this change is well known.   Hooker
asked that the corps of ten thousand men at Harper's Ferry
might be placed under his orders, with the view of adding
this force to the corps of Slocum, which he had sent forward
from Frederick towards Harper's Ferry, and with this column making a demonstration against Lee's rear by a movement up the Cumberland Valley.   General Halleck, who
then, for the country's sins, exercised the functions of General-in-Chief at Washington, would not consent to the evacuation of Harper's Ferry, whereupon Hooker requested that he
should be relieved from the command of the army.   His request was granted, and General G. G. Meade, commander
of the Fifth Corps, was nominated in his stead.   The appointment of this officer took the army by surprise, but it
astonished no one more than General Meade himself, for he
had spoken with such manly frankness his conviction of
Hooker's incapacity at Chancellorsville, that that officer had
threatened to have him arrested, and when at a late hour of
the night of the 27th of June, Meade was awakened from
sleep in his tent, near Frederick, by the messenger from
Washington, his first question to General Hardie, who brought
the commission, was, whether he had come with the order for
his arrest.   Hardie, evading the question, told him to strike a
light, and then placed in his hand a paper, which opening,
he found it to be an order appointing him to the command of
the Army of the Potomac, and committing to him all the

powers of the Executive and the Constitution, to the end that
he might wield untrammelled all the resources of the nation
to meet the emergency of the invasion. Though not what is
called a popular officer, he was much respected by his comrades in arms. He was an able commander, forty-eight years
of age, in person tall and slim, with a long, grayish, thoughtful face, an excellent tactician, and imbued with sound military ideas; and though he afterwards manifested an undue
shrinking from responsibility, the gravity of the hour had the
effect to quicken and elevate his powers, and he immediately put
the army in motion, with the determination to speedily bring
Lee to battle. Spite of the malicious detraction of his
adversaries, who have tried to make it appear that he
shrank from the issue of arms at Gettysburg, it was in
reality the moral firmness of General Meade that determined the great combat in the form in which it actually occurred.

On the morning of the 29th of June, Meade put his columns in motion from Frederick. He renounced all thought
of moving to the west side of the South Mountain, and resolved to press northward on the east side of that range, ascending the course of the Monocacy towards the Susquehanna,
till he should compel Lee to loose his hold on the Susquehanna, and turn and give fight. Mark, now, the curious
conjunction of events that was bringing the two hostile
masses, though quite ignorant of each other's movements, towards each other, till unexpectedly they found themselves
grappling in deadly wrestle, in an obscure hamlet of Western
Pennsylvania! Meade thought the Confederates were pressing northward to the Susquehanna, where he knew of the
presence of Ewell's corps at York and Carlisle; Lee thought
the Union army was marching westward from Frederick.
But in point of fact, Lee turned eastward the same morning
of the 29th, on which Meade moved northward, and as the
direction of the rival armies was at right angles with each

other, it was inevitable that they should come to an encounter in the course of two or three marches.

Eight miles east of Chambersburg, the great road to Baltimore debouches through the South Mountain range at the furnace of Thad. Stevens. Thence, continuing eastward, it passes through the town of Gettysburg, which is a point of convergence of many roads leading as well northward to the Susquehanna as southward to the Potomac. Thither Lee, on the morning of June 29th, directed the Chambersburg column, composed of the corps of Longstreet and Hill, and to that point also he ordered Ewell's column to countermarch from the Susquehanna. Gettysburg was not in any manner the objective of this operation : the purpose was simply to move in that direction as a measure of concentration. To give battle there was the last idea Lee had in mind ; and the manner in which, contrary alike to his inclination and his desire, he was led to do so, forms one of the most remarkable illustrations of the absence of truth in that saying of Napoleon, that " war is not an accidental science."

After the army of the Potomac had made two marches, that is, on the night of the 30th of June, Meade became satisfied that Lee was concentrating his forces east of the mountains to meet him. Under these circumstances, he set about to select a position on which by a movement of concentration, he might be prepared to receive battle on advantageous terms. With this view, the general line of Pipe Creek, on the dividing ridge between the Monocacy and the waters flowing into Chesapeake Bay, was selected as a favorable position, though its ultimate adoption was held contingent on developments that might arise. Accordingly orders were issued on the night of the 30th for the movement of the different corps on the following day. The Sixth Corps (Sedgwick) forming the right wing of the army, was ordered to Manchester, in rear of Pipe Creek ; head-quarters of the Second Corps (Hancock) were directed to Taneytown ; the

Twelfth Corps (Slocum) and the Fifth Corps (Sykes) forming the centre on Two Taverns and Hanover, somewhat in advance of Pipe Creek; while the left wing formed of the First (Reynolds), Third (Sickles), and Eleventh Corps (Howard), all under Gen. Reynolds, was ordered to Gettysburg, which had that morning been occupied by General Buford, who with a division of horse covered the front of the left wing of the army.

Now the van of Lee's main column that, as has been seen, had started from Chambersburg, bivouacked on the night of the 29th at Cashtown, five or six miles west of Gettysburg; and on the following morning, the morning of the 30th, General Heth commanding the advanced division, sent forward Pettigrew's brigade to Gettysburg to procure some supplies. Pettigrew, on nearing the town, found it occupied by a hostile force — which was, in fact, Buford's cavalry; and fearing to risk an attack with his single brigade, he returned to Cashtown, after a mere far-off reconnoissance of the Union force. Having reported to his corps commander, General Hill, that officer determined to move the next morning to Gettysburg, with a couple of divisions for the purpose of disposing of the body of cavalry. But Reynolds, with his corps, bivouacked that same night of the 30th of June, on the right bank of Marsh Creek, distant only some four miles from Gettysburg, which he was to make the next morning; and though in Meade's plan of operations it was not proposed that Reynolds should stay at Gettysburg, or be followed thither by the other corps, his presence there being indeed simply designed as a mask behind which the army should take position on Pipe Creek — still the movements of the opposing forces were such that though they knew it not, a collision was inevitable in the vicinity of Gettysburg. On such turns of fortune hinges the issue of mighty campaigns!

II.

THE BATTLE OF GETTYSBURG.

When Lee crossed the frontier to enter upon the invasion of Pennsylvania, he promised his lieutenants he would so act as to throw the cost and peril of attack upon the enemy. This resolution arose from a wise appreciation of the lesson of many an encounter between the rival armies in Virginia; for to this day the largest logic to be drawn from the history of the hundred combats waged between the two great armies is that victory accrued to that side which secured for itself the advantage of fighting on the defensive behind a fortified position. Exceptions there are indeed to this generalization, but they are only sufficient to give a greater prominence to the rule that repulse attended that army which was compelled to oppose its naked valor in the storming of lines which its opponent had had a day or a night to fortify by the improvised works so readily and so constantly constructed. Penetrated with this principle, and desirous of husbanding his strength for the execution of his ulterior purpose (since it was not a mere blow and return that the Confederates meditated, but a permanent lodgment on Northern soil), Lee had resolved so to manœuvre as to compel his opponent to attack him — rightly adjudging that the prizes of Baltimore and Washington could only be snatched after the Army of the Potomac should have suffered defeat in the open field.

Now Lee was faithfully following out the line of this purpose in concentrating his columns on the east side of the South Mountain; for, in so moving, he would soon, provided the motions of the Army of the Potomac were such as he supposed them to be, compel that army to turn and give battle for the safety of its own communications, seriously compromised by his manœuvres. But he was not aware that Meade, by a rapid forward leap, had changed the whole situation;

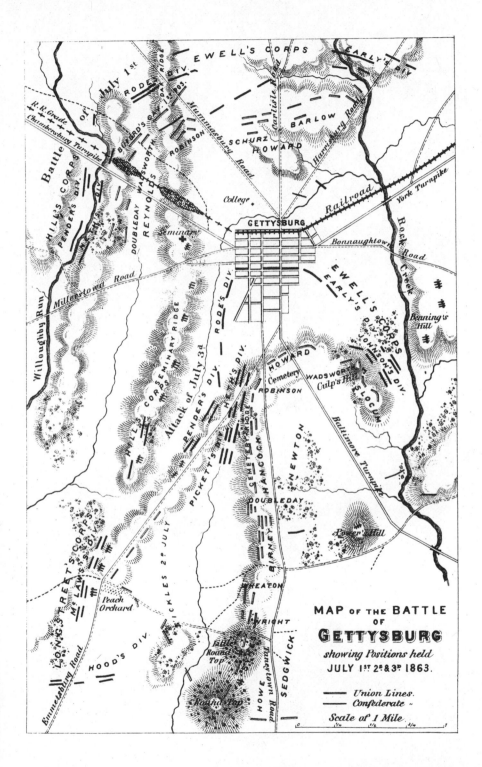

MAP OF THE BATTLE
OF
GETTYSBURG
showing Positions held
JULY 1ˢᵗ 2ᵈ & 3ᵈ 1863.

—— *Union Lines*
—— *Confederate* "

Scale of 1 Mile

above all, he was not aware of what was passing at the front that morning of the first day of July. Lee was not aware, and Meade was not aware.

The pretty little old-fashioned town of Gettysburg nestles at the base of a series of heights and hills whose names have since been lifted to that historic immortality wherewithal grand battles consecrate the ground on which they are fought. The configuration of the *terrain* presents the character of a ridge with several detached hills, trending four or five miles south of Gettysburg — not in a straight line, however, but curved back on the north end, giving in rough the form of a fish-hook. In this figure Wolf's and Culp's Hills will represent the curved part, Cemetery Hill, that portion that rounds into the straight line, which latter is formed by Cemetery Ridge, running a couple of miles due south, when it abuts in a high conical hill, covered with a dense growth of oaks and pines, named Round Top. Round Top shoots up from a bald granite spur known as Little Round Top. On the west side the ridge falls off in a cultivated, undulating valley, which it commands, and at the distance of a mile or less is a parallel crest named Seminary Ridge. This position was occupied by the Confederates in the great encounter that succeeded the action of the first day. Still farther to the west, other parallel swells of ground stretch out like the lines in a musical score all the way to South Mountain, which lies in blue beauty on the rim of the horizon, ten miles off.

From this direction came, on the morning of Wednesday the 1st of July, General A. P. Hill, with two divisions of his corps, determined to dispose of the Union cavalry that Pettegrew had espied occupying the town of Gettysburg the day before. This cavalry, the troopers of the gallant John Buford, had that morning moved out from the town, beyond Seminary Ridge, to the next ridge to the westward, taking position on the hither side of Willoughby Run, about two miles west of Gettysburg. His line was drawn up across

the Chambersburg road, and as Hill approached Gettysburg
by this road, the two found themselves about nine in the
morning precipitated into action.   Buford alone on the Union
side was present on the field; but he knew that Reynolds,
who had bivouacked the night before four miles off, was on
his way to Gettysburg, whither indeed that officer, with the
leading division of his corps under Wadsworth was moving
according to prescribed orders, though with little thought of
battle in his mind.   By skilful deployments Buford held in
check the van of the Confederate force, which as yet consist·
ed only of Heth's division, till Reynolds's, with Wadsworth's
division arrived at ten o'clock.

Reynolds had no orders to bring on a battle; he had no
orders to hold Gettysburg, which was a place concerning the
military value of which neither Meade nor any one else in the
army knew aught: indeed he had in his pocket a paper in-
structing him to follow the movement of concentration on
Pipe Creek.   But to his mind, all instructions were now
superseded by the actual facts of the situation.   Buford was
hard pressed, and he must support him.   Perhaps, too, mysterious influences, of which he himself knew little, moved
him — some foreshadowing glimpse of the great glory of
victory he was not permitted to live to see; for having put
himself at the head of his leading division to hasten forward
its march to the field where Buford was skirmishing, he
dispatched orders sending forward the Third and Eleventh
Corps in all haste to Gettysburg.   Doubtless his fine military
eye took in at a glance the features of the rocky ridge of
Gettysburg as an eminent vantage-ground for a defensive
battle, and if he could only hold the head of the enemy's
column in check on the plain beyond the town where the
cavalry was essaying to arrest its advance, the army would
have time to come up and base itself on the fastness of hills.

"It was," says Wadsworth, "a matter of momentary consultation between General Reynolds and myself whether we

would go into the town, or take a position in front of the town. He decided that if we went into the town, the enemy would shell it and destroy it, and that we had better take a position in front of the town. We moved across the field to — and beyond — the Seminary Ridge. Before we had time to form our line, we were engaged with the enemy. The only battery in my division was placed in position by the side of the road leading to Cashtown. At the time only one brigade was up. General Reynolds told me to take three regiments to support the battery on the right, and he would go to the left and place the balance of the division there." The balance of the division consisted of the Fourteenth Brooklyn (Col. Fowler) and the Ninety-Fifth New York (Colonel Biddle), together with Meredith's "Iron Brigade." The former regiments were immediately thrown into a skirt of woods, and engaged in a warm skirmish with Archer's Confederate brigade, which was crossing Willoughby Run; the "Iron Brigade" was formed on the left flank. Being determined to bring matters to an immediate issue, Reynolds, with animating words, gave the regiments in the skirt of woods, the command to charge. But scarcely was this begun when, struck by a bullet, he fell mortally wounded, dying ere he could be removed from the field. The loss of this brave officer, who died too early for his country's good but not for his own fame, might well have affected the behavior of his men most seriously; but the impulse he had given his troops swept everything before them. All of Archer's brigade that had crossed Willoughby Run, including several hundreds, together with the commander, were captured; and the Fourteenth Brooklyn and the Ninety-Fifth New York, joined by the Sixth Wisconsin, having made a change of front charged upon Davis's Mississippi brigade that was coming in on the right, and had, owing to the falling back of some of Wadsworth's regiments, nearly captured the battery. The Mississippians sought shelter in the cut of an unfinished railway grading, hard by the Chambersburg road, and being there surrounded, were compelled to surrender with their battle-flags.

Pending these operations, the remaining two divisions of the First Union Corps (the divisions of Doubleday and Robinson), and Pender's division on the Confederate side arrived, thus giving a greater development to the still fiercely embattled lines.   But the Union troops, inspired by the most determined spirit, held to their ground with unflinching tenacity; and when the sun stood at high noon, the heroic First Corps was still opposing an unshaken front to the enemy.   Though much reduced in numbers, it had inflicted yet heavier punishment on the foe, and it had yielded not a foot of ground.   In fact, the action of the morning may be considered a decided success to the Union arms; and there was good prospect of maintaining this unbroken, for an hour after noon Howard's Eleventh Corps arrived on the field, having been ordered by Reynolds before he fell to hasten forward to Gettysburg. Howard, leaving one of his divisions in reserve on Cemetery Hill, formed the divisions of Schurz and Barlow on a prolongation of the right flank of the First Corps, thus covering a wide sweep of ground to the west and north of the town.

But at the same time, marching in the direction whence the sound of firing was heard were the old antagonists of the Eleventh Corps — the veterans of Jackson that at Chancellorsville had driven these same troops in such disastrous flight.   It will be remembered that Ewell, who commanded this corps, had been directed to countermarch from the Susquehanna and make a junction with the remainder of the Confederate army either at Cashtown or Gettysburg, or as circumstances might dictate.   Now he had with the divisions of Rodes and Early bivouacked the night before near Heidlersburg, ten miles north of Getteysburg, and having, on the morning of the 1st of July resumed his march, he soon caught the echoes of the combat from the field of Gettysburg.

Marching *au canon*, he reached the scene of action between one and two o'clock, threw Rodes's division round to connect on the left of Hill's corps and disposed Early's division on the right face of the Eleventh Corps. The accession of strength brought by Ewell was opportune to the Confederates, and it played a part as important as Blucher's arrival on the field of Waterloo. The Eleventh Corps make but a feeble resistance and, it is said, gave way before the enemy's skirmishers. Yet the disaster that followed was not entirely due to the inferior mettle of the troops; but in part, at least, to their faulty disposition in an excessively extended line. Moreover, Rodes's division on its arrival succeeded in securing a commanding height opposite the centre of the Union line where the flanks of the two corps approached each other : and when toward three o'clock the Confederates made a final advance, they easily burst through at this point, thus taking both corps *en revers*. Regiment after regiment from each corps fell away, and at length so shattered and disentangled did the mass become that it broke into retreat. This grew into rout as the Confederates, scenting the disorder, pursued with loud yells, and the fugitives becoming entangled in the streets of Gettysburg, five thousand of them were taken prisoners. The remnants of the two corps, less than a moiety of their original strength, were finally rallied on Cemetery Hill, in rear of the town. But the day was irretrievably lost — so gloomy a sequel followed the bright promise of the morning!

While these momentous events were passing at Gettysburg, General Meade was still at his head-quarters at Taneytown, distant thirteen miles. So rapidly indeed had the crisis been precipitated that it was not till afternoon that he became aware that a re-encounter had taken place at the front — then the tidings came accompanied with the announcement of the death of Reynolds. Hereupon General Meade ordered General Hancock to proceed to the scene of contest to assume general command, and make an examination of the ground in the neighborhood of Gettysburg, and if it should be found suitable for battle, the rest of the army would be ordered up. Riding forward in all haste Hancock arrived on the field at half past three. "I found," says he, "that, practically, the fight was then over. The rear of our column, with the enemy in pursuit, was then coming through the town of Gettysburg. General Howard was on Cemetery Hill, and there had evidently been an attempt on his part to stop and form some troops there." In this duty General Howard's success had not been eminent; but Hancock soon made the magnetism of his presence felt — "his personal appearance there," says Warren, "doing a great deal toward restoring order." He extended the lines to the right so as to take possession of Culp's Hill, and was soon able to present so formidable a front that the Confederate skirmishers, who were already breasting the hill slope, were called off.

Never was pause at the door of victory more fatal to the hopes of a commander. Had the enemy followed up his advantage by seizing the crest of Cemetery Hill or Culp's Hill, there would have been no Gettysburg; and indeed it is difficult to forecast what in this case they might not have done; for the Union corps were much scattered, and no place of concentration had been secured. That they could have gained these positions there is little doubt, and indeed Ewell was even advancing a line against Culp's Hill when Lee reached the field and stayed the movement. What was it that thus lowered his upraised arm? I shall state it in his own words; and, if at this distance there are facts which induce the belief that his reasoning was unsound, his decision will only point the moral of the fallibility of the wisest judgment in war. "It was ascertained from the prisoners that we had been engaged with two corps of the army formerly commanded by General Hooker, and that the remainder of that army, under General Meade, was approaching Gettysburg. Without information as to its proximity, the strong position which the enemy had assumed could not be attacked without danger of exposing the four divisions present, already weakened and exhausted by a long and bloody struggle, to overwhelming numbers of fresh troops. General Ewell was therefore instructed to carry the hill occupied by the enemy, if he found it practicable, but to avoid a general engagement until the arrival of the other divisions which were ordered to hasten forward. In the mean time the enemy occupied the point which General Ewell designed to seize (Culp's Hill), but in what force could not be ascertained, owing to the darkness. Under these circumstances, it was decided not to attack till the arrival of Longstreet " — who, to abridge the story, did not arrive that night. Then the action of the first of July terminated.

During the afternoon of the 1st of July General Meade received from Hancock such report of the nature of the ground in the neighborhood of Gettysburg, as determined him to fight a battle there. He therefore ordered all the corps forward, and, by a vigorous night-march, all were concentrated by morning — all save the Sixth Corps, which, having a march of thirty-six miles to make, could not arrive till mid-day. By morning, also, the whole of Lee's army, with the exception of Pickett's division of Longstreet's corps, had reached the ground. And so dawn revealed to the eyes of the opposing armies the massive array of each drawn up within range of their respective artillery. The clouds that had parted on the Rappahannock were now brought together, charged with electric elements, amid the hills of Western Pennsylvania.

This, verily, was very far from what Lee had promised himself. He had resolved so to manœuvre as to compel the enemy to attack him; had assured his lieutenants he would not assume a tactical offensive : nevertheless, here he found himself fronting the host of his adversary, who was posted in a coign of vantage, where attack must needs be most perilous, and yet, such was the situation, that the Confederate commander could not decline battle; for in the high-strung condition of his army, elated by the inspiration of the invasion, and puffed up by the success of the previous day's rencounter, to have withdrawn would have been an intolerable confession of weakness.

Impelled by his fate, Lee resolved to attack, and his plan of battle was, in his own words, as follows: "It was determined to make the principal attack upon the enemy's left, and endeavor to gain a position from which it was thought that our artillery could be brought to bear with effect. Longstreet was directed to place the divisions of Hood and McLaws on the right of Hill, partially enveloping the enemy's left, which he was to drive in. General Hill was ordered to threaten the enemy's centre to prevent reinforcements from being drawn to either wing, and co-operate with his right division in Longstreet's attack. General Ewell was instructed to make a simultaneous demonstration upon the enemy's right, to be converted into a real attack, should opportunity offer." To make the details of this plan intelligible, let us see in what manner the opposing forces were positioned. On the Union side, the right wing, composed of the Twelfth Corps, with Wadsworth's division of the First Corps, based itself on the rough and wooded eminence of Culp's Hill; the Eleventh Corps, with Robinson's and Doubleday's divisions of the First Corps, held Cemetery Hill; the prolongation of the line to the left along the crest of Cemetery Ridge was occupied by Hancock's Second Corps; the Third Corps, under Sickles, formed the left wing, running from Hancock's flank to Round Top. On the Confederate side Longstreet held the right, opposite Sickles (the Union left), his line drawn along the well-wooded crown of Seminary Ridge, Hill continued the line along the same ridge to the Seminary, being opposite the Union centre under Hancock, and Ewell's corps, the Confederate left, stretched from the Seminary through the town, and enveloped the base of Culp's Hill. Accordingly, when Lee states that Longstreet was to "drive in the enemy's left," the relative situation of the opposing forces was such that the onset must fall upon Sickles's corps. Now a certain circumstance, explained in the following extract from General Meade's evidence before the Committee on the Conduct of the War, had rendered this part of the Union line more vulnerable than any other. "I had sent instructions in the morning to General Sickles, commanding the Third Corps, directing him to form his corps in line of battle on the left of Hancock's corps, and I had indicated to him in general terms that his right flank was to rest upon Hancock's left; and his left was to extend to the Round Top Mountain, plainly visible, if it was practicable to occupy it. During the morning I sent a staff officer to inquire of General Sickles whether he was in position. The reply was returned to me that General Sickles said there was no position there. I then sent back to him my general instructions, which had been previously given. . . When I arrived upon the ground, which I did a few minutes before four o'clock in the afternoon, I found that General Sickles had taken up a position very much in advance of what it had been my intention he should take; that he had thrown forward his right flank, instead of connecting with the left of General Hancock, something like a half or three quarters of a mile in front of General Hancock, thus leaving a large gap between his right and General Hancock's left, and that his left, instead of being near the Round Top Mountain, was in advance of the Round Top, and that his line instead of being a prolongation of General Hancock's line, as I expected it would be, made an angle of about forty-five degrees with General Hancock's line. As soon as I got upon the ground I sent for General Sickles and asked him to indicate to me his general position. When he had done so, I told him it was not the position I had expected him to take; that he had advanced his line beyond the support of my army, and that I was very fearful he would be attacked and would lose the artillery which he had put so far in front, before I could support it, or that if I undertook to support it, I would have to abandon all the rest of the line which I had adopted—that is, that I would have to fight the battle out there where he was.   General Sickles expressed regret that he should have occupied a position which did not meet with my approval, and he very promptly said that he would withdraw his forces to the line which I had intended him to take. We could see the ridge by turning around which I had indicated to him.   But I told him I was fearful that the enemy would not permit him to withdraw, and that there was no time for any further change or movement.   And before I had finished that remark or that sentence, the enemy's batteries opened upon him and the action commenced."

The precise position which Sickles thus took up may be noted in the accompanying map, where his line will be seen on a ridge along which the Emmettsburg road runs — a ridge intermediate between Cemetery Ridge, held by the Union army, and Seminary Ridge, occupied by Lee.   The question of the merit or demerit of Sickles's advanced line has been the subject of too much argumentation to require any here.   It needs that one should go on the ground in order to see how natural it was for him to take up that position, how many inducements there were for him to do so, how really laudable his motives were.   Nevertheless it was an error, for it threw his right flank much out of position in reference to Hancock's line on his right, and gave him no place on which to rest his left flank except by refusing it sharply towards the Round Top, thus forming a salient, which if broken through, would enable the enemy's artillery to enfilade both faces of his line.

It had been very still all day — noiseless shiftings, deployments, reconnoissances, and miscellaneous preparations; but a few moments before four o'clock, as the Union commander yet talked with General Sickles of the dangers incident to his position, the air was suddenly filled with the tumultuous clamor of battle, and the whole massive array of Longstreet's line, not even covered by skirmishers, moved forward. The attack fell upon the left front of the Third Corps, from where Sickles's line receded from the advanced ridge at Sherfy's peach orchard on the Emmettsburg road, and ran back through a low ground of woods, wheat-fields and woods, towards Round Top—the position being held by the brigades of DeTrobriand and Ward of Birney's division. But as Longstreet's front had a much greater development than the Union force on the wing, his flank extended quite beyond the left of Sickles — in fact overlapped it by two brigades.

This extension was manifestly designed on the part of the Confederates; for if by a forward rush they could crown the crest of the rocky spur, Little Round Top, they would hold in their hands the key of the whole position. Nor apparently was there aught to prevent their seizing this point, seeing that it was wholly unguarded when the enemy moved forward; but before he could gain it, defenders arrived. When the action commenced, the Fifth Corps (Sykes), which had been in reserve on the right, was moving over, under orders from General Meade, to form a reserve on the left, and as the head of the column composed of Barne's division was passing out to reinforce Sickles, General Warren, Chief Engineer of the Army, having seen the nakedness of the key-point of Little Round Top, and marked the near approach of the hostile force that overlapped Sickles, detached Vincent's brigade to garnish the position. Moving rapidly up the posterior slope of Little Round Top, this brigade had barely time to come forward into line when the Confederates, all exultant with their supposed success in flanking the Third Corps, came rushing up the ravine. The combatants immediately met in deadly clinch, in a grapple of such desperate fury as was seldom seen on any battle-field. But the position was saved by the bravery of Vincent's men, and of Weed's brigade, which reinforced them, though both Vincent and Weed gave their lives for its defence.

While, happily, the flanking force of Longstreet was thus held in check, the main part of his line, covering the left front of Sickles, met with greater success. The most terrific fighting occurred near the salient of the line at the peach orchard — a point the vital importance of which caused it to be contested with a wonderful determination. But no valor in the defence could countervail the faulty location of Sickles's corps; so that, when the Confederate artillery had succeeded in gaining a position whence it would enfilade his line, and the infantry was advanced under cover of its fire, the peach orchard was carried. The troops of Birney's division, to the left of that, fell back, and retired in much confusion over the main ridge behind, leaving Humphreys' division, together with Graham's brigade, alone in the advanced position along the Emmettsburg road. The situation was as critical as can well be conceived; for when Humphreys, on turning round to look at the ridge in his rear (the ridge which, if carried by the enemy, would decide the fate of the field) he saw that, for half a mile or more — that is, from the left of Hancock nearly to the Round Top — it was bare of troops, and unless he could carry back his division in face of the enemy's fiercest efforts in such order as would enable him to fill up that gap, the day was lost. Fortunately, Humphreys, by his skill and intrepidity, was equal to the occasion. The spontaneous impulse of this officer was to attack the enemy while yet the Confederates were assuming the offensive, and he felt confident of his ability to break their front. But, after the peach orchard was carried, Birney, who had succeeded to the command of the corps (Sickles having been carried from the field severely wounded), directed him to make a change of front to the rear, and form a new line, extending toward the Round Top. Knowing the almost impossibility of making the movement with any success in a situation that placed the enemy as well on both his flanks as in front, he would have disregarded the order had it not been coupled with the information that Birney's division would make a corresponding movement in connection with him. But Birney was unable to hold his troops to their work, for they fell back over the ridge, and were out of sight before Humphreys began to retire. This he still determined to effect in such manner as would enable him to fill up the gap in his rear; so he withdrew his small command of five thousand men by frequent stands of resistance, and many a fierce buffet, and he formed them, the three thousand that were left, in compact array, on the original crest. Here, joined by Hancock's troops and others from the right, they repulsed all further attempts of the enemy. These, indeed, were not of a determined character, for the Confederates were thoroughly exhausted, and day was already passing into the dusk of evening.

We must now look a little to what happened on the left of Humphreys, after the troops of Birney had been driven back. Following up their success the Confederates pressed forward into the low wooded ground in front of Round Top, and the fire of the attack was yet so fierce that the two brigades of Barnes's division that were sent in to support Sickles's left went down before it. Then Caldwell's division, detached by Hancock from his own left, marched by a detour toward Little Round Top, skirting which, it fared forth to the low woodland where hot battle boiled and bubbled as though it were some great hell-cauldron. The division fought with desperate fury, gained some advantage, and then, overpowered, came out with the loss of half its strength — two of its brigade commanders, the gallant Cross and Zook being killed. Then Ayres's division of Regulars took the place, opposing their disciplined valor to the enemy's advance: thus, till at length the Confederates succeeded in working their way round the right flank of the division to its rear, when the Regulars were forced to change front and fight their way through the hostile ranks, back to Little Round Top. There was then no Union force left on all the intermediate ground — nothing between the enemy and the main crest. This, however, was now well garnished by troops of the Fifth and Sixth Corps, which, when the Confederates perceived on debouching from the woods (for from the direction in which the enemy was approaching the crest is not visible until one issues from the woods), they halted in dismay at what yet remained to be done. Disorganized by the advance and fearfully punished in gaining what they had already won, they were not minded to brave the perils of scaling the beetling heights that, crowned with troops and artillery, now rose before their gaze. While they thus hesitated, Crawford's division of Pennsylvania reserves moving down the crest determined their conduct : they fell back to the wheat-field where they lay for the night.

It has been seen that in the plan of battle devised by Lee, Ewell on the left was to make demonstrations while Longstreet on the other flank attacked. Accordingly, after several shows of offence, Ewell about six in the evening formed his columns for a simultaneous attack both against Cemetery Hill and Culp's Hill. Against the latter position, where rested the right of the Union line, Johnson's division advanced ; and as Slocum's corps which had been holding it, was during the afternoon mainly withdrawn to brace up the forces on the left the Confederates succeeded in effecting a lodgment within the abandoned breastworks which they held during the night. The ascent of Cemetery Hill was made by three of Early's brigades and was met with so little firmness by the troops of the Eleventh Corps there stationed that the head of the charging column gained a foothold on the crest within the Union batteries. The artillerists resisted manfully, and presently Carroll's brigade of the Second Corps coming up made a countercharge that quickly threw back the intrusive force, which indeed was too weak for the task it had undertaken. Moreover it appeared that a grave mishap befell in the execution. " General Ewell," says Lee, "had directed Rodes to act in concert with Early, covering his right, and had requested Brigadier-General Lane, then commanding Pender's division, to co-operate on the right of Rodes. When the time to attack arrived General Rodes, not having his troops in position, was unprepared to co-operate with General Early, and before he could get in readiness, the latter had been obliged to retire from want of expected support on his right. Lane was prepared to give the assistance required of him, and so informed General Rodes, but the latter deemed it useless to advance after the failure of Early's attack."

Such was the course of the action of the 2d of July. It was without important result to the Confederates. They had indeed driven Sickles from his advance position; but this had only the effect to give a more solid integrity to the Union line drawn on the main crest. Some slight advantages perhaps they had acquired. The gain of the intermediate ridge along which runs the Emmettsburg road gave them a forward position for the artillery and they had secured a foothold within the breastworks of the extreme right on Culp's Hill. The chief fault in the enemy's conduct was the insufficient weight of the main attack under Longstreet, and the want of co-operation between the two wings. Any how, the result was such that Lee resolved to make another effort on the morrow. "The operations of the 2d," says he, "induced the belief that, with proper concert of action, and with the increased support which the positions gained on the right would enable the artillery to render the assaulting columns, we should ultimately succeed, and it was, accordingly, determined to continue the attack."

The general plan of Lee for the operations of the 3d of July remained unchanged; but there were some important modifications of details. Longstreet had during the night been reinforced by the division of Pickett, and it was proposed to make this the centre and main substance of the assaulting column.   Instead of directing the attack against the extreme left of the Union line, posted on the rocky summit of Little Round Top, as had been done the day before, Longstreet determined to hurl his masses against the left centre on Cemetery Ridge, holding the two divisions of Hood and McLaws simply to cover the right flank of the advancing lines.   To add weight to Pickett's storming force, it was strengthened on its left by Heth's division of Hill's corps and two brigades (those of Lane and Scale) of Pender's division of the same corps, and on the rear of the right flank by Wilcox's brigade of Anderson's division, also of Hill's corps.   Such was the force prepared for the assault, and it numbered about eighteen thousand men.

In co-operation with this main attack upon the left centre of the Union line, it was also proposed that Ewell should renew his efforts against the extreme right; and as that part of his force that had the previous evening gained a lodgment within the breastworks on Culp's Hill maintained its foothold during the night, much was hoped from a vigorous effort at this point.   Ewell therefore reinforced Johnston's division, which had gained the lodgment on Culp's Hill, with three additional brigades.   But early in the morning General Meade, having in the night returned the Twelfth Corps to its original position on the right, ordered an assault for the purpose of expelling the intrusive force.   This, after a severe struggle that continued from before dawn till near noon, was at length accomplished: and as Longstreet was very much delayed in forming his dispositions, it came about that when at one o'clock he was prepared to move forward, he was compelled to do so alone.

Yet, before the infantry attack should be begun, the Confederate commander resolved to try the effect of a heavy artillery fire.   He therefore caused one hundred and fifty-five guns to be placed in position along the fronts held by Longstreet and Hill, and from this massive enginery there opened, at one P. M., a prodigious bombardment that was continued for near three hours. The fire was vigorously replied to by eighty guns placed on Cemetery Hill and the crest of Cemetery Ridge, under direction of General Hunt, the chief of artillery. As a spectacle, this, the greatest artillery combat that ever occurred on the continent, was magnificent beyond description, and realized all that is grandiose in the circumstance of war. But in regard to the accomplishment of the purpose intended by Lee — to wit, to sweep opposition from the hill slope — its effect was inconsiderable. Some damage was done the artillery *materiel*, but the troops had excellent cover and suffered but little. General Lee has indeed noticed in his report that the fire of the Union batteries slackened towards the close; but this was because the chief of artillery, wishing to reserve his ammunition for the infantry advance, imposed economy on the batteries.

Out of the smoke-veiled front of Seminary Ridge, at three o'clock of the afternoon, emerged, in magnificent array, the double battle-line of the Confederates. Not impetuously, at the run or double-quick, as has been represented in the over-colored descriptions in which the famous charges has been so often painted, but with a disciplined *steadiness* — a quality noticed by all who saw this advance as its characteristic feature. The ground to be overpassed by the Confederates in order to attain the Cemetery Ridge where the Union battle array was drawn was a perfectly open plain of cultivated fields above a mile in width, and as it sloped gently up to the crest of Cemetery Ridge, it formed a natural *glacis*, and gave the defenders a fair field for the fire of artillery and musketry. It will, in fact, be difficult for one who shall survey the ground to conclude otherwise than that the enterprise of the Confederates was hopeless. Almost from the start, the assaulting lines came under fire of the Union batteries, and then was seen the effect of the wasteful use of ammunition on the part of the Confederates during the preliminary bombardment, and on the other hand the good result of the imposed economy on the part of the Union artillerists.

Scarcely had the Confederates moved forward from their own lines, than the fire with which they were greeted began to tell on the integrity of their formation. Heth's supporting division, on the left of Pickett, indeed, began to waver at the time it was leaving its own lines, and while crossing a low stone wall behind which they had lain, some already showed such trepidation that they were jeered by the reserves that lay behind. Then, as they became exposed to the fire of artillery from Cemetery Hill, the brigade on the left flank hesitated and went back, and from that flank there was such a continual wearing away that, by the time the assaulting mass had advanced over half the width of the plain, Heth's division had broken and disappeared. There was a like result on Pickett's right, where the supporting brigade failed to keep up; so that it came about that, for the real storming column, there was left but Pickett's division alone. His right experienced the same fire from Round Top that had stayed the progress of the supporting brigade on that flank, but this did not cause the division to pause — it only caused it to double in somewhat towards its left. This brought the point of attack a little off from where it was intended, and directly in the face of the two reduced and incomplete divisions of Hancock's corps. And here I cannot resist the opportunity of transcribing from the manuscript report of General Hancock, the concise yet vivid language in which he describes the great scene that followed — a scene in which he formed so distinguished a figure.

"The column pressed on, coming within musketry range without receiving immediately our fire, our men evincing a striking disposition to withhold it until it could be delivered with deadly effect. Two regiments of Stannard's brigade (First Corps), which had been posted in a little grove in front of and at a considerable angle with the main line, first opened with an oblique fire upon the right of the enemy's column, which had the effect to make the troops on that flank double in a little towards their left. They still pressed on, however, without halting to return the fire. The rifled guns of our artillery having fired away all their canister, were now withdrawn to await the issue of the struggle between the opposing infantry. Arrived at between two and three hundred yards, the troops of the enemy were met by a destructive fire from the divisions of Gibbon and Hays, which they promptly returned, and the fight at once became fierce and general. In front of Hays's division it was not of very long duration: mowed down by canister from Woodruff's battery, and by the fire from two regiments judiciously posted by General Hays in his extreme front and right, and the fire of different lines in the rear, the enemy broke in disorder, leaving fifteen colors and nearly two thousand prisoners in the hands of this division. Those of the enemy's troops who did not fall into disorder in front of this division were moved to the right, and reinforced the line attacking Gibbon's division. The right of the attacking force having been repulsed by Hall's and Harrow's brigades, of the latter division, assisted by the fire of the Vermont regiments already referred to, doubled to its left and also reinforced the centre, and thus the attack was in the fullest strength opposite the brigade of General Webb. This brigade was disposed in two lines — two regiments, the 69th and 71st Pennsylvania, were behind a low stone wall and slight breastwork hastily constructed by them, the remainder of the brigade being behind the crest, some sixty paces to the rear, and so disposed as to fire over the heads of those in front. When the enemy's line had nearly reached the stone wall, led by General Armistead, the most of that part of Webb's brigade posted here abandoned their position, but, fortunately, did not retreat entirely. They were immediately, by the personal bravery of General Webb and his officers, formed behind the crest before referred to, which was occupied by the remnant of that brigade.

"Emboldened by seeing this indication of weakness, the enemy pushed forward more pertinaciously, numbers of them crossing over the breastwork abandoned by the troops. The fight here became very close and deadly. The enemy's battle-flags were soon seen waving on the stone wall. Passing at this time, Colonel Devereux commanding the Nineteenth Massachusetts, anxious to be in the right place, applied to me for permission to move his regiment to the right and to the front where the line had been broken. I granted it, and his regiment and Colonel Mallon's Forty-second New York on his right, proceeded there at once. But the enemy having left Colonel Hall's front, as described before, this officer promptly moved his command by the right flank to still further reinforce the position of Gen. Webb, and was immediately followed by Harrow's brigade. The movement was executed, but not without confusion, owing to many men leaving their ranks to fire at the enemy from the breastworks. The situation was now very peculiar. The men of all the brigades had in some measure lost their regimental organization, but individually they were firm. The ambition of individual commanders to promptly cover the point penetrated by the enemy, the smoke of the battle and the intensity of the close engagement caused this confuson. The point, however, was covered. In regular formation, our line would have stood four ranks deep. The colors of the different regiments were now advanced, waving in defiance of the long line of battle-flags presented by the enemy. The men pressed firmly after them under their energetic commanders and the example of their officers, and after a few moments' desperate fighting the enemy were repulsed, throwing down their arms and finding safety in flight, or throwing themselves on the ground to escape our fire. The battle-flags were ours and the victory was won. Gibbon's division secured twelve stand of colors, and prisoners enough to swell the number captured by the corps to about four thousand five hundred."

After the repulse of Pickett's assault, Wilcox's command, that had been on the right but had failed to move forward, advanced by itself to the attack, and came within a few hundred yards of Hancock's line. But in passing over the plain it met a severe artillery fire, and Stannard detached a force which took it in flank and rear, capturing several hundred prisoners; the rest fled.

Meantime within the Confederate lines reigned a great disorder. To the straggling parties that had begun to break off from the assaulting column almost from the start, were constantly added new crowds of fugitives till the whole mass giving way fled to their own lines where it required the most strenuous personal exertions of Longstreet and of Lee to rally and compose them. Of the conduct of the latter officer, an eye-witness thus wrote: "If Longstreet's behavior was admirable, that of General Lee was perfectly sublime. He was engaged in rallying and in encouraging the broken troops, and was riding about, a little in front of the wood, quite alone—his staff being engaged in a similar manner further to the rear. His face, which is always placid and cheerful, did not show signs of the slightest disappointment, care, or annoyance; and he was addressing to every soldier he met, a few words of encouragement, such: as 'All this will come out right in the end; we will talk it over afterwards; but meanwhile all good men must rally. We want all good and true men just now, etc.' He spoke to all the wounded men that passed him, and the slightly wounded he exhorted 'to bind up their hurts and take up a musket' in this emergency. Very few failed to answer his appeal, and I saw many badly wounded men take off their hats and cheer him. He said to me, 'This has been a sad day for us, Colonel—a sad day; but we can't always expect to gain victories.'"

This was the last offensive sally attempted by Lee. He

was himself thoroughly convinced of the hopelessness of the undertaking, and the fire of his troops was quenched in blood. "The severe loss sustained by the army, and the reduction of its ammunition," he mildly says, "rendered another attempt to dislodge the enemy inadvisable." The fault in the Confederate tactics in the battle of the 3d, was the same as that I have pointed out as inhering in those of the previous day's action. Their lines were too much extended, and the attack was not sufficiently powerful; or, as Longstreet has put it, "the attack should have been made with thirty thousand instead of fifteen thousand men."

It is still a point in dispute among military men whether Meade should have followed up the repulse of the Confederates on the afternoon of the 3d by an advance of his own left. On this point General Hancock gives the following interesting testimony. "I think that our lines should have advanced immediately, and I believe we should have won a great victory; I was very confident that the advance would be made. General Meade told me before the fight that if the enemy attacked me, he intended to put the Fifth and Sixth Corps on the enemy's flank: I therefore when I was wounded and lying down in my ambulance and about leaving the field, dictated a note to General Meade, and told him if he would put in the Fifth and Sixth Corps I believed he would win a great victory. I asked him afterwards, when I returned to the army, what he had done in the premises. He said he had ordered the movement, but the troops were slow in collecting, and moved so slowly, that nothing was done before night, except that some of the Pennsylvania reserves went out and met Hood's division, it was understood, of the enemy, and actually overthrew it, assisted, no doubt, in some measure, by their knowledge of their failure in the assault." But on the other hand, General Longstreet, in conversation with the writer of these pages, said in reference to the question of attack: "I had the divisions of Hood and McLaws that had not been engaged during the day; I had a heavy force of artillery, and I have no doubt I should have given the Federals as severe a repulse as that received by Pickett." And in fact the experience of nearly all the Virginia battles goes to confirm the opinion of the Confederate commander.

Although General Lee, after the failure of the attack of Friday came to the conclusion that further attack was hopeless, and had formed the resolution of withdrawing from Northern soil, he still felt confidence in his ability to repulse any assault that might be made upon him. Accordingly on the 4th, while pushing forward the laborious task of sending off his immense trains to the Potomac, he drew in his flanks, threw up breastworks, and took a defensive position in which he rather coveted than deprecated attack by the Union army. General Meade, on the morning of the 4th, ordered demonstrations along the whole front; but they were very feebly made, and when the officers met together that evening to report the state of things on their front, there was little or nothing definitely known as to the position or designs of the enemy. Lee, however, removed all doubt by withdrawing that night. The retrograde movement was begun after dark, the whole column moving by the Fairfield road. A heavy rain continued throughout the night, and so much impeded progress, that Ewell's corps, which brought up the rear, did not leave Gettysburg until late in the forenoon of Sunday the 5th. After an arduous march Lee's whole army reached Hagerstown on the afternoon of the 6th and morning of the 7th of July.

When it was definitely discovered that the enemy had withdrawn, the important question of pursuit presented itself. But it was a difficult matter to decide whether this should be made in a direct following up of the enemy, or by a flank movement east of the South Mountain by way of Frederick. However, to harass the enemy's rear, the Sixth Corps, under Sedgwick, was immediately sent forward in direct pursuit.

Having on the evening of the 6th overtaken the enemy's rear guard, posted in the Fairfield pass, it was found occupying so strong a position, that Sedgwick deemed attack inadvisable. Meantime, Meade had resolved to adopt the other line of pursuit, and therefore directed the march of the whole army by way of Frederick.

Lee's trains succeeded in reaching Williamsport on the 6th; but were unable to cross the Potomac on account of the high stage of the water, and the pontoon-bridge left at Falling Water had been destroyed by a party sent out by General French from Frederick. The wounded and prisoners were sent over the river as rapidly as possible in a few ferry-boats, while the trains awaited the subsiding of the Potomac and the construction of a new pontoon-bridge. "On the 8th of July," says Lee, "the enemy's cavalry advanced toward Hagerstown, but was repulsed by General Stuart, and pursued as far as Boonsboro'. With this exception, nothing but occasional skirmishing occurred until the 12th, when the main body of the enemy arrived. The army then took a position previously selected, covering the Potomac from Williamsport to Falling Waters, where it remained for two days with the enemy immediately in front, manifesting no disposition to attack, but throwing up intrenchments along his whole line. By the 13th, the river at Williamsport, though still deep, was fordable, and a good bridge was completed at Falling Waters, new boats having been constructed, and some of the old recovered. As further delay would enable the enemy to obtain reinforcements, and as it was found difficult to procure a sufficient supply of flour for the troops, the working of the mills being interrupted by high water, it was determined to await an attack no longer. Orders were accordingly given to cross the Potomac that night, Ewell's corps by the ford at Williamsport, and those of Longstreet and Hill on the bridge."

It will thus be seen that Lee reached the Potomac six days

in advance of Meade, which would indicate an excessive cir-
cumspection in the movements of the latter at a time when
the utmost impetuosity was called for. It is true that the
line of pursuit adopted by General Meade — namely, that by
the east side of the mountains, *via* Frederick and the South
Mountain passes — was nearly double the length of Lee's line
of retreat through the Cumberland Valley. The distance to
Williamsport by the latter route is about forty miles, and by
the latter seventy-five. Nevertheless, as it took General
Meade seven days to make the seventy-five miles, the march
must be accounted slow. Yet it would be unjust to make
this circumstance a ground of censure against General Meade,
for no one could have exerted himself more strenuously than
did that commander to overtake and finish his adversary: the
failure was really owing to the fact that the army, having lost
most severely in its best officers, was not in condition to re-
spond to the wishes of General Meade.

Whether Meade should have attacked or refrained from
attacking Lee at Williamsport, is one of those questions
on which every American considers it his right and privilege
to pronounce an *ex cathedra* opinion. It is probable that the
popular verdict will always condemn him for his hesitation to
assume the offensive. Yet it is certain that Lee wished to be
attacked at Williamsport, and if it be a cardinal maxim of
war never to do what the enemy desires you to do, it may
appear that there are at least two sides to the question.

On the retirement of Lee, Meade did not delay the passage of the Potomac. But the Confederate commander refusing battle, continued his retreat to the Rapidan on the banks
of which the opposing armies now took up position.

III.

RESULTS OF GETTYSBURG.

Such was Gettysburg — the battle the greatest in respect

of its proportions and the weightiest in respect of the issue involved, of all the actions waged during four years between the mighty rival armies of the East.   In point of losses alone, it deserves to rank with the first-class battles of history, for on the Union side the casualities were near twenty-four thousand, and on the Confederate side they exceeded twenty-seven thousand men, killed, spoiled, or taken.

With what design the invasion of the North was undertaken, in what manner it culminated in the mighty wrestle among the hills of Western Pennsylvania, and with what result to the invader it was brought to a close, have already been set forth.   It only remains to draw such general deductions as are authorized by the review of the campaign as a whole.

The circumstances under which Lee initiated the campaign, authorized him to expect the most important results from the invasion of the North.   Having many times before defeated the Army of the Potomac with a much inferior force, it was not unwarrantable for him to assume that he would again triumph now that he had an army equal in strength to that of his adversary — an army, too, in such high and daring spirit that, in the words of Longstreet, it was "capable of anything"; while the commander opposed to him at the opening of the campaign was a man for whose character and abilities he entertained a contempt which it would be difficult to say was not merited.   It must also be conceded that the plan of operations devised by Lee, while wonderfully bold, was yet thoroughly methodical and well matured.   For if the march removed his army to an indefinite distance from his base, he yet had an easily guarded line of communications by way of the Cumberland and Shenandoah Valley, to his depots at Winchester and Gordonsville, whence he could readily draw ammunition.   And in the matter of supplies he was in no wise dependant on Virginia, for the well-peopled and productive soil of Pennsylvania affords ample resources for the subsistence of an army, for a time and whilst moving, without the use of magazines, by the European method of requisitions at the cost of the inhabitants. The proof of this is furnished in the fact, that the Confederate army not only subsisted on the country during the campaign, but that in addition, it forwarded to the Potomac great quantities of cattle and corn that served to eke out their meagre larder until such time as the maturing corps furnished fresh supplies.

Being thus easy with respect to that part on which Frederick the Great has said that armies, like serpents, move — to wit, its belly — Lee, leading a powerful, valiant, and enthusiastic army, confidently moved to an anticipated victory. His aim was the capture of Washington, the defeat of the Army of the Potomac, and the retention of a footing long enough on loyal soil to so work upon the North, that under the combined pressure of its own fears, the uprising of the reactionary elements at home, and perhaps the influence of the Powers abroad, it might be disposed to sue for peace. He had ample means for the conduct of the enterprise, which was of itself not extravagant, and it is rare that any military operation presents greater assurance of success than Lee had of attaining his end of conquering a peace on northern soil.

This being so, we can rise at once to the height of the appreciation of the triumph at Gettysburg — a victory which, if we consider the tremendous issue which it involved, calls forth sentiments akin to the trembling joy with which Cromwell returned thanks to Heaven for the "crowning mercy" of Worcester. It was the crisis of the war — the salvation of the North.

In tracing out the causes of Lee's defeat we shall find that something was due to the faults of that commander himself; something to the good conduct of General Meade, much to the valor of the Army of the Potomac, and much, again, to fortune, "that name for the unknown combinations of infinite power," which maugre every seeming assurance of success, was wanting to the Confederates. It was not by the prevision nor by the manœuvres of either general that the forces were brought into collision on the 1st of July, though the Union commander is certainly entitled to great credit for the promptitude with which, accepting the issue accidentally presented. he threw forward his army to Gettysburg. Here, nature as well as circumstances, and the unusual temerity of Lee, favored the Union army. Elated by the success of the first day, the Confederate commander, contrary to his intent and promise, determined to attack. But while the position might readily have been turned, it was impregnable by direct assault, if maintained with skill and firmness. And it was so maintained; for the Army of the Potomac, realizing the tremendous issue involved, feeling that it stood there for the defence of its own soil, fought with far more determination than it had ever displayed in Virginia.

The experiment of the Pennsylvania campaign gave a complete and final quietus to the scheme of Southern invasion of the loyal States, and the enterprise was never more attempted. Nor indeed was the army of Northern Virginia ever again in condition to undertake such a movement. This was not alone due to the shock which it received in its *morale* from so disastrous a blow, but to its material losses, the portentous sum of which exceeded the aggregate of its casualties in the whole series of battles which Grant delivered from the Rapidan to the James River. This subtraction of force viewed merely in a numerical count was most grave, considering the great exhaustion of the fighting resources of the Confederates; while, when we take into account the quality of the men, the loss was irreparable; for the thirty thousand put *hors de combat* at Gettysburg were the very flower and *élite* of that incomparable Southern infantry, which, tempered by two years of battle and habituated to victory, equalled any soldiers that ever followed the eagles to conquest.

But the results of Gettysburg were not confined to the

Eastern theatre of operations : its effect was powerfully felt
throughout all the West, where, in consequence of the ab-
sorption of force for the invasion of Pennsylvania, a succession of severe disasters befell the Confederate arms.   At the
time the campaign was initiated the Army of the Mississippi
was shut up in Vicksburg, and the Army of Tennessee confronted the force of Rosecrans in daily expectation of attack,
and itself too weak to maintain its ground.   Now let us suppose that Lee, in place of recalling the corps of Longstreet
from North Carolina in order to enter on the invasion, had
confined himself to a defensive attitude on the Rappahannock
(which he could certainly have maintained, since even without Longstreet he had all the force with which he had a
month before overwhelmed Hooker at Chancellorsville), and
meanwhile, sent his energetic lieutenant, strengthened, perhaps, by an additional division or two, to the West.   This
accession of strength would have enabled Bragg to take
the offensive against Rosecrans, for it is a matter of history that, in the month of October following, Bragg, reinforced in precisely the manner indicated, was able to give his
antagonist a crushing defeat at Chickamauga.   But it is not
Rosecrans alone that might have been thrown on the defensive
— for this result accomplished, such detachments might then
have been sent from the Army in Tennessee as would have enabled Johnston to relieve Vicksburg.   As it was, Bragg saw
himself forced to fall back and abandon the whole of Tennessee
when Rosecrans advanced in the month of June, while Vicksburg, closely invested by Grant, and deprived of all hope of
relief, was compelled to surrender — an event which, by a
striking conjuncture, took place on the same day that witnessed Lee's final repulse at Gettysburg.

And thus the battle-summer rose to its climax in the clash
and clamor of Titanic war, which, spending its fury on the
soil of Pennsylvania, was echoed back from the borders of
the Mississippi and the Alpine heights of the Cumberland

IX.

THE WILDERNESS.

I.

PRELUDE TO THE WILDERNESS.

WHEN in the month of May, 1864, vernal grasses and flowers came once more to festoon the graves in battle-fields over which the contending hosts of North and South had wrestled for three years, the armies upstarting along all the front of war prepared to close again in deadly combat. It was the opening of the spring campaign of 1864; but it was more than the opening of a campaign, for the circumstances were such as to mark this as a new epoch in the history of the war.

This characteristic it owed first of all to the clearly-defined aspect of the military situation, which for the first time showed an entire unity both in the objectives to be attained by the Union armies and in the organization of the war itself.

When hostilities began between the North and South, the theatre was so vast, the circumstances were so novel, and the country so green in war, that the conduct of military operations was of necessity almost wholly experimental. The North undertook to subdue rebellion throughout a country continental in its dimensions, stretching from the Potomac to the Rio Grande — a country in which the whole population was in arms and animated by the bitterest hostility. Without military traditions, without a military establishment, without a military leader of genius, the North, strong in the faith of the Union, accepted the gage of war. It formed armies. It sent them forth to battle. Of course, the conduct of the war was crude. There were three or four different armies in Virginia, three or four between the Alleghanies and the Mississippi — eight or ten in all where there ought to have been but three. These armies were placed frequently on faulty or indecisive lines. And there was no unity in their action. Nevertheless these armies went to work. They began "hammering." And at the end of three years they had produced results somewhat notable in their way. Let us recall briefly what these were, both as regards the East and the West, to the end that we may the better realize both what remained to be done and the change now introduced into the conduct of the war.

In considering the operations in Virginia there are two facts that should be borne in mind. First, that the Army of the Potomac had there not only to combat the main army of the South, but an army that by means of the interior lines held by the enemy, might readily receive great accessions of force from the western zone. "To the Confederates," as I have elsewhere said, "Virginia bore the character of a fortress thrust forward on the flank of the theatre of war, and such was their estimate of its importance, that they were always ready to make almost any sacrifice elsewhere to insure its tenure." Secondly, that the Army of the Potomac, in addition to its offensive charge, was the custodian of the National Capital — a duty that governed all strategic combinations in Virginia. Having thus at once to make head against the most formidable, the best disciplined, and the most ably commanded army of the Confederacy, and to guard Washington, which, while a glittering prize in the eyes of the enemy, was also most unfortunately located on an exposed frontier, it is not wonderful that the Army of the Potomac had not yet been able to attain its goal — the capture of Richmond. From the fact that each army had a point of the highest importance to cover and an objective of the highest importance to gain, there resulted from the alternate aggressive movements of these two mighty and closely-matched rivals an ebb and flow, a flux and reflux of battle and bloodshed that rarely burst beyond the boundaries of the Potomac and the James. The history of the three years' operations up to this period is a history of the collisions of these two powerful bodies in combats wherein victory adhered now to the one and now to the other of the opposing standards. If the one side could claim a Manassas, a Fredericksburg, a Chancellorsville, the other could claim a Malvern, an Antietam, a Gettysburg. But it is the glory of the Army of the Potomac, that through all these weary three years it had kept good its trust, that it had preserved the Capital, that while receiving terrible blows it had not failed to inflict the like, and that it had already put *hors de combat* alone a hundred thousand of the bravest and best soldiers of the Confederacy. The opening of the spring campaign found it lying on the north bank of the Rapidan — its adversary being ensconced in works on the opposite side.

Meanwhile, the deeds of the armies of the west throughout these three years claim a more brilliant page.

It is one of the well-known generalizations of the war, that while victory so long shunned in Virginia the Union standards, she crowned them through the West with constant laurels. This inequality of fortune is partly explained by the diversity of the obstacles to be overcome, East and West, and of the proportionate means for overcoming them : for the relative skill, strength, advantage of position, and what not, in the combatants, were very different on the two fields. But, nevertheless, as if to proclaim the dominion of fate, even where at the West energy and address were replaced by carelessness and blundering, there too the star of success shone fixed in the ascendant; and whatever there lacked of sound dispositions or right use of resources, seemed made up by pure good fortune and the prestige of past triumphs more legitimately won. No Union negligences or errors, however great, would as at the East, inure to permanent disadvantage. Confederate offensive campaigns met, when at the very summit of success, unexpected and improbable checks, ruining the enterprise — as in Sydney Johnston's invasion begun and ended at Shiloh, and in Bragg's elaborate movement towards Louisville. Confederate defensive campaigns were suddenly turned to disasters, near the hour fixed for the saving contrecoup — as by Pemberton's operations at Vicksburg and the substitution of Hood for Johnston at the Chattahoochie. A rare cloud appeared on the Union path only to magically furl off, leaving at last the whole retrospect so luminous with victory from bound to goal, that one would say Fortune had been suborned to march under the Union banners.

The profit of these western successes was not confined to that region, but more than once roused the Union from the almost fatal melancholy into which the ruinous havoc repeated upon its eastern armies was plunging it. The governmental archives might, if ever penetrated, disclose the burden of gloom which western victories opportunely relieved; for often, while the cause was sinking in distress in the East, a blast from the West, blowing fresh and strong, gave it lease of life again. Beyond the Alleghanies, in an experience unknown at the East, each fought-out campaign led straight to the campaign succeeding: and a surplus of prestige from past victory gave bright augury of victory to come; till the very momentum of the Union columns rolling across their hundred-leagued campaigning grounds, was by friend and foe alike pronounced resistless. The Union triumphs at Mill Spring, Fort Henry, Fort Donelson, and Shiloh, in the spring of 1862, were followed by gradually unclinching the Mississippi forts from the sullen grip of the South, till Columbus, Island Ten, Fort Pillow and

Memphis being surrendered, and two elaborate lines of valley defence successively forced, the great Mobile highway lay open to Vicksburg. Bragg's angry lunge, in autumn, to win back lost fortunes, ended, after Murfreesboro', in a long recoil to Georgia, and in the abandonment of the north central zone, with all its cities, its arms-bearing people and its supplies. Onward with the new year 1863, moved the Union banners. Rosecrans scaled the Alleghanies toward Chattanooga, while Grant followed the guidance of the Mississippi, whose *embouchure* had been already won by the great river-fight below New Orleans. Midsummer was crowned with the conquest of Vicksburg; and when Port Hudson succumbed, in close corollary, the famous Mississippi line was fought out, and its record closed up in the war's annals. In the latter days of September, the Rosecrans column, winding its way far up the Alleghanies, aiming at Chattanooga, seized it and therewith the key of the whole mountain system. It only remained now for Grant, as commander of the whole Valley Department, to set a seal on the year by securing what was gained; and this he did (November, 1863,) in a great mountain battle, dashing Bragg from his seat on the heights which engirdled Chattanooga, and forcing off, in the same blow, Longstreet's eager grasp from Knoxville : then the Confederate hosts fell back into Georgia.

Such then was the result, territorially considered, of the three years of war. It had reduced the belligerent force of the Confederacy to two armies — the one under Johnston in Georgia, the other under Lee in Virginia. And in reducing the area of the rebellion it practically limited the functions of the Union force to the destruction of these two armies, which were the sole material support of the Confederacy. The anarchic elements of the war had been reduced to order and organic form, and if much yet remained to be done, there was at least a clear unity in the objectives to be attained.

Happily, also, the same unity had lately been imported into the conduct of the war by the appointment of General Grant in March, 1864, to the grade of Lieutenant-General and his nomination to the office of General-in-Chief. Aside from the approved good qualities of that commander, the stroke was most just and wise, for in truth for three years the war had been without a head. Since the time when, for a brief period, McClellan had exercised the functions of General-in-Chief — a period during which he had outlined but had had no opportunity to execute a comprehensive system of operations — an incredible incoherence prevailed in the general conduct of the war. It is true that since that time General Halleck had exercised the functions of a central military director at Washington. But his office was the shadow of a name. He could not get himself obeyed by the commanders in the field, and when he did actually intervene it was commonly only to entail disaster. In point of fact, as General Halleck's last annual official report had clearly shown, operations were directed sometimes by the President, with or without the approval of his military counsellors, sometimes by one or another of his military counsellors, without the approval of the President, and sometimes by the general in the field without the approval of any one. In this lamentable state of facts, it is not wonderful that the results thus far achieved fell far short of the army's lavish expenditure of blood. "The armies in the East and West," in Grant's pithy phrase, "acted independently and without concert, like a baulky team, no two ever pulling together." Indeed, between the armies in the two zones, there had hitherto been such lack of combination of effort that the Army of the Potomac and the Army of the West had commonly found themselves in their extremest crisis at the moment when the other, being reduced to inaction, left the Confederate force to concentre on the vital point. And in truth the wonder was not that the war was not already brought to a close : rather the wonder was that so much should have been accomplished.

But now Grant commanded " all the armies of the United States," and he was at once able, with all the resources of the country at his call, with near a million men in the field, and a generous and patriotic people at his back, to enter upon a comprehensive system of combined operations. The task before him was plain. Strategetic positions now played but a secondary *rôle:* armies had become objectives. In the West the successor of Bragg lay, recruiting his army after its rude bout at Chattanooga, in secure camp at Dalton, on the railroad to Atlanta. His presence at that point was simply designed to cover from further incursion the broad State of Georgia, as Lee's army behind the Rapidan was planted there for the shielding of Virginia : and both of these forces had now obviously been thrown mainly on the defensive. It was the primary scope of the two great campaigns of the year to project the Union armies respectively upon the natural line of retreat chosen by their antagonists, and, in so doing, to force the latter to give decisive battle : the battle resulting in their defeat, would drive these armies from their lines of supplies, or else quite disperse them, leaving, in either event, the cities they covered to their assailants, who would thus capture Richmond in Virginia, and, in Georgia, Atlanta, the Richmond of the West.

Raised to the supreme command, Lieutenant-General Grant committed the care of the Mississippi Valley, and all the armies between the Alleghanies and the great river, to Major-General Sherman. The campaign against Lee he determined to direct personally, and in this view he established his head-quarters with the Army of the Potomac, the immediate command of which, however, continued in the hands of General Meade. The few weeks that remained until the season favorable for military operations should arrive, were filled up with manifold activities, and by the opening of May

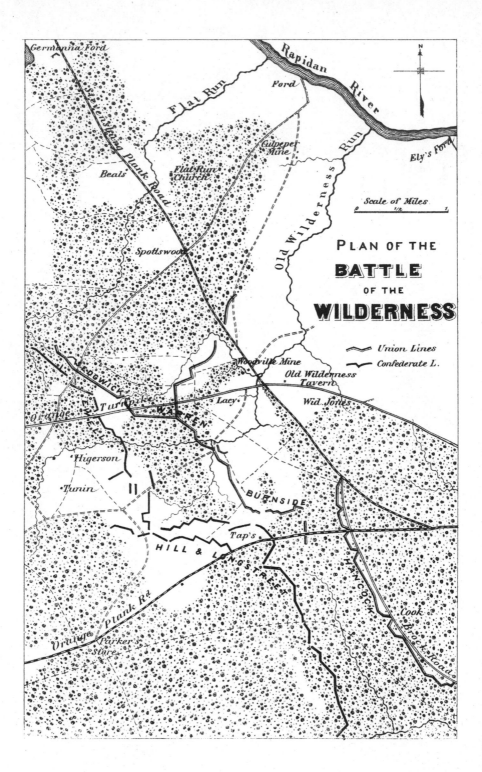

PLAN OF THE
BATTLE
OF THE
WILDERNESS

Scale of Miles

Union Lines
Confederate L.

Germanna Ford
Rapidan River
Flat Run
Ford
Ely's Ford
Culpeper Mine
Beals
Flat Run Church
Old Wilderness Run
Spottswood
Woodville Mine
Old Wilderness Tavern
SEDGWICK
Turnpike
Lacy
Wid. Jones
Orange
WARREN
Higerson
Tunin
BURNSIDE
HILL & LONGST.
Tap's
Hancock Brook Road
Cook
Plank Rd
Orange
Parker Store

all needed preparations had been completed. Then Grant gave the word "Forward," and the army in Virginia and the army in Tennessee, unleashed, joyfully entered upon those grand campaigns that will form the subject-matter of this and the succeeding chapter.

II.

THE BATTLE OF THE WILDERNESS.

On Tuesday, the 3d of May, 1864, knowing that the Army of the Potomac must soon move, and being desirous of chronicling a campaign to which in advance a surpassing public interest attached, I left Washington and proceeded by the Orange and Alexandria Railroad to Culpepper Courthouse. General Grant had established his head-quarters in a house in that dilapidated and war-worn old Virginia town, and in the evening I was received by him. It proved that I was just in time to witness the opening of the campaign, for orders had been issued for the army to move at midnight, and the commander was then giving the final touches to his preparations. His maps were before him, and he spoke with confidence of the future. He was to cross the Rapidan, turn the Confederate right, and then throw his army between Lee and Richmond.

Lee's army lay behind the Rapidan — a stream which had never been crossed by the Union army save to be quickly re-crossed. The three Confederate corps were positioned *en échelon* behind that river — Ewell's corps guarding its course; Hill's corps lying around Orange Courthouse, and Longstreet's corps being encamped about Gordonsville. The journals of the time amused their readers with most absurd speculations regarding Lee's lines, which were pictured as another Torres Vedras. But in reality the works on the Rapidan were of the simplest kind, and were not designed as a battle-line. Lee knew perfectly well that a direct passage of the Rapidan

would never be attempted; for the south banks of that
stream in its upper part rise into considerable bluffs, which
completely dominate the north bank, and precluded all
thought of attempting a crossing in the enemy's face. Besides, in Lee's method of defending rivers, it was never his
habit to plant his army on their banks for the purpose of pre-
venting a passage. It was his wont, rather, to observe the
river-line with a small force, sufficient to dispute the crossing
for a time, while, distributed at convenient points within
supporting distance, he held his masses to be hurled against
his antagonist after he had crossed. Lee's army at this time
numbered 52,626 men of all arms.

The Army of the Potomac had wintered in cantonments
along the Orange and Alexandria Railroad in the vicinity of
Culpepper Courthouse. Since Grant's arrival it had been
reorganized into three corps — the Second, Fifth, and Sixth.
The Second Corps was under Major-General W. S. Hancock,
the Fifth under Major-General G. K. Warren, and the Sixth
under Major-General John Sedgwick — three most able and
experienced lieutenants, subordinate commanders of the
highest type. With the Army of the Potomac was associated the Ninth Corps, which arrived immediately before
the opening of the campaign. It was under General A. E.
Burnside, who held command independent of General Meade
— a very faulty arrangement, which worked so ill that the
corps was afterwards merged in the Army of the Potomac.
The powerful body of cavalry, numbering over ten thousand
sabres, had been placed under General P. H. Sheridan, the
man of all others most worthy the command. There was a
great deal of raw material in the different corps, but it had been
thoroughly fused with the veteran element: so that the army
of 130,000 men which Grant held in hand was not only very
formidable in numbers, it was in excellent discipline and in
the highest spirits. "Hope elevated and joy brightened its
crest."

The camps were broken up during the 3d of May, and at midnight the columns moved out under the starlight towards the Rapidan. To those of us who lay in Culpepper Court-house there was little sleep that night; for during all its hours the air was filled with the tramp of armed men and the rumble of wagons — and indeed the anticipations of the morrow were too exciting to permit slumber. When the morning came, Generals Grant and Meade and their staffs rode forward to the Rapidan at Germanna Ford. We found that Warren's corps had already crossed there on pontoon bridges, and that Sedgwick's corps was following. Han-cock's corps, forming the left column, was at the same time filing across the Rapidan at Ely's Ford, a few miles down stream from Germanna Ford. The crossing of the river was made without the slightest opposition, for the points of pas-sage were quite beyond Lee's right flank. The few videttes had fled at the apparition of the Union cavalry which pre-ceded the infantry. The scene when we arrived, and throughout all the afternoon as the troops continued to defile across the Rapidan, was wonderfully imposing — the long columns winding down to the river's brink, traversing the bridges, and then spreading out in massive array over the hill-slopes and subjacent valleys of the south bank. Before the afternoon was spent the whole army was across, and the heads of columns, plunging into the depths of the forest, were lost to view. Hancock pushed out to Chancel-lorsville, and lay all night on the old battle-field of Hooker. Warren advanced southward by the Stevensburg plank road six miles, to Old Wilderness Tavern. Sedgwick remained close to the river. Burnside had orders to hold Culpepper Courthouse for twenty-four hours, and then follow in the path of the other corps. The head-quarters' tents were pitched for the night within a few hundred yards of the river; but the troops of Hancock and Warren bivouacked in the heart of the Wilderness.

Well aware was Lee of his opponent's move ; for from the Confederate signal station on the lofty height of Clark's Mountain the motions of the Union columns toward the Rapidan had been descried in the early dawn, and as we went forward we saw beacon-fires blazing on the mountain-top to summon the concentration of the far-scattered Confederate corps. Lee had predetermined that if Grant turned his right by crossing the Rapidan at the lower fords, he would take the offensive, launch forward his army to the Wilderness, and there join battle with his antagonist.   From the position of the three Confederate corps, the average distance to where — marching north-eastward, they might strike the Union force after crossing the Rapidan — was about twenty miles ; but the movement was facilitated by the two excellent roads (one a turnpike, the other a plank road) from Orange Courthouse to Fredericksburg.   By throwing forward his army on these roads Lee would strike Grant's line of march at right angles, and if the movement was made with sufficient celerity it would avail to intercept the Union army in the Wilderness. Lee made his dispositions accordingly, and while, during the 4th, the Union columns were defiling across the Rapidan, the Confederate army was hastening forward to meet them as fast as legs and hoofs and wheels could travel.   By dark of the 4th, so much of the intervening distance had been overpassed that Ewell, whose corps moved by the Orange turnpike, and Hill, whose corps advanced by the Orange plank road, had approached to within a very few miles of where Warren lay at Old Wilderness Tavern, which is at the junction of the Orange turnpike with the Stevensburg plank road leading southward from Germanna Ford.

At head-quarters we were up long before dawn of the 5th of May, and rode southward from Germanna Ford to reach Warren's position at Old Wilderness Tavern.   We found the road filled with Sedgwick's corps faring forth in the same direction.   The sun blazed hotly and fiery red, and many soldiers succumbed by the roadside to die ere the campaign was begun. After a few hours' ride we reached Old Wilderness Tavern. We found that Warren's corps had bivouacked here during the night — one division (Griffin's) being thrown out on the Orange turnpike about a mile to the westward to guard the approaches by which the enemy would advance if he was minded to risk battle. Warren's orders had been to resume the march early that morning, and advance by a wood-road running south-westerly from Wilderness Tavern to Parker's Store on the Orange plank road. Accordingly at daybreak Crawford's division, followed by the divisions of Wadsworth and Robinson, moved forward to attain that point — Griffin's division being still held on the turnpike. But when Crawford's division had neared Parker's Store it found a Union cavalry body that had been sent forward to preoccupy that point being driven out by a hostile column which was pushing rapidly down the plank road; and at the same time Griffin's skirmishers on the turnpike became engaged with another body of the enemy. It happened that just as we reached Old Wilderness Tavern, about 8 A. M. of the 5th, the tidings came that Griffin had encountered a Confederate force moving down the turnpike. Now there was here an appearance and a fact; and it is necessary to explain both how the commander construed the circumstances and what the circumstances actually were, for they differed most materially — and indeed thereby hangs the battle of the Wilderness.

When, on the 4th of May, the Army of the Potomac by its successful passage of the Rapidan at Germanna and Ely's fords, had turned Lee's right flank, it seemed a warrantable inference to conclude that the Confederate commander, finding his river-line now become obsolete, would not attempt to join battle near the Rapidan, but that he would be compelled, in view of the wide dispersion of his corps, to choose a point of concentration nearer Richmond. Grant and Meade therefore had no thought of being interrupted in the march through the

Wilderness, and their purpose was by a rapid march south-westward to throw themselves between Lee and his capital, or at least to catch the Confederate corps divided, and beat them in detail.   It was in execution of this purpose that on the morning of the 5th, Warren was directed on Parker's Store, and that Hancock, whose corps had bivouacked at Chancel-lorsville, was ordered, that morning, to move to Shady Grove Church, six miles south of Parker's Store.   By launching forward in the same south-westerly direction, it was supposed that the Union army would, in a few vigorous marches, bring Lee to battle somewhere between Gordonsville and Louisa Courthouse.   Now when, on the morning of the 5th, War-ren reported that Griffin had encountered a hostile force press-ing down upon him on the Orange turnpike, Grant and Meade, fully believing that Lee was executing a movement of retreat, did not attach any importance to the fact.   It was concluded that the force which now faced Griffin was only some part of the Confederate right which had been observing the line of the Rapidan, and which was now left behind as a rear-guard while the mass of Lee's army concentrated far be-low ; and I put down in my note-book an observation which, while standing beside General Meade shortly after our arrival at Wilderness Tavern, I heard that officer make to Generals Sedgwick and Warren.   "They [the enemy]," said he, " have left a division to fool us here while they concentrate and pre-pare a position toward the North Anna ; and what I want is to prevent those fellows getting back to Mine Run."   Acting on this hypothesis, the order was given to Warren to attack the enemy on the turnpike.

Such were appearances.   The reality, as has been seen, was very different.   Lee instead of falling back on learning of Grant's advance, had no sooner detected the nature of the manœuvre than he resolved to assume the offensive.   On the morning of the 4th he directed Ewell to march rapidly east-ward on the turnpike ; he gave Hill the same direction on the plank road, and he called Longstreet up from Gordonsville to follow Hill. Ewell and Hill after marching during the whole of the 4th, encamped within a few miles of where Warren lay at Old Wilderness Tavern — Ewell being on the turnpike and Hill on the plank road. The force that encountered Griffin on the morning of the 5th, was Ewell's van; the column seen by Crawford hastening down the plank road was that of Longstreet. Lee had met Grant's move with another equal in dexterity and surpassing it in boldness.

That the hope of getting between Lee and Richmond was futile soon became apparent to the Union commander, for as the forenoon wore away, the pressure on Griffin's front became more and more weighty, and on the plank road an endless column of the enemy was seen filing past with swift strides. It was now imperative to form new combinations. Hancock at least must be recalled from his march southwards towards Shady Grove Church, and brought up into position with the rest of the army. If indeed it were only possible that he should get up in time, for the enemy was gathering so strongly on the plank road, and pushing forward so strenuously, that it was doubtful whether he would not sever connection between Hancock and the rest of the army! "My advance," says Hancock, "was about two miles beyond Todd's Tavern, when at nine A. M. I received a dispatch from the Major-General commanding the Army of the Potomac to halt at the Tavern, as the enemy had been discovered in some force on the Wilderness pike. Two hours later I was directed to move my command up the Brock road to its intersection with the Orange plank road." To prevent Hill's attaining this all-important intersection, and allow Hancock, who was now full ten miles off, to come up into position on the left of Warren, Getty's division of the Sixth Corps was sent to the junction of the Brock road and the Orange plank road to hold it at all hazards; and, meanwhile, Warren was to attack Ewell on the turnpike with all his force, Sedgwick

24

assisting on his right.   Warren, mounting, rode to his command and ordered an assault.   Let us follow him.

It was the Wilderness !   This desolate region embraces a
tract of country of many miles, stretching southward from
the Rapidan, and westward beyond Mine Run — the whole
face of it being covered with a dense undergrowth of low-
limbed and scraggy pines, stiff and bristling chinkapins,
scrub-oaks, and hazel.   It is a region of gloom and the
shadow of death — such a " darkling wood " as that where
through Dante passed into the Inferno : " Savage and rough
and strong, that in the thinking it reneweth fear " :

> " Questa selva selvaggia ed aspra e forte
> Che nel pensier rinnova la paura ! "

Passing westward from Wilderness Tavern, across the insignificant brook of Wilderness Run, one ascends a. considerable ridge which slopes westward into an extensive clearing,
then pleasant and green with the verdure of spring — the one
oasis in the circumjacent wild.   On the western hill-slope
stands the house of one Major Lacy, and on the hill itself
beneath some fine trees, Generals Grant and Meade took
their station.   The cleared meadow lay around, and, beyond,
to the westward, was the thick forest into which the great
army, penetrating, had become lost to view.   Thither following, we take a look around — not a far look, indeed ; for
about and beneath and overhead, the tangled underbrush and
knotted trunks and ragged foliage of chaparral, consume the
spaces into which the eye yearns to penetrate.   Is a battle to
be fought here in this labyrinth?   There is a glory and a
grandeur, there is pride and pomp in the marshalled lines of
two mighty hosts that meet to contend on the open plain —
there is something to thrill, to inspire, to intoxicate.   Carry
battle into a jungle and listen to it without a shudder.   You
hear the Saturnalia, gloomy, hideous, desperate, raging un-

confined — you see nothing : and the very mystery augments the horror.

By noontide Warren had formed his corps. Griffin's division was across the turnpike ; Wadsworth's division was to go in and take position on the left of Griffin, with Robinson's division in support and one brigade of Crawford's division (the movement on Parker's Store being now suspended) was put in on the left of Wadsworth. From the patter of skirmish shots the fight rose presently into the loud climax of battle. But nothing was visible : only from out those gloomy depths came the ruin that had been wrought, in bleeding shapes borne in blankets or on stretchers — the ghastly harvest of war. When the fight had lulled in the afternoon I had time to find out what had been done.

Griffin's division, with Ayres's brigade on the right and Bartlett's brigade on the left of the Orange turnpike, attacked with great impetuosity ; and as at the first onset only a part of Ewell's corps had come up, Griffin for a mile carried everything before him. Then, however, the Confederates turned at bay, formed on a wooded acclivity, and there being joined by the remainder of Ewell's corps, refused to be moved any farther. Unhappily there was no connection between Griffin's division and that of Wadsworth, which went forward on its left, and a great misfortune befell the latter. In advancing Wadsworth's division, Warren was compelled, as there were no roads, to give it direction by a point of the compass. Its course was to be due west from the Lacy House, which would have brought it to the left of Griffin's division, and on a prolongation of its line. But Wadsworth started facing north-west, instead of going due west, so that by the time he had approached the enemy his left had swung so far round as to present that naked flank to the fire of the Confederates. Becoming confused in the dense forest, the division broke, and retired in much disorder. At the same time Ewell assumed the offensive against Griffin, and succeeded

in throwing back that division over all the ground it had before wrenched from the enemy.   The fate of McCandless's
brigade of Crawford's division was still worse, for occupying
an isolated position, it was nearly surrounded and was driven
from the field with the loss of almost two whole regiments.
Thus all the ground gained was given up; but the Confederates did not follow, and Warren assumed a new line across
the turnpike, a little west of Wilderness Tavern. The shock to
the Fifth Corps was very severe, and entailed a loss of above
three thousand men.

Three hours after noon there came a lull: the opening act
of the drama had been concluded with such result as we have
seen.   The air was stifling, and the sun sent down his rays
like spears.   I went to Warren's head-quarters at the Lacy
House, to rest and await further developments, and found
the house had one historic event of interest associated with
it, for it was here that Stonewall Jackson lay after he was
borne, mortally hurt, from the battle-field of Chancellorsville,
and it was here that his arm was amputated.   Picking up a
copy of Horace, which I found lying on the littered floor, I
opened it mechanically, and happened to light on where the
poet, in the Ode to Mecænas, speaks of war, —

> " Multos castra juvant, et lituo tubæ
> Permixtus sonitus, bellaque matribus
> Detestata; "

which set me a-musing, for to how many mothers whose sons
then lay in the dark woods of the Wilderness, must wars be
" *detestata*."   But such thoughts were quickly interrupted;
for from the far-off left there came a guttural, oceanic roar
of musketry, and riding thither I found that it was Hancock,
who had at length come up, had joined the faithful Getty,
guardian of the precious junction of roads, — precious as that
at Quatre-bras, — and was now attacking the enemy.   What
here befell may best be told in the words of Hancock's report, which lies before me in manuscript: —

"When I first joined General Getty, near the Orange
plank road, he informed me that two divisions of Hill's
corps were in his immediate front, and that he momentarily
anticipated an attack.   I therefore directed that breastworks
should be constructed in order to receive the assault should the
enemy advance.   Between three and four o'clock I was ordered to attack with Getty's command, supporting the advance
with my whole corps.   At 4.15 P. M. General Getty moved
forward on the right and left of the Orange plank road, having received direct orders from General Meade to commence
the attack without waiting for me.   His troops encountered
the enemy's line of battle about three hundred paces in front
of the Brock road, and at once became hotly engaged.   Finding that General Getty had met the enemy in great force, I
ordered Birney to advance his command (his own and Mott's
division) to support the movement of Getty at once, although
the formation I had directed to be made before carrying out
my instructions to advance were not yet completed.   General
Birney immediately moved forward on General Getty's right
and left — one section of Ricketts's battery moving down the
plank road, just in rear of the infantry.   The fight became
very fierce at once : the lines of battle were exceedingly
close, and the musketry was continuous along the entire line.
At 4.30 P. M. Carroll's brigade of Gibbon's division advanced to the support of Getty's right on the right of the
plank road, and a few minutes later Owen's brigade of Gibbon's division was also ordered into action in support of
Getty, on the right and left of the Orange plank road.   The
battle raged with great severity and obstinacy till about 8
P. M., without decided advantage to either party."

Thus closed the first day of the Wilderness — a deadly
combat, or series of combats, yet hardly a battle.   It was, as
I have elsewhere called it, "the fierce grapple of two mighty
wrestlers, suddenly meeting."   The action was thoroughly
indecisive.   If Grant had been arrested in his passage

through the Wilderness, Lee, at least, had been foiled in his purpose of interposing between the two divided Union columns. The whole army was brought into position, and Burnside's corps was ordered up to participate in the great struggle, now seen to be inevitable. Lee anxiously awaited Longstreet, who would doubtless arrive in the morning.

For combinations of grand tactics there was manifestly no opportunity in the Wilderness. Men might here carry on a deadly work of "bushwacking," but for an army to manœuvre in this chaparral, through which a bird could scarcely wing its way, was wholly out of the question. Grant's plan was formulated in a single sentence, — "Attack along the whole line at five in the morning."

At early dawn of the 6th we were up again on the hill near the Lacy House, to await the overture of the battle. But fifteen minutes before the appointed hour of attack arrived, the enemy, anticipating us, snatched the honor of the opening. The onset was made on the Union right (Sedgwick's corps), falling first upon Seymour's brigade, then involving the whole of Ricketts's division, and extending finally to Wright's. But it made no impression on the Sixth Corps front, and Sedgwick was able to join in the general attack. It is at this distance of time manifest enough that this sally of the enemy was made for the purpose of disconcerting the Union commander and paralyzing action on his part for a while — a point which it was extremely desirable Lee should gain, for as neither Longstreet's corps nor Anderson's division of Hill's corps were yet up, he feared the result of an assault, especially from the Union left, and in acting offensively against the other Union flank, he did so merely as a diversion. However, it failed of realizing Lee's intent, and neither hastened nor retarded Grant's attack, which was begun at 5 A. M., as had been appointed.

The battle-line, as now drawn, was about five miles in

length — running north and south and facing westward. Sedgwick held the right, Warren the centre, and Hancock the left. Burnside's corps, after a forced march, arrived during the morning, and was to be thrown in to fill up an interval between Warren and Hancock. There were, therefore, to be no reserves — a circumstance that made some of the older campaigners shake their heads.

The chief interest centred in the left, under Hancock. It was from them that the main and most forceful attack was to be directed, and with this view a very weighty accumulation of troops was made on that flank. In addition to his own powerful corps of four divisions, Hancock held in hand Getty's division of the Sixth Corps, and Wadsworth's division of the Fifth Corps, which during the previous evening had been sent through the woods to co-operate with Hancock, and had secured a position hard by the left flank of the hostile force confronting that officer. This consisted of two divisions of Hill's corps, — the divisions of Wilcox and Heth, — which held position across the Orange plank road, their left connecting with the right flank of Ewell's corps. These two divisions constituted the whole of Lee's right wing, for neither Longstreet nor Hill's other two divisions had come up when at five in the morning a blaze of musketry announced that Hancock was advancing.

From the breastworks along the Brock road Hancock sent forward his battle-line, covered by a cloud of skirmishers. The assaulting force was made up of Birney's, Mott's, and Getty's divisions, with Carroll's and Owen's brigades of Gibbon's division, the remaining brigade of Gibbon's division and the whole of Barlow's division, forming the left of Hancock's line, were retained in the works along the Brock road; for Hancock had been warned that Longstreet was approaching by the Catharpen road in such a manner that had he advanced his left, Longstreet would have fallen full on his rear. The left flank rested securely on a piece of

open and commanding ground, where a plentiful supply of
artillery had been massed.

Pushing out into the dense thicket along both sides of the
Orange plank road, the assaulting line presently encountered
the two divisions of Hill, upon which it fell with such vigor
that they soon began to waver and shake.; and as at the same
time Wadsworth terrified them by an attack in flank, the
Confederates were completely disrupted, and retired in much
disorder.   "After a desperate contest, in which our troops
conducted themselves in the most intrepid manner, the enemy's line," says Hancock, "was broken at all points, and he
was driven in confusion through the forest for almost one and
one half miles, suffering severe losses in killed and wounded
and prisoners."   In fact Hill's troops could not be stayed till
in their retreat they had overrun the trains and artillery and
even the head-quarters of the Confederate commander,
where, as Longstreet afterwards told me, he found on his
arrival a confused huddle of bewildered and broken battalions.   It required but that the Union troops should press
on in order to snatch a crowning victory; for the overthrow
of Hill's divisions uncovered the whole extent of the Confederate line.

But if the Confederates in their rout were thrown into disorder, the advance of the Union force so far through the
forest brought upon it scarcely less confusion.   For in such
wood-fighting all that gives cohesion to a battle array — the
touch of the elbow, the sight of a firm support on either
side — is wanting, and in a short time all alignment is hopelessly lost.   It thus came about that when Hancock's men in
pressing after the flying enemy had advanced into the heart
of the Wilderness, it was found that the integrity of formation had so disappeared that the commander was forced to
call a halt in order to make a readjustment of the line.   It
was now almost seven A. M., Getty's exhausted division was
replaced by Webb's brigade, drawn from Gibbon's command

on the left; Frank's brigade of Barlow's division made an advance from the same flank, and after an obstinate contest succeeded in forming a connection with the left flank of the advanced line; Stevenson's division of Burnside's corps reported to Hancock ready for duty, and Wadsworth's division after being gallantly fought by its intrepid commander across the front of that part of the Second Corps which lay on the right hand of the plank road, was now brought into proper relations with the rest of the forward line.

Two hours passed in perfecting these dispositions. But these two hours had wrought a change for the Confederates. The remaining divisions of Hill's corps had arrived, and the head of Longstreet's column was reported not far behind. Lee seizing hold of the first comers, hurried them forward to patch up his broken front; and reading a little trepidation in the faces of the men at the sight of the *débris* of Heth's and Wilcox's divisions, the Confederate commander put himself at the head of Gregg's Texans, and commanded them to follow him in a charge; but a grim and ragged soldier of the line raised his voice in determined resistance, and was immediately followed by the rank and file of the whole brigade in positive refusal to advance till the well-loved chief had gone to his proper place in the rear. After this there was no faltering. Anderson's and Field's divisions quickly deployed, and Longstreet's powerful corps soon afterward coming up, added such weight and breadth to the line that the Confederate commander was in position not only to withstand further pressure, but himself to strike. When therefore, at nine A. M., Hancock, having perfected his dispositions, resumed the advance, he struck a front of opposition that was now immovable. Though he assaulted furiously, he made no farther progress.

The situation of Hancock's force was now somewhat peculiar. His left remained on the Brock road; his centre and right were advanced a mile or more in front of that road.

But while that portion that remained in the breastworks along the Brock road had a secure stay for its flank, the left of the forward line was wholly unprotected, being quite in the air. It had been found impossible to further move the enemy, and for a defensive position the advanced line was ill placed. Yet it was soon to be thrown on the defensive by a fierce attack of the enemy.

From the close of Hancock's morning combat about nine A. M., there was a long lull till near noon. During this interval I rode from the head-quarters of Generals Grant and Meade to visit Hancock, whom I found on horseback at the junction of the Brock road and the Orange plank road. I had been there but a short time when a terrific outburst of musketry announced that the Confederates had taken the offensive, and in a few minutes a throng of fugitives came rushing back from Hancock's advanced line, and overran us on the Brock road and spread through the woods in great confusion. Hancock, flaming out with the fire of battle, rode hither and thither, directing and animating; but the disruption of the left flank spread calamity through the line, and though Hancock endeavored by throwing back that flank to still hold on to the advanced position with his right, it was found impossible to do so, and he had to content himself with rallying and reforming his troops behind the breastworks on the Brock road. Wadsworth, on the right of Hancock, opposed the most heroic efforts to the enemy's onset; but he was finally unable to hold his men to their work, and he fell mortally hurt while endeavoring to stay their flight.

It seemed indeed that irretrievable disaster was upon us; but in the very torrent and tempest of the attack, it suddenly ceased, and all was still. What could cause this surcease of effort at the very height of success, was then wholly unknown to us; but when after the close of the war, I had an opportunity of meeting General Longstreet, he solved the riddle for me. It appears that on Longstreet's arrival, Lee determined by concentrating both corps in a supreme effort to overwhelm Hancock in one decisive stroke. The forenoon was therefore spent in careful preparations; and in order to give full effect to the meditated blow, it was planned that while one force should press directly against the Union front, another should be sent by a detour to attain the rear of the Union left, and seize the Brock road. Having seen the front attack opened with most encouraging success, Longstreet, with his staff, galloped down the plank road to direct the effects of the turning force, when suddenly confronting a portion of his own turning column, the cavalcade was by it mistaken for a party of Union horse, and received a volley, under which Longstreet fell severely wounded. As that officer had made all the dispositions, his fall completely disconcerted the plan: so that Lee suspended the attack, and it was not till four in the afternoon that he got things in hand to renew it.

Returning to head-quarters under the trees on the hill-side near the Lacy house, I found Grant sitting on the grass, smoking alternately a pipe and a cigar—calm, imperturbable, quietly awaiting events and giving few orders, for indeed on such a field there were few orders to be given. I soon learnt that little had resulted from the attack of Warren and Sedgwick. And indeed the main interest centred on Hancock, to whom, from the corps of the former officer, had been sent two divisions, and from that of the latter one division—so that Hancock held in hand full half of the army. Nevertheless, with the remaining moiety of these corps both Sedgwick and Warren had vigorously attacked in the morning. It soon became apparent, however, that the enemy held one of those powerful positions that could not be carried, and against which all effort was a vain sacrifice of life. In fact, both Warren and Sedgwick were brought to a dead-lock: no impression whatever could be made on the enemy's position. Much had been hoped from an effort which was to be made by Burnside, who was to advance through an interval between Warren's left and Hancock's right in such a manner that he would have struck the rear of the hostile force confronting the latter officer. But after passing the day in a fruitless course of peripatetics through the woods, the corps in the afternoon fell back and entrenched. It thus came about, that as the fight died away along the right and centre, and as after Lee's attack upon Hancock there was quiet also on the left, the storm of war along all the opposing lines was hushed into a dead calm that continued up to four P. M.

But Grant was far from having given up the fight. "It has been my experience," he observed to the writer as we sat under the trees on the hill-side, "it has been my experience that though the southerners fight desperately at first, yet *when we hang on for a day or two we whip them awfully.*" He therefore ordered Hancock to attack once more at six in the evening.

Yet it soon appeared that neither was the aggressive ardor of Lee wholly quenched. For while Hancock was making his dispositions for the attack, the Confederates resumed the offensive against him. Lee had, at length, got things in hand, and, being resolved to complete the work begun by Longstreet, but broken off by that officer's fall, he once more launched forward his lines. A little past four, the Confederate lines in long and solid array came forward through the woods, and overrunning the Union skirmishers pressed up without halting to the edge of the abatis less than a hundred paces from Hancock's front lines. Here, pausing, they opened a furious and continuous fire of musketry, which, however, did not greatly harm the Union troops, who, kneeling behind their breastworks, returned the fire with vigor. It is not doubtful that the repulse of the enemy would have been easily effected · but an untoward accident for a time placed the result in jeopardy. The forest in front, through which the battle of the morning had been fought, chanced to take fire, and a short time before the afternoon attack was made the flames communicated to the log parapet of the left of the front line. At the critical moment of the enemy's onset a high wind blew the intense heat and smoke in the faces of the men, many of whom were from this cause kept from firing, while others were compelled to vacate the lines. The Confederates seizing the opportunity swept forward, and some of them reached the breastworks, which they crowned with their colors. But the triumph was short-lived. "At the moment when the enemy reached our lines," says Hancock, "General Birney ordered Carroll's brigade of Gibbon's division to advance upon them and drive them back. Carroll moved by the left flank and then forward at the double-quick, retaking the breastworks at once, and forcing the enemy to fall back and abandon the attack in great disorder and with heavy loss in killed and wounded."

This substantially closed the action of the second day of the Wilderness, though the enemy contrived to excite considerable alarm by a night sally made against the right flank of the army. In this affair Generals T. Seymour and Shaler were captured; but the result was, as a whole, unimportant.

The morning of Saturday, May 7th, found the opposing armies still confronting each other in the Wilderness : yet neither side showed any aggressive ardor. There was light skirmishing throughout the forenoon; but it was manifest that both armies were so worn out that they mutually feared to attack, though they were not unwilling to be attacked. It had been a deadly wrestle, yet the result so far was indecisive. The Union troops, wearied and chagrined, sent up no cheer of victory through the Wilderness. Many, indeed, believed we would recross the Rapidan.

But there was one man that was otherwise minded. During the day the corps were gathered into compact shape, the trains were drawn out of the way, and the columns were disposed for the march; for Grant, like Phocion, desired to have an army "fitted for the long race." When night came, he seized the mighty mass and launched it southward — towards Richmond !

III.

RESULTS OF THE WILDERNESS.

The story of the Southern War is filled with the records of great battles whose immediate fortunes were divided with such equal hand that both sides claimed the victory. Nor were these issues dubious in semblance only; for, if we assume as the test of decisiveness in action some material change wrought in the military problem, some positive alteration in the ratio of the contending forces, something, in a word, which has palpably deflected the current of the war by its interposition — very many of the four years' battles must be set down as tentative and fruitless. This observation holds good even when gigantic armies have wrestled in prolonged stress of combat on fields heaped with the holocausts of ineffectual sacrifice. Into the reasons on which this fact rests, it would be discursive here to enter deeply : — whether it be partly traceable to the nature of the struggle and the character and equality of the combatants, whose veins pulsed with a common blood ; whether partly to a similarity of arms, equipments, discipline, and method of action ; whether partly and principally to the physique of the battle-fields, whose sites were mainly hostile to manœuvre, now consisting of a mere maze of dense undergrowth hardly passable by its deceitful, tortuous, boggy footpaths, now a terrain upheaved into a tumble of swamp, ravine, and thicket, — often defying tactical combinations, and not seldom neutralizing cavalry, or artillery, or both, and turning pitched battle into an enormous Indian fight of man to man, with pursuit by the final victor almost impossible.

To all appearances, the battle of the Wilderness had every

characteristic of such bloody and indecisive combats. And, indeed, if we regard the individual action without reference to its sequel, it would be difficult to say of what it was decisive. The material losses on the Union side exceeded those of the Confederates, being about fifteen thousand to ten thousand. Besides, after the action was concluded in such manner as we have seen, Lee still held his position defiantly, and only withdrew when on the night of the third day he found himself flanked by his antagonist's manœuvre towards Spottsylvania Courthouse.

Nevertheless, if we deeply consider this mysterious and terrible battle in the Wilderness, we shall discover that it differed essentially from the many encounters that had taken place on the Rapidan and Rappahannock; and it will, perhaps, appear that it takes this significance from being the type of that series of operations which make up the wonderful campaign from the Rapidan to the James — a campaign unparalleled in military history for its duration, the character of the operations and the number of battles fought, and which, prosecuted with a remorseless energy, resulted in gradually throwing back the Confederate army, and finally in shutting it up within the lines of Petersburg and Richmond, whence it was not to issue save to its doom and downfall.

The Wilderness, I say, prefigured this campaign. As an action it was without brilliancy in its conduct. It was a mere collision of brute masses — or as an officer on the field pithily expressed it to me, "the bumping, bumping of two armies, to see which could bump the hardest." It might have been fought by any other commander. But the difference in the result was this: that while any other commander we had thus far seen would have fought the battle of the Wilderness and gone backward, Grant fought the battle of the Wilderness and went — *forward!*

Looking at the war as a whole, we can see that the time had came for this manner of procedure. The North, fatigued with three years of seemingly fruitless warfare in Virginia, chagrined at the constant advances followed by constant retreats, demanded a captain who, without too chary a regard for human life, should *go on:* and the people were perfectly willing that he should use the resources lavishly, provided only he produced results. If the time had come, the battle of the Wilderness showed that the man also had come.

It is not my purpose here to follow out that wondrous series of operations that make up the overland campaign — those up-piled terraces of struggle at Spottsylvania and the North Anna and Cold Harbor — those Titanic combats that made the country between the Rapidan and the James one vast red Aceldama. Let the mighty wrestle in the Wilderness stand as the type and exemplar of all the rest, as that which announced alike to friend and foe that henceforward it was war to the death.

Eng'd by H B Hall.   Photo. by Gurney.

W. T. Sherman

Dick & Fitzgerald, New York.

X.

ATLANTA.

———

I.

PRELUDE TO ATLANTA.

SURVEYING from his lofty mountain fastness at Chattanooga the broad subjacent country to the far-off Mississippi, Sherman, to whom Grant, on his removal to Virginia, had delegated the command of all that vast theatre, saw that the war in the West was already nigh its end. The basin of the Mississippi was substantially overrun, the soil of Kentucky, Tennessee, and Missouri fast and forever in Union keeping, while in Mississippi and Alabama on the hither slope of the valley, and Arkansas and Louisiana on the other, such positions were held as to make military operations there on a grand scale waste of time and troops. A profitless blaze of victory might indeed be easily kindled in many quarters; but to the distant south-west, there were no strategic points unconquered which might not better claim the attention of a body of cavalry or an invasion from a base near the Gulf. A few experimental thrustings of cavalry columns, and, in one case, of an infantry column, through the Gulf States, had verified Grierson's pithy saying, that the Confederacy there was " a shell;" and though other such expeditions might meet more discomfort than danger, the shell was not worth the puncturing.

But the Confederacy yet lived in its armies, and of these

25

one of the two that still held the field strong and defiant confronted Sherman in an entrenched camp at Dalton, where it
covered Georgia.   But Georgia was now not only the chief
granary, it was the main military workshop of the Confederacy, as Florida and Texas had been its corrals.   Down in the
heart of the State was Atlanta, the centre of a network of
manufacturing cities and villages, — such as Rome, Roswell,
Marietta, and the like, — from whose factories the Southern
armies were now drawing powder, shot, shell, caps, cannon,
small arms, clothing and equipments, wagons and harnesses,
all the paraphernalia of war.   Central Georgia was a vast
grain-growing prairie, whence loaded cars rolled constantly to
army store-houses, after harvest-time, to furnish the winter
sustenance of many Confederate armies besides that of
Johnston's.   Georgia was the key-stone of the Confederate
arch, whose firm northern buttress was Virginia.   Through
Macon and Atlanta ran the great railroad lines between the
eastern and western Confederacy : to break them would be to
sunder direct communication between the Atlantic States and
the States of the Gulf, to cleave once more the Southern territory from mountain to sea, as it had been rent asunder on
the line of the Mississippi.   To do this, and to destroy
the army of his adversary, was the task imposed upon Sherman.

Of that officer's fitness for the task its history is the best
evidence ; and beforehand there was proof abundant not only
in his skill and recognized genius on the one hand, but in his
wide experience on the other.   He was a man of martial instinct, of quick intelligence, of far-reaching habit of thought,
and even on his first field his talents had flashed out.   At Bull
Run, being for the first time under fire, he handled his brigade
with noticeable ease, and gave several specific exhibitions of
soldierly skill.   In his second battle, Shiloh, Sherman was
still more conspicuous ; for, though commanding a raw division, and while officers ranking him were on the field, the chief

control of the action seems to have been instinctively and at once accorded to him, on the first day. General Halleck, on reaching the scene of action immediately sent word to Washington that "it is the unanimous opinion here that Brigadier-General W. T. Sherman saved the fortunes of the day on the 6th," while Grant crowned many words of eulogy by declaring "to his individual efforts I am indebted for the success of that battle." Commencing his record thus brilliantly, Sherman had very naturally soon become General Grant's favorite subordinate. The last act of his famous career had been a superbly rapid and well-conducted march of four hundred miles from Vicksburg to Chattanooga in season to allow him a "full man's share" of what hard blows were to be borne in the dethronement of Bragg from Missionary Ridge; when, without taking breath, once more his fate appointed him to go to the relief of Burnside, then imprisoned at Knoxville : adding one hundred miles to his four hundred, by incredible exertions he saved the gallant garrison. Thus the very nature of his best-known achievements, in the way of moving vast armies over vast regions with the precision and smoothness of mechanism, was the best augury of success in sweeping hither and thither as he might list, throughout Georgia.

For his projected campaign, Sherman demanded one hundred thousand men in the proper ratio of the three arms; and of ordnance two hundred and fifty guns. The actual force with which he took the field was nearly as designed, the aggregate being ninety-eight thousand seven hundred and ninety-seven men and two hundred and fifty-four guns. The command consisted of three armies — Thomas's Army of the Cumberland, sixty thousand seven hundred and seventy-three strong; McPherson's Army of the Tennessee, twenty-four thousand four hundred and sixty-five; Schofield's Army of the Ohio, thirteen thousand five hundred and fifty-nine.

The positions which the opposing armies had now assumed brought into striking light the strategic character of the

region, and the military value of its primary feature, Chattanooga. The great mountain system of East Tennessee ran
like a ridge into the heart of the Confederacy: Chattanooga
was a natural bastion on the line of Confederate communications. Ousted by Rosecrans from this key-point of the central zone, Bragg felt that without regaining it and the dependent mountain system, the Confederacy would always be
vitally menaced, and accordingly essayed the movement
which Grant had so rudely rebuffed. The possession of Chattanooga transferred to the Union armies the advantage of
interior lines, while their opponents, thrown off in turn upon
exterior lines, ran the risk of being beaten in detail. South
of Chattanooga, also, the mountains of the Blue Ridge, so
hostile to operations directed across them easterly into Virginia or North Carolina, by falling into the champaign country
permitted forward movements. Knoxville, the centre of that
valley district between the Alleghanies proper and the Blue
Ridge, known as East Tennessee, and extending from Cumberland Gap to Chattanooga, was held, like the two latter
points, by Union forces, while, on the other flank, the
Tennessee River was lined with garrisons sufficient to prevent
the passage of infantry from the south. In a word, then,
the Union position at Chattanooga, itself impregnable, was
well guarded on both flanks, and tempted its possessors to
thrust strong columns into the plain below. Meanwhile it
gave the inestimable advantage of a single line of operations
combined with a double line of supplies, by means of the
two railroads running, the one north-west to Nashville, the
other due west to Memphis.

The mishap of Bragg at Chattanooga had completed the
disappointment and chagrin of that officer at his ill-starred
western campaign. With the fact of his misfortunes only too
palpable, their precise cause was still somewhat involved in
mystery, it now appearing to be his own errors, now the mis-
conduct of subordinates, now the weakness of his force, and

sometimes even a fatality which followed the Confederate cause in that region, whose influence it was hopeless to throw off. Mortified and annoyed, he withdrew to Richmond, and his superior, General J. E. Johnston, took the *bâton* of command into his own hands. He found himself in possession, at Dalton, of 45,000 effective men — 40,900 infantry and artillery, and 4000 cavalry : while several thousand cavalry were ready to be recalled, which meanwhile were prying hither and thither, through Georgia and Alabama, to see if some careless avenue had not escaped the watchful Sherman along his wide flanks, at which entering, they might get upon his enormously attenuated lines of supply. Some other reinforcements were collecting, to be poured into the gaps made by battle. These, therefore, and certain indefinite masses of possible Georgia militia, which, thanks to the impracticable intensity of States' Rights authority, had to be left to come to the field at the call of their own delicate fancy, constituted his army. The whole fortune with which it started on its new career consisted of a testamentary bequest of numerous disasters.

To what *rôle* Johnston was now limited by the evolution of past events, it was easy to see ; for his foe, in all a hundred thousand strong, lay intrenched with his main army at the apex of the grand strategic triangle before him, and covering armies drawn a little distance down on either side of the salient. One flank of this Union position was ribbed and ridged with the natural barriers of a great mountain system, the other by a broad river, studded with garrisons at the crossing-points. Of necessity content to protect what remained, rather than to idly attempt regaining what was lost, Johnston fortified himself strongly in and around Dalton, the first position of importance south of the Union advanced lines, now at Ringgold, in front of Chattanooga. But the restless government at Richmond, stung into petulance by past defeat in the West, and half impressed by the fate which seemed inevitably to cloud that horizon, resolved to shake off the spell of disaster before it was further fixed, or at least to prove that it had good cause to despair, before despairing. Accordingly, Johnston, on taking command about Christmas of 1863, was instantly pressed for an offensive campaign, to redeem the disaster of Missionary Ridge : but the condition of his army forced him to decline the undertaking, and winter was passed in recruiting. However, when March opened, it had brought to Johnston no troops of importance, and, on the other hand, detachments for minor purposes had weakened him, so that March and April passed in the rapid exchange of tele-graphic theses between Dalton and Richmond, as to whether an offensive army could be made out of nothing, and a brisk disputation on the method by which such an army should advance into Tennessee.

It is needless to inquire what might have been the upshot of these speculations, for they were rudely interrupted by Sherman's initiative. On the 4th of May the Army of the Potomac crossed the Rapidan, and on the same day Grant, pausing by the wayside, while seated upon a felled tree, wrote a terse word to be flashed over the wires to his col-league at Chattanooga. Sherman's three armies, as if loosed from the tugging leash. bounded forward, and the campaign began. Let us follow its course closely, for in respect of the skill displayed, both in the attack and defence, it forms a most interesting study.

Commanders do not always insist upon recalling, after the working out of a campaign from theory to history, precisely what their real intent was, but have their memory of what they designed to effect influenced by the palpable fact of what they did or did not effect : this habit simplifies history, though sometimes it checks confusion at the expense of strict accuracy. In the two great spring campaigns of 1864, there lay before each Union commander, in Virginia as in Georgia, first, a hostile army, his immediate objective ; secondly, a city, his remoter geographical objective : and since the decisive defeat of the former was the easy capture of the latter, such a defeat at the outset became the first object of the new campaign. To force the adversary at once by manœuvre to a great battle, and to win therefrom decisive victory, became the aim; to be unable to do so could not be fairly regarded as a defeat, but it would be a foil, and a disappointment, — a postponement of victory. Sherman's desire was, if possible, to fall upon his opponent soon after sallying from Chattanooga, and to overthrow him in a grand battle; in that case, he could drive the exhausted remnant of Confederate force either altogether from its natural line of retreat, or force it rapidly backward beyond Atlanta. If, on the other hand, it was Sherman's aim to fight the battle for Atlanta near Chattanooga, the reverse was Johnston's policy, unless, indeed, he could get such odds of position, in return for willingness to fight at once, as would compensate for withdrawal. For decisive battle and victory for Sherman was essentially the same, nearer or farther from Atlanta: in either case, such were the numbers and character of Johnston's forces that the city would be sure. But decisive battle and victory for Johnston would be infinitely more valuable far away from Sherman's base, since then the latter's communications could be ruined by the cavalry, and his army distressed for supplies. At the start, however, Johnston lay well forward in and around Dalton, on the railroad, in a position almost impregnable. In front, on the line of advance from Chattanooga, or rather from Ringgold, where Thomas's army lay, Rocky Face Mountain imposed a huge, impregnable, natural barrier, divided by a narrow ravine called Mill Creek Gap (or, more expressively, Buzzard's Roost), at the bottom of which ran the main road and railroad to Dalton, and, winding among the hills, Mill Creek, a tributary of the Oostanaula. Along the slopes of this ravine, on its natural rock epaulements, Johnston planted batteries, sweeping it in all directions, and mounted artillery especially upon a ridge at its easterly end, which, as Sherman says, ran "like a traverse directly across its *débouché*." To detain the assailants under the fire of his artillery and infantry Johnston felled abatis through the ravine, and flooded it by dams built on Mill Creek. His flanks he easily preserved by similar defences on the inaccessible spurs of the same mountain system, and so felt himself secure. Had Johnston been able to count on his opponent's willingness to fling himself in direct attack against his various prepared positions, all anxiety for the campaign would have ceased, for he could have found any required number of natural fortresses for that purpose between Dalton and Atlanta, and would have had men to spare for other desirable objects. But he could not hope that piece of fortune from his antagonist, who, being by no means foolhardy, could be safely counted on to devise in his brain a method for forcing an encounter on something like equal terms. Sherman, in a word, must certainly make a detour, with intent to turn the enemy's flank, and, getting upon his communications, would force him out of his craggy citadel. Johnston's right had assurance of safety, not only in the impracticable region, but in the obvious aim of Sherman's advance, and the line he must take in order to cover his communications with the Tennessee. His left was the point to be menaced. Accordingly, while Sherman was busily preparing his supplies, Johnston was as busily mending and cutting roads in the rear of his position, so that whatever direction Sherman's flanking column should take through the rough country, he could march faster to confront it: and he also minutely observed the physique of the whole region, and selected later positions for defence, from the Tennessee down to the Chattahoochie; for obviously the great battle of the campaign ought to occur near the banks of the latter river.

Well aware of the reception prepared for him at Rocky Face Mountain, Sherman had planned — under cover of a demonstration on the latter point so very vigorous as to deceive even his wily antagonist into the notion that the Union troops were aiming to parallel the successful storming of Missionary Ridge — to throw a strong column far to Johnston's left and rear. For this purpose he had hitherto positioned the armies of McPherson, of Thomas, and of Schofield, forming his right, his centre, and his left, respectively at Gordon's Mill on the Chickamauga, at Ringgold, and at Red Clay, due north of Dalton on the Georgia line. Schofield was to march south, upon the enemy's right flank, Thomas to actually enter Buzzard's Roost Gap, in a determined move, while McPherson was to slip hastily down on the west through Ship's Gap, past Villanow, through Snake Creek Gap, to Resaca, eighteen miles on the railroad due south of Dalton, there or in that region fall upon the railroad, and so thoroughly break it up as to cut Johnston's line of supplies. This succeeding, Johnston could not fail instantly to withdraw; when McPherson, who, after breaking the road, was to have retired a few miles to Snake Creek, and there fortified himself, would sally forth and attack Johnston in flank on the retreat. While McPherson thus hung upon him and detained him, Thomas would push through the now abandoned gap, and, with Schofield, catch up with Johnston's rear and fall upon it, and so bring on a general and decisive battle.

On the 7th of May, after two days' skirmishing, the columns went forward, and Thomas, driving the Confederate cavalry outposts from Tunnel Hill, at the mouth of Mill Creek Gap, entered it, and made a bold push, on the 8th and 9th, for the summits. Geary's division of Hooker's corps brilliantly assaulted the Confederate troops in their position at Dug Gap. Newton's division of Howard's corps forced its way well towards Dalton, and Schofield pushed down thither with his army from the north. But this gallant attack was not designed to carry the position, much less expected to do so: for everything was based on McPherson's detour. The latter officer, as ordered, had entered Snake Creek with the corps of Logan and Dodge, preceded by Kilpatrick's division of cavalry, but found there Canty's brigade of cavalry; and, on driving the latter into Resaca, discovered, to his chagrin, that Johnston, fathoming the whole scheme, had already interposed a checkmate, and made Resaca "too strong to be carried by assault." Canty's brigade, indeed, had been sent to Resaca on the 5th, and, on giving the alarm on the 9th, had been joined in the works by three full infantry divisions, which marched the same evening by roads constructed for this purpose. Moreover, while McPherson thus paused, facing Resaca, and unable to get upon the railroad either above or below, he became suddenly aware that, instead of turning the enemy's flank, his own was in danger, from roads which ran down from Dalton across his present left flank and rear. Fearing lest Johnston, suddenly abandoning Dalton, might appear on these roads, McPherson fell back across them several miles westerly, to Snake Creek, and there threw up intrenchments. And so quickly ended the first stage of the campaign.

In reviewing this movement, several reflections arise as to its conduct. The times of moving and attacking, as usual in Sherman's operations, were perfectly arranged. But McPherson, instead of doing the main part of his assigned task, that of breaking the railroad, did only the secondary part, which was to fall back from it and intrench himself. The reason assigned is the strength of Resaca, and the actual fact in the case determines the question of feasibility. The force which McPherson had was between twenty thousand and thirty thousand — considerably larger than that of the garrison on his arrival, and sufficient to overcome any but a very strong and well-defended position. Moreover, it may be suggested that since everything was made dependent on McPherson's demonstration, it might have been well at least to feel the enemy's strength, and even to make a bold adventure of attack; for if this part of the plan did not succeed, no part succeeded.

But, on the other hand, it is clear that, if Resaca were really too strong to be carried, McPherson is to be praised for not attempting it, and so dampening the campaign with defeat at the outset. Of the actual fact, McPherson's peculiar engineering genius and training enabled him very well to judge, and his position as commander authorized him to act on that judgment. Moreover, the discovery that the enemy was not, as expected, taken unawares at Resaca, but was ready for him, placed him in a false position as he halted before it; and the good roads from Dalton running in his rear, confirmed his impression that the object of his presence was understood, and would be turned to his disadvantage if he remained there, by an attack from those roads. It is true that at this point one inquires again if battle was an undesirable thing to obtain; but, at all events, having found the state of affairs different from what he had been led to expect, McPherson could rely on that fact to decline making an uncalculated assault. Above all, however, there is the decisive fact that Johnston had seen through the move from the outset, had long before prepared the defences at Resaca to check it, and had so repaired the roads as to throw back thither any required portion of his force at Dalton. It will be suggested, however, admitting this point, that a force sufficient to take Resaca should have been thrown out to the right. But it may be answered that this would have exposed still more thoroughly the plan, and have made the demonstration at Buzzard's Roost a very palpable feint. McPherson's move was the main one, yet it could not be made with the main force, for fear of attracting attention. It may farther, accordingly, be suggested that the move might have been made by a wider detour, striking the railroad still lower; or, if this would imperil too much the flanking column, that it should be made by a light cavalry column. Sherman's desire, however, had been not merely to make the enemy retreat towards Atlanta by getting on his line of supply, but to have a force ready also, on the flank, to check that retreat so soon as it was commenced, in order that the rest of the army might come up, and fight the enemy dislodged from position.

At all events, Sherman was not long in making up his mind what to do next. "Somewhat disappointed at the result," he had yet, as usual, provided for its possibility. It being useless to keep up the attack on Rocky Face Ridge, he gave orders, on the 10th, for throwing his whole army round to McPherson's position, except Howard's corps and some cavalry. To cover this move, skirmishing was carried on all day of the 10th, and a spirited attack made upon Bates's division at night. Next day the Union army was in motion to the right, and simultaneously Johnston threw Loring's division down to Resaca, following it, on the night of the 12th, with the rest of his force, the cavalry bringing up the rear. Howard marched after him through Dalton. Having divined his opponent's intent, Johnston, on the 13th, drew up his whole army in his second prepared position, in and around Resaca, with Polk's left on the Oostanaula, Hardee in the centre, and Hood's right on the Connesauga. They, and especially Loring, on the left, had sharp fighting with McPherson, who drove Loring back to the Oostanaula; and so, ensconced in his works, Johnston awaited the arrival of the rest of Sherman's army, which the next day, indeed, brought to light. Sherman, comprehending all at a glance, resolved to try his hand once more upon his opponent's communications, and this time in a somewhat different method.

From Resaca, the Oostanaula runs south-westerly to Rome, whence a branch of the main railroad runs due east to Kingston which is due south of Resaca. Between Resaca and Kingston, are the railroad towns of Calhoun and Adairsville. Supposing Johnston to hold Resaca, as he had held Dalton, with his main force, Sherman determined to attack him at once with his whole army, detailing only light and rapid columns to cut off his communications below. Accordingly, he threw pontoons over the Oostanaula at Lay's Ferry, near Calhoun, and marched one division, Sweeney's, across it against this place, while, under the mask both of his main force and Sweeney's, he threw the whole cavalry division of Gerrard much farther below, to break the railroad between Calhoun and Kingston. Without pause, on the same day, the 14th, Sherman attacked the Resaca intrenchments at all points, from noon till late at night. McPherson was on the right, Thomas in the centre, and Schofield, who had forced his way through the rough woods, on the left. Thomas pressed obstinately through Camp Creek Valley, and Hooker's corps crossed the creek. A severe engagement resulted all along the centre and right of Johnston's position, in which the troops of Thomas and Schofield, crossing the valley separating their own position from the intrenchments of Hood and Hardee, vigorously endeavored to carry the position. But the muddy bottom of Mill Creek, the natural entanglements of the undergrowth and stunted willows on its banks, interlaced with vines, and the trees felled over the ravines on both slopes, prevented advance, and nothing was gained there; and, at nightfall, Hood was able even to recover some ground seized in the morning. On the Union right, however, McPherson got handsomely across Camp Creek, and, bursting upon Polk, drove him out of position, and planted his artillery on heights which swept with a commanding fire the Confederate bridges across the river, while Sweeney crossed the Oostanaula below on the pontoon bridge, towards Calhoun. Hastening a division to the latter point, to check Sweeney, Johnston ordered Hood to attack, on the 15th, so as to counterbalance Polk's misfortune. But, on hearing that the Union right had begun to cross down at Lay's Ferry, on the pontoons, Johnston quickly countermanded his orders of attack, and passed the Oostanaula at night, burning the railroad bridge behind him. Stewart's division, however, not receiving the countermand, attacked Hooker's corps, and was badly repulsed, in the afternoon. Hooker followed up his advantage, and added to the positions he had before seized, which Stewart's attack was designed to recapture : his trophies were four guns and several hundred prisoners. In the operations around Resaca, the Union loss was from 4000 to 5000 killed and wounded, that of the Confederates much less, from the protection of their works. So ended the second stage of the campaign.

From Resaca, Johnston retreated down the railroad to Cassville, four miles east of Kingston, with the Union army after him. At Calhoun, Hardee had a brush with McPherson, who had crossed, on the 16th, at Lay's Ferry, and next at Adairsville a sharp affair with Newton's advance division, moving on the Resaca road. Meanwhile Davis marched his division westerly to Rome, and, finding it abandoned, took possession of a few heavy guns, and all the valuable rolling mills and iron works. On the 19th, Johnston had fully taken up his third position in rear of Cassville, on a steep, intrenched ridge, with a valley in front swept by his fire. His losses had hitherto been slight, and were now more than made up by reinforcements, of which French's division of Polk's corps was the chief. Inspired by this addition, he ordered an attack on the approaching Union columns ; but, through a misapprehension of General Hood, the plan miscarried, and Sherman, unsuspicious, and, indeed, probably careless of this intent, moved on into position in front of Cassville, and meanwhile ordered his artillery to play at the intrenchments. At nightfall, Polk and Hood, both brave officers, having first talked over the subject together, approached Johnston, and urged him to retreat at once across the Etowah, their reason being that their present position was untenable, under the sweep of the Union batteries. Johnston and Hardee thought otherwise, but, yielding at length to the earnest appeals of the two former officers, Johnston committed the great mistake of his march, and, abandoning, without a blow, the whole of the fine valley of the Etowah, he precipitately moved to that river at early dawn of the 20th, crossed it, and, making a longer stride in retreat than ever, passed both Allatoona and Ackworth, and made for the chain of hills which cross from east to west in front of Dallas and Marietta. So ended pacifically the third stage of the campaign.

The morning of the 20th revealed to Sherman that his enemy had fled. Astonished this time, and not a little chagrined, at the revelation, he began to doubt whether it would be possible to bring his opponent to a decisive field on the hither side of the Chattahoochie. At all events, however, he could console himself with the easy mastery of the Etowah and its bridges and the roads adjacent, and derived confidence from the numerical weakness exhibited by his enemy's declining to fight even on terms so favorable as Cassville had proposed. The only word of ambition for a conquering army is "forward"; so forward it was again for Sherman's columns. Their commander, convinced that Johnston was determined to draw him far into the interior before engaging him with anything like sincerity, nevertheless boldly accepted the issue; and though he felt that he had lost the choice of battle-ground, was confident of success on a field of his enemy's choosing. His necessity, his success hitherto, and his own adventurous spirit, alike impelled him to rapid advance. Nevertheless, he resolved to make a third effort to cut off his opponent's retreat, and so, dislodging him from his entrenchments, grapple with him on open ground. Supposing Johnston would pause in the natural stronghold of Allatoona Pass, Sherman determined to make a detour to the right, of the widest character, and this time in a method different from either of the former. Accordingly, he filled his wagons with twenty days' supplies, and on May 23d started his whole army, except the garrisons at Rome and Kingston, for Dallas, which lies to the south-west of Allatoona. The columns were so marched across the Etowah and beyond as to cloak the flanking move, but Johnston detected it on the very day of starting, and took position at New Hope Church, just east of Dallas, covering the various roads leading back to the railroad. Hood was on the right at the church, Polk in the centre, and Hardee on the left, crossing the road to Atlanta. On the 25th Hooker, in Thomas's advance, had got up near the church, and after Geary's division had skirmished severely all the afternoon, an hour before sunset he got the other two divisions in hand, and assaulted Stewart's division of Hood's corps at the church for two hours with tremendous fury, ceasing only when night and the storm made him desist. The next three days, however, were taken up with constant fighting all along the lines, resulting from Sherman's endeavors to deploy and push his troops close up to the enemy's intrenchments; and, on the afternoon of the 27th, this effort culminated in a fierce assault of Cleburne's position, which Johnston reports to have been repulsed " with great slaughter." This officer estimates his own loss in each of the two main engagements at four hundred and fifty, and that of the Union forces at about three thousand in each. On the 28th, however, Sherman says that a " bold and daring assault" on McPherson while the latter was " in good breastworks," received a " terrible and bloody repulse." Constant skirmishing continued till the 4th of June, during which interval Sherman had worked to the left and covered the roads leading back to Allatoona and Ackworth, the former of which he had resolved to use as a second base for his now attenuated line of supplies.

Ten days of this dead-lock and unprosperous grapple, however, was already too much for a soldier of Sherman's temperament, and he determined once more to turn the enemy out of his position. To move again to the right would throw the Union force too far from the railroad, which Sherman was compelled to keep open and use. He therefore began to work gradually and methodically across to the left, and Johnston, watching, followed in a parallel line also to the east, and so, face to face, the armies reached the railroad, Sherman at Ackworth, and Johnston at Marietta. In front of the latter town, Johnston took up a formidable position on the mountain chain, which, with Kenesaw on his right, Lost Mountain on the left, and Pine Mountain thrust forward in the centre, formed a complete defence for Marietta and the railroad. His troops busily threw up intrenchments and felled trees in front, while Sherman, at Ackworth, was receiving large reinforcements, consisting chiefly of two divisions under Blair, and Long's cavalry brigade; and meanwhile, he had repaired the railroad to the very rear of his camp, and unloaded ample provisions within his lines. At length, when ready to advance, Sherman found the same problem presented anew to him at Kenesaw which he had solved at Dalton, at Resaca, and at Dallas. This time, however, he was loath to risk its solution in the same way; for his army was near at the end of a greatly prolonged line of supply, and a detachment of a flanking force to the right or left was a more serious affair than it had hitherto been. The preparations of the enemy showed that this position was not to be abandoned, like the one at Cassville, but to be fought, like the one at Resaca: and so strong was it by nature and art that any detour of his might be met by an attack from forces easily detached from the small numbers required to hold Marietta. Accordingly he abandoned his previous methods for the time, and resolved to experiment directly against the hostile breastworks. He marched from Ackworth on the 9th of June, his troops full of confidence, well fed, and encouraged by reinforcements. The fighting commenced the next day, and lasted, now in skirmish and now in battle, but always without respite, till the 3d of July. Hood was on the Confederate right, Polk in the centre at Pine Mountain, and Hardee on the left; while McPherson was on the Union left, Thomas in the centre, and Schofield on the right.

26

Through dense thickets and almost impassable ravines, Sherman's troops slowly worked their way for many days, suffering much each day from the fire of their enemy, who had greater immunity, from his advantages of ground. During the battle of June 14th, General Polk was killed by a cannonball, and Loring succeeded him; next day Pine Mountain was abandoned, and a few days later, Lost Mountain. While these costly advances, however, were creditable to the gallantry of the assailants, they did not improve their position. For, in truth, Johnston's previous line had been extremely faulty by reason of its length; and the tempting natural positions of those mountains, joined to some rational expectation that his enemy would again attempt to get round his left, in which case he would probably have sallied and attacked him, had induced Johnston to grasp a reach of ground disproportionate to his force. Indeed, it was this very fact which had partly influenced Sherman, who saw it in his initial reconnoissance, to attack his position; and his main effort had been to break through between Kenesaw and Pine Mountain by a strong and well-officered force, composed of the corps of Hooker, Howard, and Palmer. But, instead of piercing the line, he had only rolled it back and condensed it; since Johnston, seeing his error, had now put his centre, Loring's corps, on Kenesaw as a salient, with Hood on the right flank drawn back across the Marietta and Canton road, and Hardee on the left aross the Marietta and Lost Mountain road. Hood was afterwards shifted to the left of Hardee, and on the 22d suddenly and savagely attacked, near the Kulp House, Hooker's corps and a brigade of Schofield who was on the right; but, after a spirited advance, he was checked and driven back with very severe loss.

Sherman, however, had now been a month south of Ackworth, and three weeks operating in vain against Kenesaw. The enemy was in stronger position than ever at the latter point, and had suffered comparatively little, while his own troops had been undergoing herculean labors, and had been cut up by the constant fire from the enemy's breastworks. It would not do to remain longer in this position, shifting and developing the lines with little profit; and yet the other alternative, that of "flanking," besides the objections which were entertained to it three weeks before, would, if now adopted, suggest the query why it had not been chosen then, with saving of time and troops. Accordingly, Sherman felt authorized to make one grand assault against the heights of Kenesaw, with the desire of piercing the position. Three days' notice was given to the subordinate commanders, that the preparations might be complete. On the 27th, the batteries, planted for the purpose, opened a terrific cannonade for several hours, and then, precisely at the moment fixed, two large armies rushed forward, Thomas and McPherson each assaulting at the prescribed points, the former mainly striking Hardee's corps and the latter Loring's. They were both completely repulsed, the killed and wounded being, according to Sherman, "about three thousand, while we inflicted comparatively little loss:" indeed, the Confederate official loss was less than five hundred, while it was thought that the Union loss was as many thousands.

Quick of apprehension, and not needing several experiments to teach him what one had demonstrated, Sherman no longer doubted as to his proper course. Feeling that his men had done all they could do for him in direct assault, he was content to resort once more to the old manœuvre: and this time he executed it with even greater tactical brilliancy than before. After a few days' skirmish he moved McPherson, on the night of July 2d, once more on a flank march by the right down toward the Chattahoochie; whereupon the same night Johnston abandoned Kenesaw and Marietta, and moved back on the railroad five miles from Marietta to Smyrna Church. Sherman eagerly pressed his columns, hoping to assail his antagonist while delayed by crossing the river; but he found that this event had been forseen, and the Chattahoochie covered with works, at the desired point, and an advance intrenched line thrown up at Smyrna.   But pressing hard against this latter point, Thomas forced the skirmish line, where it was held by Smith's division of Georgia militia, just thrown in, and this, with other menaces, compelled the garrison to fall back to the intrenched river line which, at the point where the railroad crosses at Turner's Ferry, made an admirable bridge-head : to the river, also, retired the whole Confederate line. During four days' brisk skirmishing, Sherman, by degrees, threw a large force across the Chattahoochie, above Turner's Ferry, Schofield crossing at Soap Creek, on the 7th, Howard two miles below at Power's Ferry, on the 8th, while McPherson's whole army lay ready and able to cross above, at Roswell.   All these forces built strong bridges, and intrenched their positions without much opposition, as the fordable nature of the river induced Johnson to take up his line along Peachtree Creek and the Chattahoochie below that point.   However, as a consequence, on the night of the 9th, Johnson abandoned his strong position on the west bank of the river at Turner's Ferry, and in that act left Sherman, as the guerdon of his well-manœuvred and well-fought campaign, the unchallenged mastery of all North Georgia between the Tennessee and the Chattahoochie.

II.

BATTLE OF ATLANTA.

In the latter days of the Confederacy, the grim fatality which from the outset had walked with it, side by side, along its destined course, silent and unseen, seemed to throw off, at length, the cloak of invisibility, to stab it boldly with mortal blows.   Looking at that epoch even with such light as the few subsequent years of history have thrown upon it, in the logic of events and the character of the actors, we may find ration-

MAP OF THE
ATLANTA CAMPAIGN

al necessity for all that took place. But so stupendous were some of the acts of folly then perpetrated by the Confederate leaders, that one would say that it was not enough for the insurrection to rear its front high opposed to the storm of blows which fell crushingly upon it from without, but it must succumb to keener pangs received from within. While, in the enthusiasm of the contest, it seemed hardly fanciful to declare that Fate itself, shadowing the Confederacy so long through successes, with unsuspected presence, at length revealed its sardonic figure in the moment of destiny, to fix its doom and downfall.

One such mysterious blow to the Confederacy was that by which General Johnston was removed from its Western army at the moment when he was most needful for its salvation, kept from command till an intervening general had ruined and disintegrated it, and then gravely restored to the leadership of its pitiful fragments.

By the middle of July, after a week of preparation on both sides, the well-earned rest of the two armies being broken only by detached skirmishes and the labors incident to the coming attack and defence, Sherman and Johnston were ready for the trial. Sherman, meanwhile, by way of episode, had, with Rousseau's cavalry column, broken up the Montgomery Railroad, which brought Johnston's south-western supplies for many miles west of Opelika. For his main army he arranged specific plans of march and battle, posted the cavalry, improved the roads and bridges, and brought forward reinforcements and supplies. Johnston was occupied as busily on his part. The railroad crosses the Chattahoochie at Turner's Ferry, a few miles distant from Atlanta, and at the same point Peach-tree Creek empties into that river. The Chattahoochie, above Peach-tree Creek, Johnston had abandoned partly, as he alleged, on account of its numerous fords; and partly because, in defending it, the broad and muddy channel of Peach-tree Creek would have separated the two wings of his army : at all events, Sherman easily commanded a crossing there, both north and west of Atlanta.   Johnston, with a large force of negroes superintended by his engineers, girdled Atlanta with intrenchments, mounted with heavy guns, and also selected two positions for assaulting the Union army as soon as it should appear in his front.   Of these the first was on high ground south of the creek, from four to six miles from the city, wherefrom he would attack his enemy while crossing, in the hope of driving him back across the creek and then across the Chattahoochie, profiting by the confusion incident to the passage.   Should this prove unsuccessful, his second device was to withdraw his army to one side, and uncover his second position, which was a strongly intrenched line covering Atlanta between the Decatur and Marietta roads.   Lining this with the Georgia State troops already arrived and with others promised, he would await the moment when Sherman attacked them, when with his main army he would fall upon his opponent's flank.   This plan was obviously based on his adversary's preparations to attack by crossing the Chattahoochie to the north of Turner's Ferry, and to advance against Peachtree Creek, on the east of the city.   His troops were well equipped and supplied, and his ordnance and trains in good condition.   As to numbers, he had lost from Ringgold to Atlanta ten thousand killed and wounded, and four thousand seven hundred from other causes.   He had received during the campaign about twenty thousand men, leaving him therefore, more than five thousand better than he started, and his army consisted of fifty-one thousand men, being forty-one thousand infantry and ten thousand cavalry.   He considered that Sherman's losses "could not have been less than five times as great as ours," particularly on account of the daily attacks made in line of battle upon the Confederate skirmishers in their rifle-pits, in dislodging whom "their loss was heavy and ours almost nothing."   Laying great stress, therefore, upon the belief that his troops "fighting under cover, had very trifling losses compared with those they inflicted," Johnston hoped that against his own ten thousand killed and wounded, an enormous counterbalance of Union loss must be set, swelled by losses, too, of garrisons, detachments, and expiring enlistments. To himself, on the other hand, many thousand State troops had been promised before the end of the month.

But there were some elements in the problem not herein calculated. Johnston had been unable to break Sherman's wonderful line of supply; and, therefore, the two armies met in that respect as equally as at Dalton; his State troops were not in hand but in the bush, and his enemy not the man to wait "for the end of the month" till they could be brought in; the Union army despite its losses was again filled to the brim, near a hundred thousand strong, well-equipped and flushed with triumph; and its army, corps, and division commanders included a portion of the ablest soldiers of the Union.

On the 17th of July, in the order prescribed, the Union army went forward. On the same day Johnston, by an order from Richmond, was relieved from his position, and passed the *bâton* of command into the hands of Hood, a brave man destitute of military ideas.

Developed in general line along the Peach-tree road, with Thomas on the right, Schofield in the centre, and McPherson on the left, the Union army swung around on the former as the fixed point. Thomas crossed Peach-tree Creek without difficulty in the front of the Confederate works, Schofield marched through Decatur toward Atlanta, and McPherson, coming down from Roswell, fell upon the Augusta Railroad and broke it up four miles, and continued on through Decatur to join Schofield's left. It now remained to develop all the armies in the line of battle close to Atlanta; but, before this could be well done, Hood, who, in accepting Johnston's command, had wisely adopted in general his plan, and requested him to make the dispositions of troops on Peach-tree Creek, began to play his part in the game. At four o'clock, on the afternoon of the 20th, Hood, having massed his troops, advanced on the Buckhead road which runs from

Decatur to the Chattahoochie, and struck into an interval between Thomas's left and Schofield's right, which Sherman was just then trying to fill. The blow fell on Hooker's three divisions, and the divisions of Newton and Johnson; and, suddenly given, was gallantly met. For a time the assault rolled back the Union troops; but, after a five hours' battle, it was abandoned, the attacking party losing, as was conjectured by Sherman, about five thousand men, while the troops attacked, being partly intrenched, lost but one thousand seven hundred and thirty-three.

The execution of the first of Johnston's plans, that of attacking Sherman on his passage of Peach-tree Creek, having failed, although for a moment promising success, Hood now addressed himself at once to trying the second. This was, as has been explained, substantially to withdraw the main army from the outer Peach-tree intrenchments, and, leaving Atlanta still under the protection of State troops and others in the works between it and the creek, to concentrate far out on the right, for the purpose of falling on Sherman's left flank, when it should come up, exposed, to form the general line in front of Atlanta. Accordingly, on the night of the 21st, Hood moved out to the east, beyond Decatur and the Augusta Railroad, and awaited his opportunity. The device succeeded, for, next morning, Sherman found, to his astonishment, that the lines of works on the heights commanding the southerly banks of Peach-tree were left vacant, and was induced to believe that Atlanta had been abandoned. Pushing Thomas across these lines towards the city, he hurried forward his left, McPherson, along the railroad from Decatur. McPherson, the night before, had, after severe skirmishing, moved two miles west of Decatur, and, crossing it at the south, Blair's corps had seized, after a hasty struggle, a commanding hill not far from Atlanta. In this process, his right, Logan's corps, had been brought up to connect with Schofield's left, at the Howard House, while Blair was on Logan's left. Dodge's corps was now sent round in rear to form on the left of Blair. But, before noon of the 22d, Sherman began to be undeceived ; for Thomas and Schofield found themselves confronted by works which opened noisily with artillery and musketry, according to Hood's orders, while, about 11 o'clock, the rattle of musketry on his extreme left and rear, increasing and lengthening, and soon swelled by artillery, as far back as Decatur, forced upon his mind the danger which menaced him. It was instantly seen that, while heavily engaging Thomas and Schofield by the corps of Stewart and Cheatham, Hood was aiming to turn the Union left by an attack from Hardee, and that the crisis demanded prompt action. Already Hardee' had struck and enveloped Blair's left flank, for Dodge had not reached the point for which he was moving, but, between his head of column and Blair's line was a wood half a mile broad, which Hardee had already seized. Hastily sending his staff hither and thither with the necessary orders, McPherson rode from the Howard House, where he was consulting with Sherman at the moment of the surprise, towards the front, and ordered one of Logan's brigades across into the interval between Dodge and Blair. Entering these woods himself alone, unaware of the enemy's great progress, a shot struck dead the gallant leader of the Army of the Tennessee, and his horse rushed wounded and riderless out of the forest.

While Stewart's (formerly Polk's) corps sharply engaged in front, Hardee's, and Hood's own corps now under Cheatham, continued their victorious progress on the flank. Carrying the greater part of the high hill which commanded the region around, the assailants captured the intrenching parties, and drove G. A. Smith's division back upon the division of Leggett, still clinging to the crest, where a terrific contest was kept up from noon until four o'clock. Before that hour a full regular battery had been surprised and captured while moving up through the woods, besides a section of a battery taken from Smith's division when their position was carried; and, meanwhile, Wheeler's cavalry burst in upon Decatur, in the rear, seized it, and, falling upon the trains, captured a few wagons, and drove the rest back towards the Chattahoochie. As the day waned, the contest grew hotter and the attack more desperate, and soon after four o'clock Hood again plunged into McPherson's army, now under Logan, and again broke through its lines, capturing two more guns, and then, driving a division before it four hundred yards, advanced upon two full batteries, one of them 20-pounder Parrotts, and, in the face of terrific fire, gallantly carried both of them. It had now become of great moment for the Union forces to regain this last position; and, at length, by concentrating all the available forces of Schofield and Logan, and raking the enemy's ranks with the remaining batteries, when the day was done Hood was stopped in his career exhausted: and successively withdrawing across the positions he had carried, and abandoning the last two batteries he had taken, he was forced to be content with the two guns earlier captured, for his trophies. In this desperate day of assault, the total Union loss was 3722, and that of the Confederates, as General Sherman estimated, "fully 8000."

But this day ended the direct operations against Atlanta from the north and east; and Sherman next, accordingly, began to try on the other flank.   Meanwhile, to aid the project, he resorted to the familiar plan of cutting the communications.   Garrard's cavalry, whose absence had enabled Wheeler to seize Decatur, had, during the two great battles, broken some bridges, and burned some stores near Covington, on the Augusta Railroad, forty-two miles east of Atlanta; Rousseau had broken the Montgomery road at Opelika: it now remained to break the Macon road.   For this purpose, Sherman sent out two cavalry columns, one five thousand strong under Stoneman, and the other four thousand strong under McCook, with orders to meet at Lovejoy's Station on the Macon road, far south of Atlanta, and there break it. The project failed from want of concert, except in effecting a slight and easily repaired damage to the road. Both commands were surrounded, McCook cutting his way out with the loss of five or six hundred men, and Stoneman with five hundred men being captured, and the rest for a time dispersed. After this triumph, Wheeler saw his way open to break Sherman's long line of supplies, which he did by a raid near Calhoun, capturing, also, nine hundred beef cattle.

But Sherman had not relied entirely on his horsemen, and was already preparing to move his infantry on Atlanta from a new point. Unable to get around by the left, he now abandoned that idea, and closed up that series of operations. His new endeavor was inaugurated by moving Howard's (late McPherson's) army over to its wonted position on the other flank, the 27th of July, and this army, crossing Peachtree Creek and Proctor's Ferry, established, next day, the extreme right on the Lickskillet or Bell's Ferry road, which runs due west from Atlanta; so that, from being south-east of the city, it had changed to the opposite quarter. The Confederate commander, seeing that Sherman had given up trying to enter the city from the east, also promptly moved to the other flank. About noon of the 28th Hood, in what Sherman styles a " magnificent advance," made a terrific assault on the extreme Union right, and for four hours the scenes of the 20th and the 22d were re-enacted. But, rendered wary by experience, the Union troops had no sooner been halted than, with marvellous dexterity, they had heaped up the usual breastwork of rails, logs, and earth; and repulsed from these once more the gallant attacking columns withdrew over the fields strewn with their dead. The reported Union loss was six hundred, and the conjectured Confederate loss five thousand. Sherman continued, therefore, his new line of effort, and began to subtract gradually from his left to piece out his right, till he might reach around to the Macon Railroad. In this way Schofield's army and a part of Thomas's were moved over at the opening of August, and Hood built along his own works in parallel course, the two armies gliding, and facing, and sparring, like trained wrestlers. On the 5th of August Schofield made a dash to break through Hood's line a mile below Utoy Creek; but it failed, and cost about four hundred men. During these operations, Sherman daily bombarded Atlanta with long-range guns, which frequently set it on fire.

At length Sherman, finding time flying and his enemy still intrenched before him, consented to resort to the old tactics, so often successful, and once more to plant his army on his enemy's line of supplies from the rear. Nevertheless, mindful that those flank movements of the main army, while they worked the enemy out of his position, yet had always, unhappily, failed to force a decisive combat, a matter he greatly desired, Sherman was fain to experiment first on the enemy's line with a cavalry column: for this promised success on account of the absence of Wheeler's cavalry in breaking up the Dalton road, to Sherman's rear. Accordingly, on the 18th he dispatched Kilpatrick with five thousand horsemen to the West Point Railroad, with orders to "break it good near Fairborn," and then to cross and tear up the Macon road; and meanwhile, he proposed to take more advantage than he had yet hitherto from his detours. Kilpatrick made his raid, encountered and fought the Confederate cavalry, and came back confident of having badly damaged the two roads; but Sherman, conversing pointedly with that officer, as was his wont, on precisely what had been done and what had not been done, found the result insufficient for his purpose. There was nothing now left but to move the whole army, — a course sure to procure the evacuation of Atlanta, but which would probably allow the safe withdrawal of Hood's army. The movement began with the 25th : and, marching Williams's corps into the intrenched position at the Chattahoochie, which covered the bridges, having filled his wagons with fifteen days' supplies, Sherman dexterously shifted his great army in successive movements from left to right. An expert now in manœuvre, he transferred corps and armies as deftly as a veteran player shuffles and deals his cards; and when, at length, the great army had been landed on the West Point Railroad, from Fairborn nearly up to East Point, the men fell to work by thousands in high spirits, and in a day hopelessly destroyed twelve miles of it. Conning his maps, meanwhile, for the next position, Sherman resolved to march due east to the Macon Railroad, partly because the road was nearest to him by that route, partly because its seizure there would bring him directly south of Atlanta, and force Hood, unless he had seasonably taken the alarm, to make a wide march to get out of the city. Hood, however, had extended his lines and moved his troops parallel with Sherman's, and, accordingly, when, on the night of August 30th, Howard's Army of the Tennessee, having driven Hood's skirmishers before him all day, arrived at Jonesboro', on the Macon road, that point was found intrenched and occupied in heavy force. The Union troops were now disposed along the Macon Railroad, but not on it: Howard on the right, at Jonesboro', twenty-two miles from Atlanta, Thomas in the centre, at Couch's, and Schofield on the left at Rough and Ready, eleven miles from Atlanta. Next day, the 31st, the army pressed forward at all points to attack the railroad; but Hood, conscious that this move was really the death-stroke to Atlanta, sallied from his works, about noon, at Jonesboro', and with the corps of Hardee and S. D. Lee, attacked Howard, to dislodge him. Two hours of heavy assault on the intrenchments which the Union troops had already got up, failed of their object, and with severe loss to both sides, Hood retired, and instantly, of course, prepared to evacuate his citadel.

Next day, however, the 1st of September, Sherman continued intently to destroy the Macon Railroad above Jonesboro', working his forces towards the latter point. From Jonesboro', Hood had already drawn off S. D. Lee's corps, preparatory to retreat; but Hardee still held the works. Towards evening, Davis's corps, with some supports, attacked and pierced the Confederate lines, capturing eight guns. The drama, however, was substantially over. Hood had now completed his arrangements and was drawing his whole army and its trains towards Macon, along the road which runs due south from Decatur to McDonough, nearly parallel with the railroad, and Hardee had only been left in position to cover the movement.

That night the army, slumbering along the well-earned railroad, and dreaming of the end of its toils, was roused by the sound of heavy explosions, twenty miles away to the north, succeeded by sharper and lighter discharges, as if a battle were waging there. A full hour these sounds reverberated, and, after an interval, again they burst forth. It was the exploded store-houses, trains, and magazines, of Atlanta, fired by the rear-guard of Hood, whose van was already well southward, marching with the loaded wagons of his army. Sherman had won Atlanta.

III.

RESULTS OF ATLANTA.

To the people of the North, the midsummer of 1864 was the dark hour before morn. Their two great armies had started in early May with the promise of a campaign as short and brilliant as it would be decisive in breaking the armed power of the insurrection. The prayers, the hopes, and the faith of the North attended them, nor was a doubt expressed, even if entertained, of their rapid triumph. This confidence, unlike that of the old days, was well founded: for after the winter's preparations had passed, and after a lull in grand operations in the great theatre of Virginia for very many months, the

Confederate armies which stood up for the new campaign were
of such inadequate strength, that they read in their own mus-
ter-roll the death-sentence of their cause.   Three months
passed by; and such had been their military record that the
whole Union horizon seemed darkened, and the most hopeful
were plunged in despair; while the Confederates, succeeding
beyond all hope, plucked up courage anew.   A fearful retrospect met the eye in Virginia, the great charnel-house whose
threshold the Union army had passed but to fill it afresh with
the rows of the dead.   In its grave-dotted path to the Appomattox, the noble army which had crossed the Rapidan so
cheerily had dropped the greater part of itself — most of its
best officers and its boldest men.   In other years, it had been
thought that the Northern armies had been made to suffer;
but in this brief campaign, before summer was over, more
Union soldiers had been killed and wounded than in all former
campaigns in Virginia from the beginning, under McDowell,
McClellan, Pope, Burnside, and Hooker, while Lee, meanwhile, had lost no greater number of killed and wounded than
in the single series of battles with McClellan on the Peninsula.
The disheartening feature, however, was that the campaign
in which the principal disproportion of losses had occurred,
that from the Rapidan to the Chickahominy, after taking all
summer to fight out, had been abandoned as a failure; and
now a new series of operations, in effect a new campaign,
with almost a new army, had begun, which was inaugurated
in bloody repulses.   It was not enough that the Wilderness,
Spottsylvania, the North Anna, Cold Harbor, had sapped the
strength of the Army of the Potomac, but Petersburg, which
at least it was hoped to carry, had repulsed many successive
attacks; twice had efforts to extend around it to the south
met with similar disasters, and at length the last pitch of pa-
tient endurance was reached in the mine-assault of painful
memory.   As the months wore away, the hope which had inspired the start, gave way to sober reflection, to gloom, and

at last almost to despair, when, in spite of the concealment of figures, it became known that Lee's army had already put out of the combat a number of Union soldiers equal to its own original force, and still lined its breastworks, defiant.

The Virginia cloud even overshadowed the West, and, despite the favorable news from Sherman's campaign, a decisive battle was demanded in proof that the news might be trusted.   To add to the calamity, an audacious army under Early streamed down the Shenandoah Valley, burst across the Potomac, swallowed all opposing forces, marched through the whole length of Maryland, posted itself on the railroad running between Washington and Philadelphia, and actually bombarded the forts of the National Capital; thus giving color to the assertion of Mr. Davis, in his message to his Congress, that it was not Richmond but Washington which at that moment was in a state of siege.   Moved by this unwonted depression of the public mind, and the unwonted position of national affairs, at length a political convention representing one of the two great parties into which the nation was divided, proclaimed that the " four years of failure to restore the Union by the experiment of war " required that " immediate efforts be made for a cessation of hostilities."   Shocked, even in their own depression, by this boldness, the Government at Washington could not escape listening to the ominous sounds of popular dissatisfaction.   Another draft for half a million of men had been announced in the midst of the general gloom, making this burden of the war more burdensome by the unhappy hour of its imposition, and causing the people to inquire what had become of the five hundred thousand who had started to conquer the South in the spring.   In the exigency of the moment even the President of the Union contemplated the possibility of making peace by negotiation with the political leaders of the insurrection, independent of operations in the field, and actually drew up a list of propositions to that effect.

In such an hour, Sherman's bugle-note of victory came strong and clear from out of the depths of Georgia. As by magic it startled the people from this lethargy of despair, inspired the Government with confidence, freshened in spirit the comrade-army of the East, that army of heroic constancy. In the national capital, where among the rulers all had been anxiety, alarm, distress, or despair itself, there was an incredible change of feeling, while through the country once more, after being so long dumb and listless, the cannon pealed, the bells rung, and the banners flaunted over a series of victories; and when Sherman's preparatory triumphs were in time crowned by the fall of Atlanta, and Farragut swelled the chorus of victory by his glorious bay-fight at Mobile, the joy was unbounded. Nor was this a temporary elation, since, excessive though it appeared by the very reaction from previous distress, it became sustained and justified. This steady breeze from the West drove across the sky and forever out of the horizon the dense clouds which had so long lowered, till they were in the deep bosom of the ocean buried. Thenceforward the path was clear and radiant; nor was there ever, after the autumn of 1864, any rational doubt that the days of the insurrection were numbered.

The immediate fruits of the capture of Atlanta were also very great, though so far surpassed by its moral influence as to deserve only secondary mention. Four months of vigorous campaigning, with marching and fighting by night and by day, a contested passage of the Alleghanies for two hundred miles, with ten pitched battles and scores of lesser engagements, had given Sherman the control of North Georgia. Although Johnston's main army had escaped intact across the Chattahoochie, thus foiling Sherman in his main design, yet, under the guidance of Hood, it had been surely dealt four reeling blows; and if it eventually escaped with its trains, yet Sherman had the consciousness that at least twenty thousand men had been in those four battles

27

put *hors de combat*. The country now occupied by Sherman was at once the workshop, the granary, the store-house, and the arsenal of the Confederacy, and Atlanta was the centre of a network of many towns and villages, such as Rome, Roswell, and Marietta, which had furnished forth so much of its war material to the Confederacy. Here were foundries, furnaces, rolling-mills, machine-shops, laboratories, railroad repair-shops; here were factories of cannon and small arms, of powder, cartridges, and caps; thence went army-wagons and ambulances and harnesses, and cotton clothing and woollen clothing in abundance for the army. Much of the machinery was now destroyed either by the Confederate or the Union troops, and that which was removed could no longer be used to advantage. The year's crop of the rolling valleys at his back had also come under the control of Sherman, with their plentiful grass and grain. Looking towards future operations, he had now leaped the great chain of arduous mountains, and could glide along their base or move on the smooth slope to the sea. He was planted at the skirt of the cotton-growing region of Georgia, into which he could now direct his columns. On his right, lay the railroad towns of Selma, Montgomery, Opelika, Columbus; in front Macon and Milledgeville; on the left Athens and Augusta — all exposed to his cavalry marches, while the railroad system connecting the Eastern Confederacy with the Western, — already badly broken, — could properly be said to lie at Sherman's mercy.

The central figure in the Georgian drama, the man on whom its success chiefly hung, had been well fitted to the *rôle* he was called to play. Both by native temperament and by the accidents of his experience, Sherman had been made apt for the bold and novel method of warfare which it was needful to wage. A man of soldierly instincts, Sherman had received the training of the full curriculum at West Point, where his military abilities gained him high scholastic honors. The long interim between his graduation and the outburst of the Great War, seems to have done but little additional for him, either in martial experience or in martial fame; and nevertheless that interval must have been a generous seed-time, since no man in the country at the fall of Sumter was a more thorough potential soldier. Amongst Sherman's early-displayed traits was a broad and thorough view of campaigning, which comprised at once a complete plan at the outset, and thereafter attention to the minutest details. Of Sherman it soon became insufficient to say that he knew the art of combat, but that he knew perfectly how to march, to feed, and to fight a great army, and had reduced each one of these to a distinct and complete science.

Sherman, moreover, above all Union commanders, possesses the geographical eye. His campaigning-ground lies as a grand chart before him, whereof every inch passes under his vision: its elevations, its depressions, its watercourses, its vegetation, its network of roads, and all its possibilities too, as well as its present features, he deems it not beneath him to study. At a glance the features of a landscape take on in his eye their military hue: a mountain range appears to him a natural traverse, the rising ground yonder a bastion, this precipitous pass a gorge, that river a wet ditch to be passed; and thus he may be said seldom or never to miscalculate the amount of the aid which nature tenders to him, or has lent to his adversary. Something, too, of the beauty of the natural surroundings, as well as their military significance, evidently catches the gaze of this commander, and expresses itself in words now and then, even in his official reports. But it is that other faculty of measuring and grasping the *terrain* on which he manœuvres and gives battle, though its breadth and its length be meted, as it often was, by hundreds of miles in a single campaign, of which we mainly speak. His ground he studies with an anatomist's nicety, now watching the great backbone formed by the mountain chain, now the ribs and spines it puts off on either hand, with those great arteries, the rivers, fed by the lesser water-courses, the veins.   Striking here, he knows that he will touch the heart of the country, or there, that he will paralyze the right arm of its strength.   Nor is it merely the surface elevations and depressions, nor the geological drift of the land, nor its clothing of forest and undergrowth, nor its irrigation, nor the capacity and direction of its turnpikes and paths, nor the nature of the soil, which may affect his marchings or his bivouacs, that Sherman investigates; but he evidently learns thoroughly the natural products of the land, with a view to the question of supplies for himself and for his opponents, and this, too, not by a tardy experience, but before he sets foot on the campaign, and not in his own neighborhood only, but for scores of miles on all his possible lines of advance.   Accordingly, it has been related of him, that even while campaigning on the Mississippi years before, he was intently studying the whole theatre of his Georgia triumph, and indeed all the interior of the Confederacy.   It is also said that at the very beginning of the war he obtained from the Census Bureau in Washington a map, made at his own request, of the Cotton States, with a table showing the cattle, horses, and products of each county, according to the last census returns reported from those States; so that afterwards, when the time for such enterprise arrived, he was practically familiar with the resources of the whole country on his line of march.

The natural bent of his genius, also, provoked Sherman to undertake campaigns of the audacious nature of the Georgia and Carolina excursions.   Being original in his conceptions, he habitually thought of many things which but few other commanders would have thought of, and, indeed, provided for a hundred fancied contingencies and dilemmas which his opponents never attempted to bring about.   If ever unduly elated by success, the first error of over-confidence was apt to rouse him to his customary discretion and skill; but a certain pride, joined to his bull-dog tenacity of purpose, commonly induced him to try to work through as he had begun, in order to approve himself to have been right at the start. He possessed a rare and felicitous union of method and originality, having a great devotion to order and system, which, however, he overthrew when they became trivial and constraining, as concerning petty things, and as being the marks of a mind working in a rut.

He was a martinet in his ideas of military regulations, discipline, drill, subordination, and held himself and his subalterns implicitly to obeying orders; nevertheless, neither in fashioning his campaigns, nor in executing their tactical details, was he hampered by any traditional leathern-stock method, since no small part of his success was due to the presence in his command of strict discipline and unquestioning obedience to orders on the one hand, and a certain freedom from restraint and wise latitude in the choice of means on the other. His own temperament was conscientiously exact and scrupulous, but yet bold and facile in invention, and naturally bent on some new and better way of doing an old thing, never admitting meanwhile that anything was impossible merely because it had not been done before.

He was not always correct in his judgments of men, and sometimes hasty in uttering opinions upon matters beyond his professional scope and in which he was not an expert; but with regard to the latter it may be said, that it never could be averred of anything relating to the military art, and of the former, that no incompetent subordinate ever had the chance to deceive him twice. In the constitution of his mind there was a kind of intellectual absolutism which might have led, but happily did not, to dangerous manifestations. It was controlled, indeed, by his soldier's habit of fidelity to orders: but on emergency and under the push of circumstance, might obviously have asserted its supremacy.   In this respect Sherman differed remarkably from many brother officers, most of whom looked to the way in which the people would regard their actions, kept always in mind their liability to be haled before the popular tribunal, and never quite sank the citizen in the soldier.   The tendency in Sherman of which we speak became the stronger from his being impetuous rather than imperturbable in spirit, and self-confident in ratio to his past successes.

Sherman had a fine organizing and administrative ability, which he exhibited not only in his wonderful composition and preparation of vast armies, but also in directing municipal affairs in several conquered cities like Memphis, Atlanta, and Savannah.   In the latter function, however, he showed, as was not unbecoming a soldier, the tact rather of an executive than of a legislative or judicial mind.   Being a born general, his quick eye, his deftness and his martial instincts, saved the time which many journeymen soldiers lose by awkwardness and slow comprehension.   He was prescient from the start, and being among the first to detect the approach of war, was also amongst the few who at once appreciated its gravity.   Accordingly, his scorn of three months' troops, and his bold estimate of two hundred thousand men as requisite to march from the Ohio to the Gulf, procured him a rather premature verdict of insanity from the "sixty-day" sages of Washington.

Remarkable above all was Sherman's restless energy, which kept him at work in season and out of season, and allowed no moment's respite in his measureless activity. This quality enabled him not only to superintend his campaigns, but to personally direct to a wonderful extent the evolution of their details.   He was accustomed to know thoroughly the condition of the manifold departments of his armies, and to perform many of those functions which some officers would be glad to shift upon their aides-de-camp.

Allied to this trait was his perfect self-reliance and confidence,
which made him desire, wherever possible, to take the
supreme responsibility.

There are two classes of commanders, of which one may
be said never to have gained a battle if gained, or to have
lost it if lost : it was some corps, division, or brigade commander who saw and seized the key-point, or repulsed some
unexpected assault, or made some happy unauthorized attack, or knew the ground whose nature had not been
explained to him; or else it was some accident of fortune
that gained the victory, or some error or inferiority of
the enemy, and in short, anything but original planning.
Nevertheless, even such are invaluable, if only they know
how to use the greatness of others, though they be not great
themselves.

However, Sherman belonged to the other class, and
whatever victories he gained are his own.   No aide-de-
camp drafted his plan of campaign, no subordinate detected
for him the key-points of his battle-grounds, and whatever
there is of good or bad in Sherman's soldiership, is his own,
for glory or blame.   Accustomed to thoroughly plan and prepare his campaigns at the outset, so that he had a tolerably
just perspective of their daily progress, he was left with leisure to employ great care upon details.   His field orders are
remarkably specific in their instructions, pointing out to subdivisions the roads to be taken, and the times of starting and
arrival, and the methods of manœuvre and attack, with such
minuteness as to shift much of the responsibility of the issue
to the shoulders of the general-in-chief.   Such orders form a
marked contrast to the loose and general and conditional instructions of some commanders, whence one conceives a low
idea of the influence they have exerted on the actual issue.
Sherman, however, had himself furnished fine models of the
promptness and precision which he desired in others.   For a
single example, at Vicksburg Grant had ordered Sherman to

be ready with supplies of all descriptions, to move back against Johnston on the 6th of July, for which time an assault on the city had been fixed. Sherman, without a moment's delay prepared himself, though he might have taken leisurely advantage of the interval; hence, when it so happened that Vicksburg fell on the 4th, the same day Sherman's columns were marching against the Confederate commander. Grant says, "when the place surrendered on the 4th, two days earlier than I had fixed for the attack, Sherman was found ready, and moved at once." The same trait of promptness was visible in his forced marches during the Vicksburg and Chattanooga campaigns, while, as to his precision, being a master in the art of handling troops, a hundred battalions would move to and fro beneath his skilful touch, with the smoothness of mechanism.

But here I must pause, it being no aim of mine to attempt a complete portraiture of Sherman, or even to set forth all his purely military traits; but simply to indicate the qualities which so well fitted him for the grand campaigns in Georgia and in the Carolinas. His early opponent in the former campaign, General J. E. Johnston, who might perhaps have been the Fabius Cunctator of the Confederacy, was a soldier who oftener deserved success than commanded it. Of soldierly intuition, thorough training, wide experience in his profession and among men, he was thoroughly worthy of the confidence with which he inspired the people of the Confederacy. His early Virginia campaigns illustrated his ability, while those of the West, if properly regarded, do not diminish his fame. But he was unfortunate now by reason of the overwhelming forces opposed to him, now by the folly or disobedience of subordinates, now by the exigencies of the vast region he was assigned to protect, and chiefly by the interference of the Richmond marplots, who either distorted his plans at the start, or foiled them at the moment of maturity. An excellent officer, sound in judgment, well-poised in character, wary, prudent, circumspect, he admirably husbanded his resources, and was never taken unawares. He conducted his campaigns with a vigor and intelligence which extorted admiration from his opponents, though it provoked censure from his government. After Vicksburg, Mr. Davis was desirous to remove him from command, and plunge him in oblivion; after Atlanta, he fancied that he had permanently submerged him; yet he again rose to the surface in North Carolina, whither his old antagonist in his continental campaigning had now brought the Army of the Mississippi to confront him. No higher praise could be awarded him, and no better consolation for the rebuffs of fortune, than this evidence of the trust of the people of the South, constant through all adversity.

It would not be difficult to trace a kinship of genius between the two great antagonists in the Atlanta campaign; and it is worthy of note that each had the highest appreciation of the other's talent. Sherman's official report is replete with expressions of admiration at the procedure of his "astute adversary," and I well remember that the same sentiment was frequently expressed toward Sherman by Johnston in many conversations which I had with him in North Carolina at the close of the war. They were, in fact, both consummate strategists; both operated according to large plans; both understood perfectly the true nature of war: and the campaign in which these worthy rivals pitted their skill against each other forms one of the most wonderful exhibitions of military chess-playing on record.

XI.

NASHVILLE.

———

I.

PRELUDE TO NASHVILLE..

In early autumn of 1864, the good people of Georgia and Alabama were startled by the apparition of the gaunt, cadaverous figure of Jefferson Davis, preaching among them a new crusade against the North: like Peter the Hermit, he journeyed from town to town, stirring up the minds of men and of women to his project. To say truth, the times were inauspicious for a tour of enthusiasm, people being still wonderstruck with the fall of Atlanta; but it was this event itself which inspired the Presidential peregrination. Aware that Virginia was safe in the watch-care of General Lee, and the Eastern Campaign in train of prosperous continuance till another spring, the West had become the focus of all the Confederate President's anxieties. And well it might, since there another summer of discontent was now added to those years of uniform misfortune, in whose course not only had the great Mississippi Basin been delivered over to the enemy, but even the Alleghanies, whose wooded crags and labyrinthine fastnesses promised a century's warfare, when sea, and gulf, and stream, the South over, should be conquered: these, too, had been o'ermastered from the Chattahoochie back to the Ohio.

Fearful lest some spell had fallen upon the Western people,

Eng^d by Rosslehite.   Photo. by Gurney

Geo. H. Thomas

Dick & Fitzgerald New York

by reason of their manifold disasters, and eager to wake them from the stupefaction of despair which might well have followed the conquest of Northern Georgia, the Confederate President started on his travels from Richmond. The ardor with which he undertook this mission was fanned not only by patriotic, but by personal emotions. For, if a gloom prevailed wherein the cause at the West seemed to be lost, the popular mind did not fail to lay the chief burden of fault at the governmental threshold in Richmond, whence two months before had passed the order deposing General Johnston. To bandy reasons for that policy was now idle; since, in the rude logic of his hearers, it would always appear that Johnston had greatly saved his army in order to save Atlanta, but Hood had greatly lost his army only to lose Atlanta too. The sole recourse was to vindicate the past by the future; and since hollow generalities could not draw the people from despondency, he resolved to give them specific promises: and thus it happened, that, to the chagrin of friend and the profit of foe, before this crusading mission had been long afoot, the Confederate plans of autumn campaign were disclosed by their own deviser.

Nor did he wait until the army had marched; but unburthened his secret many weeks before their real intent could possibly be divined from the manœuvres of the columns. Nor did he confine his instruction to one locality, but distributed it more or less generously, in various public speeches, in the Carolinas, in Georgia, and in Alabama, as at Salisbury, Columbia, Macon, Augusta, Montgomery, and in the camps of Hood's army at Palmetto. "Be of good cheer," he cried, turning to Cheatham's division, when, in the twilight of the 26th of September, a great concourse of Hood's soldiers had gathered at head-quarters, to hear their President, "Be of good cheer, for within a short while your faces will be turned homewards, and your feet pressing Tennessee soil." And Hood, taking up the strain, ingenuously added,

"Within a few days I expect to give the command 'forward,' even if we live on parched corn and beef." To the people of Augusta, four days earlier, Davis had declared that "the enemy must be driven from the soil of Georgia." To the people of Montgomery he defended the removal of Johnston, from whom, at Dalton, he had expected "a successful advance through Tennessee into Kentucky," and whom, had he suspected a retrograde, he would never have reinforced by Polk, but would have left the latter "to assail Sherman upon his flank by North Alabama." To the people of Macon, he said that "the fate that befell the army of the French empire in its retreat from Moscow will be reacted. Our cavalry and our people will harass and destroy Sherman's army as did the Cossacks that of Napoleon; and the Yankee General, like him, will escape with only a body guard." There should be nothing more like that "deep disgrace" of the "falling back from Dalton," by Johnston. "I put a man in command whom I knew would strike a manly blow for the city, and many a Yankee's blood was made to nourish the soil before the prize was won. . . It has been said that I abandoned Georgia to her fate. Shame upon such falsehood! Where could the author have been when Walker, when Polk, and when S. D. Lee were sent to her assistance? Miserable man! The man who uttered this was a scoundrel. . . Your prisoners are kept as a sort of Yankee capital. Butler, the Beast, with whom no Commissioner of Exchange would hold intercourse, had published in the newspapers that if we would consent to the exchange of negroes all difficulties might be removed. This is reported as an effort of his to get himself whitewashed, by holding intercourse with gentlemen." A week after this remarkable harangue, Hood was not yet in motion; and, accordingly, Mr. Davis was able still to announce with some freshness at Augusta, "We must march into Tennessee; there we will draw from 20,000 to 30,000 men to our standard, and so strengthened, we must push the enemy back to the

Ohio." By October 4th, he had reached, in his perambula-
tions, Columbia, South Carolina, to whose people he said,
that ." General Hood's strategy had been good," and that
"his eye is now fixed upon a point far beyond that where he
was assailed by the enemy," so that, "within thirty days,
that army, which has so boastfully taken up its winter quarters in the heart of the Confederacy, will be in search of a
crossing on the Tennessee River."

Never was victor of a grand campaign more perplexed by
his conquest than the triumphant master of Atlanta. Even
while the world rang with his praises, and his fame was as
brilliant in the Eastern Hemisphere as in the Western, while
the North was intoxicated with the magnificence of his conquest,
and the South had found in its depths of gloom the lower depth
of despair, he who had wrought the miracle was already anxiously casting his horoscope for the future, and read therein
the presage of doubt, perchance of disaster. Ever restless,
he paused no moment to enjoy his victories, and far-sighted
always, he was long since gazing ruefully at the autumn's
prospects.

Whence sprang the anxiety which clouded his victory? He
held Northern Georgia with one hundred thousand stalwart
soldiers; but these were chiefly pushed out to the end of an
enormously-extended single line of supply, of which every rod
was in hostile, and but recently overrun territory. To per-
serve this line would paralyze his strength, by requiring detachments to garrison it from end to end. The remnant then
left at its extremity would be powerless to advance, because
a few miles in front lay its intrenched enemy, never yet en-
trapped into decisive battle, who had been reinforced until numerically as strong as when four months before he lay
at Dalton. Indeed, the grand Atlanta campaign had been
ended at a fortunate moment, and in a manner which did
credit to Sherman's prudence as well as to his genius. For,
pursuing Hood from Jonesboro' to Lovejoy's, after the re-

treat from Atlanta, he had found him admirably posted in strong works, in a region wild, broken, with its ridges clothed with dense thickets, and its valleys spongy and patched with the morasses where the head waters of many little tributaries of the Flint River collected. Thither Thomas pursued, with Stanley's corps in advance and Wood's division leading. A gallant assault by this division was severely repulsed, and General Wood himself was among the many officers wounded; and in a dispiriting rain the troops fell back and encamped. But with that keen instinct which always warned Sherman when to stop in a hopeless task, he drew his troops back into Atlanta, and issued his proclamation of victory. In the applause which followed this announcement, the demonstration at Lovejoy's was forgotten: Sherman however remembered it, and knew that he had a powerful enemy in his front. Already now that enemy, falling by detachments here and there upon the Union line of supplies, gave earnest of more dangerous moves to come.

Looking back, Sherman saw the trains that supported Atlanta journeying to him over hundreds of miles. From Atlanta to Chattanooga there was but one stem of single track, with no loop-lines to support it, a measured distance of one hundred and thirty-eight miles. Allatoona, his sub-base, where a million of rations were accumulated, was ninety-eight miles from Chattanooga and forty from Atlanta. But since neither Allatoona nor Chattanooga was safe from siege and capture, with the main army at Atlanta, these could be regarded only as depots, and his true base was at least as far back as Nashville. Now from Nashville to Chattanooga the distance by rail is one hundred and fifty-one miles, and to Atlanta two hundred and eighty-nine miles. To transport supplies, however, for so great an army and for the protection of his garrisoned rear, required also the use of the routes from Nashville to Huntsville and from Huntsville to Stevenson; and, finally, since, as events proved, not even

26

Nashville was safe from attack, Sherman's absolute source of supplies could be traced to the Ohio, at Louisville. The directest single railroad route from Louisville to Atlanta was four hundred and seventy-four miles in length, and that was, therefore, the measure of Sherman's line. But he was, in fact, forced to rely also on the Knoxville and Chattanooga road, a length of one hundred and twelve miles, thus swelling the sum to five hundred and eighty-six miles, and again upon all possible feeders in Tennessee; so that, in fine, the actual railroad lines kept open by garrison and used for the Atlanta campaign, was something over nine hundred miles. The food, the forage, the clothing, the ammunition, all the military stores and outfit, in short, of at least one hundred and twenty thousand persons and fifty thousand animals, passed over these lines, and the quartermaster's department at Nashville alone, on the day of the capture of Atlanta, had fifteen thousand operatives at the former city, and ten thousand more on its nine hundred and fifty-six miles of railroad, by whose aid it loaded and despatched one hundred and fifty cars each day. Now, of this enormous network of communication more than five hundred miles could be instantly menaced throughout by a single bold move of the Confederate army; and a great part of the region spanned by the track was made doubly hostile by its mountainous character, and by the temper of the neighboring people.

In the very tempest of general admiration, therefore, over Sherman's marvellous skill in keeping these vast lines substantially intact during a four months' vigorous campaign, guarding what he held at the start and adding thereto a hundred miles and more — so that repairs were often made in the face of the breaking column, and that habitually, in Sherman's words, "the locomotive whistle was heard in our advanced camps almost before the echoes of the skirmish fire had ceased" — there was yet, to the reflective critic, an anxious query when this prolongation of the line of march would end. To Sherman's retrospective glance, it seemed absolutely sure that his communications could be snapped in fifty places by a judicious use of the Confederate army : nor was it wise to count upon any other use being made. But, even supposing it possible to hold the lines already gained, of what future avail? Whither should he turn his columns? To Macon, the next prominent city in his course? it was a hundred miles away, and Montgomery or Augusta, to the right or left, more distant yet. If his present line of supplies were too long, a longer would be preposterous : while, with an enemy strong in front, he could hardly send detached columns hither and thither, and, even if he could, his own attenuated line and fortified city demanded all his thought.

In this perplexity, Sherman, as usual, first bent himself to the immediate necessities of the hour, and within ruminated the question of the future, — doubtless looking often and often, let us add, to the lines of operation running easterly from East Tennessee. During the first week in September, he occupied Atlanta with Thomas's army, putting Howard's on the right at East Point, and Schofield's on the left at Decatur : the cavalry were on the flanks. Hood had divided his force, advancing a part on the Macon Railroad as far as Jonesboro', while his main army encamped on the West Point road at Palmetto Station, so as to meet an advance from Atlanta in either direction. A fortnight later, Forrest, that daring trooper called by his admirers "the Wizard of the Saddle," made his bold raid upon the Tennessee garrisons and railroads, confirming Sherman's fears. Then it was that, on the 26th of September, Davis achieved his pilgrimage to Hood's camp at Palmetto, and published the Confederate programme for the autumn campaign. A few days later, on the 28th of September, the news had reached Sherman's corps, and at once a burden rolled from the mind of that commander, and light streamed upon his future path. With unconcealed joy, he heard the tidings that Hood was to withdraw his whole army from the front of Atlanta, and throw it into Tennessee : it now only remained to use his opponent's move for extricating himself. The next day he sent Thomas, with some spare troops, to protect Tennessee.

Already, indeed, Hood's camps were broken and his columns on the move; and with the announcement of his intent came the news of his passage of the Chattahoochie in force. The gleam of fortune revealed to Sherman had been the possibility of a clear path through Georgia to the sea. To hold Atlanta he had found impossible; to retrograde would seem to undo the summer campaign, and would be disastrous to the *morale* of his army; to advance was sufficiently hazardous, with an enemy strong enough to cut off his supplies in the rear, and to prevent foraging parties from getting them in the country around. But now, every step of Hood made it possible to sweep unimpeded to the coast, and open communication with gun-boats and water supplies; and, though the march might be bloodless, yet it would be a " change of base" from a point whose tenure was doubtful, to one whose tenure was sure, and all the while would wear the guise of conquest. With exultation, therefore, Sherman saw Hood throwing himself north-west of Atlanta, and aiming, with all his legs, to increase the gap between them. "If Hood will go to Tennessee," he exclaimed, "I will give him the rations to go with."

Nevertheless, Sherman at once turned in the other direction, moved by several reasons. The object for which he had come into Georgia was not to feed his army, not to march over broad plantations: it was to meet, fight, and destroy the Western Confederate forces. Accordingly, should Hood march triumphantly north, while the spectacle of the two combatants hurrying not toward, but away from, each other, would hardly be edifying, still more discreditable would be the exchange of Nashville and Louisville for Macon and Savannah. And if it were replied that Sherman's object was to reinforce Grant, the rejoinder would be swift, that it was

28

more needful first to conquer Hood, and then the question of march or transportation to the East would become very simple. Moreover, to allow Hood to go on his way rejoicing would be the surrender of a score of garrisons, and immeasurable wealth of stores and ammunition. Accordingly, Sherman instantly turned on Hood, in the hope to force a general battle, whose success would resolve all questions and allow a march to the ocean or the gulf or whithersoever else a march might appear a victory.

Before Sherman could get out of Atlanta, Hood was far north of it, and Stewart's corps and the cavalry, marching to the railroad, had destroyed it thoroughly for over twenty miles between Allatoona and Marietta, capturing the garrisons of Big Shanty and Ackworth, and breaking all communication between Sherman and Thomas. Hood, meanwhile, with his other two corps, marched briskly off to the Coosa river, crossed it below Rome, and moved towards Summerville and Lafayette, where his position threatened both Chattanooga and Bridgeport. Stewart continued his railroad adventures, and, on October 5th, sent French's division to attack Allatoona, just reinforced by Corse, who most brilliantly and stubbornly defended it, until, Sherman's main army appearing from Atlanta, the Confederates drew off. Sherman, indeed, had, on the day previous, taken his army, consisting of the Fourth, Fourteenth, Fifteenth, and Seventeenth Corps, out of Atlanta, leaving the Twentieth to hold the works. He now started after Stewart up the railroad; but the latter sped quickly towards Dalton, which he captured on the 14th, with its garrison, destroying more railroad, from Tilton on one side of Dalton to the Tunnel on the other: then, his work done, he withdrew through Nickajack Gap to Hood's main army, now near Summerville. Hood, well pleased with his success thus far, and laughing a little at the wild-goose chase on which he appeared to be leading his opponent, put his columns in motion for Gadsden, on the Coosa. And Sherman, in the lack of anything better to do, followed, though somewhat disgusted at finding that his opponent, as he phrased it, "evidently wanted to avoid a fight." On the 19th, Sherman had got to Gaylesville, higher up on the Coosa than Gadsden, in Northern Alabama, near the Georgia line. Seven days at Gaylesville, Sherman waited to see what Hood would do at Gadsden. Then, on the 26th, he found that the latter had, while clothing and reshoeing a part of his troops, sent a column of infantry west to Decatur, to clear the way, doubtless, for an advance in force against Nashville. To follow up Hood could no longer be thought of, because experience showed that he could move the faster, Sherman's columns being more cumbersome. Moreover, Hood, at present, was playing the winning game, since he had broken Sherman's line of supplies, captured some of his garrisons, and drawn him clear out of Georgia into Alabama, all without a battle. His present move aimed to coax the Union general into Tennessee; but to this Sherman took exception, for to dance attendance upon a general whom he had just disastrously defeated, and to fight a defensive campaign for the retention of Chattanooga, Murfreesboro', and Nashville, after he had captured Atlanta, was something his temper could no longer brook. His northern movement must be stopped somewhere, and the sooner the better; so, leaving Hood in good hands, he reversed his columns and marched to the Atlantic.

It was the 26th of October when Sherman began to gird and strip for the journey to the sea. He sent the Fourth and Twenty-third Corps to Tennessee, turned back the rest of his army from Gaylesville to Smyrna Church and Kingston, and, in the fortnight succeeding, organized and equipped his expedition, sent back all surplus artillery, stores, baggage, with the sick and wounded and refugees, to Chattanooga, and then destroyed the railroad from Atlanta to the Etowah, and from Resaca to Dalton. At the same time, in Rome, Atlanta, and elsewhere, all remaining shops, foundries, mills, depots, and supplies were burned, lest they might become useful to the Confederates, to whose repossession North Georgia was now surrendered. Sherman had taken with himself 60,-000 veteran infantry, sixty guns, and 5,500 cavalry. A much smaller force could have accomplished all that was required, but it was advisable, for moral effect, to move all the troops forward that could be spared, and to send the fewest possible in retrograde. Had Thomas's army proved insufficient for its task, the disposition would have been censurable, no matter what the success of the march to the sea; but the sequel vindicated all. As stout Cortez broke his ships behind him, on the Mexican coast, that the dream of retreat might not enter the minds of his men, so Sherman, as he turned his cohorts southward, put the torch to the camps and the city of Atlanta. With mighty tongues of flame leaping from the crashing edifices of the ruined " Gate City of Georgia," and blazing by night in portentous beacon-fires for miles along the untried paths, the columns of Sherman, cutting loose from the world behind, on the 13th of November, plunged into the forests, and were lost to sight.

The officer who now reigned for the time over the broad Mississippi Valley, with a shield for Tennessee and a sword for the advancing foe, was Major-General George H. Thomas. Long before famous among the choicest soldiers of the Union army, Thomas had added to the laurels of Mill Spring, Murfreesboro', Chickamauga, and Missionary Ridge, those of the late Atlanta campaign, during which he had the handling and immediate command of 60,000 men, being more than three fifths of Sherman's whole army. He was Sherman's senior subordinate, Sherman's own senior in years, an approved officer of the highest type, and one who had bettered by twenty months' longer experience the encomium passed upon him by Rosecrans at the opening of 1863 — " true and prudent; distinguished in counsel, and on many battle-fields celebrated by his courage." The importance of defeating Hood was illustrated by the assignment to this task of so excellent a soldier, with whom, also, was Schofield, an admirable ally; so that with the coastward excursion rode not one of the three army commanders who fought at Dalton and Kenesaw.

It was on the 29th of September that Thomas left Atlanta for Nashville, and the 3d of October when he arrived at the latter capital. His mission then was merely to protect Tennessee and its many cities, forts, and garrisons, and the railroad and river communications of the army in front, against the bold raids of Forrest and Buford, who had been prowling through the neighborhood during the previous fortnight. Startled, however, by the prompt demonstrations of Generals Rousseau, Steedman, Granger, Morgan, and Washburne, Forrest's two Confederate columns made off across the Tennessee again, about the time when Thomas assumed command. While the latter officer was posting the troops just enumerated along the Tennessee and the railroads, in support of the chief garrisons established on those lines, Hood launched forward from Palmetto, on his northerly invasion.

Once more now, precisely as in the spring of 1862, nearly three years gone, General Beauregard had been sent from Virginia to Mississippi, to restore the failing fortunes of the West. Once again his mission involved the superintendence of an offensive campaign into Tennessee, for which purpose he again fixed his head-quarters for a time, as of old, at historic Corinth. But how had the scene changed since that earlier experiment! Then, the wide-spreading Mississippi Valley was in Confederate keeping from Arkansas to Georgia; the Alleghanies were Confederate altogether, no Union column daring to look towards East Tennessee; while the Great River was fast in Southern tenure from Columbus to New Orleans. Feeling their way down into Kentucky from the Ohio, the Union columns were then not less astonished at their own temerity, than were the Confederates confident of punishing it. And now, three disastrous years had made havoc so sad of Confederate possessions! Indeed, the very remembrance of the ill-starred campaign of aggression which began and ended on the field of Shiloh, might well have cast an ominous shadow on the mind of Beauregard, and presaged disaster for the campaign to come. But the hour was one for action, not for gloomy meditation over a changed landscape. To Beauregard, in mid-October, had been assigned the grand "Division of the West," including all possible paths of Hood's army. Through October, workmen were busy in repairing the old Mobile and Ohio Railroad and its feeders and connections, till at length trains ran up as far as Corinth, and thence due east to Cherokee Station, where they poured supplies of every sort, collected through Alabama and Mississippi, — from Mobile, Selma, and Montgomery, — into Hood's camp. Besides clothing, shoes, arms, equipments, ammunition, food, forage, there came also to Hood, under Beauregard's effective rallying, large reinforcements of troops. But with the end of these preparations, Beauregard disappears forever from the scene of the Tennessee campaign, wherein, indeed, he appears to have held not even the *rôle* of stage-manager, far less that of an actor in the drama; but, as it were, the place of property-man, dispensing the costumes and the weapons, and furnishing forth the appointments for Hood's ensuing tragedy.

It was not only in clothing and shoeing his troops and filling his wagons that Hood was busy at Gadsden, while Sherman waited at Gaylesville. He sent before him those who should prepare his way into Tennessee; Cheatham hovered about Decatur and Florence, and Forrest was once more in the saddle, and blowing his bugle along the Lower Tennessee. Thomas now had but one desire for the present, which was to keep the Confederates south of the Tennessee till at least Stanley's Fourth Corps could arrive on the scene of campaign. But Hood had moved before the Union plan was adopted, and, accordingly, while Stanley was hurrying from Sherman, Hood, between the 29th and 31st of October, easily crossed the river three miles above Florence, his cavalry repulsing Croxton's brigade, which was all the force that could be then stationed at that point. At the same time, Forrest swung down the westerly bank of the Tennessee, with seventeen regiments of cavalry, and nine guns, carrying all before him to Johnsonville, a Union base of supply and railroad terminus, and there captured a quantity of supplies, barges, and gun-boats, while to the remainder of the flotilla and the store-houses the garrison put the torch, destroying some millions' worth of materials of war.

But now, on the first day of November, the Fourth Corps arrived at Pulaski, where it was joined soon after by the Twenty-third — too late, however, to prevent the lodgment of Hood's infantry north of the Tennessee. Pulaski was selected by Thomas as the outpost from which to observe Hood's movements. and all the available cavalry were picketing the north bank of the Tennessee : while Schofield took command at Pulaski, Thomas was vigorously at work at Nashville. Hood, meanwhile, had already occupied Florence with the corps of Stewart and Cheatham, while to the opposite or north bank of the Tennessee he had thrown S. D. Lee's corps, with a division of cavalry on either flank patrolling the neighboring fords, and the banks and the regions beyond.

Very anxiously, during the first two weeks in November, did Thomas, with his scanty forces, watch his enemy ; but the latter lay quietly at Florence and Tuscumbia, and his only hostile manœuvres were with Forrest's cavalry, which pushed out to Shoal Creek and there incessantly skirmished with the squadrons of Hatch and Croxton. However, Thomas was not eager to hurry his antagonist, since every hour to him was golden, in collecting his forces. While he thus watched and waited, Sherman, whose presence at Kingston was to Thomas of great moral support, cut the line of communication on the 12th, and vanished from the scene.

The days which succeeded Sherman's departure from Kingston were full of solicitude. Should Hood, taking the alarm, abandon his design and march off to harass Sherman, Thomas was instantly to follow upon his trail: otherwise he was to defend Tennessee and meet and overwhelm the Confederate army. Hour after hour the Confederate camp-fires were watched; at length it was evident that Hood clung to his own enterprise, and would turn his banners northward.

The situation of Thomas was one of enormous responsibility, calculated to weigh down a less firm and self-sustained spirit. To his care was committed the Military Division extending from the Ohio to the Gulf, from the Mississippi to the mountains; the task of holding Tennessee, defending the line of the Tennessee River, and the railroad lines from Chattanooga to Nashville; finally, the destruction of the Western Confederate army, the grand object of the whole war west of the Alleghanies. Sherman's instructions were that he should " exercise command over all the troops and garrisons not absolutely in the presence of the general-in-chief." To accomplish his ends, Thomas had not only to make a campaign, but to create an army — or, at least, to collect and crystallize one from materials scattered hundreds of miles; and this before the alert enemy should learn his difficulties and take advantage of them. It is by reflecting on what was to be done and what there was with which to do it, that the energy of those days may be appreciated. " At this time," says Thomas, " I found myself confronted by the army which, under General J. E. Johnston, had so skilfully resisted the advance of the whole active army of the Military Division of the Mississippi from Dalton to the Chattahoochie, reinforced by a well-equipped and enthusiastic cavalry command of over twelve thousand men, led by one of the boldest and most successful cavalry commanders in the rebel army." He estimated Hood's strength at from forty to forty-five thousand infantry, and from twelve to fifteen thousand cavalry, while Sherman fixed it at thirty-five thousand infantry and ten thousand cavalry. One commander looked at the force he met and destroyed, the other to the force he left behind for another to vanquish; it is not safe, however, to place Hood's effective force, when greatest, much above fifty thousand men. To meet it Thomas had at Pulaski and thereabouts an effective force of but thirty thousand men. Of the six corps in Sherman's army, he had left Thomas but two — the Fourth, about twelve thousand strong, and the Twenty-third, about ten thousand strong; to these were added Hatch's division of cavalry, four thousand strong, Croxton's brigade, twenty-five hundred, and Capron's brigade, about twelve hundred — in all, twenty-two thousand infantry and seven thousand seven hundred cavalry. The rest of Thomas's force was posted along the railroad and river, as at Murfreesboro', Stevenson, Bridgeport, Huntsville, Decatur, and Chattanooga, to hold the lines of communication until Hood's purpose should be developed, and his path divined. All, however, that Thomas wanted was time; for two infantry divisions under A. J. Smith, were on their way from Missouri, and other detachments were pouring into Nashville, while Wilson was busily moulding the fragmentary cavalry of Kentucky and Tennessee, and remounting the regiments which Sherman had dismounted so as to take their horses for his own troopers in the march of Savannah. Schofield at Pulaski was ordered to retard the enemy when he should advance, but without risking a general engagement till the reinforcements were up.

At length, November 17th, Hood leaped the river with his main force, from Tuscumbia to Florence, and two days later moved from the latter point, on two parallel roads, towards Waynesboro', and drove Hatch's cavalry out of Laurenceburg on the 22d. From Laurenceburg as well as Pulaski, a road runs back to Columbia; and the Confederates were aiming to arrive

first at this latter point by the Laurenceburg road, in order to
cut off Schofield's retreat. The latter officer, accordingly, by
Thomas's direction, fell back skirmishing from Pulaski along
the turnpike, on the 23d, and next day safely reached Columbia, on Duck River; but there was no time to spare, for the
leading division, Cox's, had barely leisure to move down the
stream and check the Confederate cavalry column which was
struggling to get across the Union line of retreat.

Looking at the map of manœuvre, one would declare that
skilful and brilliant strategy on the Confederate part, joined
with a measure of good fortune, would have made Schofield's
position at Pulaski, despite his promptitude, very perilous.
The latter was, with all his trains, many days' march south
of Nashville. Now, until he should reach Nashville, neither
that city nor his own army was safe. It may be said that
Schofield had a long start of his opponent; but time and distance were not the only elements of the race. Schofield was
tied to his trains, and most of his force was taken up with
guarding them; on the other hand, Hood had no anxiety for
his trains, and as his rear could not be touched by hostile
raids, he had most of his army light and free for a rapid flanking movements. Again, Hood far outnumbered Schofield, and
above all outnumbered him in cavalry, the Union horsemen
being no match for Forrest. It may be asserted, therefore,
that considering the opposing numbers, the length of the retreat, the excellence of Hood's flanking column, and the certainty that Schofield's trains would, if set upon by the enemy,
block the way and delay and confuse the Union forces — the
situation of Schofield was for many days precarious.

Hood's main plan was to push into Kentucky and there
recruit his army and fill his wagons; and he seems actually
to have dreamed of swelling his force to 90,000 men. But it
was first needful to defeat Thomas, and the latter's poverty in
troops gave him a good chance of success. The miry roads
and the lack of maps and previous reconnoissances, defeated

the scheme of cutting off Schofield between Pulaski and Columbia, and the second effort was made between Columbia and Franklin.   Had Hood then succeeded in gliding between Schofield's army and Nashville, the city would probably have fallen.

There was skirmishing between Hood's advance and Schofield in front of Columbia, from the 24th to the 27th, and on the latter day Hood's whole army was up and in position. That evening, therefore, Schofield abandoned the town, which is on the south bank of Duck River, and crossing to the other shore, took up a very strong position a mile and a half distant.   At midnight of the 28th, Forrest drove off Wilson's cavalry, which guarded the Lewisburg pike, six miles above Columbia, and there crossed Duck River.   Stuart's and Cheatham' scorps and Johnson's division of Lee's corps followed before dawn, one division of Lee's corps being alone left in Schofield's front at Columbia.

The point at which Hood aimed was Spring Hill, fifteen miles north of Columbia, on the turnpike leading back to Franklin.   His troops were in light marching order, with but one battery to a corps, and marched on roads parallel to the turnpike.   Hood was already on Schofield's flank, and had cut communication between the latter and Wilson, before the retreat of the Union troops from Columbia was commenced. It seemed that nothing could save the latter.

It was now a "race for Franklin."   As Hood had, by parallel roads, endeavored to get past the Union flank, Stanley with the second division of his Fourth Corps, was hurried at once back to Spring Hill, fifteen miles north of Columbia (at which point the Confederate flanking column would debouch on the Franklin turnpike), in order to guard the rear. He was just in time to save the trains, as well as the line of retreat, from the clutch of Forrest.

Forrest reached Spring Hill at mid-day, but Stanley's troops, who had that moment formed around the trains, barely managed to keep him away. The contest, however, went on till four o'clock, when Cheatham's corps arrived on the field, two miles from Spring Hill, at which point Stanley had a small force deployed along the pike. Cheatham was ordered by Hood to make a vigorous attack, and, had he done so, beyond all question Schofield's retreat must have been cut off, for a part alone of Stanley's corps was struggling against the whole of Forrest's and the whole of Cheatham's, and all the rest of Hood's army, except one division, was marching up to the field. But Cheatham made only a feeble demonstration with only a part of his command. Yet even this Stanley's exhausted command might not longer have withstood after their heroic labors, had not tidings of their condition reached Schofield, who, at a late hour in the afternoon, started with Ruger's division of the Twenty-Third Corps to Stanley's relief.

Chagrined at Cheatham's sluggishness, which had consumed the day, Hood after dark endeavored to throw Stuart's corps, which had arrived, across the turnpike. But the latter officer also did not move upon the required position, and at eleven o'clock went into bivouac within 800 yards of the road. So, a second time, an opportunity for blocking Schofield's retreat was lost; and the simple story is the best comment on the condition of the Confederate army. The division commanders seemed lacking in respect for their superior.

Schofield appears to have been under the impression that Hood's main force was still around Columbia, and all day looked for an attack near that point. Thomas says, "Although not attacked from the direction of Huey's Mills, General Schofield was busily occupied all day at Columbia, resisting the enemy's attempts to cross Duck River, which he successfully accomplished, repulsing the enemy many times with heavy loss." As we have seen, only one of Hood's divisions was left to make the feint against Columbia. But, whatever the success of this division, the fatal blundering of Hood's flanking column threw away victory, when it might have been made sure.

However, when darkness had fallen, the Union troops at Columbia, obedient to the instructions left by Schofield, stole back on the turnpike road to Franklin. The march was hurried, for though the railroad bridge across Duck River had been destroyed, the pontoon bridge, hastily fired, had been abandoned to the enemy, who might be expected to cross in prompt pursuit, the more especially as Lee's division had been pressing vigorously all day to detect a withdrawal. At midnight, Hood's pickets at Spring Hill sent back word that the enemy was moving "in great confusion" along the pike, with trains and troops mingled. Hood quickly ordered Cheatham to move a heavy line of skirmishers against the pike, to delay this retreat. This was done; and so incomprehensibly negligent did the Confederate corps lay within easy march of the turnpike, over which the Union troops and trains which they had come thither to destroy were distinctly heard to rattle and hurry hour after hour. Indeed, it was believed, and no wonder, for a long time thereafter by the Union commanders, not only that the smaller part of Hood's army was at Spring Hill, but that even that part were asleep or heedless when their enemies marched past them. This was the third and last chance for Hood to destroy Schofield and capture Nashville.

To Schofield it was a night of intense anxiety, especially when, going with Ruger to Stanley's aid, he had discovered the enemy bivouacking in force at Spring Hill, less than eight hundred yards from the turnpike, and fifteen miles north of the main army at Columbia. Three miles beyond, at Thompson's, were the still-burning fires of another cavalry camp just abandoned. Quietly posting a brigade at each of these points, to prevent an irruption from the crossroads on the line of retreat, Ruger anxiously awaited the passing of the main army. Swiftly the latter moved back on the pike, enveloped in the favoring darkness, and passed Spring Hill at midnight, while the Confederates seemed to slumber in their camps near by after their day's labors; meanwhile Wilson's cavalry clattered back on the Lewisburg pike. At dawn of the 30th, the Confederates moved upon the pike in search of their foe; but he was gone, foot and horse, baggage, artillery, and ammunition. The baffled troopers dashed angrily along the road, only to find Schofield drawn up, next morning, after a hard night march of twenty-five miles, in firm line of battle around the town of Franklin; and, except a few burned wagons, his trains were safe behind him, beyond the Harpeth.

The town lies on the left or southerly bank of a bend in the Harpeth River, a tributary of the Cumberland, and eighteen miles south of Nashville, by the great turnpike along which the retreat had been conducted. The stream winds in horse-shoe shape at this point, so as to cover the north and east of the town, leaving only the south and west exposed; accordingly, Schofield formed line of battle with his two corps across this front, and resting both flanks upon the river, the one above the town, the other below, still maintained a tolerably dense and solid line. No sooner was the column deployed, than with that marvellous celerity which long practice had begot, the troops, though jaded and sleepless, fell to intrenching with axe and spade; and by four o'clock they had thrown up a handsome parapet of logs and earth. This line was dotted with artillery at available points, while on the northerly bank of the stream, in the rear, the rest of the artillery was posted along a range of intrenched heights, which swept the broad plain in front of the main position. In his semicircular line, Schofield posted Stanley's Fourth Corps on the right, and his own Twenty-third Corps, under Cox, on the left, while Wilson's cavalry was disposed along the northerly shore, beyond both wings, to guard the neighboring fords from the passage of flanking columns of Forrest's cavalry. The position was a strong *tête-de-pont*, covering the bridge and turnpike in the rear, along which, meanwhile, labored the rumbling trains which Schofield had made it a point of honor to preserve.

Before noon of the 30th, Hood's skirmishers were up and pressing the Union outposts, while the latter struggled to give time for the rapid intrenchment going on behind them. The region on both sides of the turnpike for some miles south of the river is level and cleared, with a few bushy patches here and there, which served as partial curtains for Hood's deployments; but the arrival and formation of his columns were in the main obvious from the Union lines. By four o'clock in the afternoon Hood was all up, and, with Stewart on the right and Cheatham on the left, S. D. Lee in support, and Forrest's cavalry on the flanks, he began a general assault. The broad undulating interval, open in the main, but broken by bushy hillocks and clumps of undergrowth, was passed under destructive fire, with splendid gallantry. The first brunt of battle fell upon two brigades of Wagner's division, of the Fourth Corps, which, according to some strange theory of combat, had been posted about eight hundred yards in front of the main intrenched line, there to act as a sort of cushion to receive and deaden the initial violence of the charge. It was the same division which had stubbornly fought at Spring Hill the day before, and now comported itself with the like obstinate gallantry. But Cheatham's corps, rolling in a billowy mass over the plain, dashed full upon the outlying brigades, and, curling around their flanks, swept off six hundred and fifty prisoners, and stretched several hundred more wounded on the earth. In a few moments, Maney's division was in full possession of Wagner's intrenchments, and the remnant of the two luckless brigades were flying in confusion back to the main line. It was clear enough now that this outpost had better at once have drawn behind the line of battle; for, besides the havoc in its ranks, its tumultuous rush to the rear threw the main line into disorder at that point, and by covering the enemy behind, prevented the troops in the works from opening fire upon him. Close upon the heels of the flying brigades pressed the exultant Confederates, and pursued and pursuers leaped together over the intrenchments. It was a critical moment; a wide entrance had been effected into the Union works; the position was imperilled, and two 4-gun batteries already captured by the Confederates. At this moment the remaining brigade of Wagner's division (Opdycke's), which had been held in reserve inside the lines, threw itself impetuously into the gap, and by a sudden charge, with Conrad's brigade in support, recaptured the two batteries, and drove Cheatham's men across the intrenchments, with the loss of several hundred prisoners. In this gallant struggle General Stanley was wounded, after having in person rallied Wagner's men, and led them to the expulsion of the enemy.

And now the battle redoubled in fury, and the roll of musketry burst from wing to wing of either army, while the batteries echoed their deeper diapason. With officers of all grades leading the charge, the Confederates fairly leaped upon the parapet, and men in gray and men in blue grappled in deadly wrestle across the breast-high mound which divided them. Stewart's corps, on the Confederate right, was raked with a merciless cross-fire from Cox's corps and the intrenched artillery on the northern river bank, which, threatening to sweep away that wing, checked its repeated assaults. On the other flank, Cheatham, encouraged by having once broken into the Union right and centre, surged desperately thrice more against the lines, receiving each time a withering storm of canister and grape upon both flanks, and the musketry fire of the Fourth Corps in front. Four distinct assaults, it was thought, were made, in Hood's desperate style; for the assailants with surprising gallantry came again and again to the breastworks, now here, now there, as if loath to quit the prey whereof they had so long been baffled; and between the compact assaults fierce artillery exchanges took place — and infantry exchanges too; since the Confederate riflemen clung constantly to the field, close up to the works, wherever the roughnesses of the ground would shelter them. When darkness fell, desperate charges gave way to a general interchange of fire, but it was only at ten o'clock that the assaults ceased and the battle was over.

In this engagement at Franklin, Hood's loss was 6252, of which 702 were prisoners, while Schofield's loss was 2326, whereof 1104 were prisoners. The Confederate losses included thirteen general officers, of whom six were killed on the field, six wounded, and one captured: among the killed was Major-General Patrick Cleburne, who had risen from the ranks of an Arkansas regiment, and was, it may be said, the best soldier in Hood's army.

Schofield's aim in joining battle at Franklin, was now achieved: for whereas to have fled without a stand on the banks of the Harpeth, would have turned retreat to rout, and in the intermingling of troops and trains, would have brought ruin on one or both, now he could make his way to Nashville in safety and order. A full day's journey had been secured for his trains, and, the battle being over, before midnight Schofield put his troops once more in motion, and withdrew as noiselessly and successfully from Franklin as he had from Columbia. He marched, too, with the consoling reflection that he had inflicted a terrible loss on his opponent, and checked his career at the outset by an unexpected and bewildering blow.

Before Hood, the headstrong, got breath again from the buffet at Franklin, the city he aimed at was safe; for the next day Thomas's reinforcements came. However, as if with appetite edged by frequent disappointment, the Confederates, on finding Schofield gone, hurried along the turnpike so stealthily emptied of their enemy, and paused only in sight of his main citadel, which they straightway began to environ.

II.

BATTLE OF NASHVILLE.

In a military view there was little to give the city of Nashville the significance it early assumed in the war and always maintained. There was not much in the physique of the region around it of strategic value, while historically it was proved to be a dependent post, whose evacuation could be procured by operations scores of miles away. Fortified with much care, it yet became self-supporting only with the presence of a large army, to which in turn it was as likely to prove a cage as a castle. Its lines of communication were not proof against skilful menace, so that at a well-directed shock on the flank, Nashville would succumb; as yield indeed it did to Buell, upon the fall of Donelson, when Sydney Johnston's army withdrew without a shot. It was, doubtless, this fact which influenced the conduct of Hood, who, as we shall see, having with much pains got up to Nashville, sat ten days before it, waiting to see it fall, as it might of yore, at the waving of his *báton* towards its lines of supply.

However, considerations social, political, and geographical, made Nashville the great prize in Tennessee. It is the chief city of the Mississippi Valley between the Ohio and the ocean — the largest in population, the wealthiest, the leading mart of trade, the centre of social influence, and the chief focus of politics for all the region about. Within, it displays in sumptuous buildings and worthy institutions the proofs of civic prosperity and refinement, and its environs are studded with beautiful country-seats; ten handsome macadamized roads radiate to the surrounding villages, and railroads starting in all directions, link it directly to all neighboring cities. It at once became the Union depot for the great campaigns in Tennessee and Georgia, and its repossession was coveted

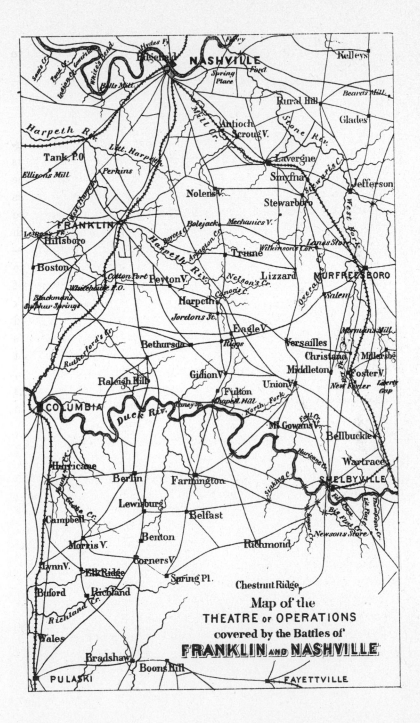

Map of the
THEATRE of OPERATIONS
covered by the Battles of
FRANKLIN and NASHVILLE

by the Confederates, both for prestige and actual value, beyond that of any other city in that part of the disputed field.

But Nashville was not to be had back for the asking. Though its safety could not be guaranteed by natural strength of its own, nor could any network of intrenched lines ally it to positions which might be pronounced impregnable for a given campaign, yet it was capable of effective fortification. The city lies on the picturesque heights rising from the southerly bank of a bend in the Cumberland; and, as at Franklin on the Harpeth, strong works are easily thrown up from river to river again, across the southerly side of the city, while all the rest is covered by the stream. The river was a sentry-beat for the Union gun-boats, which, ceaselessly moving to and fro, watched the banks, and prevented a hostile crossing: the heights about the city swept the interval over which a storming party must pass.

Self-poised and deliberate, General Thomas arrayed his forces around Nashville, conscious that he was master of the situation. The period of doubt had passed. The army of observation at Pulaski had been safely drawn back, with all its trains, after dealing a severe blow at its opponent. On the day of the battle of Franklin the advance of A. J. Smith's command reached Nashville from St. Louis, followed the day after by a body of five thousand returned convalescents and furloughed men of Sherman's column, from Chattanooga, who had been collected there by degrees, under Steedman: with the latter came also a colored brigade from the same point. Bodies of detached troops of all sizes, from companies to brigades, gathered from all quarters — from Missouri and Louisiana, from Kentucky and Georgia; released garrisons marched easterly from the Mississippi and westerly from the mountains; from the frontier the outposts were drawn back to the interior, and from the rear recruits streamed forward in great numbers. A volunteer division, over four thousand strong, of employees of the Quartermaster's forces, was organized in Nashville under Donaldson. No less than twenty new one-year regiments joined Thomas at the same point, many of which were absorbed in replacing old regiments whose terms of service had expired. Now, too, that Hood's path was known, the garrisons in Southern Tennessee and Alabama had been concentrated, those of Athens, Decatur, and Huntsville withdrawing to Stevenson, and that of Johnsonville to Clarksville: Milroy abandoned Tullahoma and joined his forces to Rousseau's at Murfreesboro', whither also were sent five new regiments from Stevenson. In short, Thomas, in early December, had his straggling troops collected, his army in hand, and an effective force of about fifty thousand men ready not only for defence but to take the field in offensive campaign.

Meanwhile, both Nashville and Murfreesboro' had been strongly fortified. Five thousand of the Quartermaster's men, under General Tower, reinforced by citizens, had been busily intrenching around the former city for many days, and two regular lines of earthworks, known as the exterior and the interior lines, with forts connected by strong curtains at proper intervals, and rifle trenches in front, girdled the city at distances of two miles and less therefrom. Eight gunboats watchfully patrolled the Cumberland, which was fortunately high enough to give them free course, and like so many moving fortresses guarded with their heavy guns the left bank of the river from Forrest's attempts to cross it. Line of battle was formed, on Schofield's arrival, along the commanding heights surrounding Nashville. Smith, eleven thousand strong, held the right, with his right flank on the Cumberland below the city; the Fourth Corps under Wood the right centre; Schofield's Twenty-third Corps the left centre, with his left on the Nolensville pike; and Steedman the interval to the river above the city: Wilson's cavalry took post on the north bank, at Edgefield.

By noon of the 2d of December, Hood's cavalry showed in

front of the Union intrenchments and began skirmishing: next day his infantry was up and drove the Union pickets into the works. The same day Hood entirely invested the city on its southern, south-eastern and south-western sides, establishing his main line entirely across the river-bend, and crowding it well towards the opposing intrenchments. He threw up three lines of earthworks on a range of hills south of those occupied by the Union forces, and somewhat inferior, his salient being on the crest of Montgomery Hill, less than six hundred yards from the Union centre. His infantry occupied the high ground on the south-east side of Brown's Creek, his right resting on the Nolensville pike, and the line thence stretching westerly across the Franklin and Granny White pikes, to the hills south and south-west of Richland Creek, and along that creek to the Hillsboro' pike, where his left rested: cavalry filled the interval between each flank and the river.

While thus occupied, Hood also began to cut the communications of Nashville. Those with Johnsonville and Decatur were already severed, and Forrest's cavalry dashed upon the Chattanooga road and broke that also, capturing a few car-loads of troops in Steedman's last train from Chattanooga. Hood then blockaded the Cumberland by planting batteries along the shore, and so closed that source of supply. The only line now left open was the Louisville road, a single stem of track one hundred and eighty-five miles long, exposed to guerillas throughout its length, and menaced by Forrest's troopers, who were only waiting for the Cumberland to fall in order to cross the river and break it. The Cumberland, indeed, had now become an exciting diorama, with the Confederate horsemen moving relentlessly along its southern shore, chafing at the swollen stream, and eagerly searching where they might ford or bridge it; on the opposite bank, the Union cavalry watching and following every movement; between them a fleet of gun-boats steaming to and fro with sleepless activity, and checking each attempt of the Confederate horse to enter the stream. Soon, Forrest dispatched a strong body northward to Lebanon to vault the river there at the earliest possible moment, while Wilson posted a force of Union troopers at Gallatin to guard the country there.

Meanwhile, Hood attempted the reduction of Murfreesboro', and, the day after his arrival, sent Bates's division of Cheatham's corps to attack the blockhouse on Overall's Creek; but Milroy coming up with a column from Murfreesboro', five miles distant, the Confederates hastily drew off, their battery having done the blockhouse no damage. During the next three days, Bates, aided by one of S. D. Lee's divisions and a strong body of cavalry, demonstrated heavily against Fort Rosecrans, at Murfreesboro', garrisoned by 8000 men, under Rosseau. But on the 8th, the expected assault not being made, Milroy, with seven infantry regiments, sallied out and attacked the investing force, and drove it from its breastworks, capturing 207 prisoners and two guns, his own loss being 205. Simultaneously the Confederate cavalry had effected an entrance into the town of Murfreesboro', but was soon expelled.

In these preliminaries the first two weeks of December slipped away. The silence of Thomas was interpreted by his enemy as a sign of weakness; for the former had lain quiet behind his works since the artillery salvo wherewith he had greeted Hood's arrival, to which compliment the Confederate batteries had deigned no reply. In great confidence Hood awaited the moment when, the river having fallen, Forrest should cross and cut the Louisville Railroad, whereupon he expected to give a Roland for an Oliver, and repeat at Nashville the Sherman tactics at Atlanta. Some dim suspicion, however, that all was not well, ought, one would think, to have crossed him, on reflecting that his enemy was in a city full of supplies, and fortified with great care, with his flanks protected by gun-boats, and with an effective force in Nashville, or within call, actually outnumbering the assailants in infantry and rapidly approaching them in cavalry — facts which gave Hood's sojourn a novel aspect when regarded as a "siege." Yet his misconception of Thomas's inertness was perhaps pardonable, since a similar one prevailed in some Union quarters distant from the field of operations, and General Grant himself, chagrined first at the retreat inside the works of Nashville, and still more so at Thomas's persistent defensive, actually dispatched an order for his removal from command — an order which fortunately for the Union cause was suspended for a time, and during the reprieve was fought the Battle of Nashville.

Delay indeed there had been, but it was easily explicable. Thomas was cutting out his work, not for a reconnoissance, but for a sure and overwhelming victory, and not even for a victory alone, but for a pursuit of the routed army, ending either in its surrender or its dispersion south of the Tennessee. To accomplish this, he must have above all a strong body of cavalry, in which arm the necessities of Sherman's expedition had left him far inferior to his opponent. The work of remounting the dismounted cavalry, in spite of Wilson's vigor, could not be finished until a week after Hood's arrival at Nashville; and until it was finished, Thomas, with the unshakable resolution which marks the man, declined to experiment against the enemy's works. However, all things were at length ready, and the 9th of December appointed for an attack upon the besieging forces; but, on the night of the 8th, a violent storm sheeted the earth with ice, and made the movement of troops impossible. On the 12th, the cavalry corps marched or slid from their position at Edgefield, crossed the Cumberland, and took post within the defences on the Hardin and Charlotte pikes. It was now 12,000 strong, of whom, however, 9000 only were mounted, and about a fifth of these badly; the rest were in fine condition.

A thaw came on the 13th, and before sunset of the 14th the ice embargo was removed. Accordingly, in the afternoon, General Thomas called his corps commanders to his head-quarters, and, in a careful discussion, gave them their instructions for an attack the next day. Thursday, the 15th of December, dawned auspiciously, and at an early hour the Union army drew out of its intrenchments and formed precisely according to the method explained the night before; its movements were shrouded from the enemy, not only by the broken ground, but by a heavy fog which did not lift till noon.

The plan of battle was simple and effective. Under cover of a violent demonstration against the Confederate right, the main army was to be massed and hurled against the Confederate left, the weakest point; the position having been turned on this flank, it was next proposed to attack the line the enemy would be forced to assume, using the advantage thus gained upon his left and rear to detach him from his hold on the right, and so expelling him from all his intrenchments. To Steedman was intrusted the defence of Nashville, with Donaldson's division of Quartermaster's troops, the regular garrison under Miller, and a part of his own Chattanooga command; but with the main body of the latter he was to make the prescribed feint on the enemy's right. Schofield and Wood also left strong skirmish lines in their trenches. The rest of the army moved directly in front of its works, and this disposition brought Wilson's cavalry on the extreme right of the line; A. J. Smith's divisions of the Sixteenth Corps next, on the Harding pike; Wood's Fourth Corps next, on the Hillsboro' pike, confronting Montgomery Hill; Schofield's Twenty-third Corps on the left and rear of Wood, in reserve; and Steedman on the extreme left. The battle was to open with Steedman's feint on the Confederate right, and then, at the proper moment, Smith and Wilson were to vigorously turn the Confederate left, one division of

Wilson moving down the Charlotte pike meanwhile to protect the Union right rear; then Wood was to assault the frowning salient on Montgomery Hill, where the enemy's centre protruded like a wedge, and, taking it on the left and rear, to break through his line. Such was the scheme.

Before dawn, Steedman moved out east of the Nolensville pike, and, under cover of a noisy fire from the forts and batteries, aided by the clamor of the gun-boats, pushed across the Murfreesboro' pike, and reached the Confederate pickets. His force comprised three brigades, Thompson's, Morgan's, and Grosvenor's, the two former being well-drilled colored troops, and these were deployed in skirmishing order. The Confederate skirmishers were driven in after a very sharp engagement, and the main works were reached and charged, where a battery swept a rocky gap on the railroad line. A protracted and gallant attempt to carry this position failed, and the assailants fell back with severe loss. But, in the purpose assigned to it, that of misleading the enemy and attracting his attention and his troops, Steedman's demonstration was a complete success, and permitted the Union right to swing resistlessly forward at the other end of the line.

Brentwood Hills, on which Hood's left was posted, extend, with spurs and intervals, nearly or quite to the Cumberland, and accordingly the country over which Smith and Wilson were to move, was difficult, being broken and thickly timbered; a very few rods of marching, indeed, showed that if the attack had been made while the snow and sleet incrusted the ground, it would have been a dead failure. When Steedman had well engaged his enemy's attention, Smith and Wilson moved out on either side of the Harding pike, and then wheeled to the left across both the Harding and Hillsboro' pikes, in order to envelop and carry the Confederate left flank, and if possible to reach the Franklin pike near Brentwood Station. Whether or not it was that Hood had not expected an attack at all, as the absence of his cavalry at Murfreesboro' and along the Cumberland would imply, he seems at all events not to have attended the assault on his left flank, and the friendly fog which enveloped the Union march, together with Steedman's feint, allowed Smith and Wilson to get well across the interval without hindrance.   The cavalry, who were dismounted, and the infantry, vied in the *élan* with which they sprang upon their astonished enemies ; McArthur's division was in the advance of Smith's corps, with the remainder closely following, and side by side with McArthur, on his right, was Hatch's cavalry division, with Croxton's brigade beyond, and Knipe's division in close support.   They first struck the Confederate picket line along Richland Creek near Harding's house, and swept it off with whirlwind rapidity, and, swinging to the left, came upon a redoubt mounting four guns.   McArthur was advancing splendidly in solid columns, but Hatch's men, being deployed in skirmish line, plunged rapidly ahead, and at a single dash, swept the redoubt, and seized the guns, which were soon turned upon the fugitive enemy.   Without losing momentum, Hatch pushed against a second redoubt, at the summit of a steep hill, and carried that in like manner with the first, capturing four more guns and two hundred and seventy-five prisoners.   Thus, at one o'clock, Smith and Wilson were sharing the glory of piercing and turning the Confederate left, and driving their enemy back over his ranges of fortified hills towards the Franklin pike.

At the same hour, the Fourth Corps was comporting itself with its traditional spirit, and winning fresh laurels elsewhere on the field.   To it had been been assigned the task of assaulting the enemy's centre at his strong advanced post on Montgomery Hill, whose flanks and summit were lined with intrenchments, and its gorges and approaches swept with artillery.   Whatever doubt may have clouded Hood's mind as to the meaning of Steedman's demonstration had long since vanished, and he was fast hurrying his troops to the support of his left and centre.   Beatty's Third division was in advance, with Kimball's and Elliott's closely supporting, and Post's brigade of the former, with Streight's supporting, and Kneppler's in reserve, at one o'clock moved up the rough acclivity. In a most gallant charge, Post ascended the heights, carried the intrenchments, and turned the position, with the capture of many prisoners.

While the Confederates retreated to their interior line, the right of the Fourth Corps, Elliott's division, connected with the left of the Sixteenth Corps, Garrard's division, and, there being no space for Schofield to interpose, — Smith not being so far to the right as was designed, — Schofield's corps was moved from the reserve to the right of Smith, in a movement which threw the cavalry still farther around on the Confederate left and rear.

And now, all the forces being drawn up in connected line, the whole pressed vigorously forward during the afternoon. For Wilson, Schofield, and Smith, the work was mainly henceforth that of pursuit, but Wood had still a second line of strong intrenchments to capture, before his day's work was done. Advancing with all three divisions, the Fourth Corps carried by assault the entire line in its front, capturing eight pieces of artillery, five caissons, several hundred small arms, and about five hundred prisoners. Rapidly reforming the columns which had been thrown into confusion by the assault, Wood hastened after his retreating enemy, aiming for his natural line of retreat along the Franklin turnpike; but before this could be reached the brief winter's day was done, and a darkness fell which put an end to the march.

Well satisfied with his first day's work, Thomas found that he had driven his enemy from his original line of works to a new position several miles distant along the base of Harpeth hills, where he held a line of retreat on the main Franklin pike through Brentwood, and on the Granny White pike. The day's captures summed up twelve hundred prisoners, sixteen guns, forty wagons, and many small arms; and these had

been achieved with a heavy Confederate loss in killed and
wounded, while the Union loss was light. Above all, the
Union forces, though so newly moulded into an army, had
behaved with a steadiness and spirit which gave bright augury
for the morrow. Their line, when readjusted at nightfall,
ran parallel to the Hillsboro' pike and east of it, where the
battle had left them with Wilson on the right, and, successively, Schofield, Smith, Wood, and Steedman. Johnson's
cavalry division was absent from the right, having passed the
evening, aided by the gun-boats, in engaging a Confederate
battery at Bell's Landing, eight miles down the river.

All along the line the bivouac fires flared out into the bleak
wintry air, and around them the tired troops dreamt of a
brighter victory in the morning. Thomas rode back to tele-
graph the first chapter of his story. " I shall attack the enemy again to-morrow," he said, " if he stands to fight, and if
he retreats during the night I will pursue him."

Day dawned amid a clamor of artillery. Promptly at six
o'clock Wood threw his corps forward from the Union line
toward the Franklin pike, and soon found that Hood had
drawn back his centre and right in order to conform them to
the necessities of his left. As the interval, however, was too
strong to be entirely abandoned, Hood had lined it with his
skirmishers, whom encountering, the Fourth Corps by rapid
fighting drove before it to the Franklin pike ; then, deploying
in line of battle across the pike, Wood swept southward from
Nashville until he had driven the enemy's skirmishers within
their intrenchments, and developed the main Confederate line.
This achievement required of course a new formation of General Thomas's troops, in order to assault the Confederate position. Steedman marched out from Nashville by the Nolensville pike, and connected with Wood's left, while Smith on the
other flank moved up to Wood's right. While this line of
battle faced southerly, Schofield remained facing easterly

toward the Confederate left flank, his line striking that of
General Smith at right angles. Wilson's cavalry was dismounted, and moved up from the Hillsboro' pike to Schofield's right, also facing easterly. Hatch's division joined
Schofield, and Knipe, on Hatch's right, pushed by noon entirely across the Granny White pike, one of the Confederate
lines of retreat, and stretched at least a mile in rear of Hood's
left.

The new Confederate position was exceedingly strong. Its
right rested on Overton's hill, about five miles south of the city,
its centre occupied the valley through which runs the Franklin pike, and its left a range of the Brentwood hills which
border on the Granny White pike. The densely wooded
sides and summits of all these hills had been rapidly intrenched,
and trees were felled in front to entangle the assailants. The
centre was naturally the weakest point in the line, and next
the left, which, though well posted, was made uneasy by the
menace of the prolonged Union right flank, while the right as
on the day before was by far the strongest of all : the line had
been shortened till it was now about three miles in extent.
In view of the tremendous stake for which he played, it being empire on the one hand or ruin on the other, even Hood's
fiery blood might have chilled for an instant at the momentous
results which an hour would bring forth. With an elder
Hotspur he might well have considered " it were not good to
set so rich a main on the nice hazard of one doubtful hour."
But it was now too late for prudent thoughts, which perhaps
in any case had been spurned.

The afternoon was well advanced ; the Union line had been
everywhere joined, and had pushed up at all points to within
six hundred yards of the enemy ; and, on the right, Wilson
had felt his way well around Hood's rear. The decisive moment having come, Wood ordered Post's brigade, supported
by Streight's, of Beatty's division — the troops which had
carried the salient on Montgomery hill — to assault Over-

ton's knob, and Morgan's colored brigade of Steedman's command formed in co-operation on the left.   The attacking columns, at three o'clock, formed in full view in the open plain, and instantly the troops could be seen hurrying from the enemy's centre and left to mass on his threatened right. The intrenchments of the knob ran athwart its northern face considerably below the summit, and then, turning southerly, across its eastern side, withdrew covering the right of the Confederate line by a retired flank.   Forward plunged the storming parties, and rose steadily higher and higher up the slope through the entanglements, under a tremendous fire of grape, canister and musketry, white men and black (all clad in blue) vying in gallantry.   With banners bowing forward, the line swept straight up to the breastworks, though great gaps were torn in it by the cruel fire ; but there, the Confederate reserves, rising up, poured into it a sheeted flame ; and pausing, and wavering, and as it were shuddering along its length, it fell back, broken as a long wave is broken on the shore, and blown off in spray.   "They left their dead and wounded," says Thomas, "black and white indiscriminately mingled — lying amid the abatis, the gallant Colonel Post among the wounded."

But Smith and Schofield, as soon as the Fourth Corps had grappled the enemy's right, rushed on his centre and left, "carrying all before them," says the general-in-chief, "and irreparably breaking his lines in a dozen places."   They seized all of the artillery that had fired upon them, captured thousands of prisoners, including four general officers, and drove the astounded and dismayed Confederates from the crest of Brentwood hills down the reverse slope in tumultuous retreat. Pursuing the routed enemy, Schofield and Smith quickly encountered Hatch and Knipe, who, dismounted, had by a wide circuit gained the Confederate rear, and struck it at the very moment their comrades were ascending the hill in the front.

Excited by the victorious cheers on the right and the intermingling crack of rifle and carbine which told of the joint triumph of infantry and cavalry, the Fourth Corps and Steedman's command, which had been already handsomely reformed, and were chafing for the final signal, burst, once more, with a vigor which nothing could stay, against the stronghold upon Overton's hill. Once more, too, a terrific storm of musketry and grape swept down the slopes of this dread acclivity; but the enthusiasm of the Union forces was beyond all control, and without a pause they carried the crest, with its artillery and a great part of its garrison, and drove the remnant in utter rout through the Brentwood pass to Brentwood hamlet.

A few hours of day were all that the Union legions now craved, to complete the ruin of their opponents. The latter, clogging the path behind them with wagons, broken caissons, muskets, knapsacks, blankets, whatever threatened to delay, poured in confusion down the Franklin pike, the only road left open to them. Close at their heels hurried the relentless Fourth Corps, in a chase of several miles, gathering prisoners and spoils till night descended to save the beaten army. On the Granny White pike the cavalry saw, almost within their clutch, a confused mass of fugitives; but, being dismounted, and unwonted to pursue briskly on foot, they impatiently awaited their horses. These at length came, and Hatch's division, hastily mounted, rode down the Granny White pike with Croxton and Knipe behind them. Before two miles were past, Hatch ran upon Chalmers's cavalry division, which was posted across the road behind barricades. Dark as it was, Hatch's men were eager for attack, and charging, with Spaulding's Twelfth Tennessee in advance, broke through the barriers, and scattered the Confederates, capturing General Rucker amongst the other prisoners: it set the seal on the triumphs of the day.

With the Confederate army routed, its dead and wounded left on the field, four thousand five hundred prisoners, fifty-three guns, and thousands of small arms left to the Union forces, the two days' battle at Nashville ended.

The morning after the battle dawned cold, rainy, and dreary — dreariest of all to the routed Confederate troops, now streaming back to the Tennessee. At daylight Wilson's cavalry and the Fourth Corps were on the march, the latter on the Franklin pike and the former along the Granny White pike to the junction with the Franklin pike, where it took the advance; Steedman moved in rear of the Fourth Corps, and Schofield and Smith in rear of the cavalry. Four miles north of Franklin, Knipe struck Stevenson's division, the Confederate rear-guard, and in a brisk charge by the whole column, Knipe, Hatch, and Croxton, in front and flank, the position was carried, with the capture of four hundred and thirteen prisoners. Meanwhile Johnson's division, dispatched by Wilson direct to the Harpeth, had crossed and come rapidly up on the south bank of the river and menaced Franklin; so that, to save its flank, Hood's rear-guard fell back from the river-crossing and abandoned the town, leaving in its hospitals over two thousand wounded. Without a pause, the Union cavalry thundered down the Columbia pike, and along such by-paths as were practicable, in relentless pursuit, the Confederate rear-guard sullenly retiring before them.

At length, five miles south of Franklin, Stevenson, whose division (lately S. D. Lee's) formed the rear of the column, deployed in an open field, putting a battery in position on rising ground, and stood at bay. It was already quite dark, a mist enveloping everything, and the rain still descending. But Wilson, deploying Hatch on the left of the pike and Knipe on the right, with their batteries, posted his own body-guard, the Fourth Regular Cavalry, one hundred and eighty strong, on the road to charge the enemy. The batteries opened with grape and canister, and then, at the word "forward," the gallant Fourth Cavalry dashed down the pike

in columns of fours, charging with drawn sabres, breaking
the Confederate centre, riding over their guns, and pursuing
for nearly a mile. Simultaneously Hatch and Knipe had
enveloped the Confederate flanks, and a part of Hammond's
command of Knipe's division even pushed across the West
Harpeth. But darkness had already fallen, and in the confused running fight, pursuers were as likely to be captured
as pursued, and, indeed, Lieutenant Hedges, commanding the
Fourth Cavalry, was thrice made prisoner before he finally
escaped. As for the Confederates, they were in a sorry
plight, having little cavalry to cover their retreat : they
abandoned four guns in the enemy's skirmish, and afterwards
threw others into Duck River, which their opponents recovered when the water went down. Meanwhile, Wood's Fourth
Corps, pressing impetuously forward to Harpeth River, had
found the bridges destroyed and the stream impassable.
There, accordingly, on its banks they bivouacked, with
Steedman near by, and Smith and Schofield some miles
back.

Next day, the 18th, with the rain still dismally falling,
Wilson pushed his cavalry after the flying enemy to Rutherford's Creek, three miles from Columbia. The stream was
impassable, and "running a perfect torrent." In an instant,
the unwelcome conviction flashed upon Thomas that the fragment of an army which had seemed beyond escape, had
probably eluded his grasp. The pursuers had no pontoons,
and Rutherford's Creek and Duck River were impassable
without bridges. One pontoon train had indeed been hastily
built at Nashville, and was on its way, but its incompleteness
and the bad condition of the roads retarded its arrival. The
delay was fatal. Three full days were lost to the Union
troops at this time, and Hood improved the respite to save
the debris of his army. He urged his trains through the
miry roads ; he tugged away at his pontoons and got them to
Duck River, and thence to the Tennessee ; in fine, he organ-

30

ized a new and powerful rear-guard, containing all the serviceable troops in his army. Forrest's cavalry was able to reach him at Columbia, where also other detached troops joined him, and with these horsemen and four thousand infantry under Walthall, he formed a splendid rear-guard of eight small brigades. As for Thomas, that officer waited impatiently and with ill-concealed mortification for his pontoons to come up, rough bridges to be extemporized, the roads to mend, and the flooded rivers to subside. It is with a bitter significance that his report declares, "I would here remark that the splendid pontoon train properly belonging to my command, with its trained corps of pontooneers, was absent with General Sherman." Meanwhile he hurried off Steedman by rail to Decatur, so as to cross the Tennessee and threaten Hood's railroad communications west of Florence; and Wood's corps closed up with the cavalry, while the latter were delaying. On the 20th, Hatch and Wood improvised bridges on the ruins of the old railroad and road bridges at Rutherford's Creek, crossed, and hurried on to Duck River: Hood's rear had got over the night before and taken up their pontoons behind them. It was two days more before another bridge could be improvised for Duck River, and Wood's corps moved across; and Wilson passed the stream a day later, on the 23d. The rain had given way to bitter cold.

Thus beset with difficulties, checked by untoward delays, and deprived of proper resources, a less resolute soldier had relinquished the pursuit, content with the triumph already gained. Thomas still gave the order "forward."

Wilson and Wood were now the pursuers, Schofield and Smith more leisurely following. On the 24th, they twice reached and drove the Confederate rear-guard, and pressed it so sorely as to save the bridges over Richland Creek. On Christmas morning they drove their jaded enemy out of Pulaski, and, on the same evening, Harrison's brigade startled him from the point which he had intrenched for the night's bivouac. Three days of forced marching succeeded, over terrible roads and in a constant, cheerless rain, with short rations for the pursued and almost none for the pursuers, since the latter had outrun their trains. The wretched Confederates threw away anything which could help their retreat. At Pulaski, they abandoned two hundred wounded in the hospitals, and threw four guns into Richland Creek; a mile beyond they destroyed twenty wagons loaded with ammunition, belonging to Cheatham's corps. The road from Pulaski to the Tennessee was strewn with wagons, limbers, small arms, blankets, and other debris of a demoralized army, while stragglers filled the woods. "With the exception of his rear guard," says Thomas, "his army had become a disheartened and disorganized rabble of half-armed and barefooted men, who sought every opportunity to fall out by the wayside and desert their cause to put an end to their sufferings. The rear-guard, however, was undaunted and firm, and did its work bravely to the last." At length, the fugitive army reached the long-expected and welcome Tennessee, and crossed it at Bainbridge, six miles above Florence, where the Union gun-boats could not reach it; and thanks to the rains which had turned the streams to torrents and the roads to sloughs, thanks, also, to the lack of pontoons by his pursuers, Hood escaped, with the wreck of his army, into Alabama.

The rout of Hood was accompanied by another Confederate disaster in East Tennessee. Breckinridge having, in November, defeated Gillem's command in that section, Thomas directed General Stoneman to recover the lost region, and to drive the forces of Breckinridge, Duke, and Vaughan into West Virginia, and, if possible, to destroy the famous salt works at Saltville. All this Stoneman, with the commands of Gillem and Burbridge, handsomely accomplished, by a series of extraordinary forced marches and arduous labors in the worst of weather. Gillem routed Duke

at Kingsport and Vaughan at Marion, the latter on the day of
the battle of Nashville; Breckinridge was driven into North
Carolina; the works at Saltville ruined; the region traversed
laid waste.   Still later, six hundred cavalry, under Colonel
W. J. Palmer, moved upon Hood's line of retreat in Mississippi, destroyed, near Russelville, his pontoon train of two
hundred wagons and seventy-eight boats, and meeting a
supply train near Aberdeen, consisting of one hundred and
ten wagons and five hundred mules, burned the former and
shot the latter: one hundred and fifty prisoners, besides,
were captured, and one thousand small arms destroyed.   In
fine, Lyon, who with eight hundred horsemen had been
operating briskly on Thomas's railroad lines in Kentucky,
was driven back into Alabama with about a fourth of his
command, the rest being scattered; and the camp of this
remnant was surprised by Colonel Palmer, and the greater
part of the men captured.

III.

RESULTS OF NASHVILLE.

The word of the prophet Davis had come to pass; the
early snow of winter had, of a truth, witnessed "a Moscow
retreat."   It was not, however, the Union but the Confederate hosts that were ruined, and not Sherman but Hood, that
exhibited his pitiful travesty on the Great Napoleon.   To
complete the vision of the soothsayer, there were "Cossacks"
too, in plenty, harrying the flanks and rear of the flying battalions: but these were Union troopers, and, as they swarmed
around the ill-starred Confederate army, their sabres hacked
it without mercy.

At the end of December, Hood and his army, and all the
co-operating columns, were driven out of Tennessee.   But
so small was the fraction that escaped, so large the proportion
of killed and captured left behind, that when the year went

out the Confederate army of the West may be said to have expired with it.

Aware that in the wintry season, and on roads impassable, to hunt still further after the wrecks of the Confederate forces would be a game not worth the candle, Thomas announced to his troops the close of the campaign, and promised them their well-earned winter quarters; but General Grant, not so well comprehending at his distance the completeness of the victory and the ruin which had befallen Hood's army, ordered a renewal of the campaign. It was promptly undertaken; but there was nothing to campaign against. What was left of the Confederate forces began to dribble away each day in desertion, a calamity more fatal than hostile operations. The original Confederate army seemed to have vanished from the scene, suddenly and totally, as if through a trap-door. The career of its whilom commander was ended, and, as if to cap a monstrous satire upon military policy, the scattered pieces of the army which Hood had received from Johnston, were now coolly handed back to the latter, after the manipulations of the former could no longer do them harm. To Johnston was assigned the task of sweeping together the relics of all past and gone Confederate armies south of Virginia, for the coming spring. He swept from Mississippi to Alabama, from Alabama to Georgia, through Georgia to South Carolina, across both Carolinas to the region of Raleigh and Goldsboro', where, for the first time, he had swept together mass enough to make a stand on the field of Averasboro'.

When Thomas came to audit his accounts for the new year, he found that, in the series of actions already sketched, extending from September 7th to January 30th, he had captured 13,189 prisoners of war, including eight general officers and nearly one thousand others, seventy-two pieces of artillery fit for service, and many battle-flags. Besides these, there had been taken more than three thousand small arms and many infantry accoutrements, filled ammunition chests, and wagons loaded with ammunition and supplies. As to the material destroyed in the retreat, both by pursued and pursuers, no computation was made or was possible; nor was it easy to estimate the number of Confederate troops who, collected for the conquest of Tennessee, strayed off, as occasion served, to their own homes, and doffed forever the gray uniform. But besides these latter, in the interval already spoken of, 2200 deserters appeared within Thomas's lines, and took the oath of allegiance. Of all these swelling figures, the chief part, of course, belonged to the battle of Nashville and the pursuit, — sixty-four of the seventy-two captured guns, all the small arms and accoutrements, and most of the prisoners. In addition must be reckoned the Confederate losses in killed and wounded, which were very severe. These achievements Thomas declares to have been accomplished on his part with a total loss of not over ten thousand men.

The first result, therefore, of this magnificent victory was to roll back a daring invasion, which aimed at the recovery of Confederate prestige, the possession of the Tennessee and the Cumberland, and all the garrisoned towns thereon, and Nashville, Knoxville, Chattanooga, and Louisville itself. Had this campaign succeeded, not only would Kentucky and Tennessee have become Confederate States, but the war would have been gravely prolonged for years: not improbably even Lee's surrender in Virginia the following April would have been succeeded by a transfer of the contest to the Gulf States, or beyond the Mississippi.

Next, the Nashville campaign was the annihilation of the Western Confederate army, the object for which Sherman and his hundred thousand had descended from Chattanooga in May, now accomplished eight months later by the arm of Thomas. The Confederacy lived in its armies, which continuing, its territory might be traversed and laid waste in vain; but from the ruin of these armies there was no recuperation, since the fighting stock of the Confederacy was already exhausted. Thomas solved one branch of the problem, and eliminated one army from the military equation. When Hood's forces were dispersed, when Sherman's magnificent columns reached Savannah, when Thomas, with fifty thousand men, was forced to look far away for other fields to conquer, it was discovered that the latter soldier had taken a Confederate piece from the board, and left the Union game one entire army ahead. Moreover, since Georgia, Alabama, and Mississippi had been drained and dredged of material to furnish forth the ranks of Hood, the splendidly-appointed legions which Sherman led out of Atlanta were able to journey unmolested to the sea. They marched whithersoever they listed; the few squads of gray beards and boys whom they met got briskly out of their way or were trampled under foot. It was indeed less a campaign than a tour of triumph; and when Hazen had gallantly stormed Fort McAllister, the city of Savannah fell. This "holiday march," nevertheless, had been a frightful blunder, if Hood had triumphed in Tennessee.

It was, however, when spring opened, — the last springtime of the war, — that the results of the splendid victory around Nashville were most obvious to all eyes. The war had ceased over all the Western campaigning grounds, and even as far East as the Carolinas the hardy troops of Sherman waded swamp, and forded river, and trudged along narrow causeway, far beyond Fayetteville, without finding a noticeable foe. As for Thomas, with his great army master of all the territory about him, it only remained to break up his columns, and send them on expeditions thousands of miles away. Schofield's corps went to the Atlantic seaboard, and, embarking in transports, landed in North Carolina. A second great infantry column was despatched down the Mississippi to New Orleans, where Canby employed it to reduce Mobile. Stoneman rode almost unmolested with a great troop of horsemen into north-western North Carolina; and when Wilson took the field again with his cavalry corps, he swept like a whirlwind through Alabama and Georgia, scattering the scanty militia before him, and proving by a second demonstration that, with its defeats around Nashville, the Confederacy at the West had already tumbled to the dust.

The figure of Thomas looms up in many respects without a superior, in most respects without a rival even, among the Union Generals created by the war.

When the Rebellion opened Major Thomas was a soldier of twenty years' experience, during which he had not only not turned aside to the attractions of civil life, but had accepted only two furloughs. It was during his latter leave of absence that the Insurrection broke out, and Thomas received the colonelcy of his regiment, now styled the Fifth Cavalry.

From this time the fame of General Thomas becomes national. His complete and admirable victory at Mill Spring was the first triumph of magnitude for the North since the disaster at Bull Run, and brought back a needed prestige to the Union arms. As commander of the Fourteenth Army Corps, under Rosecrans, he was conspicuous in the marching and fighting which preceded Murfreesboro', and all-glorious in that decisive battle. Him Rosecrans then portrayed as "true and prudent, distinguished in council and celebrated on many battle-fields for his courage." It was he who alone and unaided saved the army of the Cumberland at Chickamauga, when the example of all around him might have excused him for flying from a lost field. And again, accordingly, the enthusiastic tribute of praise comes up in the report of Rosecrans : " To Major-General Thomas, the true soldier, the prudent and undaunted commander, the modest and incorruptible patriot, the thanks and gratitude of the country are due for his conduct at the battle of Chickamauga." It was Thomas, whose troops "forming on the plain below with the precision of parade," made the wonderful charge on Missionary Ridge, which threw Bragg back into Georgia. It was he who, in the grand Atlanta campaign, commanded under Sherman more than three-fifths of that army, and who delivered the opening battle at Buzzard's Roost and the closing battle at Lovejoy's. It was Thomas, in fine, who set the seal of success on the Georgia campaign, 300 miles away at Nashville.

Imposing in stature, massive in thew and limb, the face and figure of General Thomas consort well with the impression made by his character — the firm mouth, the square jaw, the steady blue eye, the grave expression habitual on the impassive countenance, being indexes to well-known traits. The war showed that his gifts, like his qualities, were in the main of that more solid and substantial sort which gain less immediate applause than what is specious and glittering, but which lead on to enduring fame. Yet there was noticeable in him a rare and felicitous union of qualities which do not often appear with full vigor in the same organization. Cautious in undertaking, yet, once resolved, he was bold in execution; deliberate in forming his plan, and patiently waiting for events to mature, yet when the fixed hour struck, he leaped into great activity. Discretion in him was obviously spurred on by earnestness, and earnestness tempered by discretion. Prudent by nature, not boastful, reticent, he was not the less free from the weakness of will and tameness of spirit which are as fatal to success as rashness. He was, in short, one of those "whose blood and judgment are so well co-mingled that they are not a pipe for Fortune's finger to sound what stop she please."

Of his complete mastery of his profession in all its details, of his consummate skill as a general, the best monument is the story of his battles; for he never lost a campaign, or a field;

he never met his enemy without giving him cause to grieve for the rencontre : and he culled laurels from fields on which brother officers were covered with disgrace, and more than once plucked up drowning honor by the locks, as at Chickamauga. As he did not himself fail, so he did not suffer himself to be ruined by incompetency in superiors, much less in subordinates, for he was accustomed to consider beforehand such possibilities, and to guard against them. His successes were won by art, not tossed to him by fortune, and whenever victory came to him he was conscious of having earned it. Such successes indicate temperaments at once solid and acute, and in which wisdom and valor concur, — Nestor of the council, and Hector of the field.

He was a soldier who conned his maps before he marched his army, who planned his campaign before he fought it, who would not hurry, who would not learn by thoughtless experiments what study could teach, who believed in the duty of a general to organize victory at each step. He was a lover of system, and was nothing if not systematic. He approved what was regular, and required proof of what was irregular ; had that fondness for routine which does not ill become an old army officer ; and even in exigences desired everything to proceed duly and in order. He was not a slave to method, but naturally distrusted what was unmethodical ; and that he invariably won battles by virtue of time-honored principles, and in accordance with the rules of the art of war, was, besides its value to the country, a truth invaluable to military science in the land, whose teachings had been somewhat unjustly cast into contempt by the conduct of other successful soldiers.

His Nashville campaign gave more than one instance of the trait just noted. Superiors were vexed at his constant retreat from the Tennessee, at his flight behind the parapets of Nashville, at his delay to attack the investing force ; but neither this vexation nor the danger of removal which threat-

ened him could avail with Thomas, for that soldier would
not be badgered into premature battle. Soon after, the wisdom of Thomas in delaying attack in order to mount his
cavalry, approved itself, for never before in the war had grand
victory been so energetically followed by pursuit. In the
battle itself, too, spectators fancied that he was pausing too
long before engaging his right flank, but he held that wing
poised as it were in the air, till the fit moment, when he swung
it like a mighty sledge upon the Confederate, and smote him
to the dust.

The best justification of his system was its success, for if
discreet he was safe ; if slow, sure. One of his earlier friendly nicknames was "Old Slow Trot," and another, "Old
Reliable," while later troops sometimes called him "Old Pap
Safety." He provided for dilemmas and obstacles, he suffered
no surprises, made no disastrous experiments at the sacrifice
of position, of prestige, or of the lives of his troops : and indeed he was wont to make his enemy pay dearly for the privilege of defeat, and usually lost fewer troops in action than
his adversary, whether pursuing the offensive or the defensive.
Thus, if the processes of his thought were slow of evolution,
they at least attained to their goal.

His natural impulse would seem to be to stand *inebranlable*
on the defensive, and having taken manfully his enemy's
blows till the assailant was exhausted, then to turn upon him
in furious aggression ; so it was with his first national victory
at Mill Spring, and so with his latest at Nashville, while his
fight at bay at Chickamauga is immortal. A fine analyzer of
character might perhaps trace a sympathy between this military method on the one hand, and the well-known personal
traits of the soldier on the other — his modesty, his unassum-
ing, unpretending spirit, his absence of self-assertion and
habit of remaining in the background ; and therewith his vigor
when roused, and his bold championship of any cause entrusted to him. At all events, the fame of his persistency, of his

firmness, almost amounting to obstinacy, of the unyielding grip with which he held his antagonist, became world-wide. When Grant hurried to the relief of beleaguered Chattanooga, there to supplant Rosecrans, he telegraphed to Thomas, then in command, "Hold on to Chattanooga at all hazards;" to which message came the sententious response — "Have no fear. Will hold the town till we starve." When steadfast he stood in Frick's Gap, on the field of Chickamauga, after the columns on both his flanks had given way, — the torrent of Bragg's onset, the hail of fire that swept the Union ranks, moved him not a jot from his firm base, and the billow that swamped the rest of the field recoiled from him. "The rain descended, and the floods came, and beat upon that house; and it fell not: for it was founded upon a rock." Thereafter, the soldiers of his Army of the Cumberland were wont to call him "The Rock of Chickamauga."

Grave and wise at the council board, yet it is on the well-contested field that Thomas shines most conspicuous. In the ordinary tide of battle he is emphatically the Imperturbable — calm, poised, entirely cool, self-possessed, one on whom the shifting fortunes of the day have only a subdued effect, and whose equanimity even success cannot dangerously disturb. But he is greatest in extremity, that "trier of spirits." In the supreme moment of exigency which demands a great soul to grasp it, — such an one as came to o'ertasked Hooker at Chancellorsville, — Thomas shines out pre-eminent, and asserts his superiority. Phlegmatic at most hours, the desperate crises of battle are alone sufficient to stir his temperament into fullest action, and then his quiet, steady eyes flame a little with battle-fire.

He had the great quality of inspiring in his troops perfect confidence and great devotion. Indeed, his soldierly skill was well set off by the air and manner of a soldier — unaffected, manly, far from the pettiness bred by long pampering in the drawing-room, but with a simplicity, robustness, and hardiness of character, like that of his own physique, the inheritance of thirty years in field and garrison. Dignified and decorous, his brother officers found him free from show and pretence, frank, open, and magnanimous; while to his troops he was kindly and amiable. He excited no envy or jealousy in his rivals, who found him straightforward and conscientious; and his men had cause to know that he was observant of merit and rewarded it. His reputation was without reproach, his controlled temper superior to the vicissitudes of camp and battle, and joined to them was a courage which set life at a pin's fee. A Virginian, and of such social ties as might well have made him " a Pharisee of the Pharisees," he had proved at the outset the quality of the allegiance he bore to the Republic, by casting in his lot with the Union arms. His loyalty was disinterested, and the result of conviction not of political aspiration.

The progress of the war, too, gave him, as it did so many officers, a chance to show the quantity and stability of his patriotism. Even while the country resounded with the glories of Chickamauga and Missionary Ridge, Sherman, his junior in experience, in length of service, and in years, and his equal only in rank, was appointed over him to the command vacated by General Grant. Without murmur, perhaps without thought of injury, Thomas took his place under Sherman with the cheerful obedience of a true soldier. On the eve of Nashville, he was to have been relieved of command, but desired, for the sake of the country, that he might execute a long-formed plan, after which he would be at such disposal as might seem fit.

Such was General Thomas, the completely rounded, skilful, judicious, modest soldier — a man compact of genuine stuff, a trustworthy man —

Rich in saving common sense,
And as the greatest only are,
In his simplicity sublime.

XII.

FIVE FORKS.

I.

PRELUDE TO FIVE FORKS.

THE end of the Confederacy was nigh. Four years had Virginia, buttress and sea-wall of the South, withstood the tide of invasion which ceaselessly rolled in upon her, spurning it from her battlements, shattered and spent, as the rock flings back the billow beaten into foam. Six times the tumultuous flood had surged with whelming front against her firm barrier, and six times baffled had recoiled : now it was McDowell; now McClellan; now Pope; now Burnside; now Hooker; now Meade; now Grant.

Grant it was, indeed, whose great host came, at length, like the mighty seventh wave, topping its fellows, to crush into ruin even the ramparts of rock-bound Virginia.

Once more at the end as in the beginning, the armed champions of North and South gathered towards that battle-ploughed State, on whose soil was fated to end, as there it had begun, the arbitrament of arms. From North, from South, from West, Federal and Confederate alike drew nearer to the historic campaigning ground. Savannah, Wilmington, and Charleston, falling in succession, had left the Atlantic a sealed ocean to the Confederacy, with no port along three thousand

Eng^d by Campbell.   Photo. by Gurney.

Dick & Fitzgerald, New York.

miles of seaboard and gulf-board — save where, far down the south-western horizon, the Union gun-boats and armies thundered in Mobile Bay, and pitched the final war-note for an echo of deeper diapason around Petersburg and Richmond. The coastwise garrisons shrunk back to join each other in the Carolinas — Hardee and Bragg and Beauregard — whom, with whatever other Confederate soldiery could be found extant, east of the Mississippi, the veteran Johnston laid hold of, and drew back closer to their comrades at Petersburg. Finally, the General-in-Chief of the Confederacy, whose own unflinching army had been so long the Ægis of its beloved Virginia, collected all from mountain and valley around his capital, and girded him for the death-struggle.

While thus the armies of the Confederacy drew together within the circle, around them and always converging approached the serried rows of Union bayonets and sabres.

Bursting in a tornado through the Shenandoah Valley, and scattering like chaff the paltry handful of opposing horsemen, Sheridan with ten thousand troopers thence trailed in majestic circuit around to the left of the Army of the Potomac — like some peerless knight who paces about the field of the tourney before he enters the lists.

In Alabama and Georgia, Wilson, with thirteen thousand men, rode rampant through the centre of the Confederacy, capturing all the towns and troops and stores in his path, and sweeping the land with the besom of vengeance : then paused in position at Macon, and held the lower avenues of Confederate retreat from Virginia to the West.

From Knoxville, Stoneman led a third cavalry column, five thousand strong, through the passes of the Alleghanies; and having laid waste western North Carolina as Wilson had Alabama, waited and watched there in turn for the mighty issue in Virginia.

And lo ! approaching hither, appears the great " Army of the Mississippi," come, in lack of Western fields to conquer, to fill up the measure of its fame along the Neuse and the Roanoke. Marching down the banks of the Great River, this renowned host had unlocked its manifold fetters, and let it run rejoicing to the sea; thence moving across the central zone, it gave back the Border States to the Union; descending southerly, it overran the broad Mississippi Valley; turning easterly, it scaled the Alleghanies, and planted its banners on their cloud-capped crests; then, plunging through Georgia, it lighted its Christmas bivouac-fires in conquered Savannah: it turned north when the sun turned; busily waded river and footed causeway; and when the doomed Confederate armies, compassed in fatal toils, looked southerly for an outlet of escape, there came rolling across the plains of the Carolinas, beating nearer and nearer, the drums of Champion Hills and Shiloh!

In the early days of March, 1865, Robert E. Lee resolved to abandon the cities of Petersburg and Richmond, and to join his Army of Northern Virginia to the companion army of Johnston in northern North Carolina. To this end, the two officers arranged the prior manœuvres, the choice of routes, the bridging of intervening streams, and the storing of rations. It was a grave change in Confederate strategy, and told the pressure of more than one impelling cause. The Confederate general saw that, with opening spring, the sunshine and the gales were fitting the roads for a new campaign, wherein no longer a single but a fivefold danger threatened his army and his capital — no longer Grant alone, but Sheridan, Sherman, Wilson, Stoneman, were marching or waiting to march upon him; and as he glanced around the sky there was menace in every quarter of the compass. Nor was it more the numbers of the Union forces than their new possibilities of manœuvre which disturbed the Confederate chieftain. With ten thousand fresh sabres which would take the remnant of Confederate cavalry at a mouthful, and with overwhelming masses of infantry in support, no doubt remained that, sooner or later, Grant would cut the Danville Railroad. But that stroke would be fatal, since this was the channel of supply for Lee's army, already too scantily rationed.

The ruin that menaced the Danville road had already befallen the railroad lines of Georgia and both Carolinas, thanks to the energy of Sherman and the destructive genius of his men. Bitterly satirical was the comment already written by history upon the strategy of the winter's Tennessee campaign. It had accomplished many things : annihilated Hood's army ; ruined the Confederacy at the West ; given existence to one Union army at Nashville, and escorted another safely to Savannah ; stopped up the conduits of supplies of the Virginia army ; and placed Sherman within supporting distance of Grant. Rash Hood ! short-sighted Davis ! in that blindness of arrogance which strove at this stage of affairs to invade the North, so as to "make the enemy feel the war in his own borders," by way of reformatory punishment rather than in pursuit of strategic advantages, this pair of strategists brought a new army from the womb of the exhaustless North, to ruin a contest already desperate. Not content with forcing Sherman back to whence he came, by legitimate appliances, they wanted not Georgia alone but Tennessee, not Tennessee alone but Kentucky ; nay, Atlanta and Chattanooga were nothing without Nashville, Knoxville, Louisville, and a campaign along the Ohio. This exploit left General Lee, in spring, the moiety of two States for his military domain.

On paper, in March, 1865, Lee's immediate army numbered one hundred and sixty thousand ; in fact, owing to enormous desertions, added to the usual depletions, it numbered fifty thousand effectives ; and of these, deducting the detached troops, there remained wherewith to line his long trenches, forty thousand. Johnston, also, had promising rolls, but an army only forty thousand strong — of whom somewhat over

31

twenty thousand were effective. For these sixty thousand to
eighty thousand men, pitted against double their numbers,
Lee was to plan his campaign. But of supplies there were
less than troops; for while the Confederate conscription was
a monstrous abuse and failure, the Confederate commissariat
was worse than its conscription, — which, upon the whole, is
the most expressive thing to say of it.

Such then was the look of the board before the closing
move, and such the warning voice which called on the Confederate commander to abandon the field he had so long disputed. He might then have been pardoned for a flood of
despair over calamities which others, not he, had brought on;
for that which he saw prophetically as danger to the Confederacy, we see historically as downfall. But though the air
was full of disastrous auguries, he, like the hero of Homer,
asked "no omen but his country's cause." With unbroken
confidence, Lee prepared to withdraw from his capital.

Across the Appomattox, another soldier, quiet, undemon-
strative, resolute, was studying the same map of war, and
forming quite another schedule of conclusions than that of
General Lee. Earlier than his rival, Grant had forecast the
fall of Richmond in the spring, knowing better than Lee
could know the enormous results to be expected from the
winter campaigns of Sherman and Thomas. His plan, however, was not to force, nor to suffer, but to prevent, the
abandonment of Petersburg and Richmond. He sought, instead, to keep his adversary there, to push the affair to another
Vicksburg or Donelson, to surround him, cut off his supplies,
and force him to surrender. What he purposed himself to
do for Lee's army, he designed that Sherman should do for
Johnston's, so that, in one tremendous campaign, between
the Neuse and the James, he might bring the Confederacy to
the ground.

To retreat unscathed from Richmond, Lee must so manœuvre
or strike as to outwit an antagonist lying in wait to prevent

that very movement. Moreover, to avoid being overtaken in marching to join Johnston, it was desirable to move on the shortest road, which was not north, but south, of the Appomattox, namely, the Cox road, towards which the Union left wing was thrown out. Accordingly, Lee resolved to initiate an attack on the opposite Union flank, partly in general to cloak his retreat, and partly in particular that the troops lying nearest the Cox road might be moved away to succor the Union right. This accomplished, he would slip down that road with his army and laugh at pursuit. The point selected for attack on the Union right was Fort Steadman, on the line of the Ninth Corps; and, on the 25th of March, two divisions, under Gordon, handsomely surprised and stormed the work. But, by a fatal blunder, the assaulting column was not supported, and, the Union works being so built as to command from the rear and flanks the position already carried, at the end of their brief triumph most of Gordon's troops were cut off by a cross-fire, and one thousand nine hundred of them laid down their arms. Gordon's loss was heavy, too, in killed and wounded; that of the Union troops being four hundred and five, besides five hundred and six captured. At once, Meade followed his parry with a thrust, and, pushing out the Second and Sixth Corps, they captured the picket lines in their fronts, and eight hundred and thirty-four prisoners. In the desperate struggle at this point the Union loss was eleven hundred and twenty-three; the Confederate loss severe. The Union left had not stirred towards the right; and Lee's initiative was a costly failure.

Neither sooner nor later for this attack, but on the day appointed, like a fate which seizes but cannot itself be seized or evaded, Grant's own scheme rolled forward to consummation. In general the manœuvre was the familiar movement "by the left," designed to swing a heavy column across the extreme Confederate right, against the Southside Railroad. The troops of the turning column were the Second and Fifth

Corps of the Army of the Potomac, and Sheridan's cavalry, nine thousand sabres. The Ninth Corps and three divisions of Ord's Army of the James, remained to guard the trenches, and formed the pivot for the wheeling column. The 29th of March was assigned for opening the manœuvre, and on that day it began.

The reader who may please to follow upon the map which accompanies this sketch, the journey of the Union columns from their familiar trenches to the cross-roads known as Five Forks, will find the initial marches easy of comprehension. But it must be noted that the battle-field destined to be forever famous was not at the start the objective of the Union columns, nor was even a pause expected there, much less a battle. But the Union general, as we shall see, boldly and wisely changed his plan on the first day of its execution, and Five Forks became what it is in history. The Confederate works ran south-westerly from Petersburg so as to cover the Boydton plank road as far as Hatcher's Run, and then turned off westerly and covered the White Oak road to where the Claybourn road intersects the latter, and there ended. The two infantry columns were designed to lie close up to the Confederate right flank, while Sheridan rode farther west, through Dinwiddie, on a wide detour to break up the railroad.

Warren, having on the morning of the 29th of March crossed Hatcher's Run, moved his Fifth Corps up the Quaker road, sweeping away the enemy's skirmishers, and, when about two miles from the latter's main works, Griffin's division, in advance, encountered that of Bushrod Johnson, which he defeated in a spirited engagement, the Confederate dead and wounded and over a hundred prisoners being left in his hands: his own loss was three hundred and seventy, chiefly in Chamberlain's brigade. Upon this success, Warren pressed well forward towards the main Confederate line. Humphreys, with the Second Corps, crossed Hatcher's Run, and moved up through the woods on Warren's right; and

Sheridan, six miles to Warren's left and rear, occupied Din-widdie. Thus, at nightfall of the 29th, the expedition was well afloat, with bright prospects of success. It was then that General Grant's courier, reaching Sheridan at Dinwiddie, countermanded the order to cut the roads, and directed him instead "to push around the enemy, and get on to his right rear," declaring in characteristic words, "I now feel like end-ing the matter."

However, night brought a rain which fell dismally all day of the 30th, and worked the Virginia roads back into their normal state of quagmires. All that Sheridan, Warren, and Humphreys could do was to reconnoitre the Confederate positions, which was accomplished by heavy skirmishing, without assault. So, too, the 31st must inevitably have passed (for such were the orders) in a suspension of hostili-ties, till horses could march and wains be drawn; but, on that day, another actor came to move the scene, and, true to a policy as old as the olden days of the Peninsula, himself took the initiative.

With a skilful audacity, which, even if not justified by oft experience, his hard necessities would have justified now, Lee had once more stript his almost barren intrenchments of everything but a strong skirmish line, in order to procure a force wherewith to check the Union flanking column. So swiftly, however, had the three Union corps moved out by their left and rear, that Lee's dispositions might have been incomplete, but for the rain of the 30th, which halted the Union march. But, on the morning of the 31st, Lee had massed fifteen thousand men on his right, comprising the divisions of Pickett and Johnson, with a few other troops; with these he sought, as usual, to drive back the Union left.

At the left of Grant's infantry line was, as we have seen, Warren's corps, which had handsomely advanced nearly to the White Oak road, opposite the extreme right of the Con-federate intrenched line. On Warren's right was Humphreys, but his left was unprotected, Sheridan being six miles distant at Dinwiddie. Ayres's division was in advance, Crawford's behind, and Griffin's in the rear, the three divisions being *en échelon*. Although general operations had been suspended, Warren prudently threw forward Winthrop's brigade of Ayres's division, to reconnoitre the White Oak road west of the Confederate intrenchments, with the view of subsequently occupying that road if the report should be favorable. It so happened that, at the very moment of the reconnoissance, Lee was sweeping forward his massed column for a desperate attempt to drive back the whole Union left. His sudden and swift attack in dense woods easily disrupted not only Winthrop's brigade but the rest of Ayres's division, who were attacked both in front and on the left. The confused retreat of Ayres's men disordered Crawford's, who in turn gave way, and were soon, in Griffin's words, "running to the rear in a most demoralized and disorganized condition." But, thanks to Warren's careful dispositions in massing his troops, Griffin's division not only stood firm, but, with the aid of Miles's, which Humphreys sent up on its right, repulsed the assaulting force and drove it entirely across the White Oak road. In this *contrecoup*, Warren threw in his whole available corps, but Chamberlain's gallant brigade was the only one earnestly engaged, and it captured one hundred and thirty-five prisoners of the 56th Virginia, with its flag. This was the battle of White Oak Ridge, the precursor of Five Forks. In it the loss of the Fifth Corps was not far from 1200 men, its total loss in the three days' operations thus far, being 1800.

The storm that burst on Warren spent but half its fury there: the remainder was reserved for Sheridan, who, on the same day, and against a part of the same troops, fought the battle of Dinwiddie Courthouse. The road from Dinwiddie to the Southside Railroad is crossed by the White Oak road at Five Forks, which point, accordingly, Sheridan aimed to seize. The day before he had made an unsuccessful effort with Devin's division and Davies's brigade of Crook's, to capture these cross-roads; but on the morning of the 31st the same troops renewed the attempt, and with success, the force which had held it on the 30th, being at that moment mainly absent and engaged with Warren. Soon, however, the Confederate infantry went tramping hastily down the White Oak road from their affair with the Fifth Corps, to repossess Five Forks. Overborne by this column, Devin and Davies fell back in confusion towards Dinwiddie. Pickett and Johnson, pursuing, followed down the west side of Chamberlain's Creek, but were repulsed in an attempt to cross by Smith's brigade of Crook's division, which had been skirmishing at that point with some Confederate cavalry. But in these manœuvres Sheridan's men had not only been engaged with a force too strong for them, but of necessity the whole cavalry column became awkwardly dislocated, and required new dispositions.

It was then that the genius of Sheridan — a soldier always boldest, promptest, most fertile of expedients, most irresistibly brilliant, in the supreme hour of peril — shone out conspicuous. Despite the enemy's pressure, he disentangled his troops and got them all in hand again, though on the retreat, and that being accomplished, dismounted his troopers behind the light parapets which had been thrown up near Dinwiddie, and so held the Confederates in check till nightfall forced their withdrawal: nor had the Union carbines then failed to pay some return instalment of the severe loss the cavalry had earlier suffered.

His comrades of the infantry meanwhile, anxious as well they might be, when the news came at nightfall of Sheridan's danger, prepared to aid him; and Warren, though the Fifth Corps was exhausted with its own battle, at once sent Ayres's division on the road to Dinwiddie, and prepared to follow with the rest. But Sheridan had already worked out his own salvation, and risen superior to dubious fortune at Dinwiddie

Courthouse, as he had earlier at Cedar Creek and Murfrees-boro'. Before midnight he had the satisfaction of knowing that his baffled enemy had retreated from his front, leaving but a skirmish line behind.

II.

BATTLE OF FIVE FORKS.

The vast line of Confederate earthworks which once en-girdled Petersburg and Richmond, after stretching from left to right full thirty-five miles, paused on the White Oak road where the Claybourn road crosses, and thence carried its re-tired flank a few miles northerly along the latter highway. To what point on the continent this parapet might have been pro-longed, under some circumstances, one dares not affirm; but it found a terminus at last from the lack of defenders. With 40,000 effective men, General Lee had long held it against a double investing force, though his cordon of trenches spanned two rivers, covered two cities, and protected a line of rail-road which, once destroyed, would have ruined his position.

But when his persistent adversary opened a fresh campaign by moving once more far out on the Confederate right a flank-ing column, which embraced not only two infantry corps, but 9000 well-mounted horsemen, Lee's resources were so strained that no dexterity of management could relieve them.

Four miles due west of the terminus of the main Confed-erate line, was a cross-roads as important as any which that line covered in its course; it was the intersection of the White Oak road with the one running from Dinwiddie to the Southside Railroad, and the junction was known as Five Forks, since there five paths radiate. The possession of Five Forks by the Union forces, would enable them to march thence by what is called the Ford road against the Southside Rail-road; it became, therefore, a point of strategic importance.

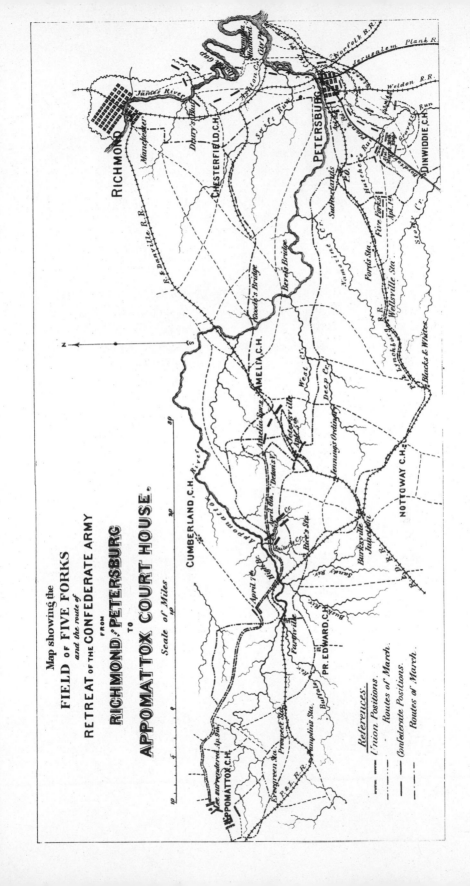

Map showing the
FIELD OF FIVE FORKS
and the route of
RETREAT OF THE CONFEDERATE ARMY
FROM
RICHMOND & PETERSBURG
TO
APPOMATTOX COURT HOUSE.

Scale of Miles

References:
Union Positions.
Routes of March.
Confederate Positions.
Routes of March.

To furnish forth a garrison for the Five Forks, which might also serve to confront the Union column which was marching to turn the Confederate right, Lee resorted to the well-worn device of stripping the Petersburg intrenchments. The force he had so collected, consisted of Pickett's division, 7000 strong, which for nine months had seen comparatively little service, Bushrod Johnson's division, 6000 strong, and the two small brigades of Wilcox and Wise, in all 15,000 men. It was this force which made the attacks in the battles of White Oak Ridge and Dinwiddie Courthouse, as already narrated.

On the morning of April 1st, Sheridan began a new movement against Five Forks. To him, during the night, General Meade had wisely assigned the command of all the forces designed for the attempt, consisting of his own cavalry, now about 8000 strong, McKenzie's cavalry division, 1000 strong, and the Fifth Corps now 12,000 to 13,000 strong — the losses of Warren and Sheridan during the three days previous having been from 2500 to 3000 men. A movement of such a character required a single head, and neither General Grant nor General Meade was to be present at its execution, their head-quarters being many miles distant from the battle-ground. The remainder of his army, the forces of Parke, Ord, Wright, and Humphreys, General Grant retained in their intrenched lines, awaiting the issue of Sheridan's contest; for although well aware that the garrison of Petersburg had been weakened for concentration on Lee's right, he preferred in place of a co-operative attack to attend Sheridan's fortune, and, that being made sure, to assault the next day.

The plan of battle was brilliant in its simplicity. It was to drive the enemy by means of the cavalry back to Five Forks, to keep him within the works there, and to make a cavalry feint of turning his right: then, under that curtain of horse which Sheridan so well knew how to draw, while behind its impenetrable screen he manœuvred the footmen, he would secretly move the Fifth Corps up on the enemy's left, and swing it full against that flank, cutting off the whole force from Petersburg and capturing it.

The topography of the region around Five Forks gives the clew to the Confederate movements. The general position assumed by its garrison, and by the forces of Sheridan at Dinwiddie and of Warren at White Oak Ridge, on the 31st, had been that of a triangle, of which the Union column occupied two angles and the Confederates a third. Partly to secure the obvious advantage of the offensive, and partly to prevent the Union forces from advancing with impunity against Five Forks, both by the Dinwiddie and White Oak roads, and so executing the manœuvre which Sheridan did the next day execute, Lee fell upon Warren's corps on the morning of the 31st as we have seen. But this manœuvre had uncovered the strategic position itself to Sheridan, who, advancing on the Dinwiddie road, had seized Five Forks. No advantage gained against Warren would make amends for giving Sheridan free course ; and accordingly the Confederates hastily rushed back, and drove Sheridan's advance from Five Forks, a movement' more readily made after their severe check by Miles and Griffin : it is easily seen how in the subsequent advance, General Warren says he "met with but little opposition." In the same way, after having driven Sheridan to Dinwiddie that same night, the Confederates were again obliged to withdraw their main force towards Five Forks, to. prevent the Fifth Corps from marching on the White Oak road, and so seizing that point and cutting off their retreat.

Accordingly, Sheridan had little difficulty, during the morning of April 1st, in executing the first part of his scheme. At daylight, Merritt's two divisions, with Devin on the right and Custer on the left, Crook being in the rear, easily drove the force left in their front from Dinwiddie to the Five Forks. Merritt, by impetuous charges, then expelled the Confederates from both their skirmish lines, and, in fine, at two o'clock

Sheridan had sealed them up within their main works and had drawn across their front his mask of cavalry skirmishers, behind which he now proceeded to the second part of his plan — the secret moving of the infantry.

General Warren had been directed, until the cavalry movement should be consummated, to halt at the point where he joined Sheridan, in order to refresh his men. At one o'clock, he received orders from Sheridan to march the Fifth Corps to Gravelly Run Church, about three miles distant, forming with two divisions in front and one in reserve. This formation was at once begun. Meanwhile, Merritt was demonstrating strongly against the Confederate right at Five Forks to deceive the enemy. Lynx-eyed, and attent to every quarter of the field, Sheridan now prepared to guard against any sally from the main Petersburg works upon what, after his line should be formed, would become his right and rear. This task was entrusted to McKenzie. The precaution was timely, for McKenzie, marching along the White Oak road towards the angle of the Confederate works at the Claybourn road, met a hostile force thence issuing, and attacking it boldly and skilfully drove it towards Petersburg.

The Fifth Corps was now formed, and eager to advance and strike. Crawford was on the right, Ayres on the left, and Griffin massed in column of regiments behind Crawford; Ayres and Crawford were each formed with two brigades in front and the third in rear, each brigade being in two lines. Then Warren pushed straight on to the White Oak road, which was speedily reached, being about half a mile distant, and changed front forward so that in place of being parallel to the road his line crossed it at right angles, and faced westward. This manœuvre was a left wheel, in which Ayres was the pivot and Crawford with Griffin behind the wheeling flank. The Fifth Corps was now directly upon the left of the Confederate position, overlapping it for a long distance, and McKenzie, having countermarched and returned on the White

Oak road, as Warren advanced to attack, was sent by Sheridan round to the latter's right.

The breastworks at Five Forks were of the usual character — a strong parapet of logs and earth, with redoubts at intervals, and heavy slashings thrown down in front: a thick pine undergrowth covered its approaches. The main line ran along the White Oak road upwards of a mile on each side of the road from Dinwiddie; and the breastwork was retired northerly on its left flank about one hundred yards, in a crochet; the interval thence to Hatcher's Run was guarded only by a skirmish line.

It happened therefore, that, when the Fifth Corps wheeled into position across the White Oak road, close upon the Confederate left, Ayres's division covered the ground fronting the refused line of breastworks, while Crawford and Griffin overlapped it. Before the two latter divisions had completed their change of front, Ayres became sharply engaged with the Confederate skirmishers, and driving them back, worked his men well up to the breastworks. There, however, the enemy opened a hot fire, which reached not only Ayres but the left of Crawford. The latter officer, in order to get by the enemy's flank, as he had been directed, in order to seize the Ford road, obliqued to the right, so as to draw his other flank from the severe fire it was receiving across open ground. But this manœuvre uncovered the right of Ayres, which staggered and finally broke under a flank fire. In this crisis, Warren promptly repaired the line by throwing Griffin into the interval between Ayres and Crawford, and this disposition had a second good effect in allowing Crawford to swing out with confidence upon the enemy's rear.

Ayres now charged the intrenchments with his whole division, Gwin's brigade on the right, the Marylanders in the centre, and Winthrop's brigade on the left. The troops dashed in with splendid impetuosity and captured the works, over a thousand prisoners, and several flags. Griffin, on the right of Ayres, falling upon the enemy's left and rear, carried the works there and fifteen hundred prisoners. Meanwhile, Crawford had struck and crossed the all-important Ford road, in the enemy's rear. This latter success rendered of course the whole position of the enemy untenable, and, to make assurance doubly sure, Warren directed Crawford to change front, and move briskly down the Ford road. Coulter's brigade led, with Kellogg's on its right and rear and Baxter's beyond, and, encountering a four-gun battery posted to command the road, charged and captured it, Coulter suffering severely in the gallant exploit.

At this juncture, the Confederate position was almost entirely surrounded; for, while Warren was attacking from the east, Merritt, who took the cue for assault from the roll of the infantry fire, was charging from the south. But one avenue of escape remained open, that to the west, along the White Oak road. But before this could be gained, the exultant Union columns had broken in upon all sides, and most of the Confederates were forced to surrender.

The Forks having been carried, Warren directed Crawford to change front again to the right, and to pursue south-westerly so as to take the enemy a second time in flank and rear; and thither also he sent a mounted cavalry brigade, which had approached on the Ford road. About a mile west of the Forks, and two miles west of the intrenchments which he had first carried, Warren found a similar line, designed to protect the left flank of what remained of the enemy, while the latter held the western extremity of his intrenched front against the Union cavalry on the south. Sheridan's orders had been that, if the enemy was routed, there should be no halt to reform broken lines; but the infantry, although full of spirit and enthusiasm, had become disorganized somewhat by their own victory, and by marching and fighting in the woods; and pausing before the enemy's new line, they were losing the momentum of pursuit in a straggling skirmish fire. At that moment Warren rode through to the front, and called those near him to follow. The officers and color-bearers sprang out, the straggling fire ceased, and in an enthusiastic charge the last position was captured, with such of the enemy as had remained to defend it. In this charge Warren's horse was shot within a few paces of the enemy's line, an orderly killed by his side, and Colonel Richardson of the 7th Wisconsin, who had heroically sprung forward to shield Warren, was grievously wounded.

The day was now done and the battle ended. But for a distance of six miles along the White Oak road, Merritt and McKenzie chased the fugitives, until night protected them. What loss Pickett, who commanded at Five Forks, suffered in killed and wounded, is not recorded, but he left over five thousand prisoners, with four guns, and many colors, in the hands of the impetuous Sheridan. The lightness of the Union loss formed a novel sensation to the Army of the Potomac, compared to the inestimable value of the victory; for it was not above one thousand in all, of which six hundred and thirty-four fell upon Warren's corps.

So ended Five Forks — a battle which may be pronounced the finest in point of tactical execution, on the Union side, of any ever delivered in Virginia, and in which, nevertheless, brilliancy of execution is eclipsed by the magnificence of its issue. It was a fit climax to that Shenandoah career which had already made illustrious the name of Sheridan.

III.

RESULTS OF FIVE FORKS.

Now at length the Army of the Potomac — glorious array of soldiery! — immortal alike in its gallantry and its fortitude, much-enduring, ofttimes in disaster but never in despair, the pattern of loyalty, the bright exemplar of citizen soldiery — after so many toils was nearing its goal. Through four years these and a greater host of fallen comrades, who died bequeathing them the unfinished task, had sought the prize set before them. The pangs of Tantalus had been theirs, — always to touch the guerdon but never to clutch it, to see the shining spires of Richmond but not to reach them, to graze the battlements of Petersburg, not to surmount them; and to receive grievous wounds from each vain struggle. They had come across a sea of troubles, and vivid in memory were its Fredericksburgs and Cold Harbors, grim vortex-pools whose greedy maws had sucked up thousands of brave soldiers, till the waters rolled over them and they were gone. But the hour had come to fight the last fight, and to run the last race.

The joyful news from Sheridan quickly reached the headquarters of General Grant, and ran electrically along, the Union trenches. A general assault was ordered for dawn of the 2d, and, meanwhile, a terrific cannonade was opened from every available gun along the vast line, until the moment of advance. A forecast of victory seemed to impress the troops, who took thence unusual confidence and alertness. The fate of the insurrection seemed as clear as if it had been writ up in flaming letters on the sky. All the formations were speedily made, and the troops waited for the signal-gun.

The news of Pickett's disaster had reached Lee, too, and he felt its weight of meaning. His right flank was turned, a powerful column of horsemen, sustained by a corps of foot, was already moving unchecked towards the rear of his position. His main lines would be assaulted on the morrow. He resolved at once to abandon Petersburg and Richmond.

But time was needed to provide for orderly withdrawal; it was needful, too, to strike some last staggering blow at the Union columns, to paralyze as far as might be their immediate pursuit. For that purpose nothing was fitter than the net of intrenchments, parapet behind parapet, whence he had so often bloodily repulsed the Union columns. He would make the last assault cost dear, and gain a breathing time from the crippling of the assailants. Longstreet had two divisions north of the James, not having detected the weakness of the Union lines there : he now sent several brigades over to the right. The same night Mahone, who held the Chesterfield front, received a message from General Lee, asking if he could give him some men, and in response put a brigade on the road to Petersburg, one of whose regiments, the Mississippians, he threw into Fort Gregg, which next day they defended to the last. Besides these reinforcements, Lee had but two incomplete divisions in the trenches : the attack on Fort Steadman had gained nothing, and lost four thousand men, a thing of all things which Lee could not even once afford to do ; and Five Forks trebled that disaster. However, with such as he had, Lee stood to do battle, for he was used to contending with inequality of numbers. His most hopeful aim was to keep his enemy outside of the works till another nightfall, when all should be abandoned, and the retreat begun.

At four o'clock of Sunday morning, the 2d, a tremendous assault was made from the whole Union line between the Appomattox and Hatcher's Run. Parke's Ninth Corps, on the right, carried the outer Confederate line. Wright's Sixth Corps, in the centre, swept the works in its front like a whirlwind, and in less than one hour its advance had crossed the Boydton road and struck and torn up the Southside Railroad, the long-coveted line of supplies. Ord's column moved with equal spirit on the left of the Sixth Corps, and then both Wright and Ord turned and marched up the Boydton road towards Petersburg. Upon this, Humphreys, who with the Second Corps held the extreme left, west of Hatcher's Run, swept clean the Confederate position there, with the divisions of Hays and Mott, and Miles's division pursued the enemy northerly to Sutherland Station, where he overtook and wholly routed him, capturing two guns and six hundred men : meanwhile, Humphreys marched the other two divisions on Wright's left towards the city.

When Ord had reached the Petersburg lines, the command of Gibbon attacked Forts Gregg and Alexander, two of the strongest redoubts amongst the Petersburg defences. The latter quickly fell, but in the former Mahone's men fought with customary desperation, and again and again sent their assailants reeling from the works. At last it fell, but its 250 defenders had been reduced to 30, and of Gibbon's men 500 lay stretched in front of the redoubt.

But now, before eight o'clock, all the network of exterior defences had been swept by the Union troops, who, rapidly advancing, drove their exhausted opponents far back to the last strong chain of works which immediately girdled Petersburg. At this time, within the city, General Lee, General A. P. Hill, and General Mahone, were talking over the perils and prospects of the day at the head-quarters of the former officer. As the firing drew near and ominously nearer from the front, General Lee, listening, said to Hill, "How is this, general? your men are giving way." Instantly General Hill mounted his horse, and dashed down the road to the front. General Lee's words were true : the Union forces were already crossing the lines at all points. As Hill rode along, he suddenly came upon two or three men in blue uniform, who, taking position behind a tree, levelled their pieces at him. "Throw down your arms," cried the general. The men were staggered for an instant by the very audacity of the demand, but recovering, gave back their answer from their rifles' mouths ; and A. P. Hill, who had fought throughout Virginia, from the first hour of Bull Run to the last hour of Petersburg, fell from his horse, dead.

The fate of the city was not yet accomplished. Its inner cordon of works, well built and posted on commanding heights, forced the assailants to recoil with great loss, re-

32

calling the sanguinary assaults of early days.   One of Longstreet's brigades, coming up from Richmond, even sallied
from the works, and for a time the famous Fort Mahone fell
again into Confederate possession, again however to be captured.   Before noon the bloody strife on the Confederate left
had ceased, and comparative quiet reigned along the line. It
was the Ninth Corps that had suffered most severely in the
attack, those of Ord and Humphreys much less ; the loss of
the Sixth Corps was about 1100.   The Confederate loss, too,
had not been light, especially in prisoners, of which the
Sixth Corps alone captured more than 2000, with many guns.
Lee had gained his desired day of respite, but had only
postponed, not averted, his fate.

At dawn of April 3d, the Union skirmishers were alert,
and creeping stealthily towards the enemy.   They passed
the open interval, got to the foot of the works, ascended the
outer slope, and, half astonished, leaped the frowning parapets.   The enemy was gone ! no sight or sound of him remaining ; and quickly over conquered Petersburg floated the
Union banner.   At the same moment, terrific explosions resounded from Richmond, and thither the Union pickets,
hurrying forward, found the Confederate iron-clads and
bridges on the James blown up, and Richmond in flames.
A wild carnival of triumph might well have succeeded in
the Union camps the fall of proud Richmond, but no moment
was spared for the joy of victory.   Instantly, all the Union
columns were formed and headed to the west, Ord along the
Southside Railroad towards Burkesville, and more northerly
and in a straighter course, Sheridan and the Fifth Corps,
followed by the Second and Sixth, on the road to Jetersville.
To Burkesville, too, was hastening the ruined army of
Northern Virginia, forced to march by the longer road
thither, north of the Appomattox.   Moving noiselessly under
cover of darkness, what was left of Lee's army met for flight

not far from Chesterfield — Ewell marching southerly from
Richmond, Mahone westerly from Bermuda Hundred, and
Field and Gordon, and the rest of the Petersburg troops,
northward from that city.   The remnant of Pickett's troops
had retreated from Five Forks, northwesterly to the Appomattox.   By daylight Lee was sixteen miles away.

Of 40,000 infantry wherewith Lee began the fatal campaign, more than 12,000 were gone when the sun set upon
Sheridan's battle.   But this was not all that Five Forks had
accomplished ; it had struck the signal for the storming of
Petersburg, where thousands more were snatched from Lee's
scanty hoard of men ; it had turned the right flank of his
position ; it had blocked up his best and only sure line of
retreat, since the Fifth Corps occupied the railroad at Sutherland's, ten miles west of Petersburg, on the night of his
retreat, with the cavalry at Ford's, ten miles farther west.

It is an unbroken chapter of Confederate calamities that I
am now relating ; a series of disasters indeed was needed to
hurl to ruin an army which had shown itself on many fields
too elastic and fire-tempered to break under any single misfortune.   With Richmond and Petersburg abandoned, with
an army reduced almost to 20,000 effective men, and forced
to retreat over roads longer than those on which his enemy,
having a powerful body of horsemen in front, was pursuing,
Lee had commenced his ill-starred journey.   His object
was to unite with General Johnston, and first, therefore, to
reach Burkesville, the intersection of the Southside and Danville railroads, of which the latter was his line of retreat.
On the morning of April 4th, Lee reached Amelia Courthouse, thirty-eight miles west of Richmond, and found that,
by a fatal blunder, the rations there collected to feed his
army during its retreat, had been sent to Richmond.   Till
the night of the 5th, therefore, he was forced to wait there,
and to break his command up into foraging parties.

This was the next link in the chain of disaster, for on the

afternoon of Lee's arrival at Amelia, Sheridan struck the Danville Railroad, seven miles beyond, at Jetersville. It only remained for the Confederate General to fall upon Sheridan, or to give up his retreat southwesterly to Burkesville, and to keep on due west. But Sheridan, with the cavalry and Fifth Corps, the victors of Five Forks, was 18,000 strong, and Lee, with his troops broken into detachments, had not that number at command. Thus again was Lee's direct line of retreat blocked up, and again did Five Forks throw its fatal shadow over the fortunes of this army.

Next day, the 5th, Sheridan, while intrenching at Jetersville, had his cavalry scouts on Lee's western line of retreat, and Davies's command, advancing to Paine's Cross-roads, came upon a train of one hundred and eighty wagons, defeated its cavalry escort, burned the wagons, and captured five guns and many prisoners. Gregg and Smith were sent to Davies's support, and the Confederate infantry dispatched to cut the latter off, were, after severe fighting, foiled. The same evening, Meade, with his Second and Sixth Corps, joined Sheridan.

Accordingly, on the night of the 5th, Lee hurried westerly again to where, thirty-five miles distant, his road crossed the Appomattox at High Bridge. His aim was no longer Danville and Johnston, but Lynchburg and the cover of the mountains. Close after him came the pursuers, with whatever speed was possible to foot, hoof, or wheel. Leading the hunt with a terrible energy which knew no pause, no rest, no sleep, and which foretold death to the flying game on whose flanks he so remorselessly hung, was Sheridan. Near Sailor's Creek, a stream that flows northerly into the Appomattox, five miles east of High Bridge, he sprang upon Lee's wagon train, and from its formidable guard seized four hundred wagons, sixteen guns, and hundreds of prisoners. But he would be content with nothing but the capture of the hostile column entire. Stagg's brigade was sent to charge at

Ewell's corps, which, as the rear-guard of the train, would be cut off from retreat, if detained till the Union infantry in its rear could come up. Wright soon came up, and, near Deatonsville, the divisions of Seymour and Wheaton, aided by Sheridan's impulsive cavalry, attacked Ewell, and, after heroic resistance and a sanguinary battle, captured the whole remaining force, consisting of several thousand prisoners, including Ewell, Custis Lee, and other general officers.

Meanwhile, on the right of the Sixth Corps, the Second had had a running fight to near the mouth of Sailor's Creek, capturing many guns, prisoners, flags, and two hundred wagons. On the same morning, General Read's brigade, sent forward by Ord towards Farmville, heroically attacked the head of Lee's column near that place, and, with the loss of its gallant commander and many of his men, detained the Confederates till Ord came up.

That night of the 6th of April was a sorrowful one for the Confederate army. There was little left now upon which to rely. Mahone's division, five thousand strong, vivid example of the worth of discipline and the power of enthusiasm, was still as effective, as fanatical in the belief that it could not be whipped as when it drew out of its abandoned trenches; Field's division, too, four thousand strong, was in good condition. But as much could not be said of any other division in the army. Pickett had but a fragment left from Five Forks; Johnson a handful from the same field; Anderson only his own military staff; Gordon's relics of Fort Steadman were in a poor condition to fight; Ewell's corps had just been nearly annihilated at Deatonsville and Sailor's Creek. The enemy pressed on all sides, often in front as well as rear. The men sunk down from want of rest, sleep, and food. The forage parties were constantly set upon by cavalry, and their scanty collects plundered before their eyes by Union troopers. Wagons by the hundreds, almost by the thousands, had been lost. Horses dropped dead in their tracks from starvation. With escape almost hopeless, and a flushed and relentless enemy forcing a running battle from dawn till dark, it would not be long before the leaven of disorganization would ferment even in the mass that still remained solid and true.

So reflecting, each within himself, a knot of Confederate generals, Lee's subordinates, conferred that gloomy night in the tent of General Anderson. They were all of one mind, and that was that the hour was hastening on for the surrender of the army of Northern Virginia. They resolved to communicate that opinion to General Lee, with the assurance that his officers would take the entire responsibility of having suggested and requested the surrender. One of their number was appointed for this mission, and it was determined that he should first seek as an intermediary General Longstreet, who was thought to be the most intimate in General Lee's counsel, and therefore fitted to convey the message with the better grace. This officer mounted his horse and set out for Longstreet's head-quarters.

Meanwhile, Lee, after the day's battle, was already pressing the night retreat, and had already crossed his advance over the Appomattox, at High Bridge, which important structure had been saved. For some days past, Mahone and Field had guarded the rear with their strong divisions. A great herd of stragglers, the debris of the day's battles, many without guns, many without equipments, and even without hats, were collected in a confused mass in front of the High Bridge waiting to cross — the very sight of them showed that the game was up. General Anderson, a brave and resolute officer, and one apt to stick precisely to the specific text of his orders, whatever they were, and even when he did not entirely take in their aim, was in charge of the stragglers, and on this occasion was under the strange impression that General Lee did not wish them to be at once crossed over the High Bridge. Mahone riding up thither, saw a great crowd of these disorganized soldiers, sutlers, and camp-followers, mixed up in the valley or bottom, with horses, artillery, and wagons, while a sentinel was posted on the bridge with orders to let no person whatever pass over. Hastening back through the confused mass, Mahone consulted with Anderson, and the result was that the disorderly mass poured across the bridge.

It now remained, so soon as the stragglers should have crossed, or even before, to burn High Bridge, for the Union columns would doubtless be up to save it in early morning, and it was better to leave a thousand men than to leave the bridge in their hands. This task was undertaken by General Gordon, who, in the temporary absence of Anderson, had charge of the stragglers. Meanwhile, Mahone had established a line of battle, forming the rear line of the army, on a rising ground three fourths of a mile beyond the bridge and facing it. Having passed the rest of the night in riding back from the river and picking out successive lines, on which to form in retreat, Mahone at dawn, having made the tour, returned to the river, and there found, to his mortification and rage, an officer in command who asked him in great simplicity when the bridge should be destroyed, as he had no orders naming the time. It was but another of the series of misfortunes in the retreat. Instantly the fuel was huddled together and the match lighted, and at the same moment Barlow's infantry appeared on the opposite slope, and his skirmishers catching sight of the bridge rushed in with a rattling fire. The bridge guard rapidly retreated as the bullets whistled across the stream, and, on the other side, shots piercing the tent of General Gordon, drove out that officer, who at that precise moment was in the hands of his barber, partially shaved. Mahone, from his position, was unable to command the crossing, and Barlow, who had so vigorously and promptly advanced, was able to secure it. The wagon-road bridge was secured, and eighteen guns along the banks were captured by the Second Corps. Humphreys continued the pursuit on two roads; Barlow reached Farmville, whence the enemy retreated, burning one hundred and twenty wagons; Miles found Mahone very strongly intrenched five miles north of Farmville, and attacking, was completely repulsed, with the loss of more than six hundred men.

But the long contest, the battle by day and flight by night, was nearly ended. In a spirit of magnanimity as worthy of praise as his victories in the field, the Union commander had already addressed his defeated rival, proposing the surrender of the Confederate army. Moved deeply by the generosity of these overtures, by the opinions of his subordinates, and above all by the condition of his troops, General Lee continued, during the 7th and the 8th, the correspondence which has become so very famous : and meanwhile the race for life went on.

On the morning of the 9th of April, the victors of Five Forks planted themselves squarely across the front of Lee's head of column and sealed up the retreat. The iron cavalry leader had during a thirty-mile march, the day before, captured four trains of cars loaded with Lee's supplies at Appomattox depot, and forcing his way thence by hard fighting, had, after taking many prisoners, twenty-five guns, a hospital train, and a park of wagons, drawn his lines across the road, on which the enemy was marching to Lynchburg. At dawn, in a last desperate attempt, Lee ordered his advance guard, a few thousand men under Gordon, to cut its way through. The half-starved troops, charging with the old-time gallantry, forced back the dismounted cavalry ; but these, drawing away to the right,· as a curtain is drawn, disclosed the infantry lines of the Fifth Corps and of Ord, at which spectacle the Confederates paused.

With infantry pressing full upon its front and with greater hostile masses closing up the rear, with Sheridan's horsemen mounted on the flank and ready to swoop upon the trains and confused forces of the Confederate army, the last day of the struggle had well nigh been a day of slaughter. For the environed army, with a valor all Spartan, stood ready to die after the example of Thermopylæ, not indeed in response to civic laws denying surrender, but obedient to the lofty impulse of honor.

But the sacrifice was not to be. While Gordon was throwing his troops to the front, behind them, at General Lee's head-quarters, three Confederate officers were holding a final consultation on the desperate strait of their fortunes. They were Lee, Longstreet, and Mahone: it was but little after daybreak of a very raw April morning, and they gathered around the former officer's camp-fire by the side of the road: some staff-officers were present at a little distance from the consultation. Mahone had just come up from his post in the rear of the column to the front, at the summons of General Lee. Longstreet, who had one arm in a sling, sat on the trunk of a felled tree gravely smoking a cigar. Lee, cordial and pleasant, and clad in the new uniform he had donned just before leaving Petersburg, was as serene and cheerful as ever, his face, at least, betraying not the slightest discomposure at this crisis in his career. General Lee explained to Mahone the purport of the note received from General Grant proposing surrender, for although the division commanders had surmised the object of Grant's flags in entering their lines, they had not been certainly informed. He then asked for his opinion as that of a subordinate on the condition of the army. Mahone replied that while his own division and one or two others were still able to fight, the rest of the army was so worn down as to be only fit for surrender. And, indeed, a single glance showed this army to consist only of about eight thousand effective fighting men, who, half in front and half in rear, were covering a confused ruck of ruined trains, fragments of batteries — the wrecks of the Army of Northern Virginia. To fly was as hopeless as to fight, since there was no route possible except to the North, · and no friendly night to cover, for day had just dawned : the fugitive host was caught in a basin, with no escape from the grasp of its pursuers unless the surrounding hills had fallen upon them.

Longstreet and Mahone nevertheless declared that the army deserved and would accept honorable terms alone. General Lee answered that the proposals of General Grant had been very generous, and showed that the latter officer had been prepared to give such terms as the Army of the Potomac could afford to offer, and the Army of Northern Virginia could afford to accept. But it was no longer certain that after two days' rejection those terms could be procured. There was no doubt, however, of the duty to make the effort, and General Lee, rising, and mounting his horse, turned to say, " General Longstreet, I leave you in charge here ; I am going to hold a conference with General Grant." Hardly had General Lee gone to the rear, when General Custer dashed at full speed down the road from the opposite quarter, bearing a white flag. He flung himself from his horse, and, saluting General Longstreet, asked if he were in command. General Longstreet replying in the affirmative, General Custer responded, " I demand the surrender of this army to General Sheridan's cavalry." The other rejoined, " I do not command the army for that purpose : General Lee is now at the rear under a flag of truce, communicating with General Grant for the purpose of surrender." General Custer retired, and, at the instance of the Confederates, the attack threatened in front was stopped.

So, on the 9th of April, the work begun at Five Forks was finished in triumph at Appomattox Courthouse. The long toil was over ; and an emotion commingled of relief from arduous labor and of exultation at the crowning victory, tempered by a soldier's respect for the bravery of the van- quished, overflowed the hearts of the conquerors on that memorable day. But those who stood bodily there were not all the conquerors. Ten thousand gallant hearts lay cold in soldiers' graves, since a twelvemonth gone the army crossed the Rapidan; ten thousand heroes, scarred and maimed, were far away in the cities and villages of the north; and tens and tens of thousands more, poisoned by the deadly swamp-breath or worn down by the toils of campaign, had dropped by the wayside, languished long on hospital pallets, or deserving quick death in victory had yielded to the torture of disease. Nor only those who fell in the Wilderness, at Spottsylvania, along the North Anna, at Cold Harbor, in the trenches or the environs of Petersburg, — but the heroic dead who slept on the ridges of Fredericksburg and Gettysburg, whose rude beds lay hid in the gloom of the woods of Chancellorsville, or adown the Shenandoah Valley, or along the banks of the Chickahominy, or dotting the plains of Manassas, or whose baptismal blood rained on the pavement of Baltimore — these all were conquerors on the 9th of April; and a vast host, silent, invisible, tasted the triumph of that day.

When Lee had surrendered, in natural consequence and without a blow ensued the capitulations of Johnston, Taylor, Thompson, Kirby Smith. Thenceforth, not so much as a lawless guerilla-shot vexed the air. Crag, fen, and everglade, bayou of Arkansas and Texan pampas, whatever wild spot might have become for desperate men an outlaw haunt through centuries, was given up, for so great was the influence of the example in Virginia. Before May had passed, nature had covered with kindly mantle the telltale vestiges of War's grim track. Over the continental wrestling-floor where giants strove, there was peace.

With the same magic swiftness in which the armies gathered, they dispersed. A million and a half of soldiers, when peace came, melted as silently back into the general nation as the snows of New England glide away under the vernal sun, and naught but a worn garment of blue or gray, here and

there, or a marked soldierly port, betrayed the heroes of hard-
fought fields.   There was, indeed, no longer need of citizen
soldiery; for, when the storm had passed over the Union,
though some of its limbs were reft of their glory, yet the
roots were fixed.

One who now revisits the fields whereon he saw great armies
contending, or haply was himself in the van, marvels at the
changed scene.   The dread battle-sounds have died away;
the black-mouthed cannon are dumb; in the furrows once
ploughed by caisson-wheels, the daisy or tender violet
springs; no longer the hills echo the roar of artillery, and the
plains resound with the clatter of hoof-beats and the clink of
sabres: a four-years' story seems like a fearful dream that is
gone.   But as the fancy kindles, lo, the ghastly scars of the
earth reopen, and again the field is peopled with embattled
armies, — the dun pall draws back over the landscape, and
out of its depths rise the cheer of the victors and the cries of
the wounded — the tattered ensigns, blazoned with glorious
legends, epitomes of history, toss once more in the battle-
smoke, — the clangor of arms goes up.   So in story and
imagination, the heroes contend again; as wayfarers at night,
through many centuries, heard the neighing of the Persian
war-horses and the shouts and blows of the warriors, on the
plain of Marathon.

INDEX.

BULL RUN, 13; the prelude, 13; conference between Beauregard and Johnston, 13; meeting of the armies, 14; motives of the combatants, 14; contrast with European wars, 16; the national uprising, 17; character of the war, 18; military condition of the country, 18; over-confidence on both sides, 18; the danger to the capital, 21; the influence of the Potomac on shaping the war, 21; ordinance of secession passed by Virginia, 21; the first passage of troops through Baltimore, 21; the danger to Washington at the beginning of the war, 21; the flag of Sumter hauled down, 21; the President's call for military, 21; Virginia the selected battle-ground of the South, 22; the Confederate Government removed to Richmond, 23; the cry of "Onward to Richmond," 24; popular clamor for a battle, 24; positions of the two main armies and their co-operating forces, 25; Patterson's position at Harper's Ferry, 15; Butler's position at Fort Monroe, 25; composition of McDowell's army, 26; he moves into Virginia, 26; Tyler's repulse at Blackburn's Ford, 27; Johnston's movement to join Beauregard, 28; McDowell's plan of battle, 30; Confederates' intended attack prevented by McDowell's turning their left flank, 30; Tyler's attack at Stone Bridge, 31; Confederate left flank to be turned at Sudley's Ford, 31; Hunter's move in reverse of Sudley's Ford, 32; Hunter attacked by Evans, 33; Hunter and Keyes cross Stone Bridge, 35; Hunter's success—critical condition of the Confederates, 35; arrival of Johnston and Beauregard with re-enforcements, 35; position of the armies after Hunter's success, 36; the fight for the plateau, 37; arrival of Confederate re-enforcements from the Shenandoah Valley, 39; the Union flank and rear struck by Smith's brigades, 40; the panic and the rotreat, 40; results of the battle, 42; official intentional misstatements, and absurd lay criticisms, 43; excellence of the Union plan of campaign, 44; McDowell not to blame, 44; Johnston's praiseworthy junction with Beauregard, 44; inexperience of both armies, 45; disorganization of both armies, 46; Confederates justified in not pursuing, 47; Johnston, J. E., on impossibility of pursuit at Bull Run, 47; the victory was the winning of a campaign, 48; the losses and spoils at Bull Run, 48; the North learned what was before it, 49; Confederate force at the spring of 1862, 55; moral influences of the battle, 49; the people prepare for war in earnest, 50; both North and South organize during the winter, 51; Dr. Arnold on the Lessons of Military History, 51; the formation of the Potomac Army, 51; influence of Bull Run upon the South, 52; the new Union army—its strength, 52; insignificant origin of the cavalry, 52; the battle unified the South, 53; the tendency of foreigners toward recognition and aid, 54; Southern pride, inflated by Bull Run, prepared the way for Southern defeat. 54.

DONELSON—the prelude, 56; the physical geography of the West, 56; the secession of the States of the lower central zone, 56; Kentucky became loyal, and was invested by the Confederates, 57; who seize and fortify Columbus and Bowling

40

war, 89; difficulties of the Confederate march, 91; wretched organization of the Confederate army, 92; Mississippi Valley, the second line of Confederate defense, 93; Mississippi the line of—its importance and facilities, 94; two lines of Union advance developed by the fall of Donelson, 94; the line through Nashville to Chattanooga and the ocean, 94; Memphis and Charleston Railroad—Johnston's second line of defense, 95; the Union design to separate Johnston and Beauregard, 95; its frustration by their junction at Shiloh, 95; Halleck's original plan of advance up the Mississippi, 96; subsequent plan, 97; Grant's command turned over to C. F. Smith, 97; restored on death of Smith, 98; Buell's march from St. Louis to Savannah, 98; Confederate plan to attack Pittsburg Landing before arrival of Buell, 100; Beauregard leaves forts with small garrison, concentrating his main force in the field, 100; deficiencies of the Confederate organization, 101; Confederate Army of the Mississippi, its formation at Corinth, 101; The Confederate march to Pittsburg Landing, 102; the roads and the weather, 102; the close approach of Buell, 102; topography of the Union position, 103; the sixth of April, 103; the lines of Grant's army, 104; something wrong in the Union front, 105; Johnston's advance stealthily advances, 105; Confederate fire drawn by reconnoitering party, 105; Hardee's whole force advances, 105; the Union army springs to arms, 106; the confused conflict lasts for three hours, 107; Bragg re-enforces Hardee, 107; the whole Confederate force up, 108; Prentiss driven from all his camps, 108; the first Confederate onset successful, 110; the Union line as now, 111; the defense of Sherman's left; it is turned, 110; the rally of Prentiss's troops, 112; the Union troops slowly forced back to the Landing, 113; the efforts to pierce the Union center and left, 114; the confusion in both Union and Confederate

lines, 114; death of A. S. Johnston; estimate of his character, 116; the Union army a wreck, 117; the rush for the river, 117; Wallace killed, 117; the Union gunboats re-enforce the army, 119; Confederate efforts to capture the Landing, 119; the siege guns on the bluff turned against the Confederates, 119; the desperate final charges of the Confederates, 120; the disorganization by plundering, 120; their position at this time, 120; Buell's advance arrives, 120; Beauregard decides to withdraw for the night, 122; Buell's energetic advance, 123; condition of the two armies, 123; April 7, Buell and Grant's advance upon the Confederates, 125; the losses and remaining forces, 124-5; the attack on Beauregard, 126; Beauregard abandons his right, 128; the final Union advance, 130; the Confederate retreat; the battle over, 130; indecisive character of many battles, 131; the result of Shiloh, 131; its indecisive character, 132; the losses, 132; the great Confederate possibilities lost, 133; Beauregard's original plans, and how frustrated, 133; the defense of the Memphis road, 134; Grant's error in retaining the troops on the left bank, 135; the second line of Confederate defense was lost by the battles of Shiloh, 136; Buell's zeal even outstripped his orders, 136; the evacuation of Corinth, 137; the surrender of Forts Randolph and Pillow, 137; Central and Eastern Tennessee now opened to the Union armies, 138.

ANTIETAM—the prelude, 139; origin of the campaign, 139; Lee's resolve to move into Maryland, 139; the Peninsular campaign and its consequences, 140; the supposed danger to Washington, 140; McClellan's unfortunate pause before Yorktown, 141; Johnston's Shenandoah Valley campaign, 142; Fremont and Banks attacked in succession by Jackson, 142; the fatuitous division of the Union forces in Virginia, 142; the Mountain, the Shenandoah, and the Rappahannock Departments, 142; Fair Oaks, the battle of, 143; McDowell hurries to the Valley to "bag" Jackson, who slips away, 143; the Potomac Army on both banks of the Rappahannock, 143; Johnston attacks the two corps on the right bank, and fails, 143; Johnston wounded and succeeded by Lee, 143–4; history of Robert E. Lee, 144; his plan for the defense of Richmond, 144; Malvern Hill, the battle of, 145; Gaines's Mill, the battle of, 145; Jackson withdrawn to Lee's main army, 145; Porter compelled to retire to the Chickahominy right bank; the battle of Gaines's Mill, 145; McClellan's position now, 145; the change of base to the James, 145; the battle of Malvern Hill, 146; the armies of Fremont, Banks, and McDowell formed into the Army of Virginia, under Pope, 146; Jackson sent against him, 146; Lee's position between t e two armies, 146; Lee retires toward Richmond, 146; McClellan ordered by Halleck to Alexandria to cover Washington, 146; Lee resolves to attack Pope, 147; the death of Stevens at Chantilly, 148; the death of Kearney, at Chantilly, 148; the second battle of Bull Run and Pope's defeat, 148; the battle of Chantilly, 148; Pope's forces reel back to the fortifications of Washington, 148; Lee's confidence in his own powers, 148; his motives for Maryland invasion, as stated by himself, 149; the great danger to Washington, 149; McClellan restored to command, 150; Lee concentrates at Frederick, Md., 151; fails to excite enthusiasm, 151; and moves westward beyond the mountains, 151; the Confederate intended attack on Martinsburg and Harper's Ferry, 152; McClellan finds a copy of the plan of attack, 152; and advances, 152; Longstreet and Hill wait west of the South Mountains for the reduction of Harper's Ferry, 153; McClellan suddenly discovered approaching, 153; Lee covers the siege of Harper's Ferry by holding Turner's and Crampton's Gaps, 154; Harper's Ferry hopelessly environed, 154; McClellan's duty

to relieve the garrison, 155; McClellan forces his way into Pleasant Valley, 155; Longstreet and Hill retire to Sharpsburg, 155; Harper's Ferry surrendered, with McClellan within six miles, 155; Jackson's account of the surrender, 156; the Valley of the Antietam, 157; Lee posts himself on the west bank of the Antietam, 158; McClellan arrives on the east bank of the stream with two divisions, 160; the whole army except Franklin's corps arrives, 161; position of Lee's forces, 161; topography of the field, 161: Lee stood on the defensive, compelling McClellan to cross the stream, 162; the bridges across the Antietam, 162; McClellan's plan of attack, 163; Hooker and Mansfield crossed toward Lee's extreme left, 163; the 17th of September, 163; Hooker attacks, 164; Ewell is thrown back, 164; Jackson's reserves re-enforce Ewell, 165; Mansfield comes up and is met by Hill, 165; both sides retire much shattered, 165; the losses on this part of the field as stated by Jackson, 165; Sumner attacks the Confederate shattered left with Sedgwick's division, 168; Hood beaten and commenced retiring, 169; Sedgwick assailed by McLaws, 169; McLaws' account of his attack on Sumner, 169; Burnside's orders to carry the lower stone bridge, 171; how he was held in check, 171; consequence of Burnside's delay, 172; arrival of A. P. Hill, 172; he sweeps Burnside back, 172; the battle over, 173; Lee retreats on the night of the 18th, 173; result of Antietam, 173; losses in the battle, 174: the real value of the battle to the North and what had preceded it, 174; it was a signal defeat, and a crowning victory, 176; consequences of a Union defeat, 175; the issue of the Emancipation Proclamation, 176; Lincoln, President, his account of the issue of the Emancipation Proclamation, 176.

MURFREESBORO—the prelude, 178; Buell, with the Army of the Ohio, to move against Chattanooga, 179; Grant to operate in the Mississippi Valley,

179; the relation of the battle to Shiloh and Chattanooga, 179; the adoption of the Chattanooga line by both combatants after the occupation of Corinth, 179; Memphis and Charleston Railroad now in Union possession, 179; Bragg concentrates upon Chattanooga, 180; Price and Van Dorn left to oppose Grant, 180; particulars of Buell's march, 180; the Memphis and Charleston road as a line of advance on Chattanooga, chimerical, 181; Buell's total force, 181; Florence, Decatur and Cumberland Gap occupied, 181; the problem of Buell's advance, 181; Bragg arrives at Chattanooga, 182; his force and dispositions, 182; Kirby Smith at Knoxville, with 13,000 men, 182; raids of Forrest and Morgan on Buell's line of advance, 182; Kirby Smith advances into Central Kentucky, routs Gen. Nelson at Richmond and pushes toward the Ohio, 183; Bragg crosses the Tennessee, into the Sequatchy Valley and turned Buell's left, 184; Bragg's advantages in holding the Cumberland range, 184; the inadequacy of Buell's force to hold his communications, 184; Halleck's whole scheme of the Chattanooga campaign chimerical, 185; Buell compelled to retreat and concentrate at Murfreesboro, 185; then at Nashville—then to cover Louisville, 185; the position of the two armies, 186; Bragg reaches Munfordsville and finally captures it, 186; Bragg now directly on Buell's line of retreat, 186; Bragg diverges east from Louisville, his objective, and moves to Frankfort, 186; Buell then occupies Louisville, 187; result of Bragg's operations thus far, 187; reasons for his changed movement, 187; the Union force at Louisville, 187; Bragg's error as to the political reconstruction of Tennessee and Kentucky, 188; Buell's retreat marked by great skill, 189; his task now, 190; his army reorganized and ready to move, 190; relieved of command and George H. Thomas appointed, 190; Thomas refuses to supersede him, 190; Buell advances toward Frank-

fort and Bardstown, 190; Bragg's retreat to Perryville, 191; the battle of Perryville or Champion Hills, 191; Bragg withdraws south beyond Loudon, 192; Buell superseded by Gen. Rosecrans, 192; Rosecrans committed to an offensive, 192; Buell was said to have let Bragg escape, 192; Rosecrans concentrated at Nashville, 194; Bragg's intrenched position at Murfreesboro, 194; Rosecrans advances toward him, 194; arrives in his front, 195; positions of the two armies, 195; Rosecrans's plan of battle and its merits, 196; Bragg's plan of battle and its merits, 198; Rosecrans commences crossing his left over Stone River, 199; Bragg's left attacks the Union right and carries its position, 199; the Union disaster unknown to Rosecrans, 201; on discovering it, he withdraws his left and strengthens his right, 201; Sheridan's left division of McCook repulses the further attack, 202; Sheridan's maneuver for a new front, 203; his resistance in the new position gains an hour, 204; his terrible fighting against an overwhelming force, and final withdrawal to west of the Nashville road, 205; he reports to Rosecrans, 205; Rosecrans's new dispositions, 206; Palmer's division the only one on the original front, 207; all of the division swept away except Hazen's Brigade, 207; Hazen's great service; slackening of his defense would have lost the battle, 208; Bragg now makes a new assault, 209; Rosecrans meets it with massed artillery and infantry fire, 209; Bragg, foiled in his attack on the front, essays the Union left flank, 210; Bragg's attack fails and the battle is over, 211; the battle was a drawn one, 211; Rosecrans's "Gentlemen, we fight, or die right here," 211; the next day Rosecrans again throws a force to the east of the river, 212; Breckinridge attacks it; finally driven by artillery fire across the river, 212; Bragg withdraws to Shelbyville and Tullahoma, 213; results of Murfreesboro, 213; the losses, 213; the battle similar to the battle of Prague,

Hill, 331; but the day was lost to the Union side, 331; Meade, thirteen miles distant, hears of the battle, 331; sends Hancock to the scene, 331; Hancock restores order, 332, takes possession of Culp's Hill, 332; the Confederates' pause fatal to their hopes, 332; why Lee stayed the advance, 332; next day Meade determined to fight at Gettysburg, 333; both armies were concentrated by next morning, 333; Lee could not withdraw without discredit, 334, the principal attack to be made on the Union left, 334; positions of the two armies, 334; Sickles on the left wing advanced too far, leaving a gap between his right and Hancock's left, 335; and was attacked the first, 336; his motives were laudable, 336; the position at Little Round Top, 337; the opportune arrival of Vincent there, 337; the fighting in Sickles's left front, 338; Peach Orchard lost, 338; Humphreys and Hancock repulse further attempts, 339; nothing between the Confederates and the main crest, 340; Ewell now formed for attack on Cemetery and Culp's Hills, 340; does attack and hold part of the latter, but is repulsed from the former, 340; results of the action of July 2, 341; Lee's plan for July 3 unchanged, 341; proposed attack in force on Cemetery Ridge, 342; Confederates driven from Culp's Hill, 342; the artillery duel between the opposing lines—the greatest on this continent, 343; the Confederates from Seminary Ridge toward Cemetery Ridge, 343; they are met by tremendous fire, 344; Hancock's account of the fight, 345; the Confederate right, repulsed, reënforced the center, 345; the heaviest attack now opposite Webb's Brigade, 345; the formation of the brigade, 345; it partially wavers, but is reformed, 346; the Confederates make desperate efforts, but are repulsed, 346; great disorder in the Confederate lines, 347; Lee's efforts to rally the troops, 347; expediency of a Union advance, 348; Lee threw up breastworks, waiting attack, 349; Meade demonstrates feebly, 349; at night

Lee withdraws to Hagerstown, 349; Meade now directed march *via* Frederick, 350; Lee reached the Potomac at Williamsport and Falling Waters, 350.

WILDERNESS—the prelude, 356; Virginia as a theater of war, 357; the covering of Washington and Richmond, 357; the Union Western successes constant, 358; in Virginia victory long waited, 358; Sherman intrusted with the Western armies, 362; Grant joins the Potomac army, Meade still commanding, 362; results of the three years of the war, 360; Grant appointed General-in-Chief, 361; Wilderness, the battle of the, 363; Lee's position behind the Rapidan, 363; strength of the two armies, 364; Lee's method in relation to the river, 364; Potomac Army's organization, 364; Grant moved at midnight, May 3, 365; the army across, 365; Hancock at Chancellorsville, and Warren at old Wilderness Tavern, 365; Burnside's orders to hold Culpepper Court House 24 hours, 365; Lee's plan to strike Grant in the Wilderness, 366; Ewell and Hill very near Warren by dark, 366; tidings of Confederate attacks on Warren's advance next day, 367; Grant and Meade had not calculated on a battle near the Rapidan, 367; their purpose was to move between Lee and Richmond, 368; the attack on Griffin supposed to be a feint, 368; but Lee had assumed the offensive, 368; and marched Ewell and Lee eastward on the Wilderness pike, 368; Warren ordered an assault, 370; description of the Wilderness, 370; Warren's position, 371; Griffin at first drives part of Ewell's Corps, 371; Griffin checked, 371; Wadsworth started facing northwest, 371; his left flank exposed and broken, 371; Griffin now forced back, 372; Warren forms a new line west of the tavern, 372; losses of the Fifth Corps in this fight, 372; Hancock comes up, 372; his report of what followed, 372; Hill's account of his share in first day of the Wilderness, 373; the first day closed without decided advantage, 373; the next day—